CECIL KUHNE

NEAR DEATH
IN THE
DESERT

Cecil Kuhne is the editor of five previous
adventure anthologies, *On the Edge*, *The Armchair Paddler*, *Near Death on the High Seas*, *Near
Death in the Mountains*, and *Near Death in the
Arctic*. A former white-water rafting guide,
he has also written nine books about rafting,
kayaking, and canoeing. He lives in Dallas.

ALSO EDITED BY CECIL KUHNE

Near Death on the High Seas

Near Death in the Mountains

Near Death in the Arctic

On the Edge

The Armchair Paddler

NEAR DEATH
IN THE
DESERT

NEAR DEATH
IN THE
DESERT

TRUE STORIES OF
DISASTER AND SURVIVAL

EDITED BY
CECIL KUHNE

VINTAGE DEPARTURES
Vintage Books
A Division of Random House, Inc.
New York

A VINTAGE DEPARTURES ORIGINAL, JULY 2009

Copyright © 2009 by Cecil Kuhne

Permissions appear at the end of the book.

Library of Congress Cataloging-in-Publication Data
Kuhne, Cecil, 1952–
Near death in the desert : true stories of disaster and survival /
by Cecil Kuhne.
p. cm.
ISBN 978-0-307-27936-1 (alk. paper)
1. Desert survival.   2. Wilderness survival.   I. Title.
GV200.5.H84 2009
613.6'9–dc22   2009006592

Book design by Rebecca Aidlin

www.vintagebooks.com

Printed in the United States of America
10 9 8 7 6 5 4 3 2 1

CONTENTS

PREFACE

Roaming the desert in a frantic search for water is a situation not to be taken lightly. You first feel the scratching thirst in the back of your throat, and then your mouth becomes so parched you have trouble swallowing. Before long, the craving for even a single drop of water becomes all-consuming, and eventually that desperate feeling drowns out all other thought.

The trouble here is a physiological one. The human body can last several weeks without food—it can last only a few days without water. When starved of moisture, the internal organs start to shut down, and the end cannot be far away.

The problem of course is weight: water weighs more than eight pounds a gallon, so taking enough for a journey of any length is difficult, especially if you are carrying it yourself. When water sources that were once reliable are no longer there, you are in a very precarious situation.

In spite of its dangers, the austere simplicity of the desert has a beauty all its own, and there can be startling moments of serendipity. The desert has the delightful effect of sharpening and intensifying the landscape, and its stark and rugged outlines are made more dramatic by the subtle hues of earth. Late afternoon sunsets, with their surreal pink and lilac tones, often end with a bright orange fireball on the horizon. Then a brief shower brings to life wildflowers that were formerly invisible, as well as refreshing smells of sage and soil found nowhere else. When the moon casts its lovely glow on the lunarlike landscape, there is cause for true joy.

But that joy is often short-lived. One dilemma facing those who venture into the desert is that in its midst everything can start to look the same. Reference points disappear, and you can easily become unsettled by the immense spaces around you. Getting lost is a real possibility, and the more you panic, the more water you consume, leading to a vicious cycle downward.

Many of the travelers in this volume went in search of the beauty and challenges offered in crossing these empty lands. Others found equally fascinating the native peoples who live in places that by logic are no more fit for human habitation than distant planets. How these locals adapt to such extreme circumstances astounds those of us used to the safeguards of modern society.

In 1898, John C. Van Dyke traveled to the Sonoran Desert and quickly became mesmerized by its subtle, but potentially deadly, charms. His words capture perfectly the spell that can overtake even the most jaded: "Never again shall you see such light and air and color, never such opaline mirage, such rosy dawn, such fiery twilight. And wherever you go, by land or by sea, you shall not forget that which you saw not but rather felt—the desolation and the silence of the desert."

Cecil Kuhne
Dallas, Texas

FOREWORD

Robyn Davidson

It is difficult to describe Australian desert ranges, as their beauty is not just visual. They have an awesome grandeur that can fill you with exaltation or dread, and usually a combination of both.

I camped that first night in a washaway, near the ruin of a cottage. I awoke to the muttering of a single crow staring at me not ten feet away. The pre-dawn light, all pastel misty blue and translucent, filtered through the leaves and created a fairyland. The character of such country changes wonderfully throughout the day, and each change has its effect on one's mood.

I set off clutching map and compass. Every hour or so, my shoulders would tighten and my stomach knot as I searched for the right path. I got lost only once, ending up in a box canyon and having to backtrack to where the path had been obliterated by a series of cattle and donkey tracks. But the constant tension was sapping my energy and I sweated and strained. This went on for two days.

One afternoon, after our midday break, something dropped off Bub's back and he flew into a flat panic. I now had Zeleika in the lead, because of her sore nose, and Bub at the rear. He bucked and he bucked and the more he bucked, the more bits of pack went flying and the more frenzied he became. By the time he stopped, the saddle was dangling under his quivering belly and the goods were scattered everywhere. I switched into automatic. The other camels were ready to leap out of their skins and head for home. Goliath was galloping between them and generally causing havoc. There was not a tree in sight to tie them to. If I blew this, they might take off and I would never see them again. I couldn't get back to Bub so I whooshed the lead camel down and tied her nose-line to her foreleg, so that if she tried to get up, she would be pulled down. I did the same with Dook, clouted Goliath across the nose with a branch of mulga so that he took off in a cloud of dust, and then went back to Bub. His eyes had rolled with fear and I had to talk to him and pacify him until I knew he trusted me and wouldn't kick. Then I lifted the saddle with my knees and undid the girth on top of his back. Then I gently took it off and whooshed him down like the others. I found a tree a little farther on, and beat the living daylights out of him. The whole operation had been quick, sure, steady, and precise, like Austrian clockwork—perfect. But now, whatever toxins had been stirred up by the flow of adrenalin hit my bloodstream like the Cuyahoga River. I lay by the tree, trembling as hard as Bub. I had been out of control when I beat him and began to recognize a certain Kurtishness in my behavior. This weakness, my inability to be terrified with any dignity, came to the forefront often during the trip, and my animals took the brunt of it. If, as Hemingway suggested, "courage is grace under pressure," then the trip proved once and for all that I was sadly lacking in the stuff. I felt ashamed.

I learnt a couple of other things from that incident. I learnt to conserve energy by allowing at least part of myself to believe I could cope with any emergency. And I realized that this trip was not a game. There is nothing so real as having to think about survival. It strips you of airy-fairy notions. Believing in omens and fate is all right as long as you know exactly what you are doing. I was becoming very careful and I was coming right back down to earth, where the desert was larger than I could comprehend. And not only was space an ungraspable concept, but my description of time needed reassessment. I was treating the trip like a nine-to-five job. Up bright and early (oh, the guilt if I slept in), boil the billy, drink tea, hurry up it's getting late, nice place for lunch but I can't stay too long . . . I simply could not rid myself of this regimentation. I was furious with myself, but I let it run its course. Better to watch it now, then fight it later when I was feeling stronger. I had a clock which I told myself was for navigation purposes only, but at which I stole furtive glances from time to time. It played tricks on me. In the heat of the afternoon, when I was tired, aching, and miserable, the clock would not move, hours lapsed between ticks and tocks. I recognized a need for these absurd arbitrary structures at that stage. I did not know why, but I knew I was afraid of something like chaos. It was as if it were waiting for me to let down my guard and then it would pounce.

On the third day, and to my great relief, I found the well-used station track to Tempe. I called Areyonga on my radio set, that unwanted baggage, that encumbrance, that infringement of my privacy, that big smudgy patch on the purity of my gesture. I screamed into it that I was all right and got nothing but static as a reply.

Arriving in Tempe, I had a pleasant lunch with the people who ran the station, then filled my canteen with precious sweet rainwater from their tanks and continued on my way.

NEAR DEATH
IN THE
DESERT

Michael Asher and his new bride Mariantonietta Peru embarked upon the apogee of all desert journeys as they traveled east across the Sahara from Morocco to Sudan. The natural dangers they encountered were certainly intimidating, but what they had not anticipated were the number of bizarre and often surreal encounters with the natives.

TWO AGAINST THE SAHARA

On Camelback from Nouakchott to the Nile

MICHAEL ASHER

Mafoudh

We left Chinguetti on 6 August. Mafoudh turned up at first light, bringing with him nothing but a blanket, a camel stick and a much patched knapsack containing a teapot, a glass and a spare *gandourah*.

I envied him his simple gear. Ours seemed to cover every bit of ground outside the house: saddles, sacks, cushions, saddle bags, tent, poles and waterskins. We had even exchanged one of our butterfly saddles for the more comfortable woman's litter. Loading it was a marathon. A crowd of women and children gathered around to watch the spectacle. Sid' Ahmed made an appearance and started shouting instructions. Not to be outdone, Mafoudh shouted back, while every child who could walk tramped joyfully through our belongings, picking them up, putting them down and arguing with any adult who tried to stop them.

Slowly the piles of equipment grew smaller as each item found a place on one of the camels. Miraculously there was a place for everything. We got the animals to their feet, groaning and grumbling. "Isn't it a bit heavy?" I asked.

"Nonsense!" Mafoudh replied. "This is nothing. You should see what a *real* caravan carries, by God!" Then he grabbed the headrope of the leading camel. "In the name of God," he said, "the way is long. Let's go!"

As he led the caravan off, there were cries of "Go in peace!," which struck me as comically inappropriate amid the clamour, Sid'Ahmed walked us down to the bank of the wadi, saying, "Omar is the boss, Mafoudh. When he says go, you go, and when he says stop, you stop." Then he shook hands with us and said, "Send me a letter when you reach the Nile. God go with you!" We left him standing there, a solid, proud old warrior on the edge of his domain.

Moments later we had crossed the wadi and plunged over the ridge of dunes, which for three months we had seen on waking. Now we were among them, and Chinguetti was blotted out, gone for ever. "I feel like Jonah in the belly of the whale," Marinetta said. "We've just entered the whale's belly."

All morning we trudged through the dunes. They were the visible expression of the unseen force of the wind, delicately moulded, rippled and coloured with watery pastels. There were places where the sand had been scooped out of the desert floor and layered over the rocks so that the sharp edges showed through the smooth carpet like ground-down teeth. We crossed bridges of sand where the surface cracked like ice and fell away; the camels stumbled down at incredible angles, drifting into narrow corridors where the dunes towered above us, dwarfing our tiny *azalai* with its arrogant mission of conquering the great Sahara.

Once I stopped to pick up a barbed arrow head. It was just like the ones that the people of Chinguetti had tried to sell us so often. I wondered how many thousands of years it had lain there, waiting for me to pick it up. It had belonged to a hunter, some time long ago, when this desert was a forest. The forest had gone, and the hunters had gone with it, but men had survived in this desolate land by changing their ways and adapting to the new order. Change was certain, but man survives by adapting. If we adapted to the ways of the Sahara, we too could survive.

At midday we reached the palm groves at Aghayla, where Mafoudh owned some young trees. The dates were red and squashy, ripe for the cutting. A host of people helped us to unload and set our gear down in the shade. Marinetta took the cooking things and went off to make lunch. Four old men came to talk, sitting cross-legged on our blankets, and I invited them to eat with us. They looked pleased, but I wondered if they would remain so when they saw the standard of the cooking.

Half an hour passed. The men shifted restlessly. Then the unmistakable smell of burnt rice drifted through the palm trees. A few moments later Marinetta appeared and slapped in front of us a tray of the familiar scorched pellets. Lost within the desert of rice were a few oases of dried meat, now reduced to lumps of charcoal. The men looked at the dish, and I saw their faces drop. Mafoudh grinned at me cheerfully. "It's the wind," he said. "It makes the fire too hot. Come on, everyone, eat!" The old men each took a small amount with their fingertips and began to chew. They chewed and chewed, and the tension mounted as I wondered if anyone would take another handful. None of them did. One by one they whispered thanks and got up to leave. Before we departed, though, they brought us a gift of ripe dates. Was there a touch of pity in their eyes as they handed them over?

The afternoon was steaming-hot. Every half hour my mouth became so clogged with mucus that I had to take a sip of water from one of our canteens. Marinetta had the same problem. "This water tastes like honey," she gasped. "I never knew water could taste so good." For hours we stumbled on through one band of dunes after another, but before sunset we had emerged on to a plateau of black stone that allowed us to ride for the first time. We couched the camels, and I helped Marinetta into her new litter. I had chosen to ride the red camel, Shigar, even though he now carried an uncomfortable pack saddle with almost all the provisions. Mafoudh climbed aboard the smaller Li'shal, carrying a butterfly saddle, and led the way. We rode on silently until the last sparklers of the sun burned out and left the plain in thick darkness.

It was all confusion in the camp that night. It seemed strange to have a third person with us, and neither of us knew quite what to do. Mafoudh took everything in his stride, however. He collected firewood, lit a fire and made tea while we were still sorting out our equipment. "I have to drink tea first," he explained apologetically, "or I get a tight feeling in my head. It makes me feel angry." We all felt better after we had drunk tea and eaten a plate of macaroni and sardines. We sat back in the warm sand to watch the last flux of the fire. The dark screen of the night was awash with the familiar pattern of the stars. The camels, unseen in the darkness, made shuffling sounds as they hunted for shoots of grass. "There may be some rain tomorrow," Mafoudh predicted, sniffing the air. "It's been hot today. The rain follows the heat at this time of year."

"You think it's a mistake to travel at this time?" I asked him.

"In some ways the rainy season is better than winter for travellers," he said, "because although it's hot, the rain leaves pools of water in the desert. When you've got water you don't need to be afraid of the heat. Water is God's blessing."

It was soon time for sleep, and I worried about the sleeping arrangements. It seemed ridiculous to concern myself with this in the middle of the world's greatest desert. There was no lack of space, but I felt protective about Marinetta. I was wary even of leaving the camp to relieve myself, afraid that Mafoudh might take advantage of her in my absence. Mafoudh solved the problem by taking his blanket and going off to sleep in the sand a good distance away. Marinetta and I spread out our blankets among the saddles and gear. We cuddled up close in the darkness, more contented with each other than we had been for weeks. "Well, that was day one," I commented. "Do you think we'll make it to the Nile?"

"Yes," she answered. A few minutes later she was asleep.

We saw the first signs of the storm the next afternoon as we crossed the Agfeytit valley. Before us was a vast line of grey cliffs stretching as far as the horizon. The base of the valley was a serpent of black powder on which lay a school of small, humpy dunes that reminded me of jellyfish washed up on a beach. The sky suddenly filled with a scud of cloud, and the wind carried a touch of dampness. Sloughs of silvery dust began to squirm across the ground, and we heard the distant boom of thunder. The sky was a ragged quilt of grey and blue, and there were places around us where the clouds seemed to be reaching down into the desert. The wind began to buffet us in waves that rose and fell successively. Suddenly there was a shocking crack of lightning directly in our path.

For a split second I saw the distant flash pattern, like a many-branched, electric-blue tree as it forked down into the earth. It was followed by a shell blast of thunder, which made us jump. "Jesus Christ!" Marinetta said. "We'll all be fulminated!" We waited for the rain to come.

"We'd better make camp," Mafoudh advised.

"No," I said. "Let's risk it and go on till sunset."

That evening we erected our Arab tent in case the rain started. It didn't begin until the next morning at about 5 A.M., but when it came it hit us like an explosion. The wind railed through the camp, knocking down the tent with a single blow. The violence of the storm was frightening. Every few moments the darkness was slashed by brilliant streaks of lightning, and the thunder growled overhead like a barrage. Then the rain came gushing out of the night, roiling into the sand, soaking everything, dripping cold down our necks and running three inches above the ground so that we sat like ducks in the current. Every time the thunder boomed Marinetta let out a gasp and tried to crawl closer to me. We were already completely entwined in each other's arms, and it was somehow very comforting to feel her small, damp, warm body close to mine. How many times had we watched storms like this from the cosy safety of my flat in Khartoum? How different it was to be out in it.

"My God, the cameras!" Marinetta said suddenly. I pulled the cotton sheet of the tent aside and rushed out, barefoot, from its spurious protection. Mafoudh's body was a wet sausage under his blanket. He was lying on a hillock of sand, above the running water, and he had moved the most vulnerable of our equipment up there with him and had covered it with a plastic sheet. His narrow, drenched features peered at me through the night. We laughed at each other. "God is generous!" he said. But it didn't sound as though he meant it.

The dawn came, bleak and freezing. The rain stopped and was replaced by the cutting edge of the wind. We shivered uncontrollably in our wet clothes as Mafoudh tried to make a fire for the morning tea. The rain had washed off the light top-soil and liberated the colours beneath, which showed in a mandala of patterns across the plain. Our tea was soaked; our loaves of sugar had dissolved into a damp mass mixed with sand and grit. Marinetta's flip-flops had been carried off, and my leather sandals were so wet that they folded up as soon as I put them on. Mafoudh said that we should dry out every-thing well before we started, as the saddles would fall to pieces if we tried to use them while they were wet.

"I've never seen a night like *that!*" Marinetta said, and laughed.

"God is generous!" Mafoudh repeated, then he laughed too. "But the rain is hell, isn't it?" he said.

For the next three days we crossed a landscape where water had taken over the job of sculptor from the wind. The black plain had become a blotch of blood-red, amber, orange and gold, overlaid in places by slicks of mud as smooth and creamy as milk chocolate. The rain had excavated narrow canals that fed into pools among the rocks. We never lost an opportunity to fill our *girbas* from them. Mafoudh reckoned that rain water was far better than well water, since it was never salty or sulphurous. That it tasted of camel urine and was full of camel droppings didn't seem to bother him.

"In fifteen days there will be grass everywhere," he informed us. "That rain was enough for all Adrar." We heard later that the wadi in Chinguetti had been awash like a river, and in Atar the flood water had boiled through the market, demolishing buildings and drowning four people. "You can't win in the desert," Marinetta commented. "Either you get too little water or too much. We were lucky the lightning didn't strike us."

"That all depends on the will of God," Mafoudh replied. "I once knew a man who was just sitting inside his tent and the lightning killed him. Burnt a hole through the roof as clean as a bullet, by God! Another time I saw seventy sheep killed by lightning while they were sheltering under a tree. Killed the lot! You never know when your time has come."

As we travelled, we gradually got used to each other's ways. Mafoudh had a great deal to put up with. He sometimes watched me tying on the luggage in the morning, shaking his head sorrowfully as I tried to tie knots as secure as his. "You'll have to learn to tie knots better than that if you want to travel in the desert," he told me once. "When I was a boy working on the caravans, the custom was that anyone whose knot came undone had to buy a goat or a cone of sugar. That's what we should do." I agreed and threw myself into the knot-tying with new vigour. By the end of that day I owed two goats. "Don't worry, Omar," Mafoudh said, smirking. "Everyone has to learn."

The following day a *girba* that he had tied came undone and showered water across the sand. Later we almost left one of the camels behind when the headrope came unfastened. Mafoudh had tied that one too. "I think that's two goats each," I said smugly.

He looked as though he regretted having mentioned it. "Goats were a lot cheaper in those days," he said.

We generally walked for the first three hours, then rode until noon. As midday approached we would start looking for a tree around which we could build our shelter of ropes and blankets. There were few trees that were more than brittle skeletons, yet still we argued about which was the best. "That one's no good," Mafoudh might comment. "It's got no branches to hang the waterbags on."

"We can't camp there," I would respond. "There's not enough shade." When the intense heat finally drove us to accept one or the other, we couched the camels near it. Tired, thirsty and very hot, we had to spend long minutes picking at the knots that had slowly tightened during the morning. Even Mafoudh, his head already throbbing from the lack of tea, would get angry and swear like a trooper as he struggled with the rope. We drank *zrig*, and then Mafoudh would make tea. He always looked tense and harassed until he had downed his first glass. Then he relaxed, and a smile spread across his face. We drank the tea, nibbling dates or biscuits.

Marinetta made lunch, choosing from our menu of rice, pasta, couscous, tinned sardines and dried gazelle meat. It was usually too hot to eat much at midday, and often we ended up tipping the remains of the food into the desert. Mafoudh would shake his head and declare that this was "forbidden." It was worse when Marinetta threw away excess water from the cooking pot. "Getting water is hard work in the desert," he told her. "It's a crime to throw it away."

We ate from a communal steel plate with our right hands, in the Arab fashion. Although the Moors didn't generally eat with women other than their wives, Mafoudh never turned a hair at eating with Marinetta. He told me once that it would have been a disgrace to refuse. What did cause him to raise his eyebrows was her appalling manners. The rice was invisibly divided into "territories," and it was as impolite to reach into someone else's "territory" as it would have been for us to take food off someone else's plate. Marinetta constantly dived into Mafoudh's portion for tasty morsels of dried meat or sardine. "Keep to your own bit!" I had to tell her several times before she understood.

Eating rice was a problem that she found hard to resolve. You were supposed to thrust your fist into the food, squeezing the rice into a ball between fingers and thumb. Then you transferred the ball to your mouth and popped it inside with the thumb. It was unseemly for the fingers to enter the mouth. When Marinetta tried to make a ball, it would inevitably crumble before it got anywhere near her mouth, leaving a scattering of rice across the sand. Furiously, she would crush the gluey stuff into her palm and chew it out of her closed fist, drawing disgusted glances from Mafoudh.

The reason why the Moors used only the right hand for eating was that the left was exclusively for cleaning themselves after defecating. They thought toilet paper disgusting and used water to clean themselves when it was available. In the desert they used sand or stones. Marinetta tried sand and found it painfully abrasive. Often she pined for "Scottex Supersoft." Answering nature's call was always a dilemma for her. In the daytime there was nowhere to hide, and she had to pull her long Arab shirt over her knees and hope no one was watching too closely.

After we had eaten, Mafoudh would whip through his afternoon prayer. He prayed at sunrise, noon, afternoon, sunset and evening. The prayer consisted of bowing, kneeling and the repetition of certain verses from the Quran, like a meditation. Before each prayer he would make ritual ablutions, covering his hands and face with sand. He always seemed to be in a hurry with his prayers, though, as if they were something to be got out of the way before he drank his tea.

As the days passed, any doubts that I may have entertained about Mafoudh dissolved. He seemed completely trustworthy. I felt foolish for having been over-protective about Marinetta. Still, we had to behave very formally with each other while he was around, never touching or showing any sign of affection, which might have upset his sense of propriety. In Chinguetti, with a measure of privacy, we had fought like cat and dog, rowed and argued and raged. Perversely, now that there was no privacy at all, our desire for each other increased in leaps and bounds, and I found Marinetta more attractive every day as her clothes became more stained and dishevelled and her appearance wilder. Often when Mafoudh's back was turned we found ourselves exchanging secret smiles and, occasionally, the forbidden delight of a kiss. Mostly, though, we maintained the distance of strangers, hardly able even to talk.

Marinetta always kept her hair covered in the Moorish fashion. For a woman to show her hair in their culture was as much a green light to men as flashing a naked breast in ours. She had always detested hats of any kind, and keeping her thick headcloth on, even in the cool of evening, was the worst torture she had to bear. Throughout the journey she dressed like a man, and the bulky Arab shirt and *sirwel* neatly disguised any alluring feminine curves she might have shown. This brought us problems of its own. When we arrived at a well on 11 August two women who were watering goats there refused to greet her. They backed away, giggling, when she held her hand out. "They think she's a man," Mafoudh chortled. "Moor women never shake hands with a man." Both the women were dressed in faded indigo shifts and even more faded cotton skirts. One of them was quite an old lady with a face like parchment, but the other was young, slim and willowy with creamy, smooth shoulders and pert breasts. To me she looked decidedly sensuous as she dipped the rubber bucket in the well. But Mafoudh hardly gave her a second glance. Watching Marinetta beside her, I realized with a jolt what a weird, hermaphroditic figure she must have seemed to them, with her feminine smallness and her masculine dress.

When they learned that she was a woman their behaviour changed dramatically. They hustled up to her, examining her clothes and touching her skin. They fingered her wedding ring and earrings and peered into her camera bag, continually demanding presents. They seemed like wild things. Once she presented the young girl with a cheap bracelet from Chinguetti; the girl said, "This is nothing!" and asked for more. When they became aggressive in their demands I went to her rescue and told them gruffly to leave her alone. They did so immediately. I found myself wondering about this culture in which women could touch any other woman, even a complete stranger, but a man couldn't touch his own wife.

The well was in the Khatt, the great fault in the desert crust that divides the regions of Adrar and Tagant. The water was salty, but the women said it was all they had, since no rain had fallen here or farther south. "That means there'll be no tents for us to rest in," Mafoudh said testily. "We'd better fill a *girba*, even though the water's bad. A man who doesn't fill his waterbags when he gets the chance knows nothing about the desert."

The heat was back with a vengeance, and a hot wind raked us, scorching the sand and drumming up a shroud of dust that raged in the sky like sea-froth, obscuring the sun. "This is the worst type of day to travel on," our guide declared. "It's hot, and with this mist you can't tell the north from the south." The heat got us all down. Mafoudh became prickly and argumentative, lapsing into sullen moods of silence, then waking up and yelling, "Come on! Come on!" even though we were right behind him and going no more slowly than usual. Instead of laughing, he glared at me nastily when one of my knots came undone and, when he saw me tying a *girba*, commented crabbily, "I thought you knew how to tie a *girba*. You should tie it on the left, not the right."

"Rubbish!" I snapped back. "It doesn't make any difference. You just want everything done your way!"

The heat did this: it made you argue. Yet I knew that beneath the arguments was the ancient, ugly question that has plagued all men at all times: "Who's the boss?" No one travelling in the desert with desert people can avoid that issue for long. Sooner or later, in ways subtle or obvious, there will be a struggle for power.

Ours came that night, when Mafoudh told me, "The way you march is wrong. We should get up two hours before dawn and travel in the coolest time. That way is better for camels and men. We should rest most of the day and travel at night. The day is our enemy in this heat. When you find grazing you should stop for a day or even two."

I told him that I had developed my own system of marching in the Sudan. I knew that Arabs marched haphazardly, resting for two days when they found grazing, then rushing on madly for twenty hours to make up. That style was no good for our journey of 4,500 miles. It was a journey that most Arabs would not have undertaken. I was convinced that it required a more methodical approach, a blend of the Orient and the Western. Mafoudh would be with us only till Walata, then we should have another guide, then another, and another. We couldn't change our ways continually to accommodate the whims of each new guide. Our guides would have to adopt our way. And our way was to march by watch and compass, going by day and covering the same distance daily, come hell or high wind, from Chinguetti to the Nile. I remembered the story of Harry St. John Philby, the explorer of Arabia's Empty Quarter. His bedouin guides had threatened to kill him because he insisted on travelling by day. He had won only by refusing to eat with them. I doubted if such drastic measures would be needed with Mafoudh. I reminded him of what Sid' Ahmed had said before we left, and he stomped off to bed, muttering. By the following day it was forgotten.

The next morning we saw the palm groves of Talmoust sprouting from a depression in the middle of a dusty black plain. The palm trees looked temptingly green, but when we got nearer we saw that they bore no dates. The Moors who were at the well inside the groves told us that there had been no rain there for five years and that dates no longer grew. "The palms need water just like the grass," one old man said. "If we don't get rain next year, Talmoust will be finished." There were no Haratin in Talmoust. The people here were *bidan* of the Kunta, an Arab tribe of noble origin found throughout the Sahara. They herded goats and camels around Tijikja and retired to these palm groves in the season of the date harvest. Their tents were rolled up and stored on wooden frames outside the huts of palm fibre that they used in summer. The village of huts was bleak. The buildings were grey and derelict, inhabited by naked brown children and shy women in the usual faded blue. The men were very Arab-looking, stringy as thorn trees, with wisps of beard and ragged *gandourahs*. A few scraggy camels were being watered at the well, and around it lay butterfly saddles, stained and broken, and heaps of old ropes and saddle bags.

The men crowded round to greet us, and Mafoudh and I shook hands with each of them. The greeting always followed the same ritual. First you wished the whole crowd, "Peace be on you!" and they would reply in chorus, "And on you be peace!" Then you grasped each man firmly by the hand and, putting on your most earnest expression, repeated, "How is your condition? Nothing evil, I trust!" "How is the news? Only good, I trust!" You jabbered this as if in competition with an opponent, and your adversary would repeat, "No evil, thank God!" "The news is good, praise God!" The news was always good, even if your father had died or your entire camel herd had contracted the mange.

When all this had finally died down, someone would diffi- dently inquire which tribe you belonged to. It was really an inquiry after your social position because in Mauritania your status depended on how high up the social scale your tribe stood. Mafoudh belonged to a marabout tribe, which, while still nobility, didn't figure very highly in relation to these Kunta. They considered themselves descendants of the family of the Prophet Mohammed, a distinction that earned them the title of Shurfa. The Shurfa were top-drawer in Moorish soci- ety. Curiously enough, *nsara* were considered nobility because it was said that they were descended from a branch of the Prophet's tribe that had left Arabia before the time of Islam.

When status had been established, they would get down to the real news. The first question was always about grazing. Had there been rain? Where had it fallen, and how much? Had the grass bloomed yet? Where was it, and of which type? When that topic had been exhausted, they would move on to questions about people and places. Had you seen so-and-so in Chinguetti? He was a cousin. Had you seen a she-camel of such-and-such a description? Someone had lost one a few days before. They were always avid for the news, and their grapevine was very efficient, yet they much appreciated the luxury of a radio. Mafoudh constantly chided us for not hav- ing one. "It tells you everything," he said, "even where the rain has fallen. It can be very useful."

Next morning, in a stream of thick, silent heat, we saw Tijikja below us. It lay in a rocky groove in the middle of a valley from which the purple stain of date palms spread for several miles in both directions.

"Well, you've made it to Tijikja," Mafoudh said.

"You said I'd never make it?" Marinetta laughed at me.

"Anyone can be wrong," I said, "and there's still another 4,350 miles to go."

We made camp by a thorn tree above the town. It was like coming into a great harbour and dropping anchor without reaching the quayside. As soon as we had unloaded, Mafoudh said he wanted to look up an old friend and set off on foot. Marinetta and I put the tent up. It was our first moment of privacy since we had set out. She looked very attractive, and it was all I could do to stop myself dragging her into the tent that moment. "How do you feel?" I asked her, massaging her shoulder.

"I certainly don't feel flat any more," she admitted, smiling.

I was just about to move a little closer when there was a buzz of voices. We looked up to see a crowd of Haratin children who immediately surrounded us, shouting, "*Nsara! Nsara* with camels!"

"There's the end of our privacy," Marinetta said. "We'll never get rid of them now." And she was right. We never did.

From the moment we entered the town the next day, the children never left us alone. They followed us, chanting, clapping and even throwing stones. I heard one boy, a miniature adult in *gandourah* and headcloth, tell his friend, "They are unbelievers who will surely fall into the fire." Few tourists visited Tijikja, but there was an American Peace Corps volunteer there who had adopted a Muslim name and prayed in the mosque five times a day. This was fine by me, except that the man was a Christian who, instead of declaring, "There is no God but God, and Mohammed is his Prophet," as Muslims were required to do before each prayer, proclaimed, "There is no God but God, and Jesus is his Prophet." This was not designed to elicit much sympathy from the Moors, and perhaps it had poisoned their minds against all *nsara*.

We got out of the town as quickly as we could. Every minute in this crowded environment seemed a torture. We bought more dates, powdered milk for our crucial *zrig* and a few pounds of flour to make bread. We also bought another sack of grain for the camels, piled it all on to a donkey cart and beat a hasty retreat, still pursued by cat-calling, stone-throwing children. Their leader seemed to be the miniature adult, a boy of about twelve, who resisted all my attempts to get rid of him. When we passed the last house, he was still following determinedly. I rounded on him furiously. "Where are you going?" I demanded.

"I'm going after you!"

"Oh no, you're not!" I said, feeling inclined to kick his backside very firmly. The other children lined up behind him. I glared at him and he glared back. To give him his due, he didn't seem afraid.

I was just wondering if I really would have to use force, when a little old Haratin woman came hobbling up, shouting, "Hey, you children! Let the strangers go in peace!" Incredibly, all of them ran away.

When we had unloaded our new acquisitions Mafoudh told me that some of his relations had visited the camp. "They won't believe you're going to Egypt," he said. "They say it's impossible." I sat down in the shade and lit my pipe. Then I took out our Michelin map and followed our planned route with my eyes. Before us lay the rest of Mauritania, Mali, Niger, the whole of Chad and most of the Sudan. "The way is long!" Mafoudh said.

At that moment I was filled with an inexplicable sense of dread. I had the feeling that I had stepped out of the normal barriers of time and space, that I had lost touch with reality, not knowing where I had come from or where I was going. Suddenly I felt absolutely certain that I had been here before, that I had seen everything before, even that I had already reached Egypt and that time was playing backwards. I tried desperately to remember if I had dreamed this, but it danced like a shimmer of light just beyond my memory, and I walked in abject terror beyond the bounds of time, filled with images of the past, the years of struggle, the planning, the dreaming and the work it had taken to get here. And then the images passed. The terror subsided. I looked at Mafoudh and realized that only a moment had ticked by. "Yes," I told him, "the way is long indeed."

Postscript: Michael Asher was the first to complete the west-to-east crossing of the Sahara on foot without technical or other reinforcements. The 4,500-mile journey took nine months.

An important part of the Nigerian culture is the bush taxi. Peter Chilson discovered the travails of such travel, replete with bad tires, failing motors, and overloaded human cargo, all of which led to a stream of horrendous, catastrophic accidents. He also encountered a further hazard—numerous checkpoints manned by armed soldiers who were corrupt to the core.

RIDING THE DEMON
On the Road in West Africa

PETER CHILSON

Zinder Notes

I *needed, after a few weeks shar-*ing a car with Issoufou Garba, to drink in order to sleep. Evenings, wherever we ended up, I downed three 1.5-liter bottles of Biére Niger, a product of the national brewery. I drank mostly in village bars, where they cooled the beer in a damp pit covered by wet cloth. In Zinder, I went to the Hotel Central bar, with its prostitutes from southern Nigeria and one regular customer, a despondent soldier. Every night he leaned on the bar, automatic rifle propped against the stone countertop, quietly sipping his beer and talking to no one. I

drank without Issoufou, whose Muslim faith forbade him to
use alcohol. I never got drunk, only tired enough to sleep. I
was too wired, I suppose, to become giddy.

I had a room at a hostel, which was the large home of a Zinder family who rented space to travelers. Mornings I walked to
the motor park coffee table popular with drivers, including
Issoufou. We waited for passengers, drank coffee—instant
Nescafé canned in Ivory Coast—told stories, exchanged news.
We found out who had crashed or broken down, who had
been in trouble at checkpoints and how much it had cost them,
which driver had been arrested or beaten. "You heard about
Moussa?" someone asked. "Salif says he hit a bull yesterday
near Tessaoua. He still hasn't come back."

The coffee table scene was like a mission debriefing: checking off goals, tallying casualties. Cars, like shot-up aircraft,
limped back from someplace—Agadez, Nguigmi, Diffa,
Maradi, Kano, Niamey, bush villages—every hour, chewed up
and spit out by the road. The image of the West African
motor park and its legions of beat-up cars and drivers sug-
gests a conflict with the unknowable. I think again of Saint-
Exupéry, who wrote of a pilot's struggle against the elements:
"It isn't the individual that's responsible, but a sort of hidden
force."

Issoufou Garba wanted to see a Mad Max movie, *Beyond
Thunderdome*, at the Hotel Central theater, an outdoor courtyard where a man projects movies on a whitewashed wall. He
invited me to join him. The idea of seeing Tina Turner on a
big screen, larger than life, pleased him. "It's Tina," Issoufou
said, sitting that morning at the coffee table. "We're going to
see Teeena tonight."

At 8:00 P.M., men packed the theater, which normally
shows Kung Fu movies, French police dramas, Hindu love

stories. I shared a long wooden bench with Issoufou and a half dozen other drivers wearing simple cotton robes or leisure-style African business suits in shades of gray, navy blue, brown. They laughed a little conspiratorially, a little nervously, looking about the place with arms folded. There was, after all, some guilt involved. These men, supporters of wives and children (at least thirty-five children between them), had paid the three-hundred-franc entry fee, money that could buy a family enough rice for a couple of days. But this was a road movie, a way for drivers to fantasize—about Tina Turner, yes, but about themselves as well. They wanted to see the last scene, the surreal, apocalyptic road battle fought in the Australian desert at high speed with homemade automobile hybrids—reinvented cars that functioned in a brutal, cynical, decayed, post–nuclear war desert world very similar to the scenario around them, subtracting nuclear war.

I watched, expecting something to happen—wild shouting, perhaps, some sort of road culture audience participation; cheers, maybe. Yet my companions sat and looked on politely, silently enthralled for an hour and a quarter, until the road chase, when Mel Gibson's character climbs from one vehicle to another. Then I heard gasps. laughs, sounds of excited approval: *"Oooh la, la, c'est pas vrai ça,"* or a slightly drawn out *"Alllahh!"* or *"Monnn Dieu!"* or the sharp Hausa exclamation, *"Kai!"*

On the way out, a driver named Mamane asked me, half joking, half seriously: "Is it that way in America?"

I liked the Hotel Central because, in an old Muslim market city and sultanate, the hotel represents vice like a quiet bordello in the Vatican. Long verandahs with low cement arches frame two sides of a gravel courtyard; behind each arch is a door to an empty room, twelve in all. At the courtyard's far end is a half-circle stone bar under a millet-thatch awning. Next door, high white cement walls enclose the outdoor theater. In Zinder—where I saw men publicly beat and stone women who did not cover their heads with cloth as the imams required, where in the summer of 1992 a mob of men burned the offices of a women's center—the Hotel Central offered me sanctuary from events in a city that sometimes appeared to be going mad.

The motor park is next door to the hotel, which seemed to me a natural extension of that world. Carnival manifestations of the road wash up in front of those white walls: the occasional road movie, a traveling automobile spectacle. One day, two German used-car dealers arrived from Cotonou (Benin) in two eighteen-wheelers loaded with used Peugeot 504 sedans and station wagons recently offloaded from freighters that had sailed from Brussels.

"Karl" and "Walter," as the prostitutes called the Germans, wore jeans with cowboy boots and brown leather vests over T-shirts. For three weeks they hung out between the bar and their rooms, where they negotiated with buyers and spent nights with the barmaids, the only other people they seemed to know. Karl was thin, balding, with a wispy red beard, sunken cheeks and eyes, quivering hands. At the bar he held his beer with two hands. He had on a stiff, new brown fedora with a brown leather band. I tried talking to him one night.

"I'm told you're selling cars."

He looked at me, folding his arms. "Got a cigarette?" he asked.

"Sorry."

He looked at me again, up and down. I was at least as scrawny as he was, at least as hollow faced, and, apparently, unable to hide the fact I had no intention of buying a car. In crisp English, he said, "Run along little doggy." Karl sipped his beer, and I shrugged and walked away.

Souley, the old hotel barman, later told me, "They sell more than cars." He raised both fists and put them together to make the staccato sound and movement of automatic weapons: "*Ta-ta-ta-ta-ta-ta*. Guns, guns."

At the coffee table, I told Issoufou the story. It became his favorite. Two or three times a day he slowly repeated my imitation of Karl's English, "Run a-long leetle doggy," and laughed.

Some mornings Issoufou sent me on spare parts errands, normally the job of a *karamota*. The apprentice mechanic, usually a boy between ten and eighteen, races like a dog after the machine he works on (usually a minibus) has started moving, and then jumps in a side or rear door. Once inside, the *karamota*–"dog of the car"–crouches with his back against the closed door. For my errands, the drivers awarded me the honorary Hausa nickname "Anasara karamota." *Anasara*, a term derived from Arabic, means something like "Christian," and the Hausa use it as a name for white people.

Often we didn't leave until evening.

Days came when I felt used to the road. On others I was sick and frightened. I never told Issoufou.

One evening, a crowd of men gathered around a brightly lit platform in a sandy lot outside the Hotel Central. Mounted on the platform was a two-door compact Renault with oversized tires like a dune buggy. The car sat inside a blue steel frame that wrapped around it like a big claw, bolted to the top and sides. An amusement park ride. On the hotel wall hung a giant blue-and-white cloth poster with "Rothman's"–a popular French cigarette brand–printed in blue across the center. The same letters stretched across both sides of the car.

A Frenchman in tight jeans and sneakers stood on the platform. He had thick brown hair and a beard, and he wore a white Rothman's T-shirt that struggled to hold in his belly.

Holding a microphone, he leaned back against the driver's door, blank-faced as he read from a paper, his voice nearly lost in static. A tall, bone-thin young man in dark trousers and shirt pushed his way to the front, holding high a blue raffle ticket. He'd apparently won a drawing. The man pulled him by the hand onto the platform and pushed him to the car. The young man got behind the wheel and waited as the Frenchman, cigarette hanging from his lips, buckled and snapped straps across the winner's torso and thighs. The Frenchman shut the door and walked to the rear of the platform, to a small box bolted to the metal frame holding the car, pressed several buttons, pulled a lever, and jumped into the sand. He glanced at his watch and walked into the bar.

The frame's hydraulic arms slowly lifted the vehicle off the platform and tilted the car nose-up as the winner, his face revealed by the glow of an inside light, stared straight ahead, hands gripping the wheel. His expression was nil, like someone struggling to maintain his youthful male dignity in a moment of bewilderment.

There came a hydraulic hissing and the car suddenly began rolling up and down, quickly but not violently, as if climbing and descending a succession of small steep hills or desert dunes. All this happened within the firm grip of the hydraulic frame. No automobile engine sound, just hissing and whirring. The car, of course, never left the platform. It dipped to one side and then the other, like a vehicle rounding a hillside, before straightening into a spasm of violent shaking in sharp little jerks, mimicking movement on a bumpy road. The crowd of about two hundred men and boys watched patiently, coldly, for several minutes, as if thinking, "Yes, this is interesting, but what's the point?" Our winner's head bobbed and bounced as he kept his grip on the wheel and his forward glare. The car stopped for a few seconds, then resumed the hill-climbing routine, ending in a steep, bumpy descent. The metal claw leveled the car and raised it several more feet, and then, like a last cruel joke, sent it into a wobbly spin, rolling four times before coming to a clanking, hissing rest.

For a moment, the winner broke character: mouth open, wide-eyed, he looked out his side window. Then he faced forward again. The Frenchman, knowing the routine's timing, emerged from the bar scratching his beard. He put his beer bottle on the platform before climbing back on. He went straight to the little box, pushed the lever up, and opened the car door to unstrap the young man, who stepped out steadily, to my surprise, and put on his bored look as he rejoined the crowd. The young man ignored the Frenchman, who ignored him. That was the "Rothman's Rally."

The spectacle was in town for three days to promote Rothman's sponsorship of the Paris–Dakar Rally scheduled in March. The race—billed as a contest of man against his environment—would cross the Sahara through Morocco and Mauritania to Dakar. Dozens of souped-up cars and motorcycles with support vehicles and aircraft would streak across desert and savanna, through villages and farm fields (as racers had done in many rallies before in Niger and Mali), maiming or killing the occasional farm animal, and sometimes the unwary person. A fist in the face from Europe, like an invited guest who casually wrecks the house.

I got lost one afternoon in Zinder looking for the offices of the regional medical officer, who had information about road accidents. I ended up wandering through ruins on the city's edge, building after crumbling building the French colonizers had built for themselves. I decided to keep wandering—through offices, barracks, armories, and handsome stone homes dating back to the beginning of the colony in 1900, when Zinder was the colonial capital.

The French had occupied a hilltop in the eastern section of the city, up the road from the Hotel Central and the *bureau de poste* and past the Musée Regionale. This is the same road that joins Route 1 as it heads out of the city and runs east another 375 miles to Lake Chad: Forced labor crews had plastered the buildings with white stucco over mud bricks six inches thick. The stucco, now yellowed, was flaking off under the erosive forces of rain and wind. Triangular decorative battlements, like teeth, concealed corrugated iron roofs. Many of the roofs and walls had collapsed. The remaining structures looked like dried-out broken eggs tossed aside, the yolk left to rot.

People once entered these buildings up wide stairs, across broad patios, and through high archways flanked by six-foot French windows. I entered the buildings by stepping over the remains of a wall or through a window opening.

Time had erased the more human traces of the French in these places. No furniture or shelving remained, not even a rusting bed frame; no papers, bits of photographs, clothing, wall hangings, or cookware—nothing to connect me personally to people who lived and worked in these buildings on a hilltop thirty-two years before. I found only vague random clues: bits of pipe, pieces of a white commode bolted to the floor, a chunk of a sink, electrical wiring, sections of checkered black-and-white floor tiles.

The structures, by design, demanded attention and created a military advantage. From this summit the French once administered a system that forced villagers to surrender quotas of cotton and peanuts for export, young men for colonial military service, and huge labor crews to build roads all across Niger. Elders in Zinder told me that hundreds died building Route 1 and other roads, but the French kept no records of

casualties. Men, women, and children worked in teams, the
women and young ones hauling buckets of laterite rock from
the bush while the men pounded and graded the material into
the road. French engineers surveyed the work on horseback
and kept crews under the armed watch of colonial military
conscripts from Mali and Senegal. The French paid the workers a few francs a day and required village chiefs to provide
food and water without compensation. This hardship, the
French insisted, was for the common good, for the betterment
of the region. The crews slept where they worked, and people
died of thirst, starvation, and disease. Beatings were routine
for those who lagged behind. Some were shot. None of this
can be verified through the records the French left behind.
Why, after all, would they incriminate themselves? I had only
the word of the very old in Zinder.

The French did more than draft labor crews. That much is
well documented. Young men from villages with names like
Gouré, Magaria, Droum, and Mirria were made to put on
French uniforms and taken to die in incomprehensible wars
defined in Paris, Berlin, London, and Brussels, their bodies
fallen in places like Verdun and Dien Bien Phu—all for the
glory of France.

Zinder's regional archive, a small building behind the governor's office (Zinder is now the capital of one of Niger's
seven regional departments), holds great volumes of decaying
official history. Inside, on wooden shelves and in a pyramid
pile on the floor, are reports, letters, orders. I read, in a green
cardboard binder, a directive dated June 28, 1916, typed on
onionskin under the title "Police des Routes." The commandant in Zinder sent it unsigned, as if in a hurry, to the post
commander in Tanout, seventy miles north on the road to
Agadez: "Mail convoys are again reporting pillaging by the
Mousgous and Kel-Fadey [Tuareg groups]. I have ordered

measures be taken to put an end to all hostilities. It is up to
you to assure the effective policing of the roads and Tuareg
camps."

Now, in the buildings where the colonizers had once lived
and worked, the cracking cement and tile floors were strewn
with shit. Walking through one stone building, I imagined a
Frenchman in white uniform at his desk calculating the cotton
harvest, considering the discipline of a village chief, but oblivious to an African dressed in a white coat and standing in a
corner, pumping a large bellows to cool him.

The ruins serve a purpose similar to the war ruins deliberately left unrepaired in Europe and Japan. They remind us of
something awful. But these ruins mock through negligence, a
gesture of contempt through decay.

The French have ceased to matter in this place. The culture of the colonizer has undergone a visual metamorphosis,
like the remains of a heavy snow shoveled to one side and left
to melt. It is preserved, isolated, only in the cities, such as
Niamey, where French, spoken by less than 2 percent of
Niger's population, is more commonly heard.

In February 1944, Charles de Gaulle, on a tour of the
French African colonies not controlled by the Nazi puppet
regime in Vichy, stepped off a twin-engine military transport
plane at a dirt airstrip just outside Zinder. The French community of about forty people, joined by groups of African
schoolchildren, dignitaries, and colonial soldiers, cheered him
down the gangway. The Africans were mostly non-French-
speakers dressed traditionally and ordered to be present—
village chiefs, provincial sultans, imams, musicians. African
civil servants, clerks, and teachers assigned to Zinder from
France's colonies all over Africa, also attended. They were the
only Africans who understood French.

De Gaulle shook hands and complimented the people on

their Frenchness, reminding them of the greatness of France, the benevolence of France, assuring them that France would soon end the terrible war—victorious, of course. Minutes later, he walked back up the steps to his plane and flew away, like a man who had quickly understood that he had landed in the wrong place. All along Route 1, the French governed in this absentminded way, neglect punctuated by bursts of fury and paranoia, as if they realized a mistake and didn't want to spend too much energy governing, but couldn't quite make up their minds how to do it. Government by fits and starts.

Not all the colonial buildings have crumbled. A couple of old barracks still house soldiers. A primary school holds classes within the walls of the former French hospital. And the dominant power symbol visible around the city—a rectangular crenellated mud tower built atop a large outcropping of rounded rocks (Zinder's highest point)—marks the headquarters of the regional military garrison (once the French garrison). The garrison includes several hundred men of the regular army and the Garde Republicaine, which provides security for government buildings. They have a single light tank donated by the French.

As I wandered through yet another building, I became aware, suddenly, of two little boys, maybe eight years old, in dust-stained T-shirts and shorts. They stood outside on the patio, staring at me. *"C'est la toilette, Monsieur,"* the taller boy said, not with mockery, but seriously, with the tone of someone who wanted to clear up a slight misunderstanding. They looked at me with faces like empty pages, then hurried away.

I became confused one day when Issoufou Garba called me "Bodo." We were streaking down Route 1 from Maradi to Zinder in the dark when he looked at me, making notes in the passenger seat, keeping my eyes off the road, my mind off the speed. He threw several frowning glances my way, glances he stole from the road, as if he had just noticed something for the first time. He took in my notebook and pen. I was aware of this but did not look back at him.

Issoufou said: *"Toi, tu es Bodo."*

"Quor?"

"Tu es Bodo, grand Bodo."

Puzzled, I just looked at him. "I don't understand," I said.

"Bodo was a Frenchman," he explained. "He lived here once and worked very hard. Now, when we see someone like that, we call him 'Bodo.' It's part of our language. You should know about him. He helped build the roads."

Memories linger. Bodo is the Hausa storytellers' name for Jean Boudot, a French district officer who long ago entered Zinder legend and lexicon. His personality is the subject of story and song in Niger, and Bodo is a complimentary nickname for those who work very hard. *"Lui là, c'est un grand Bodo,"* people on the street respectfully say of a farmer marching to his fields.

I found that the story still lived in the head of one of Niger's most famous cultural figures, Mazo dan Alalo, the *griot*, or personal praise singer, of every sultan of Zinder since 1940. Mazo told me about Boudot while sitting in an old lawn chair in the sandy compound of his Zinder home, a whitewashed mud mansion built by his father, who had also been a *griot*. Mazo and the elders of Zinder remember the Frenchman with ironic affection and by the title Mazo gave him: Anasara Bodo Sarkin Ayki, "The Christian Boudot, Prince of Work." They remember him for his management of the forced labor crews who worked the roads and fields and built many of the colonial buildings in Niger. Forced labor built France's colonies the world over. Forced labor built Route 1.

Mazo dan Alalo was in his mid-nineties when I spoke with him (he was not sure of his exact age). He stood six feet tall. The day I met him he was exquisitely robed in bright cotton, white and blue, with tan leather slippers and a thick white turban wound high above his head. His face looked like a scarred fingerprint, marked by wrinkle patterns of crazy slits and lines that converged to center on his nose and mouth. Mazo sang for Boudot, sang about him and against him—that nervous, lanky commandant in white shorts and open-collared shirt, thick shock of coal black hair, explosive temper. *"Un homme toujours faché"*—An always angry man—so Zinder residents still describe him. Boudot had a way of bursting from his office to yell, no matter the occasion, at the nearest person, European or African, man, woman, or child: *"C'est quoi, ça? Tu n'as rien a faire? Pas de travail?"*—What's this? You've nothing to do? No work?

Jean Boudot was *commandant de cercle*—district commandant—of Zinder for only eleven months in 1943 and 1944. His name survives as a metaphor for work. He is also remembered for his peculiar harshness, though he had decades of competition. There was Lieutenant Colombani, for instance, who, in 1925, reportedly kicked a village chief to death on Route 1, just two and a half miles from Zinder. The chief had failed to raise the labor requested for road repairs, and he was too old to rise from his straw mat when the lieutenant stood before him demanding an explanation. Colombani, Mazo and other elders told me, screamed at the chief: "I'll teach you respect!" He kicked the chief off his mat, and kicked again repeatedly at the old man's abdomen. The chief bled to death internally right there on the road. The colonial records reveal nothing of the incident, though the lieutenant's work progress reports survive.

Curiously, few remember Colombani, but everyone knows

of Boudot, whose image survives thanks to the *griot*. School-children learn the Boudot story from the words of Mazo's songs. On loan from the sultan of Zinder, Mazo toured the countryside on horseback with the Frenchman, singing his praises—"Bodo, the friend of the sultan / All the chiefs know his work"—or the praises of his programs, always in Hausa (Mazo still speaks no French, and I interviewed him through an interpreter). Mazo rode his horse right behind the commandant, beating a drum and singing with a half dozen men backing him up, on foot, with voices and drums. They sang as Boudot and his colonial soldiers marched men and women and children out of villages at gunpoint to serve on labor crews, as Boudot ordered a man beaten for taking a rest from his job crushing laterite on the road, as he handed a cash reward—five francs—to a man whose work pleased him. Mazo sang on. He had no choice, really. His situation was similar to that of a regional balladeer conscripted by a state governor to campaign for him in melody.

> Bodo Anasara Sarkin Ayki
> He who forced us to plant manioc and peanuts
> He who forced us to make the roads
> Bodo, the son of nonbelievers
> The friend of the Sultan
>
> Sarkin Bodo Anasara Sarkin Ayki
> He freed no one from work
> Who but Bodo would make the old
> the lepers, the blind, the prostitutes
> the soldiers and their wives do work
> Even the marabouts and the roosters
> who wake us for prayer went to work
>
> Anasara Bodo Sarkin Ayki . . .

The *griot* as an African institution is much more than singer and storyteller. He is also historian and journalist. Mazo was the sultan's unofficial adviser on matters of state, culture, society. He was a listener and reporter of sorts who took the country's social and political pulse. To his sultan, Mazo was spin doctor, ad man, image maker, intelligence gatherer. Spy.

Boudot fell ill often, Mazo told me—stomach problems or malaria. Yet the Frenchman insisted on daily project inspections and personally visited villages to raise work crews. "He would look at a man's hands," Mazo told me, "and if they didn't show the wear of work, Bodo would take him for labor. Sometimes he would beat the man. Bodo had no consideration." Then Mazo added, borrowing a line from his own song, "For Bodo, everything was work."

Subversion permeates Mazo's work, which music dealers sell on cassettes all around Niger. There are many versions of the Bodo song, all Mazo's recordings: he modifies the story as he sings. The listener hears Mazo telling the sultan what he saw and heard, and, in the commandant's very presence, forming a musical caricature to please the sultan, to manipulate villagers' hearts and minds, the balance of power—"Bodo who sends the roosters and lepers to work"; and this variation: "Bodo, who makes even the sultan work." The sultan, of course, never did physical labor. Mazo sang his signature into a story with words that mocked but went right past the ears of the unwary white man who spoke no Hausa. "Who but Bodo would make the old, the lepers, the blind go to work."

Zinder's Birni quarter—the city's oldest neighborhood—is built among clusters of huge rounded rocks that sprout from the flat, sandy landscape, seeming to grow out of one another like cauliflower. The rocks once made useful fortifications and still make good natural walls for houses. Many believe their size indicates the presence of significant power within.

One morning in the summer of 1911 (the year is approximate), two small boys, one Hausa and the other Arab, were playing on a rock the size of a school bus but shaped like the sloping narrow tail of a prehistoric beast. The rock conveniently intruded into the home compound of the Hausa boy, Mahamane dan Chalaga, whose father managed the sultan's vast horse stables. With a little sand tossed on the surface, the rock made a good slide for straw mats.

Mahamane and Hamed Charif, son of a wealthy Arab merchant, chased each other up and down that rock. They tumbled down together and landed in a pile at the bottom, laughing. The rains had been good that summer, and the air was cool after months of heavy, stubborn dry-season heat.

For a few moments, Mahamane sat still in the sand below the great stone. He frowned, not frightened, but listening hard. "Hamed," he said. "Do you hear that?"

A distant buzzing interrupted by clanking, and then that low buzzing again, unlike any sound they knew. They ran from the compound to investigate, and a short distance down a narrow alleyway almost collided with the thing they had heard—a parked car, driverless, with its motor idling. "When I first saw the car," Mahamane (now in his nineties) told me, "it was alone outside the house of Hamed's family. No one was in it, and it was vibrating all alone, shaking as if it were angry like a beast." I smiled at the fact that these two boys nearly ran over the first car they ever saw, rather than the other way around. "Hamed and I ran back to my family's compound to find my father. We thought we had done something wrong and that the thing was looking for us. We didn't understand what it was." The car's owner, in fact, was Hamed's father, the cloth merchant Charif Dodo.

Zinder is full of road tales, old stories of death and daring on cross-desert trade routes, and the occasional bizarre anecdote, like Mahamane's story of the car he saw as a boy. That machine must have been one of the first automobiles to enter Niger, arriving in the years just before World War I. Mahamane, who was born between 1900 and 1905, told me he was around eleven or twelve years old when he saw the car; he couldn't remember precisely. By 1912, cars were becoming more common in colonial port cities along the West African coast, but they hadn't yet rolled into the interior in noticeable numbers. The French supplied outposts like Zinder by camel and donkey caravans.

The story's details have to be carefully mined from the very old, then sifted and cross-checked. Pieces of hard fact occasionally emerge. Still, nothing is certain. In Zinder, I sought the counsel of the very old, anyone who might have a bit of information. Mazo dan Alalo first mentioned the car to me, but said his memory of it was very poor. He told me about Mahamane and instructed me to look for him at the Sultanate, where many of the city's eldest men and women collect in the morning shade of the high brown walls. I found Mahamane sitting alone on a straw mat with a cane resting across his legs. He was chewing kola nut and fingering prayer beads while clutching a camelhair blanket about him against the cold-season air. Like his father before him, Mahamane had been the caretaker of the sultan's horses—only a dozen now, though they had numbered more than a thousand during his father's time.

That car, Mahamane and others told me (people whose parents and grandparents had seen it), could carry four passengers: the driver and one more up front, two in back. It was an American car, Mahamane and Mazo insisted, which Charif had bought in Kano, British Nigeria, eighty miles to the south. In the absence of roads, he arranged for it to be towed through the bush to Zinder by a pair of camels, a week's journey.

Most likely the car was a Ford, probably a Model T, which Ford introduced in 1908 and followed up with variations, including one that completed the 1912 Peking-to-Paris Rally. The Model T became one of the most widely driven cars in the world before World War I; fifteen million were sold before Ford switched to the Model A in 1928. What the people saw in Zinder resembled a horseless buggy with thin, airless rubber tires that stuck easily in sand. An impractical machine in the Sahel, but an important symbol of wealth.

Mahamane, as far as I could tell, was the only surviving witness with a clear memory of what may have been Niger's first automobile the very day it arrived in Zinder. Such a bizarre object, a thing so otherworldly in a city that for centuries had depended on the trade of camel caravans, could not have been a secret for any amount of time. Mahamane and Hamed ran through the city to spread the news of the "shaking beast."

The morning I met Mahamane, we walked to his home, the very same house where he grew up. He showed me the great rock. Mahamane walked with his cane, taking long, slow strides, carefully placing the tip with every step, his body stooped under his blanket. "It was many days," he told me, standing again at the foot of the rock, "before Hamed and I had the courage to touch that car without running away." But he could not remember the year he saw the vehicle. "Was it around 1912?" I asked. He shrugged.

Mahamane showed me, too, where Charif Dodo and his family had lived. The house was a ruin. The skeleton of a Peugeot sedan lay crumpled and half buried within waist-high mud walls that were melting steadily under wind and rain.

The car's front half protruded like a tombstone, facing the street as if glaring at passersby. The family had faded into rumor ("They all died" or "They returned to Algeria"). Not even Mahamane recalled. Only the memory of the car, perhaps the most remarkable thing about Charif Dodo, remained.

Charif, who had the money to risk eccentricity, bought bundles of dried grass and millet stalks and hired men to lay a mile or so of track around the city. Thus, Niger's first functional motor roads were dual platforms of tightly bound and flattened grass bundles, spliced end to end along the routes Charif wanted to drive—to the Sultanate, the homes of friends, his shops, the colonial offices. The French and the sultan, always jealous and suspicious of one another's influence, had no motor vehicles of their own. The French commandant is said to have borrowed the car for tours of the city and for road inspections.

It is a point of no small significance that an Arab, a member of a group who for hundreds of years were the masters of cross–Saharan trade, was possibly the first to own a car and build motor roads in Niger. Although the French had established a wagon and caravan route along what is now Route I, they did not yet maintain it for automobiles.

Mahamane spoke skeptically of the automobile he saw as a boy. "What good was it?" he said. "They couldn't take the thing out in the bush." When I met him, he still preferred to walk. Mahamane had been in a car only a half dozen times in his life.

The French soon brought in their own cars and began building more roads and, during the late 1920s, the Zinder airstrip. Charif Dodo eventually sold his car, people say, and what happened to it after that is anybody's guess. I like to think the machine is still around in spirit and substance, scattered about West Africa in pieces, some of them still on the road. A spring fitted in one vehicle somewhere, a bolt that proved useful in another somewhere else; or perhaps a chunk of sheet metal from its body shades a family's doorway.

One afternoon around Christmas 1987 (near the end of my Peace Corps service), on Zinder's windswept streets near the *bureau de poste*, a large, snub-nosed truck with a gray cab rumbled past me. The truck was Nigerian, what they call a mammy wagon, with high wooden walls around the rear bed, like a big box, and painted in many colors. I recall pictures of lions, men in battle with big guns, and an English slogan, GOD SAVE US!

What had caught my attention, however, was something painted long before on the driver's-side door—a German Army cross, thick black and trimmed on the outside edges with thin white borders. Only a shadow of the cross remained. Just enough. The truck was moving slowly enough that I could run back and verify that the trademark sign on the radiator grille said Ford, not Mercedes, and that the door was a darker shade of gray than the rest of the body. It was a modified truck, and not unusual, except for the door and its insignia, whose origins fascinated me. A stray fragment, perhaps, of Rommel's Afrika Corps, which fought the British on the other side of the Sahara; a door rescued from shreds of hardware blown to bits in a tank battle between machines painted the color of sand, fighting in white heat like scorpions; or perhaps a door from a truck captured and sold, whole or piece by piece, at the war's end.

The memory returned in February 1993, when I was walking through Zinder's open market, in the section known as Kasuan Tsakuwa—the metal market. Metalsmiths, dozens of them spread over two acres, working with scrap metal or, literally, road metal, bits of metal from everywhere, but primarily the road. They reshape metal pieces into bed frames, cooking utensils, plates, bowls, axes, hoes. plow blades, nails and hammers, screws and screwdrivers, hinges, doors, roofing, tables, chairs, daggers and swords, tea trays, cooking stoves, travel chests, bicycle frames, eyeglasses, and back into car parts such as doors and engine hoods. And from tires and inner tubes they make sandals, shoe soles, rubber hoses, watch straps, saddlebags, and well buckets.

A playground of ingenuity, genius born of need.

The material comes from car wrecks, from parts hunted and plucked carefully like wild mushrooms, judged for value and carried to market alongside vegetables and grains, part of the general national harvest. A station wagon may kill seven passengers, but in death it preserves the livelihood of a family or two from the closest village—the first to arrive at the scene after the bodies have been cleared away and the gendarmes have finished their note-taking. It could happen no other way.

In Africa, everything is adaptable. Old bicycle frames, oil barrels from Nigeria, cans, corrugated iron, and automobile scraps such as car bodies or a heavy steel chassis too mangled to be repaired. The metal market assumes the character of a slaughterhouse, where nothing is wasted and from which everything emerges with a new identity, like cuts of meat so neatly, antiseptically packaged for the supermarket. The metalsmiths buy the raw metal; the salvageable engine parts go to mechanics and parts dealers.

The smiths handle Western technology a little like instant coffee, if you stretch the image. Their working material is soluble, filtered through mutilation, reshaped, redefined, reborn, redistributed, and redigested again and again and again. Nothing, perhaps, is quite what it seems or was intended to

be. It is simple; it is African, a question of ingenuity and survival. You use what you have, what you can find.   ·

> The road, the aged road
> Retched on this fresh plunder
> Of my youth.
> —Wole Soyinka, "In Memory of Segun Awolowo"

Driving to Madness

"There he is," Issoufou Garba said, gazing out the car wind-
shield into gritty haze. "There's my little imbecile. Do you see
him?"

"Non," I said. I didn't see him, the man Issoufou called *"mon
petit imbécile."* For some reason the words seem clearer now in
the original French, as if my memory of the man we sought is
frozen in the phonetics. An ice cube of thought. In French, the
syllables of *imbécile* bounce louder from the lips, and they can
be drawn out, emphasized with a sharp kick of the tongue
at the end. *Ilimmbéeccüla.* Which was what Issoufou was doing,
drawling the word to himself as he watched the man I
couldn't see—a *komasho.* Issoufou's own.

I looked out the window again. "Where is he?" I squinted
and leaned over on the seat, looking past Issoufou.

He frowned at me, a little impatient, and pointed once
more, casually flicking his left hand behind him with the
index finger out, the way one might point out the village idiot.
"Tu vois? C'est lui, là." Issoufou laughed just a little, nodding his
head slightly, suggesting he had made eye contact with this
person. He turned off the engine.

We were sitting in Issoufou's Peugeot station wagon, on a
road just outside the crowded motor park in Maradi, a market
city near the border with Nigeria. Two vast fields separated by

a long, low cement wall in the center make up the motor park. As a border town, Maradi is economically more complex, bigger, dirtier, wealthier, more dangerous than Niger's other cities. An African Tijuana. You can buy anything in Maradi: Snickers bars, grains and vegetables, genuine or fake designer jeans, baseball gloves (no one plays in Niger), automatic arms, smuggled gasoline. The stuff comes up from Nigeria, that African catchall, economic Goliath.

In the street, dense streams of people—women and girls balancing pots of rice and beans atop their heads, people on market business, people with no business, children, travelers, idlers—drifted and collected, moving this way and that, congealing at shops, in the shade of trees, at street-side coffee tables where rows of men—only men—sat and talked. Women in small groups walked by on errands or stood to chat for a few minutes as they passed one another on the street. One woman sat at a cooking fire frying millet flour cakes in peanut oil. She wrapped them by the dozen in newspaper and sold them to passersby. Only men seemed to lounge with nothing to do. The street was so crowded, the din of voices and engines and animals so constant, that I couldn't tell whom Issoufou was pointing at.

When we reached Maradi early that morning, the gendarmes at the city entrance hadn't bothered with us. I didn't know why. As we arrived at the checkpoint, a soldier, clutching himself against the cool February Harmattan winds, simply lowered the rope and waved us on. Four other soldiers were huddled around the driver of an eighteen-wheeler. Bigger prey, maybe.

Around 1:00 P.M. we found ourselves back among the *komasho*, a dozen young men and boys who right away saw we were looking for someone. Issoufou was pointing. The *komasho* closed in. They pounded on the windows, they thumped the roof, they shouted. *"Monsieur, c'est moi! Tu me con-nais, tu me connais, c'est moi!"*—It's me, you know me, you know me, it's me!

Now, just ahead of us, I saw a man who looked a little evil. It was, I suppose, his face. He coasted briskly along my side of the car at the head of a group of four men, like pirates prepar-ing to board and loot. The evil one, the leader, was short, overly muscular, slightly stooped, frowning from a lumpy face, like a troll. A Maradi *komasho*.

His name was Abdou, and he was one of Issoufou's con-tacts. I had never met him before, but I knew enough to be careful. Judging by his appearance, his strength, the newness of his clothing, he did better than most *komasho*. He stood there with his face in my window, grinning and rapping his knuckles softly on the glass. He didn't have to shout.

Abdou wore a heavy, ill-fitting brown canvas suit, homespun and new. His sandals were blue plastic, a cheap Chinese import. He had shaved his head, and his face was smooth skinned, lean, and square. The prominent nose and chin com-bined with high cheekbones and jutting forehead to make his visage appear lumpy, like a big potato. Thick tendons like lengths of bark ran up his forearms. His sunglasses were a style normally worn by women, the top-heavy plastic kind with bows attached to the bottom of wide oval lens frames. The inside seams of Abdou's trousers wiggled out of control down his thighs, and the cuffs were uneven by an inch. Issoufou's contempt, his use of the French-English cognate imbécile, and that nervous chuckle came to my mind. But I didn't feel like laughing.

Too risky.

All at once, Issoufou leaned over and thrust an arm behind my seat to unlock the rear door. Abdou yanked it open immediately. He slid in the backseat and slammed and locked the door against his competitors, who orbited the car, arguing amongst themselves. They peered at us through the windows, some frowning and others waving and smiling at me while the troll sat behind Issoufou and leaned forward to clamp his right hand on my friend's shoulder, still grinning. The grin's persistence carried a psychopathic quality, emphasizing that the hand-on-shoulder was not a gesture of friendship but a reminder of the strength of the hand's owner.

One of the men outside the car put his ear to my window; another did the same on the driver's side. But Issoufou and Abdou ignored all this. They dispensed with greetings, going straight to business while Issoufou simultaneously studied the streets, in case one of Abdou's more earnest competitors should decide to challenge Abdou more pointedly. The *komasho* did this occasionally to destroy one another's business contacts.

"I've got two, Issoufou," Abdou said hoarsely, just above a whisper, aware of the ears outside. He ignored me. I was just another white traveler to him—a tourist? a missionary? a Peace Corps volunteer? It didn't matter. I was Issoufou's own merchandise, a nonissue. Already sold freight.

The man at my window pressed his lips against the glass, then his tongue, laying it flat against the surface like a pink snail. He backed off a moment, laughing, watching for my reaction. I watched him blankly as he prodded me with a wide toothy smile, raising his eyebrows repeatedly. Another man sat calmly on the hood, hunched over in the shape of a gargoyle, his chin on his knees and his legs crossed at the ankles. Others circled the car. I folded my arms across my chest, a gesture of defense, of digging in.

Abdou and Issoufou continued talking in low tones. I heard Abdou say: "They weren't easy to find, Issouf. This will cost you."

I remember the actions of many *komasho* in Niger, and in Nigeria and Ivory Coast and Senegal: their bobbing, swirling, biting presence, but not what they all looked like. The details mix in my head: bare feet, sores, ragged dust-stained clothes, mostly trousers and American T-shirts. No faces. This is important: The man at my window suddenly grabbed his shirttail, vigorously wiped the smoky smear of his saliva from the glass where his tongue had been, and walked away. As if he were suddenly sorry. Another man took his place, kneeling at the window to look at me. This man wore a T-shirt, dirty white, with FOREST RANGERS DO IT IN TREES in large green block letters on the front.

Issoufou asked: "Where are my passengers?" He looked at Abdou in his rearview mirror and smiled broadly, trying to match the *kómasho*'s persistent grin and keep the tone calm and easy.

Abdou leaned forward, unimpressed, his hand still heavy on Issoufou's shoulder. He drilled a glare and an order into Issoufou's ear. "They are coming, Issouf." He slapped the top of the seat. Issoufou looked at him for a moment, and then over at me. Issoufou smiled. "We wait," he said.

Niger has a highway police unit, the Brigade Routière, a part of the Gendarmerie Nationale. Speed limit signs are posted, but Niger's open roads are unpatrolled, and drivers unmonitored for their attention to speed and traffic laws. This is true in most African countries. Governments don't have the resources to support full-fledged highway patrols. In Niger, there are only ragtag bands of men at checkpoints, wearing old fatigues and the green berets of gendarmes. The Brigade Routière.

In a motor park garage, just a parcel of open ground under a tree, I once watched a gendarme sergeant bring in his personal car to have the fuel filter changed, and later drive away without paying, leaving only this promise: "I'll find you if my car breaks down."

In Niamey, I went one day to meet the brigade commandant, but an aide outside his office told me I would have to get permission first. He didn't know where I could obtain such permission. For weeks I was passed down a line of gendarmerie and army officers ("I'm sorry, I don't have the authority to talk to you," I was told. "Go see Lieutenant So-and-so"), and bounced back and forth between ministries (Defense, Transport, Interior).

One Friday afternoon, after spending a day working my way up three floors of the Gendarmerie Nationale, where I had become a minor fixture ("Ah, it's you again. Haven't you found the commandant?"), I was standing in a small room with a lieutenant, a man named Idrissa. He was tall and thin and serious, his head clean-shaven, and he wore a dress khaki tunic and trousers, and polished black leather shoes. The room had a desk and chair, and Lieutenant Idrissa received me without offering his hand or asking me to sit. I was being interrogated, albeit halfheartedly. We spoke in French.

"What is your research?"

"I'm writing about road transport."

"Why? What is so special about Niger?"

I tried to be cheerful, personable, standing with my hands folded politely in front of me. "You are said to have the best road system in West Africa," I explained. In fact, Niger's roads, built with profits from its Saharan uranium mines, are among West Africa's best. "Maybe there is something to be learned from Niger's experience."

He frowned, shook his head. "I doubt it." Then, "Do you have a research authorization?" I smiled, though uneasy, and handed him a copy of the document, which had the minister of education's signature. He put the paper on his desk after a glance and looked back at me. "Have you ever been in the military?"

"No." I added a hopeful detail: "I was in the Peace Corps, here in Niger." This did not soften him. He did not seem to hear me. Then he said, "I'll keep your authorization." (It was only a copy.) "The commandant will see you Monday morning at eight. And he'll want to see a list of your questions before he talks with you."

I wondered whether this meeting had been just a formality, that they didn't know what else to do with me except give me the interview.

It was 4:00 P.M. Issoufou had stopped the Peugeot at a small mosque on the edge of Gazaoua, a village that straddles Route I. He wanted to pray because he had missed the midday prayer. The mud brick buildings spread and then quickly faded out over a thinly forested plain fifty miles east of the city of Maradi, seven miles north of Nigeria, and 360 miles south of Algeria.

As it turned out, Abdou did have the passengers he had promised—four men who had been waiting for us at a coffee table a few hundred yards down the street. After thirty minutes, Abdou brought them, each carrying a nylon or plastic handbag. Another half hour passed as he and Issoufou, standing beside the car, argued over price. The other *komasho* had wandered away in search of new opportunities. Abdou would lean forward into Issoufou's face—"Issouf, I could have sold them to someone else"—while Issoufou stood, arms folded, calmly toeing the dirt, smiling and waiting. Finally, Issoufou paid him twenty-five hundred CFA francs—five hundred francs more than Issoufou had first offered, and five hundred francs less than what Abdou had first demanded—and we started back to Zinder on an afternoon so windy and hazy that it almost appeared to be snowing.

Now, in Gazaoua, I was standing while the others prayed, on the road, watching sand blow over my boots. I was wearing a gray cotton turban that protected my face and mouth. The sand moving below my knees was different from the haze that hung around me: a dust storm, fine, gritty fog, light and dense, lifted high in the atmosphere by steady winds.

Sand washed around my ankles, blowing southwest in gentle brown streams and creating the illusion that the earth's surface had softened to the texture of cotton. A sandstorm requires meaner winds, twenty miles per hour or more, to move heavier particles in low sheets, usually no higher than chest level. The sandstorms of the West African Sahel look sometimes like thin creeks and at other times like broad rivers of hissing sand. These storms are not all benign. Sandstorms can quickly build deep drifts and small dunes. They occasionally bury stranded cars, even abandoned villages. The storm at my feet, though, moved mildly.

Issoufou, religious and conscientious, liked to stop in Gazaoua, a few miles west of a government checkpoint at the town of Tessaoua. We stopped there on every return trip, sometimes to pray or to find food and water. And now, watching him finish his prayers, a kerchief tied around his face from the nose down, it occurred to me that Issoufou had made this stop to prepare himself. The Tessaoua gendarmes harassed Zinder drivers only on their way home from Maradi—when they knew drivers had more money to give up. Issoufou won his battles through quiet stubbornness—that folded-arms-toeing-the-dirt pose he seemed able to hold indefinitely. He swore the gendarmes at Tessaoua hated bush taxi drivers, resented their freedom and the money they made. Issoufou rarely revealed nervousness, but I saw it that afternoon as he repeatedly dried his hands on the breast of his blue cotton tunic.

A rumor I'd heard many times in the motor parks claimed that the Tessaoua soldiers had in the past year beaten to death a bush taxi driver who was making the trip east from Niamey at night. I could never confirm the story. Yet the rumor survived among the drivers, fed by fresh details of other offenses, a sort of indirect evidence.

I collected my own such corroboration. I once saw a soldier inexplicably beat a young man at one checkpoint, and at many others I watched soldiers yank people off vehicles for reasons never made clear. On several occasions I saw drivers beaten for not having "proper registration papers." On a trip we took a month before this one, the Tessaoua gendarmes kept Issoufou's car documents for two hours without explanation. They took all the passengers' papers, including my passport. The gendarmes ignored Issoufou's inquiries and asked nothing. As we waited, they sat and played cards beside the documents, which they had stacked on a bench.

A simple demonstration of power.

After the gendarmes gave back our papers, Issoufou returned to the car in quiet rage that barely broke the crust of his personality. He spit his words as he started the engine. "Those soldiers, without these roads they would have nothing to do. Nothing!"

When I first began traveling with Issoufou, he made me promise that I was not a CIA spy or white mercenary. He didn't want additional problems with gendarmes. I laughed at this. "Issoufou, what could I possibly be spying on around here?" He merely looked at me, not seeing the humor. I gave him my word, but for some weeks he kept me at a distance when we were on the road. In the presence of other passengers or drivers, it was difficult to talk with him, especially to discuss his work or ask questions.

Niger has little experience with mercenaries, but conspiracy theories are popular. There are many authentic examples of white mercenaries—opportunists and French Foreign Legionnaires—bringing down or manipulating African governments. In 1979, French soldiers managed the overthrow of Emperor Bokassa in the Central African Republic. They have intervened in Chad and Gabon, and thousands are based in the Ivory Coast and Senegal. Bob Denard, the French mercenary and former Legionnaire who twice took power and named himself head of the government of the Comoros Islands, is legendary in Africa. In Niger, every stranger, every white person, is a suspect agent of the American CIA or the French Sûreté. Everyone blames the Tuareg rebellion on French treachery. Once, a passenger in Issoufou's car told me he was sure the Sahel's persistent drought and the advancing Sahara Desert were the work of some high-tech French effort to control its former colonies. Passengers who saw my notebook and heard my questions ("Issoufou, how much do you spend on car repairs every week?") glared at me.

"Who are you?" a passenger asked me one day. "Why do you ask so many questions? Are you CIA? Are you working for the rebellion?"

Later that same day, Issoufou told me: "You have to be careful of what you say and what you ask in this country." I felt ashamed of my naiveté. I learned to shut up. The more I traveled in Niger, the more it became obvious that the ubiquitous checkpoints did not serve the purpose of extortion alone but also satisfied a paranoid fear of strangers, of anything foreign, in a country divided by eight languages and ethnic groups. Separated from each other by language, the people of Niger live in a continuous state of mutual distrust and jealousy. There was also the very real security threat posed by the Tuareg rebels.

Almost weekly there were new motor park rumors and

radio reports of rebel ambushes. On a remote road in a village called Keita, hundreds of miles northwest of Zinder, rebels seized several vehicles from a development project. A petrol tanker was blown up on Route 2 near Agadez, and another was seized on the road from Zinder to Agadez. Clashes between soldiers and rebels were routine in the desert north of Agadez, but when rebels began hitting farther south in the area around Zinder, the paranoia got worse. Rebels attacked a bush taxi fleet near a rural marketplace one hundred miles north of Zinder and ambushed the army patrol sent to hunt them down. One soldier was killed and another wounded. That same day, rebels shot to death a village chief in that area. People speculated that a big attack was planned on Route 1 or on Zinder itself, though it never happened. In fact, I never witnessed a rebel action, though my presence, the possibility that I was a mercenary, was always suspect. Gendarmes took extra time to examine my papers.

Issoufou's uneasiness about me gradually relaxed, though it took a couple of months. I hung around and tried to show my interest unobtrusively, sympathetically. We endured dozens of checkpoint confrontations and spent hours together broken down in the wind and heat, waiting for help from a passing car on some isolated patch of road on our way to Maradi or the smaller towns of Tanout to the north and Gouré to the east. We spent nights in the Maradi motor park, sleeping in the car, doors locked against thieves known to roam the park at night with knives. Once, when we ran out of gas on the way to Gouré (the fuel gauge was broken and Issoufou had miscalculated his reserves), we left the passengers behind and hiked three miles through the bush to a village where he knew gas smugglers he could buy from. Through every mishap and hour of discomfort, Issoufou preserved his calm and optimism, uttering, "*Hakuri, hakuri,*" the

Hausa word for "patience," as if to keep himself and me in check. Frustrations that certainly would have broken me in time, he took in his stride. Anger could only add to the clutter.

So the memory of his outrage at the Tessaoua gendarmes— "Those soldiers, without these roads, they would have nothing"—stayed with me, surfacing every time we passed a checkpoint. I thought of it now in Gazaoua, turning to face the car, where Issoufou was folding his prayer rug.

At the rural high school in the village of Bouza, Niger, where I was a Peace Corps English teacher, the headmaster would receive a telegram announcing a Ministry of Education inspection. On the appointed day a deputy minister would come up the dirt road from Route I (thirty-six miles south of the village) in a fleet of three Land Rovers, one of them holding a few soldiers. The official would cancel classes and call a staff meeting to explain a vaccination program or a new policy, to discuss test scores, and so on. The soldiers, meanwhile, patrolled the grounds. The minister himself came once, bringing a light tank that crouched outside during the staff meeting. A more powerful means of communication than a memo or fuzzy phone call.

Nigerien bureaucrats are poorly trained and underpaid. Telephones barely work, electricity is unreliable or nonexistent outside regional capitals, and computers are thus impractical. Few see television. Most people have a radio, but its voice is a distant, disembodied, suspect presence.

So there is the road: a manual means to execute policy, provide services, and remind the population of a central authority. Roads are the most consistent evidence of government in Niger. District capitals, of course, straddle important motor roads, which also coincide with secondary schools, major medical services, and most large markets. Primary schools, medical dispensaries, and agricultural services are only thinly sprinkled in bush villages. The government sends officials on *tournée* to collect information, explain policy, and be seen. An imperfect, inefficient method of rule, but workable and cheap in a country where civil servants are perpetually owed five months' back pay and foreign donors provide half the $400 million national budget.

Show of strength is key. Niger's security forces number two thousand, and most of them serve on the roads—at tremendous expense, though the government won't say how much. Official extortion (what diplomats call "informal taxation") helps to pay the soldiers—in Niger and in countries across Africa—and the overall cost to the national economy may be impossible to measure precisely. I'm talking about the money siphoned off at checkpoints. Government and transport union officials in Niger, Mali, and Ivory Coast say the losses to merchants, transporters, and ordinary citizens run in the tens of millions of dollars annually, devastating losses to struggling, underdeveloped countries. A World Bank economist I met in Ivory Coast told me, "The amount of money is certainly dramatic, but to calculate a figure for West Africa would be impossible." In an April 1995 story on West Africa's economic malaise, *New York Times* reporter Howard French described a trip he took between the capitals of Burkina Faso and Ghana: "On one recent 600-mile drive from Ouagadougou to Accra, there were no fewer than 30 police and customs checks. Those who brave the route . . . say they are routinely held up for bribes or forced at each stop to surrender portions of their belongings."

The checkpoint is an African road institution, analogous to the American speed trap, where travelers expect to do battle. On Route I there is a checkpoint about every twenty-five miles. Nigerian writer Chinua Achebe's 1987 novel, *Anthills of the Savannah*, climaxes in violence at a checkpoint on a fictional African country's "Great North Road." "Security forces!" the narrative scoffs. "Who or what are they securing?" In that tragic scene, a character named Chris challenges a drunken soldier, who "unslung his gun, cocked it, narrowed his eyes while confused voices went up all around. . . . Chris stood his ground looking straight into the man's face, daring him to shoot. And he did, point blank."

Such scenarios breed easily. In Niger it is a crime to be without a national identity card, a law enforced by checking road travelers. This provides soldiers with endless opportunities for mischief. And it means that the traveler in Niger is always crossing a border and being challenged for the right to pass. The traveler must show papers that link his or her face to an identity, a profession, a country. Identity papers grant the right to be on the road, as if the road were a special place, an exclusive meeting point, like a sort of club, not just for any citizen. The penalty for not producing an identity card is loss of travel rights, jail, and a five-hundred-franc fine, which few can pay. Identity cards provide information for a running census on population size, where people live, what they do, and, most important, which ethnic group they belong to. The information is valuable for organizing services, such as estimating and providing food needs during famine, and for keeping tabs on people.

In the United States, we keep vast data networks for the same purposes: tax and driving records; criminal, bank, telephone, school, social security, birth, automobile, and health records; military draft registrations; credit histories; newspaper subscriptions; library cards. Get stopped for speeding, and in seconds the cop calls up your criminal and driving histories, if any, on a computer attached to the dashboard, or radios someone at the station to do it instead. Apply for an apartment and your credit is immediately available to the landlord.

In Niger, however, the government doesn't know you exist—no one but those in your family, village, or neighborhood do—unless you get snagged at a road checkpoint or need to, say, apply for food aid at a district capital. On a road, of course.

Issoufou kept up an easy pace during the short drive to Tessaoua. We merged into thin dust that quickly became denser than the dust we had seen in Maradi early that morning. It coated my teeth, tongue, gums. I wrapped the turban tighter around my head.

In twenty minutes we were in the market town and district capital of Tessaoua. Mud houses blended with the dust, like a world dipped in dirty skim milk. We rolled easily through the town's empty streets, passing no checkpoint. We slowed to a crawl when we began to emerge on the eastern side of town, near the checkpoint that we knew waited yards ahead. Just a cement guard hut and a crude rope hung low across the road. We were looking for it, hoping we would not overrun the rope and anger the gendarmes.

"The gendarme lives the problems of the road." I was sitting, courtesy of Lieutenant Idrissa, on the appointed Monday morning in the office of Moctar Saley, commandant of the Brigade Routière. He was telling me what I had expected to hear. "The gendarme understands the problems of the road. He is honest and very well trained."

Commandant Saley's office felt like a large closet. He worked in the brigade's one-story cement administration building inside a gendarme training compound in Niamey. There was a small window and a broken electric ceiling fan, and the walls were covered with the narrow brown dribbles of rainy-season roof leaks. Saley sat behind a metal desk empty of paperwork, wearing clean, pressed camouflage fatigues and sandals. He was in his forties, balding, very straight in his chair, trim, startlingly soft-spoken. A career soldier. Behind the desk hung a very bad watercolor portrait of him in khaki uniform poised at that desk with pen in hand, over paperwork.

Everyone I spoke to along the chain of command had handed me some generality about Moctar Saley. Scrupulously honest. A man of impressive reserve and control. A devout Muslim, husband, father of eight. A former Brigade Routière officer in five of Niger's seven regional departments, and now, for the past four years, overall brigade commandant. "Yes, a very good man," said an official of the national drivers' union. "But we think he is not very aware of reality on the road. It is a question of isolation. Commandant Saley has done his time in the field, and now he stays in Niamey."

When I arrived in Saley's office, he was cordial, rising to offer me his hand across the desk. He asked to see a written list of my questions, which I produced. He studied them silently while I waited, watching a boy in ragged shorts and T-shirt sit in the doorway polishing the commandant's boots with spittle and a dirty rag. Saley smiled and handed the list back to me, then leaned forward and clasped his hands atop his desk. He said, "*Bon, alors?*"

I sat in a bare metal chair with my notebook in my lap. "What are the most serious problems you find on Niger's roads," I began softly, testing his responses.

"The national highways are exposed to excessive speed and driver impudence," Saley said, leaning on his elbows, his arms folded, looking straight at me. I listened and made notes. "Many drivers are completely untrained and neglect the mechanical needs of their cars and the safety of their passengers. They collect the fare and drive until their cars fall apart."

Another question: "Are road conditions safer now than when you joined the brigade?"

He shook his head gravely. "The situation is worse. There are more accidents than ever." Saley did not gesture when he spoke, or even alter his tone, as if he felt his words needed no help to be understood. I looked for an opportunity to casually insert a question not on the submitted list but of great interest to me: I wanted to ask him about corruption and lack of discipline in the brigade. Saley continued. "We do not have the resources, the people, and the vehicles to patrol the roads competently."

Saley's answers came like this for half an hour, predictable, narrow, passive, no casual straying from the subject. A lecture. I was becoming restless. I said, "But," and he raised his hand to stop me. When he finished a response, he said, "*Bon, question trois?*" and later, "*Alors, question quatre?*"

"Yes," I said, late in the interview, ignoring the next question on my list, "but why do you think drivers are like this, so seemingly irresponsible, as you put it."

"They are just greedy," he said. "Drivers are not well educated or honest people. They don't take care of their cars."

The statement annoyed me. I thought of mechanics in their open-air "garages" repairing police vehicles under threat, and of the bush taxis that come in for repairs—often pushed in by passengers and the cash-poor driver, who promises the mechanic he will pay what he can when he can.

In Niger, secondhand cars are repaired with parts recycled or refashioned from other parts, over and over again. Mechanics are like battlefield surgeons inadequately trained and rushed to the front. They are few and poorly equipped. They live lives of periodic idleness and frenzy. Curled up asleep on an oily mat one moment, maybe for a whole day, and then suddenly buzzing about prioritizing the wounded, going without rest or food. Sleep and triage. They work with what they have, tools and parts strewn about the oil-stained dirt amid stripped auto carcasses—compact cars and minibuses—scattered here and there, twisted and empty like dried orange rinds.

I looked up from my notes and smiled.

"Yes," I said, "but don't you think there are similar problems of greed and corruption among gendarmes at your checkpoints? You must be aware, commandant, that drivers are always complaining of how gendarmes take money from them at checkpoints, even from passengers, and often without explanation or reason. I've seen this myself. After all, wasn't that one of the main complaints drivers brought up during the strike?" I heard my voice letting the question get out of hand, more to the point than I had planned, breaking the seal of the interview. "I understand there is even an occasional beating."

For a moment Saley stared at me, unblinking, like an actor who had been fed a line not in the script. But he was off balance only for that one moment.

"I have never heard of this happening, and I don't know what you saw," he said. "All behavior found to be unbecoming of a gendarme in the brigade is severely sanctioned. That I can assure you, Monsieur." The last sentence Saley spoke slowly, pausing briefly between each word, and rising to his feet as he finished.

Without looking up from my notebook, pretending not to see him, I asked, "Can you give me an example of when you have disciplined a gendarme?" I looked up only when the commandant did not answer.

He said, *"C'est fini, Monsieur."*

———

Issoufou suddenly punched the brakes hard, and we slid on the sandy road, stopping a foot away from the checkpoint rope. I saw it only now. Dust had all but obscured the cement guard hut. A couple of yards off the road a gendarme sat on a wooden bench, hunched over and buried in a woolen military greatcoat, lapels pulled high, arms folded, his face tucked into his chest. An old bolt-action rifle leaned between his legs, the barrel against his folded arms. He lifted a dust-caked khaki face so pale that it looked painted. The gendarme peered at us and jerked his head impatiently at the rope, and buried his face again. I reached inside my shirt to touch the amulet around my neck, to be sure it was there.

Issoufou studied the man for a moment. He pulled his kerchief over his nose against the dust and got out of the car, waving and smiling. He said in Hausa: *"Kai soja, iska lafiya"*— Hey soldier, wind is healthy. Or perhaps he meant, "May the wind give you health." I'm not sure. The gendarme simply waved back, and Issoufou, holding his smile, nodded and unhooked the rope from a wooden post. Just to be sure, perhaps to make the return trip a little easier, Issoufou walked over to the gendarme and stuffed a folded five-hundred-franc bill in a side pocket of the greatcoat.

The gendarme never looked up.

Postscript: For his travels throughout Niger, Peter Chilson fortuitously managed to escape a serious auto accident, one of Africa's leading causes of death.

The Thar is a massive expanse of granite outcroppings in northwestern India inhabited by the native Rubari people. Robyn Davidson followed a group of these migratory people, experiencing in a poignant and unforgettable way their difficult lives in a very sparse and haunting landscape.

DESERT PLACES

ROBYN DAVIDSON

I stood on the rim of the Little Rann of Kutch, the smaller of two expanses of sand, mud and salt, thousands of miles square. During the annual north-west monsoon they are inundated by floods from the Aravalli Ranges in the east and tides from the Arabian ocean in the west, thus detaching Kutch from the rest of India during the wet, and providing a lot of nothingness between Kutch and the rest of India in the dry. The Little Rann of Kutch lies below and to the east of its big sister; the Great Rann is transected by the Pakistan border, which means that it is impossible to get a permit to go there. These days only smugglers and the Border Security Forces travel across it, which seems a waste of some splendid geography. The most exciting thing about both the Ranns— apart from miniature forests of crystalline salt, poison-blue and jade-green brine held in cut-glass ponds, herds of white asses and clouds made of flamingo wings—is that they are empty.

Stretching from the shore to the horizon lay brown, white and blue emptiness. Somewhere inside my chest, a sail was unfurling. My face, I know, wore the hungry look common to people who find in earth's vacant places the primeval garden. I glanced at Chutra. He wore the look of a man condemned by the caprice of a lunatic who, that being the upside-down way of things, was his boss.

"Kitna sundar," I said, squaring my shoulders and taking a deep breath in such a way as to indicate that only people of heightened sensibility would recognize the loveliness in what lay before us, as flat and blank as earth's end. Chutra peered into it, scratched beneath his turban and said, "There's nothing there."

According to my map, which was a rough-drawn thing eight inches square purchased from the local *pan wallah*, it was less than twenty miles across this slim section of the Rann. No need to take anything other than water, a couple of roti and a few oranges. Everything else was loaded in the jeep which would cross the Rann by the more conventional method—a bridge.

Our intelligence reports varied.

1. Yes, there was quite a good track across the Rann and it was as easy to find as the map said it was. (There were several dotted lines like running stitch which the legend described as footpaths.)

2. There was no track and never had been and we might never be seen again if we didn't use the perfectly good bridge which had been built so that people could cross the Rann without dying of heat exhaustion.

3. There was no track exactly but sheep and shepherds crossed every now and then, some recently, so there should be no problem for us.

The map contained a squiggle in the centre of the Rann, which was probably higher ground. In the middle of the squiggle, *x* marked a well. As we were heading due north, we would remain to the right, or east, of that squiggle.

Naturally I wanted to go alone and might have insisted upon it had I only my dear little Ram Rahim to handle, who was so good and patient, unlike the two maharanis who, during our two-day walk here from the *dang*, had shied at every truck or bus coming up behind them. Rickshaws and cars they treated with tolerant disregard, but trucks and buses made the one try to leap on top of the other or crawl all over the person leading her. In a pointed sort of way I had not remarked upon their behaviour to Chutra. Ram Rahim had not shied.

Everyone thought that my crossing the Rann by camel was a most peculiar idea. But going alone was a kind of subcontinental heresy. "But there's no villages, no people!"

"Exactly," I would say and feel the sail ruffle. At last, some moments when I could be as close to alone as it's possible in this country—that is, alone with someone else. I was not going to pass up this shard of pleasure, wedged, as it was, between the punishments of the previous year and the difficulties which, I knew, still lay ahead. So far I had prioritized everyone and everything before myself—the magazine, Dilip, the nomads, the people who worked for me or who offered their help. Now I was going to temper my spirit in the fiery wastes and if Chutra didn't like it—with his snake-bitten finger for which I still had not forgiven him, and upon which we had wasted much time hunting down doctors and pharmacists, and which I had to clean, dress and bandage for him thrice a day, and because of which he was useless at loading the camels—he could work for someone else. My own little medical problems—two small, suppurating holes in the ankle and the missing periods—were too insignificant to think about.

On the following morning I was the first to rise. An unusual event which cost me dear but it made the point to Chutra as to who was the leader around here. I was anxious to head off in the cool of the day but Chutra dawdled infuriatingly. I had asked him to check out the route the previous night but when we finally got going and were unable to find the track, it was clear he had not done so. It was easier for me to do things myself than delegate to Chutra. Yet, if I did so, he was deeply offended. He was not a lazy man—far from it. But he had his own way of doing things and his way and mine were several centuries and a couple of oceans apart.

Around the rim of the Rann were the hovels of the salt-miners. Nothing protected them from the cruelty of that inferno or their skin from the salt which cut it like cat o' nine tails. The air did not move here. The salt mud stank and the children were juiceless, like scraps of cloth caught on sticks. They surprised you by moving. They worked all day in the mud; at night they slept on compacted mud under hessian lean-tos. Most of them were bonded labourers. Pay, if it came at all, was a pittance; work, neverending; hopes, nonexistent.

"Where is the track?" said Chutra to a scarecrow rooted in mud. He waved his arm listlessly in the direction we were going in and, despite Chutra's further volubility, would say not a word. The Little Rann had husked him.

Whenever we tried to head north, our camels began to slide around in mud. Eventually we came across a rope of animal tracks dropped across the pan, its wavy parallels disappearing into shimmer. The ground underfoot was harder, almost dry. Naturally the shepherds who had brought their flocks across must know the safest route. And, anyway, track or no track, all we had to do was head north and we couldn't very well help but bump into the northern shore. Then it was simply a matter of following footpaths to wells and villages. Heavens, I'd done this sort of thing hundreds of times. And in infinitely more treacherous terrain than this. Chutra was behaving as if this piddling little stroll was a ride across Lake Constance and he was making me nervous.

"Do you know in my country, Chutra, you can go for eight hundred miles without seeing another human being or coming across any water?" (Actually what I said was, "Chutra, my country in, eight hundred miles in, people no, water no, see.")

"Achchha," he said without shifting his gaze. I let him ride in front.

The "rope" we were following unravelled after a while into three pieces. I assumed it would splice together further ahead. We kept to the middle strand. Something slightly less flat than the flatness surrounding it appeared on the horizon. It would hover for a moment, then deliquesce into the flatness again. This cheered up Chutra so much that he decided to talk to me. He relaxed into the saddle, tipped his turban over one eye with a stick and, half turning his body towards me, said, "Madam Sahib camel very fiiiine camel; Chutra camel *not* fiiiine camel. Madam Sahib Ram Rahim beauuuutiful camel. Momal and Sumal *sundar nahin, samajhdhar nahin* (not beautiful, not intelligent)." He smirked and turned to the front. Sharp little incisors showed when he smiled, matching, in dainty repulsiveness, his naked shins.

I retorted, "Momal and Sumal better camel is . . . er . . . are. All people this . . . understand . . . able. Ram Rahim not beautiful but me like because . . . him not criminal."

These utterances did not come easily. They were costive, fatiguing utterances containing pauses during which a homunculus ran through miles of shelving in the brain, feverishly searching for vocabulary and grammatical rules. Often by the time this homunculus arrived, panting, at the speech centre, with the relevant material under its arm, the desire to say anything had left me, killed off by futility. At which point the homunculus would throw down its papers and threaten to strike.

Some hours later the "shore" seemed barely closer and the ground beneath us was getting slipperier. Salt crust cracked, revealing squelch beneath into which the camels' feet sank, and pulling them up required a lot of muscle power to balance the laws of physics. We dismounted. Now the rope of animal tracks frayed in all directions, leaving us to our own devices and at the mercy of mud. If a camel slid and fell, it could easily break pelvis or limb and that would be the end of it. Momal and Sumal behaved like ladies who had just been thrown out of their *zinana* into a street which they had never before had to cross. Ladies who had forgotten how to use their bodies for anything other than reclining on couches, holding up mirrors and spreading spite. Imperious, fractious ladies who minced along, holding up their saris. To be fair, Ram Rahim's sure-footedness had a bit to do with the fact that his feet had been toughened by the stones of Kutch, whereas the princesses' feet had trodden only the sands of Jodhpur and were consequently like bald tyres. Even so, he struggled on gallantly, while the princesses snapped at each other and generally let it be known that, had they thought it was going to be like this, they would never have come.

About two hours later the mud was calf-deep and each step a little miracle of will. Not only were my feet bruised and swollen by the mud and the salt, not only was I feeling very nauseous indeed, not only was I expecting the fatties in front to fall at any moment but, having emptied my own water canteen, I found Chutra had brought only one extra, not all three as instructed.

"But Madam Sahib said five hours."

"*Chutra, I say, said . . . Most important . . . Holding . . .* (Shit) *. . . Taking water . . . Everything . . .* (I mean *. . .* Goddamn it) *. . . Water important, five hours not important . . . Not . . .* (Oh, never mind!)"

Now, when you are on your own in deserty places and little things go wrong, you may feel dread (unreasonable in most cases because although you may get thirsty, or hungry or sick or fatigued, it is unlikely that you will die) and you may curse yourself for being a fool. However, water is the single most important resource standing between you and panic.

Every now and then I sat in the shade of my camel, head between knees and dry retched. At such times I said, between spasms, "I am absolutely fine. Don't worry." I lay on my back so that the Little Rann of Kutch would stop whirling like a top. It didn't. Chutra suggested I ride and he would lead Ram Rahim. This seemed like a good idea until we got moving. Diabolical though the walking was, it was better than ship-of-the-desert seasickness. The swelling on the horizon now seemed like dry land in the middle of an undulating ocean of light. We had been walking for five hours.

Chutra said, "North side . . ." I didn't believe him, which was sensible of me because it wasn't the northern side, it was the squiggle—an island of sand, gibbers and skeletons which we reached long, long years later and which, I worked out, was about halfway to our destination. Night was falling.

At least we were out of the mud and I had started to feel alive enough to tackle a dry roti. We tied up our beasts, sat on the rocks and ate. After food and a swallow of water I felt positively chirpy. There is nothing likelier to give you a positive outlook on life than the cessation of nausea.

If I was on my own, I thought, I would be enjoying this moment. The place was stark yet intensely present. Wild horse and donkey tracks skirted the bases of red, sedimentary hills. Wind scuffed up dust and moaned in the sandstone. I led our little quintet along a dried watercourse, out to the other shore, then veered west, having decided to avoid as long as possible whatever wetness might lie on the other side of this island by following the "beach" before striking out across the "sea." This tactic had the added advantage of lining us up with the village where the jeep would be waiting. Besides, we might be within striking distance of the well, a place to camp if necessary. Although the map had given wildly incorrect distances, surely it wouldn't show a well if there wasn't a well somewhere in the vicinity? But it was now dark. Moonless, starless, bottom of a mine-shaft dark. All day the clouds had remained in the wings, waiting for the footlights to go out so they could bustle on stage.

Luckily I always carried a small but reliable torch in my purse and this I shone on the ground ahead from time to time, looking for the animal pads that would lead us in to the well. The going now was easy, the ground flat and hard so that the sound of camel pads, softly susurrating, soothed like a lullaby. Ram Rahim was confident beneath me, a snug little boat on a big sea. So what if it took us fourteen hours rather than seven? So much the better.

I found tracks ahead. And beyond that, I thought I saw a twink of light. "Chutra, *dekho!*" I urged Ram Rahim forward, but Chutra called me back. He was very frightened. Nevertheless he followed me hesitantly towards that little glow in the night, which seemed close, then far away, then disappeared altogether.

No doubt about it—habitation. A tiny plot of tilled earth. There was a cooking fire and beside it a temporary dwelling. Chutra's camels were restive, picking up his nervousness. "Ghosts!" he warned from back there in the dark. I called across a tall thorn fence towards the shelter. A dog went berserk. A man came out, looking as frightened as Chutra, who now overcame his dread enough to ask for directions. At first the man seemed reluctant to talk, no doubt fearing we were about to slit his throat and steal his dinner, or spirit him off to a cemetery. Eventually he told us to head due north from here, past the well (just as I had predicted), and we would soon see the lights of the village.

So relieved was my *unth wallah* that he twirled his princesses around and set them off at a fast pace, singing in his fork-on-plate falsetto. I followed, thinking this a reckless and unnecessary speed at such an hour but unwilling to humiliate Ram Rahim in front of the fatties by asking Chutra to slow down. He called over his shoulder that if he didn't have to slow down for Ram Rahim, he could reach the other side in an hour.

Ten minutes later, from somewhere ahead, I heard a little yelp and camel noises. I put on my torch and saw that Momal had run straight into a thorn tree and Chutra and she and the lead ropes and Sumal were entangled painfully in it. They gazed into my torch beam like cons caught in razor wire. We had come face to face with a forest of apparently impenetrable *Prosopis juliflora* and with the discovery that Momal and Sumal were night-blind. I gave Ram Rahim his head. He picked his way in one direction, turned, picked his way carefully in the other, until he found a way through the barrier. Apparently he could see as well at night as he could by day, thus scoring points for mongrels and touchéing the *unth wallah* who said crustily, "Keep Ram Rahim in front. He can't keep up with *my* camels."

It began to rain. Sometimes I cried. I cried when at last I saw the lights and realized that we would not reach them by 2 A.M. I had given myself that limit, 2 A.M. I had said to myself, I can make it to 2 A.M. but I cannot make it to 2:05 A.M. I could not get off Ram Rahim but to stay on was torture. My feet throbbed. The tendons in my groin pained all the way to the knees in one direction and to the teeth in the other. We arrived at approximately three-thirty. We were wet and cold and stiff, and the *Prosopis juliflora* had not been kind to us. Riding into that silent medieval village in the middle of the night remains, in memory, one of the most religious experiences of my life. Would there be room at the inn?

We saw the jeep and woke a very worried driver. We couched the camels and got off. The vertebrae in my neck had fused and my feet were approximately twice their normal size. Chutra walked like Pinocchio. We watered the camels. We led the camels to our hotel—an open air cement kitchen with a room at the back. We fed the camels. I saw to Chutra's sleeping arrangements, then collapsed in the room at the back on a filthy charpoi. I lay awake for a while, listening to the owner of this establishment—a fat man with fat gold rings on fat fingers, and gold medallions on his voluptuous breast—beating his twelve-year-old servant with a stick. The boy ended up whimpering on a mat in the corner of my room, for all the world like one of the cringing, diseased, vanquished pariah dogs that prowl the village lanes. An hour and a half later I was awakened by a truck stopping at the front of the hotel. From its cabin came Hindi film music screeching at enough volume to wake the dead then kill them again. I went to the window and shouted, "Turn that fucking thing off!" Silence. I had never in my whole life yelled at anyone to turn anything off. I doubt if I had ever even asked anyone politely to turn anything off. I went back to the charpoi. I hate India, I thought and fell asleep.

At nine o'clock an angel transubstantiated at the side of my bed. I opened one eye and took the tea it offered. It was grinning. It was Koju.

And so, on a winter evening a few days before Christmas, after two days of driving, and burdened with deformed feet, fever and a sour soul, I arrived at last at Narendra's *jhumpa*, inside his aura of succour, to await the arrival of my friends and to consult a doctor. Chutra, I had left behind with instructions, an address where he should wait, and three camels. I would return to him inside a month and, with the camels, we would walk back here to Jodhpur and liberty. All he had to do was inquire of local people as to where the Rabari *dangs* were.

Narendra opened the jeep door and handed me a glass of Indian champagne. The servants popped heads out of windows, waved surreptitiously, then returned to the feast preparations. Behind the *jhumpa*, firelight was bouncing off rushes and thatching. There was the smell of frost falling and sandalwood burning. I handed Narendra his *gudio* and hobbled through the house out to the fireside. Mornat stood smiling in his grey gypsy coat and traveller's trousers, his hand at his chest, the other holding by a short chain the most beautiful dog I had ever seen. It was a Luria, a Jogi's hunting dog, which Mornat's ancestors had bred before there was history, which had travelled with the gypsies through Asia and Europe, spawning lurchers and whippets and greyhounds but remaining sturdier, silkier, more wild in the spirit. The Jogis never gave away their dogs, with whom they fiercely identified themselves. But Mornat had been prevailed upon, just this once, to sell one to Narendra to give to Memsahib as a Christmas present. His name was Seru (lion), but I decided to call him Zali, which means something like conman or vagabond. I offered the dog my hand. He held up his paw, kept his head down like a reined-in stallion and looked up at me.

"Zali, will you be my dog?" We shook hands on the deal.

My legs were propped on a stool. The feet at the end of them looked as if they belonged to someone who had spent the last few weeks on the bottom of the Thames. The left one was puffy; the right, elephantine. Serum flowed from the two ominous holes in the ankle. I did not care what was wrong with that ankle, as long as what was wrong with it wasn't Guinea worm.

"You have at least one *balan* (Guinea worm), possibly two," pronounced Rana Khan the next day. "The worm is curled up in the boil and soon it will want to come out. It exists in many segments, so that it will be necessary to go to a special *balan wallah* who will extract *all* of the segments so that reinfection will not occur. I know a good *balan wallah* in Jaisalmer, but no doubt we can find one here in Jodhpur too. "Do not," he continued, "go to an ordinary western-type doctor. He'll mess it up. These *deshi* fellows know their job." He went on to say that cobra skin ground up in jaggery was a fine cure—and there just happened to be a couple of big black cobras living around the *jhumpa*, but I couldn't see Narendra allowing to have them killed—and that a certain lizard, fairly rare, if ground up and made into a poultice, was guaranteed to suck out the most stubborn of Guinea worms. Mornat was consulted. Did he know of this lizard? Yes, he did. Could he find one? Yes, but he would have to go north of Jodhpur to the area around Koju's village.

In the meantime Rana Khan tied a black thread around my ankle and prayed to Maharajah Girda Singh of Jaisalmer (long dead) which, he assured me, was another effective remedy for worm-infestation. Rana Khan and his musicians had come to sing Marwari desert songs for us around the outside fire. Narendra and Rana were old friends; Narendra acting the traditional role of patron and the rather more modern one of trying to promote this music outside the borders of Rajasthan. In this he had had some success and these days Rana often played in the big capitals before audiences of thousands.

You simply could not be with Rana Khan and feel miserable. Music had cleansed him as a river cleans a gorge through which it tumbles. Every sweetness, sadness, foolishness, wickedness and wisdom that man had ever thought to record in ballads had flowed through him. He knew hundreds of ragas by heart, delivered them with his eyes fixed on your face, his free hand lifted towards you in entreaty, his buck teeth and rogue's features transformed into the face of love or of suffering or of saintliness. Funny songs, wise songs, romantic songs, epic songs, religious songs, Hindu songs, Muslim songs, Sufi love songs dense with meanings. When they played, the musicians and secondary singers seemed linked up with Rana Khan like nerves to a brain. If Rana became the embodiment of grief, the musicians too seemed barely able to restrain their tears. (Rana could make himself sob at will and real tears would flow.) His son, the most beautiful child on the face of the earth, played the wooden castanets; another man with a vast moustache and piano-key teeth played an empty clay pot; Rana played harmonium; and a white-bearded ancient, desiccated by too many nights sawing on his *sarungi* in the dunes of the Thar, radiated musical intelligence without moving a muscle in his face.

They all sat around the fire: a semicircle of turbans, moustaches, woollen shawls crafted deep in the desert, curious instruments and teeth. We listened enchanted for hours. Narendra got up from time to time to place money on the harmonium or to stop the singing and ask a question, challenge an interpretation of a raga or to cry "*va, va*," at a particularly exquisite interpretation—all of which only increased the liveliness of the renditions, the laughter, argument and alcoholic high spirits. At last everyone stumbled away to bed, leaving us to savour in silence the moon sheen on blue-green cabbage fields, the sleepy bird calls, and the occasional and ever more swerving emergence of Mornat from the darkness, where he had been tucking into the bottle Narendra always provided, stoking the fire with a four-foot-long metal spoon, shooting up sparks to the heavens and reflecting light upon a golden dog with golden eyes who sat, paws crossed, considering the firelight.

Here, within a world constructed by the imagination and will of an exceptional person, under stars that seemed to shine especially for these evenings, that other India might not exist. Here, everyone was well fed, happy and secure. The trouble Narendra took with all things sensual meant that there was no discord or ugliness here. All was abundance and generosity. I had not come across anyone quite like him before—the self-containment, the seemingly inexhaustible well-spring of magnanimity and courtesy. How ironic that the qualities one might expect to find in a prince, and which had been so lacking in the ones I had met so far, should find, in a man who loathed royalty and all it stood for, its apotheosis. As much as he would have hated the word, I thought of him as a truly "noble" human being.

Now that I knew something of his history and the world he had evolved from, knew the forces ranged against him, had an inkling into the reaches of his courage and how easy it would have been for him to remain safe and comfortable, my previous idea of him struck me as grotesque, as easy classifications are as soon as one gets close to another person. But in Narendra's case the difference between outward appearance and inner man was particularly easy to misinterpret. He was one of those people whom we only discover to be what they really are after we have come to know them well, and he allowed precious few people to know him at all. My admiration for him was in proportion to the effort that had been necessary to discover the truth. But what made him so different from most people I knew, not just in India but anywhere, was his lack of dependence upon the opinion of others.

The next afternoon Mornat returned with two fat and sleepy lizards. They had the faces of little old ladies who habitually attack policemen. I would not hear of them being killed. "Mornat," I said when no one could hear me, "do I have a *balan* or not?" Quietly Mornat opined that I did not. I gave the lizards back to him to let go but I have a suspicion they ended up in the Jogi cooking-pot.

There was another opinion as to my state of health from a real estate agent in jeans and T-shirt who doubled as a palmist. He was one of the torrent of constituents who came to the *jhumpa* to sit under the shade for a few hours petitioning Narendra. He scrutinized my palm and then, in front of four or five men, asked me if my breasts had ever been bitten hard by a man. Poor Narendra had to translate. I said that I could not remember whether such a thing had ever occurred and managed to stifle a blush. He explained that if I had been so bitten, then I would have had difficulty carrying children to full term, which would explain the fact that although there were five offspring inscribed on my palm none existed in real life. He suggested I wear diamonds.

The *balan* turned out to be nothing more exotic than an infected blister. The fever fell before a firing squad of new antibiotics and that other little medical matter, which I kept locked in a box at the back of my mind, would just have to wait until after my holiday when I had the energy to ponder its implications. For now there were friends, and music, and food, and Christmas, and snow-capped mountains, and Zali. And no Chutra.

The higher the altitude, the headier and happier our little group became. Zali quivered and sniffed for leopards. The

weight of the plains dropped away like haulage falling off the
back of a Tata truck, barrel by barrel down the ravines. We
parked the car in a tiny village, loaded ponies and after an
hour and a half's walk up through oak forests came the
sound, from Narendra's retreat, of hot water being sloshed
into buckets, of champagne corks popping, of a log fire crackling and of Rana Khan welcoming us with music. Pleasures
piled up thick and sweet as snow.

I had hoped that three weeks' rest in the midst of good
company would reinstate the more or less balanced self that
I remembered. But no. I had only to glimpse at the end of a
long valley, through twenty receding shades of blue, a scrap of
the plains capped with dust from which we had ascended, and
I would set my eyes resolutely in the other direction, towards
the Himalayan peaks, as if averting my gaze from something
threatening. And when anyone asked me to describe the previous eighteen months, I found myself indulging in some
fairly hysterical India-bashing.

Yet such are the enigmas of human nature that if I thought
anyone else about to denigrate India, I leapt to its defence.
And I did not think of this behaviour at the time as signalling
the beginnings of a process of identification, because when I
caught a glimpse of those plains, I felt nothing but dread. But
just as a woman cannot recall the specifics of pain during
childbirth and can only say that it was excruciating, so I could
not remember the singular sensations of being down there,
struggling and suffocating under the murk.

I wrote up my notes deep into the night, furrowing pages
with black underlinings and asterisks. Such things as: "India
is a *horrible* society, but of course I cannot say this. Instead
I have to say how marvellous it is because it continues; as if
there hadn't, throughout that continuity, been moral and aesthetic decay. Because of past glories and never mind the in-

glorious present. The corruption from top to bottom and from right to left; the giants of the Independence movement now like the giants of fairy stories—a species lost to time; the poor enduring because so few are concerned with changing the conditions which they have to endure; the structure of society is like a pyramid in which each level exploits the level beneath it and grovels to the level above (and the pyramid is bottomless). Huge masses of people are born to no purpose other than to be perpetually hungry and Hinduism has degenerated into an institutionalized abnegation of responsibility to one's fellow man."

It was a great relief to write these things. I'd *lived* the belief that just as one is unjudging towards other cultures, one has a duty to judge one's own. But where did cultural relativity stop? What morality could be universally applied? When I felt outrage was I simply a cipher for cultural prejudice? At what point would I be allowed to move from the role of uncritical guest to participant with a right to speak, the right to express anger?

If one sees a man, over-fed and crammed with gold, holding a cringing half-starved twelve-year-old by the arm and beating him with a large stick, then flinging him to the floor like a bunch of rags, then turning to the white guest and smiling, obsequiously but without shame, because what he has just done is in the order of things, is his right, while the bunch of rags crawls off to weep in the corner of a cement room on his blanket on the floor, and falls instantly asleep because he works for the fat man twenty hours a day and is malnourished and exhausted. And if no one says a word or makes any move to stop it (including oneself) because the servant belongs to the fat man and, anyway, it is the child's fate and, anyway, how would one's intervention change anything? Then?

If a highly educated and powerful Brahmin bureaucrat explains to you, seriously and passionately, why untouchables cannot be allowed into higher government positions because "for centuries they have handled excrement and it has entered their minds." Then?

Or the wife of a diplomat, who announced to her book-besotted sixteen-year-old niece, "You must marry rather than educate yourself, because if you are educated you will not adjust to marriage." Then?

There had been no therapeutic yelling, no bursting of the laces. And on those numberless occasions when a stranger had said, "And what do you think of our great country?" with that particular self-satisfaction, as if only a lunatic would find in it anything but greatness, I had never said, "Well, as a matter of fact . . ." because I knew that it was fruitless to engage in such a conversation, as what was conspicuous to me was invisible to him and vice versa.

At night, these toxic scribblings; but in the morning when I rose into bright alpine sun, the warmth of friends, of Narendra, the abundance of breakfast, the effervescent air, the affection of Koju and Hanuman and Chandrawallab and Bishan—in short, into the comforts of my class—I could gaze down to the plains and feel only admiration and wonder. Instead of muttering, "I loathe this country," I would think, No, I *love* it. I love India. Everything is contained in it. Because from this height, I could focus on the crowd and was safe from the lives of the individuals who comprised it. From this height, the words "India will continue" made sense because one saw that great river as a god might, without risking submersion, free of hope, anger or compassion, without any desire to change it.

In such a state of mind I might visit Bishan's people down in the nearby village and experience only that unique Indian warmth and sweetness, hear only the laughter, and be able to say, as an American acquaintance said after a two-week holiday in India by air-conditioned bus, that "the poor looked so . . . happy" and be able, conveniently, to forget that in this "happy" village suicide is extremely common and that only last month a woman had hanged herself in the forest. Her family, to avoid being charged with murder, had paid many thousands of rupees in bribes to the police, and many thousands of rupees in bribes to the doctor signing the death certificate, and was now entirely destitute, tripped by one twist of fate over the abyss of which every Indian, rich or poor, is acutely aware. In such a state of mind I might describe the look on Bishan's face when he says, "This always happens. Yes, every time. *Kya karen? Yaha Bharat hai*" (What to do? This is India), as an example of that enduring wisdom and acceptance of fate for which India's poor are so revered, rather than an absolute loss of faith in his country's ability to deliver justice. It was not a matter simply of corrupt police, corrupt doctors (as if it were possible for the majority of police and doctors not to be corrupt), but that the village people themselves, when given a chance, also participate in various forms of extortion on the principle that if the rich and privileged can get away with it, and the politicians and the judges and the police and the forest officers and the administrators and their own *sarpanch*, then why shouldn't we? And this moral corruption has spread so deeply and widely that there seems no way to get rid of it by any means other than a conflagration. It is not enough now to find a group to blame—the British or the politicians (vile and craven though they often are) or the industrialists or the bureaucrats—because everyone participates at some level.

When I paid the cop at the side of the road his two-hundred-rupee bribe, even though I had broken no law whatsoever, because I just didn't want to waste a day swelter-ing in a police hut at the side of the road filling out forms (or indeed risking being beaten up or raped because they were drunk and crazy), because I was already exhausted and hot and uncomfortable and fed up and fretful and harassed and there were still another eight hours of traffic and fumes and din before I could begin to breathe, to relax, to regain myself up here in the clean air of the privilege of my class, from which vantage point I would be able to discern the marvel and wonder of the crowd and of India's perpetuity, and be able to sentimentalize Indian rural life because I didn't have to live it, didn't have to notice the meanness and fear that lay beneath its "happiness," then I, too, was guilty.

If one cannot muster a godlike detachment, a sense of impotence is the next best protection from despair. India is too big. The problems too immense. What vanity to think one's own actions could make any difference to that swelling flood. The sheer volume of it suffocated every good intention. Here, life mattered, lives did not, and to achieve that famous serenity, which is now India's principal export (the frighten-ing, vaporous serenity of the New Age movement), one needed to view individual lives as insignificant, mere vehicles for DNA.

To achieve the long view, one steps further and further back from lives as they are lived to that more tranquil position from which one sees only the crowd. From that perspective human beings become a species, worth preserving. But take another step back and it is no longer necessary to preserve the species. There will be another following us, after all. Until the view lengthens to such an extent that the world disappears and one is left with only the cold reaches of space, in a private pas de deux with God. Was it possible to accommodate the contradiction between action and being, to incorporate both long view and short view in one's attitude to life, to be both reflective and active, detached and involved?

There was an odd anomaly in my attitude to India. Here I had met the best people, the best *kinds* of people I had ever known. People whose depth, warmth and dignity, whose spread and reach, made westerners seem pinched by comparison (pinched between the finger of God and the thumb of Satan). The capacity for joy here, the gratitude to life no matter what hand it had dealt you. The openness to and respect for the beingness of another, as if all the souls of the world had met many times before. In that sense I felt more at home here, more in love with life than I ever had in England. Whatever I thought about India, I would find myself, a minute later, thinking the opposite with equal conviction. Not for a moment did it allow relief from the discomforts of paradox. Not for a moment did it allow indifference.

Narendra left a day before us. Some trouble in Jodhpur with Mornat. When I joined him there, we sat out by the fire and I pestered him for the story. He said in English that Mornat's son had almost died and that he, Narendra, had rushed him to a private hospital. Mornat did not speak English but understood what was being said. He became very emotional, started crying and kept putting his hands together in that way of his. I continued asking questions such as, "But why didn't he send the boy himself? Why did he wait for you to come? Surely he knew you would pay for it? . . . Didn't he?" Until Narendra asked me pointedly to drop it. When Mornat went home, I asked why. "Because it was making me sad and Mornat sad," and he would say no more. I just could not fathom the master-servant relationship. I knew that of all the people who worked for him, Narendra probably felt the deepest affection and respect for Mornat. But what did that mean when the formal distance between them was so rigid that

Mornat would risk his son's life rather than risk offending his patron? Before sending Mornat home that night, Narendra had said to him, "That dog is eating my brains." (He felt that I spoiled Zali.) Mornat had laughed genuinely and warmly and replied, "He is young, he'll improve." And I saw the complicity and understanding between them, an understanding from which I was excluded.

Previously Narendra had referred to his servants as his family and I had scoffed at such obfuscating language. They are your workers, I had said, your serfs. But now I saw that family was the truer analogy. A hierarchical family perhaps, with a patriarch perched firmly at the top, but a family, with a family's responsibilities and duties to each other. It would be impossible, for example, for me to fire Chutra simply because he drove me crazy. If he was honest, which he was, scrupulously; if he did not shirk his work, which, it had to be said, he did not, then he was my *unth wallah* for eternity and his problems became my problems.

Narendra was the centrifugal point in the middle of my whirling. He was the interpreter of where I was. He had, in a way, *become* India to me. But to truly understand someone you have to understand his inner dialogue—that perpetual discussion with what formed him—his culture. When I had to accept that in this person I loved there were areas of foreignness which could never be mapped, and that this was mutual, I felt as if I had set myself adrift in this baffling place and would never find my way home. Once he had begged me not to ride a bicycle because it was "the easiest way for someone to murder you."

"But no one's trying to murder me," I had said, aghast.

"How do you know?" he had countered and I had searched the horizon for something familiar on which to rest my eyes. Usually there was no sense of strangeness between us and the unlikeliness of our friendship was obscured by its strength. But so remote did he sometimes seem from anything I could comprehend, it was as if I had lost my footing and was falling. It was not that our thoughts were different, that was to be expected, but that the ways in which we thought were different. But inevitably a gear would shift and I would be back with my friend in the warmth of a deeper human understanding.

When I said goodbye to him, it was a little like setting off from an island on which one has been entirely happy and safe but, once through the reef (the farm gates), turning to face an uncharted sea.

"Isn't forty-one a little . . . ?"

"Not at all," said the gynaecologist, beaming. By the look on her face she might have added, "Congratulations." It struck me that a western doctor would probably have tried at this moment of truth to arrange a look of sympathy on her face. It also struck me that I could not have chosen a better culture in which to experience this event.

Menopause. The very word has a funereal, dead-end tone. Grey women, sunk in obscurity, leeched of vitality, reaching for bottles of blue hair-rinse and packets of Valium, invisible at parties, husbands bedding secretaries, vaginas of sandpaper, any lingering sexual desires a joke for the cruel-hearted. Dear God, who would want to go there? Yet every Indian woman I spoke to, across the social spectrum, either experienced none of the physical and mental distress that so plagued her western sisters or, if she did, dismissed it as negligible. In the west the cessation of egg-laying signalled the end of female power, in India its beginning.

As it happened I had far too much on my plate to be worrying about such trivialities as "the change of life," but it did strike me as typically perverse of fate to change it now, just when I needed my strength.

Chutra was not where he was supposed to be. When my friends and I found him, on a farm near the Rajasthan–Gujarat border, he had gathered no information as to the location of Rabari *dangs* with which we might hitch a passage back, more or less, to Jodhpur, nor had he made any adjustments to our saddles and gear as I had asked him to do. His excuse for not ringing me was that he could not guard the camels and use a phone at the same time. I suggested that he might have asked someone else to ring me, since his failure to find out where any *dangs* were did rather muck up my plans. That is to say I no longer had any. And his being at a place other than the agreed meeting-place had meant an extra day of driving and anxiety for me. He countered that looking after three camels was too much work for one man and he needed assistants. I made the point that if I could walk alone with three and a half camels across seventeen hundred miles of desert, he could surely manage a hundred kilometres through settled country, where feed could be purchased and kindly people were a rupee a dozen. This was a little unfair on my part because in Australia I did not have to worry about thieves, there being so few human beings to do the thieving.

Inside five minutes my best intentions of being authoritative with him, of not allowing myself to be either irritated or bullied by him, were rubble. Happily my friends could now validate everything I had said. Yes, Chutra Ram Raika did appear to be a total arsehole.

If it should seem that one gets used to the constant tearing up and tossing away of one's plans, I am here to tell you that one does not. One chases after the scraps which malicious winds lift up and away, out of reach. And it's not so much the despair one can't cope with, it's the hope. Eventually one returns to the sitting and thinking position.

There are movements of Rabari, swirls and swoops apparently random but fractal in nature. However, to plug into this
pattern, one needed to be in many places at once, collecting
and collating information, sifting out incorrect details, driving
many hours to arrive at the office of a person who might have
an overview of the local pattern to find that the person is
away, dead or unheard of. If one could have fifty scouts, say,
all of them at the very least bilingual, and if one had a central
office where all fifty scouts could collate their material all at
the same time, and if one then found a *dang*, or a series of
dangs travelling in one's general direction, and if the *mukki* of
each *dang* could be prevailed upon to risk the inclusion of oneself, and if, then, the plans of those *mukkis* did not change at
the last second, well, then, one might get somewhere. But as it
was, I would have to set off on my own, blindly striking in the
direction of Jodhpur. At least this plan had the advantage of
taking me through parts of the Aravalli Ranges, where a soul
might take a breath before plunging back down into these
malarial plains.

It was time to leave. In the loading-up process, I had tied a
sirsingle knot in my own way, a knot I had used often and to
good effect. Chutra checked everything I had done. When he
came to the knot, he called for the attention of the entire gathering—farm owners, farm workers, relatives, neighbours, visitors, children and friends—and declaimed loudly that Madam
Sahib would be lost without him because look, ha ha, at this
crazy knot. Affectionate pity spread over his face. Still
addressing the gathering he continued, "Madam Sahib, I will
now show you the correct way to tie a knot." With exaggerat-
edly slowed-down gestures he demonstrated the tying of the
knot as if to someone with frontal lobe damage.

Arsehole. Unquestionably.

"*Chutra ji*, look, maybe *bora* no okay. *Bora* . . . (homunculus
unable to find the words for length or breadth) . . . wrong, not

right. . . . This way?" I had asked him to stitch the *bora* the night before—a large rectangle of goat and camel hair which, when thrown over the saddle, forms a pocket on either side in which goods are carried. Instead of stitching the *bora* along the horizontal, he had stitched it along the vertical. The centre of gravity of the load was therefore so high that it rolled like a badly ballasted ship whenever the camel moved.

Chutra informed me that he knew how to stitch a *bora*.

"Oh," I said. Why did I not say, "Stitch it this way and that's that"? Why did I not bypass his ego by doing it myself? I have no excuses other than fatigue of the will.

I hugged my friends goodbye on the Deesa–Mount Abu road. I would have sat right down and wept there, if I hadn't been so worried about the camels, the gear, the magazine, Dilip, Chutra, the camels, the magazine, Chutra, the magazine. And the humanity clustered around us, shoving, staring, smothering.

Chutra seemed ambivalent about the perpetually gathering crowds. Sometimes they so annoyed him that he shouted and waved his stick at them, describing them to me as "very half-mind" and tapping his forehead. On the other hand, they did provide an audience. He took charge of the princesses straight away, leaving me to lead Ram Rahim. Thinking I could not understand him, he informed everyone in convoluted but still decipherable language that the two Jaisalmer pure-breds belonged to himself while the undistinguished Kutchi bull belonged to me. He was also fond of boasting that he was contracted to be my bodyguard by the Royal House of Jodhpur. I doubt if anyone believed this because Madam Sahib, despite her paleness of skin, looked about as important as a pariah dog.

There was quite a large population of Rabari in this area. They had sold their herds and bought land and were better off than their travelling cousins. But the wilderness had left their spirit and they were just like anyone else. Once this land had been thickly wooded, ripe with bluebulls and big cats, rich with grasses for the nomads' herds. Now it was bare as picked-clean bone. The track wound beside a village which surely could support no more than fifty people.

All was quiet behind the broken wall; outside it a few chickens clucked around in the dungheaps. Then a sound which was chilling to me. Children. Avalanches of children, thousands it seemed, drawn out through gaps in the rubble as if by a piper, each with his own little face, her own little fate, beautiful, loved, unique and futureless. Because there is nothing left for them. Not enough land, or trees, or animals, or jobs; not enough money for education, or medicine, or the guarantee of a full stomach. Yet they will produce the same number of children again—and again and again—and the physical understanding of that mathematics, of the geometric progression of ever more indigent life, made the heart shrink in fear. I knew the statistics—that the resources spent on a single American child could support twenty-five Indian children. I loathed the moralism which demanded that the third world accept (and pay for) a version of environmental protection in which trees were more important than people. Anyone who used electricity or drove a car had no right to tell peasants to stop felling trees. Nevertheless it was the children of India who illuminated the obvious—unjust disparity and movements of world capital notwithstanding—*there are too many of us.* It was difficult, when I heard the cacophony of that stream of life pouring out of the most impoverished of villages, not to abhor human kind—its mindless replication. Any lingering grief at my own childlessness was assuaged by that sound, which now gradually died away as the river of life emptied back into the village, the further we moved on.

The nomads I had known tended to limit their children. But within one generation of settlement the women lose their independence, move further behind the veil and begin producing babies as fast as their wombs can manufacture them. I do not believe this is because more children are an economic advantage to settled people. Nor that children have a better survival rate in villages (rather the opposite). I think it is to do with the diminishing status of women when the wandering life ceases, to the point where they no longer have control over their own reproduction.

Everyone we passed on the road drew from Chutra the following questions: "Where are you from? What is your caste?" Depending upon their answers, he was either friendly or dismissive. (The further down the caste scale, alas, the more dismissive he became.) Yet how well I understood this ordering of the chaos when, a little further on, we saw a travelling Kutchi Rabari. My heart leapt out to greet that woman in black—my sister, my family, my *jaat*.

But her eyes were like two striking snakes. She was alone with her little flock of sheep, her companions a long way behind. I knew enough about *dang* life to know that this was unusual and dangerous. Perhaps her *dang* had had to split into smaller flocks, so that now there were not enough shepherds to go around. Or perhaps the shepherd of this flock was too ill to walk, leaving the responsibility for the animals' safety up to this lone and unprotected woman. If she lost the animals, it would mean destitution for her and her family. This was not a place in which trust and survival went together. I did not frighten her further by going over to her but lifted my hand and continued on my way.

Zali was proving to be a high-calibre companion. The long association with Jogis had bred out canine slavishness. He had an aristocratic demeanour, mitigated by terrific street cred.

Survival was his first priority and his best chance of securing that, on this journey, lay with the Memsahib whom, he had quickly worked out, he could twist around his little paw. Chutra did not signify. Chutra was inaudible and invisible.

Brave Zali. Beauuutiful Zali. Intelllligent Zali.

This perspicacity regarding the way things were communicated itself from the first night when he slept outside the front door, only to move over successive nights to sleeping outside the door of my room, to sleeping inside the door of my room, to sleeping beneath my bed, to sleeping on a corner at the bottom of my bed, to sleeping on the bottom half of my bed, to sleeping under the covers, my arm curled around him, his nose peeping out of the blankets. When Narendra condemned this behaviour, I pointed out that Zali had picked up an English vocabulary of at least a dozen commands and he obeyed all of them, which was more than could be said of the *unth wallah.*

But even with Zali's fine company, the first day was not as light-hearted as the first day of a long journey ought to be. Perhaps there were moments when there were no people clustered around, when there were no village dogs salivating at my ankles or threatening to rip out Zali's throat, when the infinite potential of a road beneath one's feet entered the spirit, so that it fearlessly called to the future around the bend, "Here I am. I am coming to you." But I do not remember them.

Being thus disappointed, I now set great store by what the first night might bring. Sleeping under the stars, camel bells tinkling in a cool breeze, perhaps some interesting roadside companions with whom to while away an hour or two, no trucks hurtling up the backsides of camels and scaring them out of their wits, no diesel fumes, no gawpers. Hope again, you see. Damned hope.

I left the finding of a camping spot up to Chutra as only he knew how to read the countryside. The place he chose was not salubrious, but the pumping of a well muffled the thunder of trucks on the road and the *mali* (a field worker employed by farm owners) seemed a sweet man. He was very excited at the prospect of such unusual guests near his well and offered to help with everything. Alas, he had no milk. He would run to the *dudh wallah* to buy some while we set ourselves up. I mimed that this was not necessary, but he insisted. I pulled out my purse and gave him some money. Chutra took the three camels off to feed. I set up my cot, laid my luggage on top, stashed my purse under it, built the bed on top of the luggage, perched upon it, invited Zali to perch upon it with me and proceeded to write by the last rays of the sun. When the *mali* came back with the milk, I would make tea on the little Primus stove. That would bring home to Chutra (towards whom I was mellowing in direct proportion as the weather was cooling) that I was not at all helpless or stupid and that he could allow me some independence without fretting.

"Madam Sahib does not understand," he had said. "India is full of crooks. Madam Sahib is too trusting." Dear old Chutra, I thought, and smiled.

The *mali* returned. He said, or rather mimed, "The stove will not light in this wind. You must bring it into the pump-house away from the wind." How very helpful, I thought. How can one not be in love with this country after all? So unlike his two companions, leering and unpleasant fellows, who had asked in a leading sort of way whether I drank alcohol. I hinted, with some very loud body language, that I was a Baptist missionary with a loaded pistol under her *kurta*. But the *mali* was harmless and I have never been one to panic over the presence of suspect men, having dealt with enough of them to know that fearlessness is usually the best defence. I handed out tea to the three men, took my own cup and went to sit on my luggage.

When Chutra came back we cooked roti and dal, then collapsed. However I soon saw that if I wanted to sleep *at all*, I would not be able to share my cot with Zali.

Steam rose off the underground water being pumped into the well, forming a thick wet shroud around us so that I could not say whether I was stifling hot or shivering cold. Somehow, I managed to be both. Zali whimpered and pushed his long nose under the covers. I reminded him that Jogi dogs were for hunting and for tearing strangers to shreds. Not for cuddling up to in the night. Neither the dog nor I slept more than three hours.

Chutra snored.

In the morning two things became apparent very quickly. Both Zali and I were ill, and my purse was missing. Had my purse contained only money, I might have neglected to tell Chutra of its disappearance, thereby hiding that inch which would lead to a mile of proof of my stupidity. But my purse contained torch, mosquito repellent, passport and all the papers needed to subdue bureaucrats from here to Delhi.

Chutra demanded an exact reconstruction of the movements of the previous night while he paced in front of me, hands clasped behind his back. He deduced that the *mali* had enticed me into making tea in the pumphouse away from the wind, then gone out to take the purse from under the luggage on the bed. Yes, perhaps I did remember him leaving while I made the tea. Yes, perhaps I had broken a cardinal rule by displaying money in my purse when I gave the *mali* some paisa for milk. And, yes, it was possible that he was watching when I buried my purse in the luggage.

The *mali* who had been so friendly the night before could not be found this morning. Chutra confronted his wife and daughter instead. He said, "As I cannot find your husband, in order to clear up this little matter of the missing purse, I'm afraid I must go to the police in Sidpur, and bring them here." The *mali* appeared shortly afterwards.

Chutra said to the *mali*, "As you know nothing about the missing purse, you will not mind coming with me to the police station to help me explain to them what has happened." But it seemed that the *mali* did mind. He would like to help us find this accursed and abominable thief but, regretfully, he had to go to work. "Ah," said Chutra, "in that case you must take me to your master and I will explain everything to him. Perhaps I will take *him* to the police." At this the *mali* shrank further into his rags and began to look far from innocent. I waited with the camels while Chutra prepared the coup de grâce.

There seemed to be lots of arm-waving and head-shaking going on. Eventually I called to Chutra and suggested that, if we gave them some time, we would most likely find the bag abandoned somewhere as they were now obviously frightened. The important things were the papers rather than the money, so perhaps we should make tea and wait. He agreed.

Less than half an hour later, the *mali*'s daughter happened to spot the purse ditched in a perfectly invisible place. Everyone gasped and rhubarbed at such phenomenal good luck and looked so painfully guilty that I felt sorry for them and doubly angry at myself. But Clouseau was relentless. He paced to and fro in front of the gaping purse, twirled his moustache with one hand and lifted his other in a gesture for silence.

"Don't touch anything," he commanded. "We will now call the police to see if the money is inside because it is rather strange that the *mali*'s daughter should have craned her neck over here, when in fact she should have been walking on the path over there." The *mali*'s daughter began to cry.

"How much was in the purse?" hissed Chutra in an aside.

"I don't remember. Probably fifteen hundred or so."

"How can you not remember? It was your money. Madam Sahib is very forgetful."

". . . About one thousand."

There followed several hours of horse-trading. By mid-afternoon the drama had reached its denouement. The *mali* was routed, I was handed eight hundred rupees and we loaded up to leave. The *mali*'s wife was wailing; his daughter had fled. Public humiliation, public shame. But Chutra had no pity. A thief is a thief no matter what his circumstance and it was the woman's bad fortune to be married to one.

I, too, was covered in shame. How could I have been so thoughtless as to leave such temptation around for a man immured in poverty, whose only knowledge of Europeans is that they are unimaginably rich? Chutra chastised me for being too trusting (read stupid). And for being forgetful. Indeed I was forgetful, pathologically so, and for this too I felt nothing but remorse.

I had so forfeited any credibility that it was beyond me to make suggestions regarding the loading or the *bora*. Hadn't Chutra just proved himself infinitely more capable than I in this venture? And shouldn't a Raika camel man know, better than I, how to load three camels so that the luggage didn't fall off? In my view it looked very precarious, but who was I to judge? A vague, gullible, idiotic "phoren."

We walked six miles to Sidpur. Chutra's victory over the *mali* had gone to his head and anyone who passed us, or indeed anyone who was five hundred yards away in a field minding his own business, would be called over and subjected to a rendition of the thief story in which our hero Chutra had, through wiliness and intelligence, retrieved for Madam Sahib (who came out of this story as a somewhat dim-witted figure, quite irrelevant to the plot except as *paisa wallah*) one thousand rupees, a sum which grew with every passing mile and every captured listener until, by the time we reached Sidpur, it had swelled to eight thousand rupees.

It was impossible not to enjoy these fabulations for the relief of hilarity they offered, but then I realized how vindictive Chutra's lying was. Everyone in the area would now know that the *mali* was a thief and that the *mali*'s wife was a thief's wife. With each thousand rupee increase, with each increment of evil attributed to the *mali*, another shovelful of earth fell on his social grave.

Zali sloped along like an old tramp. Whenever we stopped to rest from the heat, he flopped down beside me so that I had to coax him back on to his feet when it was time to leave. Animals do not lie down constantly unless they are seriously ill.

"Zali sick," I said to Chutra. He went over to the dog, filled his own clog with sand, passed this clog three times over Zali, muttered a mantra and announced that the dog would now be all right. Somehow this action overwhelmed me with futility. One might or might not survive but either way it was entirely out of one's own hands. In the streets of Sidpur I inquired about a vet. But it seemed there were no vets in Sidpur or, if there were, there was no way of penetrating the clamour, of finding a thread to follow.

On the other side of Sidpur, Momal shied at a bus. The *bora* toppled. The goods were scattered. It was hot. The road was tumultuous and full of fumes. The dog was ill. I did not know how to help the dog. I tried to lash him up on Sumal's saddle but he fell off, howling. My nose was streaming, my eyes itching, my throat raw. People stopped and stared, or laughed, or ran along beside us screaming.

Chutra found it impossible simply to do as I asked. I had to explain in my strained and exhausted Hindi, in my strained and exhausted voice, from the bottom of my strained and exhausted soul, *why* I wanted him to do it. Then, once I had got the words out, clumsily, foolishly, he would challenge what I had said or ask me to explain again, so that either I would have to struggle over the top of his will and back over the top of my exhaustion or let him do as he thought best, which was usually right, but sometimes, infuriatingly, wrong because he was incapable of taking in anything new. He had learnt one way of handling a camel, just as his parents, grand-parents, ad infinitum had learnt it and now when the situation called for something different from tradition would allow for no innovation.

I wanted two things more than anything I'd ever wanted. I wanted Chutra to go away and this ludicrous project to end. At the next STD booth I would ring Narendra and tell him I was continuing alone. But the truth was that I could not do this kind of travelling alone. It would be necessary to leave my luggage to feed the camels. The luggage would disappear. Nor could I tie the camels up somewhere to make a phone call or buy food for myself and expect the camels to be there ten min-utes later. This was the reality. Chutra and I were stuck with each other like binary stars. I knew this yet it gave me plea-sure to imagine him disappearing. To imagine the wording of the letter to the magazine describing my own disappearance. To imagine myself disappearing.

We lost the luggage again. We struggled together with the loading—sweating, grunting. I indicated how the weight should be realigned, how the luggage should be lashed. I said that the *bora* needed restitching. But I was too tired now to force the issue. To retain a semblance of composure I switched most of myself off—that strange, ever-recurring necessity dur-ing the last two years, of closing down vast landscapes, whole continents, of brain.

On the third day we pulled in to a roadside *dabar*. I sat and dropped my head into my hands. In the blackness behind them, I was composing variations on the theme of Chutra's disappearance. The rest of me was shut down. Someone arrived at my table. I did not raise my eyes for a long time. When I did, a young man in a suit said in Hinglish, "I am a Raika. I am a teacher here." I managed a smile and ventured that teaching was an unusual profession for a nomad.

"Yes, madam. But in this area we have become farmers. Madam, may I suggest that you spend tonight on Nagji bhai's farm? I will organize this. You need rest. And Nagji bhai will be able to answer many questions regarding the Raika, in fact about all the Rabari caste for hundreds of miles around. He is a knowledgeable and important man."

Hang on. A Raika teacher speaking English? And this *dabar*. Not the low roofed lean-tos filled with spit and pariah dogs and flies, brewing chemical-strength tea on little mud stoves in infernal heat, but laminex tables and advertisements for Kwality ice-cream. Civilization. Vets.

"You are so kind, sir. But I must find a vet. . . ."

"Nagji bhai will help you. Now I will give directions to your camel man. Please write well of our caste. Here we have been very fortunate but elsewhere . . . Well, you have seen for yourself."

Hope. The dog could recuperate at Nagji's while I restitched the *bora* and organized the loading. The previous three days could be summed up as a false start. Even the policeman on the corner demanding money did not subdue the cheerfulness of hope. I refused to give him anything. I mentioned the superintendent of the Rajasthan police, a friend of Narendra's, and wrote down the constable's name on a piece of paper. The constable let us pass. At this show of strength, Chutra was quite beside himself with happiness. Scraps of songs came out of his mouth as he skipped along, twirling his stick and tipping his turban to passers-by. He said, "Look, Madam Sahib, that bird there. No, there. You see?" and pointed to something feathered sitting on an overhead wire.

It is easier to believe that one can control the course of events than it is to live with the thought that we are the impotent unfurlings of initial states, that even the setting of a direction on which chance might operate is itself an effect of multitudinous previous causes lying outside comprehension, separate from will, themselves reducible to infinitely remote first causes. We must behave *as if* we were the agents of outcomes, as if character contained within it a kernel of free will, enough, at least, to allow us to choose right or left when confronted with a fork in the road, yes or no when presented with a moral choice. If determinism rules, nothing can be predicted, because causes are too multifarious ever to grasp. If free will rules, then wild cards enter the pack at every instant. Either way, in my world, the future was unfathomable.

But in Chutra's kingdom of consciousness the future was intelligible if one had the skills to decipher the codes of synchronicity—the *shaguns*. If a particular bird flew from the left of the road as we moved out of camp, or if another called from the right, we must pause a few minutes so that whatever bad luck was waiting for us would miss us (and perhaps strike someone else?), as if avian angels were forever resetting the clocks of chance. Chutra obtained proof of the veracity of these signs by ignoring those which, in retrospect, did not fit into the predictive scheme or by explaining anomalies as weaknesses in his own interpretative skills. From his point of view, there had been clear indications all the way along of our bad luck, which we had ignored out of ignorance and to our peril.

Just as, now, there were favourable *shaguns* leading us to Nagji bhai, like stars ushering kings across Sinai. The sun set, craypaz-pink. Cool air wafted from the irrigated crops; distant wells pumped like blood pulses; monkeys stole food from the fields, then leapt into the trees beside us.

Chutra hooted, bared his teeth, scratched his ribs. The monkeys jumped down from their perches, snarled at him, then sprang into branches above us to curse wildly at such effrontery. When Chutra saw that I was laughing, he redoubled his efforts until we were at war with hundreds of monkeys. We walked along for a couple of miles through a light as lovely as faded crêpe folded in an old woman's wardrobe.

By the time we reached Nagji's village the world was quiet beneath a gauze of moonlight. Buffalo were tethered and breathed warm air into the night. Outside houses old men sat silently, holding a great-grandchild or working at some craft by the shine of a lamp. Here and there a darker bundle and a glint of jewellery. Darkness threw a cloak over my strangeness, so that people let me pass with a nod or a softly called greeting. Houses, animals and people were part of one harmoniously integrated thing, like a carpet woven by gods who alone could perceive the pattern.

Come morning the gods would unravel their work, jumbling its elements into confusion, mess. And they would rip away my cloak, exposing me to the crowd. But, for the moment, the shuffling camels, the silhouetted dog, Chutra— silenced by tiredness—and myself were part of the weave.

I had not been able until a short time before to understand the Indian habit of staring. I had been wandering in the bazaars of Mount Abu and had seen a real freak. Even from the opposite end of the street, even when almost submerged beneath the swirl of people, she was the cynosure of all eyes, including my own. She wandered through the bazaar unaware of her monstrousness or perhaps inured to it. She was pale, larval and profoundly out of place. She too had tried to disguise herself in kurta pajama, had pulled her hair back as I had done. She too wore the expression I knew I wore in the streets, a kind of grim determination to deny being a European, to pretend that the people who pointed, stared and laughed must be pointing, staring and laughing at somebody else.

I had realized then, with an unpleasant little shock, that no matter how deep my identification with this country went, I would always be seen as alien. I would be like the fourth-generation Japanese American I knew whose spirit broke when he was a teenager and realized he could never be a credible Country and Western singer.

By now I was coaxing the dog along. He staggered sometimes, would lean against me, struggle on. I rode for a while, carrying Zali in front of me on the saddle until he pleaded so hard for his dignity, I let him down. Eventually in the darkness I, too, got down. The dog came to lean against my legs. "Just a little further, my friend. Then you can rest as long as you want."

But it wasn't just a little further.

The farms here were fertile. You could smell prosperity as you walked down the lanes. The scent of dense green growth, irrigation mist, massive trees not butchered for their fodder, fattened, passive cattle. How cruel to be so close to safety, in the midst of such abundance, while life eked out of a body with every step. Zali, most noble representative of his species, did not complain but kept on, sometimes touching his nose to my hand as if to give reassurance as much as seek it.

It was nearly midnight when we reached Nagji's farm. Among the faces looming out of the night, and through the fog of my exhaustion, my host was instantly recognizable.

Authority radiated from him, touching and enfolding all, intimidating and protecting all. You could lean the weight of the world on Nagji and he would not bend.

I began to unload the camels. He commanded that I stop. What was Chutra for, if not to do his job? I was to sit on a charpoi and rest. I sat. Tea was brought by women who seemed to want to shrink under the patriarch's gaze. With the noise of hurrying skirts, they vanished behind the house. The offer of food was refused but food came anyway. Nagji said, "While you are here, you do not open your food box." I expressed my gratitude as best I could. Then, swallowing embarrassment at making a request after his kindness, I brought up the subject of the dog. Did Nagji have any antibiotics? From where and how soon could a vet be engaged? Could one be called now? I was not quite sure what Nagji said but eventually it penetrated that nothing could be done tonight, and nothing tomorrow, it being Sunday. I tried to keep the despair off my face, but Nagji lowered his Old Testament head and stared right through me. "I will send for a vet tomorrow. In the meantime God will be kind, or perhaps not, but there is nothing you can do."

Chutra had been trying to big-note himself as usual. But he'd been silenced by a glance. I felt a strange protectiveness towards him. Could it be that, in spite of my wanting so desperately for him to vanish, there lurked some nascent affection for him? At last, at a lull in the conversation, during which I prepared my goodnight politenesses because I thought I might inconvenience everyone by dying if I couldn't get horizontal, Chutra found his voice. He stood up, spread his arms wide to indicate Nagji, his family, his farm, and all the people who had gathered to offer their hospitality, and declaimed, "Madam Sahib. All this I have fixed for you."

In the morning I took in my surroundings. An open farmscape of hardpacked white earth, swept each day by the women and shaded by ancient trees. Three camels tethered to a ground peg; beside them two bullocks, sleek, gleaming, enormous, fit for Shiva to ride, nosing at fresh-cut lucerne. There were thatch-roofed stables and piles of hay the size of huts. Where dark roots penetrated the soil, charpois were stacked. A whitewashed verandah contained bags of wheat and well-oiled harnesses. Bordering the acre of whiteness and shade, blue fields burst with crops. To the Indian rural aesthetic, this was paradise. Here was security. Here one would not go hungry. Out there, beyond the fence, beyond the village compound, were bandits, wild beasts, lawlessness, danger, hardships and death. Whatever beauty was in the world belonged to the villages, to domesticity, never to the jungle where man was reduced to predator and prey.

One of Nagji's daughters, having swept the compound, was now wafting incense and burning coal around the farm to ward off dirt of another order. She shot a sideways smile at me, passed the incense over Zali, then indicated tea. I was to follow her.

Nagji had eight children, six girls and two boys. His wife was away, visiting her family, but the oldest daughter, a woman in her twenties, led me into the living quarters through a small wooden door cut high in the wall, which was bolted behind me. It was like entering a cage full of parakeets. Six women were upon me, asking questions, all at once, in the local dialect, each outdoing the other, one pulling me one way to see something, another pulling me the other—all of them laughing and looking into my face with wonder. I was in a small courtyard where the animals were kept at night. To the right was a door leading to a long room. To the left, a tiny cement cubicle, the kitchen.

They pushed me into the long room where everyone slept

and in which the women lived when they weren't working, supervised, in the fields or cooking in the sweat-box. The room was dark and cool. In one corner, illuminated by the only window, were some large clay *matkis* full of water and a small *puja* stand. I was to have a bath, it seemed. At the opposite end of the room, along the wall, were rows of brass and stainless steel cooking utensils which had been polished with mud until they could catch the faintest fall of light—a visual effect which, if translated into sound, would be an organ stopped at basso profundo. Hand-stitched quilts were folded along one wall; charpois were stacked against the opposite one.

The women indicated the water, gave me a low wooden stool, handed me some soap and sat in a semi-circle as if waiting for the curtain to go up. I had been told that one should not display one's fanny, even to other women, so I bared my breasts, wrapped the towel clumsily around my waist, dropped my pajama, placed soap and *matkis* on the stand and squatted. Suppressed giggles. Oldest daughter handed me a *lungi* (sarong) and bade me sit on the stool to have my wash and put the *matki* at my feet. The *lungi* did not quite cover my pubic hair so, once again, awkwardness crippled every movement. They watched, fascinated, as I bathed.

Once that was over, I was invited to sit with them in the kitchen while they prepared food. There was no chimney and smoke filled the room. Part of it was open to the sky, so that a wedge of scalding light fell into the gloom. How could they bear this in summer? How could they possibly bear to sit in this box in forty-five-degree heat, bending over fire with no air to breathe, hour after hour, pounding dough, boiling tea? What were they made of that they could endure torture without complaint? Already I felt numbed by the heat and the smoke, queasy in the stomach. And yet, years before, I had lived in a stone ruin with half a roof, which I shared with snakes and fig trees, and it was so hot that cheese melted down off the shelves and candles disappeared into puddles without being lit. And associated with that time and place, there is not one memory of a moment of discomfort.

All the sisters were literate but only one spoke Hindi. She did the translating. They repeated questions over and over, louder and louder, closer and closer. The fire was crackling. Heavily spiced and oiled food was forced on me, which I ate to please them but felt ill. Guiltily I took some of my quota out to the dog. The women looked at each other. Waste this high-class guest food on a dog which will die anyway? Zali sniffed at the food, looked at me and lay down, leaving it untouched.

Back in the kitchen the ladies whispered together, then asked me how much I paid Chutra. I guessed immediately that he had been skiting to them, so I increased the amount by a third. The older woman turned triumphantly to her sisters and said, "I told you so!" Silly Chutra had exaggerated so wildly that only an idiot could have believed him.

Suddenly there came the sound of the tread of the patriarch. Not so much an aviary now, more a hen-house when a hawk flies over. The women scattered to the four corners or concentrated on what they were doing with frozen attention. He came in and glowered at them. They did not look up.

"You have not given her enough to eat," he bellowed, grabbing a plate and ladling yet more ghee on to a chapati.

"No, really," I said, "I cannot eat so much. They have fed me too well. Too well." I grabbed my stomach and groaned.

Nagji harrumphed and cast one more threatening look over his flock before opening the door. "Come to the front," he said to me, "when you are ready."

The moment he left, the women flew back to me like naughty schoolgirls.

I almost always preferred being with women but Nagji's daughters exhausted me. One of the effects of being locked inside a room all your life is that the ability to imagine another's state is atrophied. They could not grasp what effort it required to communicate with six people without the words to do it in. And it upset me to see how far they had fallen in so short a time, a fall directly related to the family's rise in fortunes. Conforming to the more rigid traditions such as locking up women is a privilege only the upwardly mobile can afford.

Not that the women mourned their loss. How could they? They had nothing with which to compare their lives. And if you asked them, they would find nothing missing because, after all, wasn't their father an important man? Didn't he provide well for them? Hadn't he found them husbands from good families? Hadn't he married them off on the same day and provided a big feast for the occasion? Wasn't their little brother being educated at an English medium school in distant Mount Abu? So what if they could not venture on their own to the front of the house and, if anyone came, must flee giggling to the shadows or hide in their long cell, like moles.

But I could compare them with the women of Kutch whose men looked at them with affection, respect and not a little awe, who could stride out and laugh with their heads thrown back, crack jokes and sing, haggle with the shop *wallahs*, and fight with their slings beside their men. I missed those women. Missed the space in their souls. And I longed to leave the kitchen now for the openness of the front compound.

One of the younger girls came flying through the door, breathless. "Ma has come! Ma has come!" The women rose as one. Their faces had been transformed. Gone was any coarseness. Only love was in them, shining from them. A lump came to my throat and I had to eat something to keep it down. Their mother had been away just two days, yet it was as if she had returned from a decade of travel. The daughters pressed around her, cooed to her, kissed her hands, hugged her, touched her hair. They adored her with a passion I had never before seen expressed with such intensity between mother and daughters. It was as if, in their imprisonment inside the long room, they had grown into one another, forming one organism. I did not discover Ma's history but I suspect she had had a relatively free life before her marriage. The air of empty spaces still lingered around her. How awful it must have been to be trapped in that room or watched every second as she laboured in the fields. How deeply she must have needed the tenderness of those daughters.

In the presence of their beloved Ma, I became invisible and could slip away to the front of the house, to the world of men.

Whether they came on foot or as polished Ambassadors, the stream of guests sat before Nagji like supplicants. Charpois would be brought, trays of water glasses, sometimes tea. I could not follow their conversation but the exercise of power was unmistakable. Nagji was rich, he was on the local council, even the *sarpanch* was deferential.

An old Rabari arrived, a skeleton in rags like all travelling pastoralists in this area. He was so shy, he hid his smile behind the rug he wore when I asked if he were a *mukki*. Nagji told me that he was the *mukki* of a group of people from the Sirohi area—goat and sheep herders. Nagji had convinced the village that these people should be allowed to graze their animals for several months of the year on the communally held lands. It was quite common for villages to lease out these areas to pastoralists but usually at exorbitant rates.

Had it not been for Nagji, they would have had to pay anything up to twenty thousand rupees to stay here. As it was, they paid only a thousand per year to the village, then individually to local farmers for grazing rights. Usually Nagji gave this old man his grass for free, but this year there had been very little rain. "It is a hard year for everyone. I cannot give away my grass."

When I asked if these people got any drought relief from the government, Nagji said, "I am his relief and he is my relief. It is like that. We are the same *jaat* (community). Here, God is kind. There is good soil, good rain. Where he comes from, if there is no rain, then there is no food. All day there is trouble for him from the landowners, all night from the thieves. He must patrol by night and walk by day. For him there is too much trouble and too much danger."

Nagji's grandfather had arrived in this area when the big drought decimated Rajasthan. It was at the time when land was being redistributed and made available to the ordinary man. But most Rabaris had not taken advantage of it, partly because the caste councils penalised members who gave up traditional ways of life. He said, "My grandfather was wise. He saw in to the future and sold his camels and sheep and bought this land. We are a very strong caste, a gypsy caste. My people have been in India so long no one can remember or measure the time. Did you know that gypsies came from Australia to populate this country?" I said that I did not know.

At a little pause in our conversation, I cleared my throat and said, "Nagji, you mentioned that a vet would be called. When will he come?"

Nagji looked at me a long time from beneath his brows. "The vet could not be found today. He will come tomorrow." In my mind's eye I saw the dog's life flicker out in the night and was overcome by such a sense of impotence that it was impossible to keep it from registering on my face. I turned away, so Nagji would not read what was there.

The next day was lost to me. I watched the dog dying. I fought with Chutra over restitching the *bora* until Nagji intervened and told Chutra that I was right and he was wrong. Chutra sulked. And still the vet did not come. I fretted over the dog and tried to hide my sentimentality from the women. They could not see why I should waste money on a dog. He was replaceable—any dog would warn me of danger. But Zali was not *any* dog, he was *my* dog.

At night I drove to town with the *sarpanch* to ask Narendra to please send replacements for Chutra. A dozen men watched my face as I shouted into the phone. Yes, came his voice brittle with static, he would send Koju in the jeep and try to find me a couple of other camel men. The following morning the vet came and injected Zali twice in the neck. But the dog could not stand up; it was surely too late.

Nagji was a man used to imposing his will on others. One trick he had for gaining control was to make a statement which did not make sense until something was added to it. He would make his pronouncement, then wait, glaring at you for as long as it took for you to drop your eyes, concede defeat and say, "Yes, please go on . . ."

That night he said, "What is it"—I waited, dropped my eyes before his, and said, *"Han ji, bolie"*—"you think about that gives you so much tension? You think too much."

I laughed. "Well, partly it's my habit and partly it's my . . . work." The eyes pierced and I had no choice but to venture further. "But, also, I think about the problems I face and how best to deal with them. It is difficult for me for two main reasons. One is that I cannot really *talk*. Speaking in a language I don't know, struggling to understand and to express, takes great mental effort. There are often misunderstandings which I have to let go because I cannot speak properly. When you can't express yourself, especially when there are difficulties that require quick action, a kind of pressure builds up in the mind and there is no way to release it. So that makes me worry at night, for example, and lack of sleep adds to my appearance of tension. It is like being deaf or blind, yet having to react as if you were not.

"Secondly [here I took a risk], in my country people spend time by themselves. We are used to it. I, for example, spend most of my day alone, sometimes days, even weeks, on my own. It is my preference. Even in families most of us have moms to go where we can be private. Here, the opposite is true. You are never alone and this is your preference. But for me this is very, very hard. Also it's worse than it might be because people constantly gather around me, so there is never any peace. They do not let me sleep or rest or eat or even go to the latrine without following and looking."

The strange thing about learning a language is that sometimes one achieves what almost amounts to fluency. The homunculus seems to remember where to go in the stacks. But even then, and especially if the conversation is at a more intense level than usual, it is heavy work, interrupted by the need to find a way of explaining abstract concepts using simple words or, if the words are not there, then using mime. When I couldn't understand something Nagji said, I would look to Chutra for assistance, which was strange given that Nagji spoke better Hindi than Chutra. But by now Chutra and I had developed a kind of moronic language of our own. Poor Chutra, both Nagji and I got cross with him when he couldn't translate, but he tended to labour the obvious and gallop through the difficult. Nevertheless the conversation proceeded, sometimes at a broken trot, sometimes at a crawl, sometimes circling back on itself to retrieve a meaning, but proceeding.

"Yes," Nagji rubbed his chin thoughtfully, "the public here

is very bad. And you are a woman, so it is worse. They think
of you as a statue, a perfect white statue. But all women here
are treated badly. My wife, for example, cannot go out on her
own, ever . . ."

I expressed my surprise.

"No, never. If she went out alone, the whole world would
say what, who, how, and they would tear her jewellery and
beat her." He mimed being hit across the face. The subtext of
the conversation moved on to rape. Chutra said twenty per
cent of men were bad men and that Madam Sahib was very
trusting and innocent.

Nagji said, "Nonsense, eighty per cent are bad and all are
thieves." Then he turned to me and said, "It is very, very dangerous for you. You must try to understand." He furrowed his
forehead and jutted his head forward like a bull.

"I do understand, Nagji bhai, and I appreciate your concern, but this is my work. We all must work and sometimes it
is dangerous. It is true that I might meet with trouble but it is
also true that I find people like you more often than I find bad
people. Except the police. They are always bad."

Nagji said, "You must put that in your story. Everyone is
angry that the police are corrupt. And that the poor man can
find no justice."

I said that I certainly would but doubted that it would
make any difference.

And so the conversation went on, ending, at last, in the
labyrinthine politenesses concerning how long I was to stay.
I said I should leave the following day. Nagji said ten days.
Eventually, and rather more quickly, now that we had been
so frank with each other, a sensible solution was reached. I
would be taken to the Sirohi Rabari who were camped by
Nagji's well. I could spend as long as I liked there and, when
the dog was well enough, leave from there for the forest areas

of the Aravallis, through which many Rabari villages and *dangs* were scattered.

We had been talking for over an hour and we were strained by it. Chutra chose this moment to make a long speech. On top of the effort of conversing, the accumulation of the day's worries and my own physical weakness, he placed the last straw. I grabbed my head and collapsed on the charpoi with a groan. At which, Nagji let out a lion's roar of laughter and said, "Sleep now. Tomorrow you will have peace."

Before sunrise the next morning, I found myself perched behind Nagji on a very fine cart pulled by two enormous oxen with blue horns—a form of transport originating in the steppes approximately five thousand years ago. I knew my friend was showing off as he lifted their tails, making them go faster, displaying their form, their strength—adjuncts to his own potency and power.

"You should have chosen a bullock cart," he said. "Bullocks eat anything and can go anywhere, much better than camels, and you could have had some comfort." We thundered along beside a riverbed, shaded, cool. Zali had survived the night.

The further we moved towards the Rabari camp, the more desolate the terrain became. A thousand sheep and goats were held on 250 acres. A few shepherds whom you could mistake for stones had they not been topped by turbans sat motionless under the sun. The trees, too—what were left of them—looked post-nuclear, with just a tiny tuft of leaf left here and there.

"This area used to be very dangerous," said Nagji. "Thieves lived here and wild animals. But now that I have sunk the well," he smiled and tapped his head, "the thieves have had to go. They are afraid of me."

The camp itself was a collection of grass huts lined up along a fence beneath Nagji's well. Behind them were grass pens which would hold the animals at night. A woman carried a huge bundle of lopped tree on her head. This year there were approximately fifty people from several different villages, all related.

Nagji had had flowers planted around his well—busy Lizzies and marigolds. The Rabari took off their shoes when they used it as a sign of respect and gratitude to him.

He showed me inside a hut—a cubby-house made of sticks and clumps of roly-poly grass. The earth floor had been swept so clean it was almost polished. Attached at the back was a straw room with a straw floor, the size of a double bed. This was where the mother and father slept. It was the house of the first of the three little pigs. Yet even this poverty was transformed by a veneration for beauty. Everything was neat and prettily made. Nagji told me that the people were infested with fleas and lice but the impression these huts gave was of cleanliness and order. A gorgeous woman—sexy snaggle teeth and long-boned gracility—glided over to us with tea. There were bone marriage bangles right up to her armpits, eight yards of cloth in her skirt which was red, red, red. When I returned the cup, she grabbed my hand and pulled me down beside her. She told me that on their way down here, they stopped near the foot of Mount Abu and each day carried up their milk through the jungle to the tourist hotels at the top. Ten miles straight up, at the mercy of bears, leopards and tigers. She laughed and said that, yes, it was very dangerous but what to do? She mimed carrying the *deghras* (milk cans) on her head, swaying her hips.

As usual the men were, by comparison, as plain as planks but they too, when they overcame an almost autistic shyness, were willing to talk. Because of drought and lack of feed, this year's wool was short and very coarse. It would not bring in much money. Already the people and animals were thin. If there were no rain again next year, most of the herd would die and some of the people.

When I had inspected the camp and asked my questions, it was time for Nagji to implement his idea. He ordered three black goat-hair mats for me to sit on and food to eat (rancid goat milk and dry roti). He himself sat on another mat approximately fifteen yards away. When I was settled, a shepherd brought a handful of marigolds which he strewed around me, then backed away. A woman brought incense and placed it beside me. Another brought water.

I wanted to run over to the patriarch and thank him for his largeness of spirit, his effort of empathy. Instead I sat on my mat, surrounded by marigolds, notebooks, goat droppings and incense, by huts that kept out neither dust nor wind nor rats nor even sun, by scrawny, tottering sheep, by donkeys, heads hung low and ribs like washboards, while fifteen yards away Nagji acted as guard and fifty people, smiling, and with silent respect, watched the white guest being alone.

Postscript: Robyn Davidson arrived safely back in Australia, exhausted and laden with numerous diseases (all fortunately treatable), but also with a strong desire to return to India someday.

A 1,200-mile trek across the Sahara impressed William Langewiesche with the desert's natural beauty, but the landscape also terrified him. The physical hardships of such a journey were daunting enough, but it was the decrepit towns and desperate people that grabbed his attention. His resulting travelogue is full of bandits and insurrectionists amid stark terrain where people die of thirst.

SAHARA UNVEILED

A Journey Across the Desert

WILLIAM LANGEWIESCHE

Prisoners of the Oasis

The road that night stretched across black stony flatlands, swerved, and stretched again. It went on hour after hour. The taxi was old and slow, but durable. It rattled through the darkness. I sat beside the driver, a gruff, silent man with a lined face lit by the reflection of the headlights. Behind us, the passengers slept. We came to the oasis just before dawn, when the road started down into a narrow, steep-walled valley. We took another turn, and the valley spread below us in a sprinkling of electric lights. It was the famed M'Zab: five walled towns, the home of 100,000 people and twice as many palms, where wells strike water at a hundred feet, and gardens will grow.

The M'Zab was settled a thousand years ago by an Islamic sect fleeing persecution in the north. They spoke a distinct Berber dialect, married among themselves, and developed recognizably sharp-faced features. They became known as Mozabites. Though eventually they became traders, opening shops through all the oases, they never gave up their feeling of separateness. During the war against the French, they let the fighting pass them by. The attempt by independent Algeria to sell the M'Zab to tourism never quite worked. Even today the Mozabites cling to their traditions. Old men wear antique pantaloons, and women of all ages, when they venture out, swaddle themselves in white woolen shrouds, allowing only a single eye to show. Islamic radicals recently attacked and killed a group of foreign pipeline workers here. One of the towns still closes its gates every night against strangers and infidels.

By the day's first light our taxi passed through an army checkpoint, and on into the valley. We overtook a man on a donkey cart hauling firewood from the palm grove to the market. We turned around a traffic circle and a concrete monument to national independence, swerved once to avoid a pickup truck, and swerved again to avoid a horse. The oasis was coming to life. At dawn the valley's walls echoed with amplified exaltations of Allah, the haunting calls to prayer. We arrived at the marketplace of Ghardaïa, the M'Zab's main town. The Mozabite on the donkey cart arrived later in the old-fashioned way, by beating his beast.

The M'Zab is the diving board for the deep Sahara, the point from which the bus sets off into the wilderness. The bus follows a route called the Trans-Saharan, which is shown on maps in bold ink, as if it were an established highway. You might expect gas stations and the occasional motel. But the maps reflect ambitions that have never been realized. A road from north to south across the Sahara would have to cross 2,000 miles of the most tormented land on earth, conquering drought and flash flood, canyon and mountain, salt, sand, mud, rock, and war. And then it would have to be maintained.

Attempts have been made. In the early 1990s, just before the outbreak of the Islamic revolution, the Algerian Army built and rebuilt the Trans-Saharan in sections as far as the geographic midpoint, in the mountain town called Tamanrasset. But as always the desert quickly took the road back. By the time I arrived in the M'Zab, the ruin was nearly total. Only hours south of town, the pavement of the Trans-Saharan broke apart, and forced buses into the open desert, which fed them sand and shook them apart. Because the Ministry of Transportation had no money for bus repairs, the once-ambitious schedule had been reduced to the occasional departure. I discovered that I would have days to linger in the M'Zab. There are worse ways to wait for a bus.

I found a friend of friends, a Mozabite named Hassan Hamim, who owned the state concession for the M'Zab's movie theater. Hamim was a placid clean-shaven man in slacks and Italian loafers, which he dusted insistently. He knew his customers, who tended to be young men frustrated by the smallness of oasis life. Hamim gave them cheap love stories and karate productions, and made a good business of it.

Like other successful Mozabites, he had two houses—one in town for nine months of the year, and another in the shade of the palm groves for the worst heat of summer. The house in town was three stories tall, and had thick mud walls and traditional rooftop courtyards for sleeping in the coolness of night. He invited me to stay with him.

We sat before lunch in an upstairs salon sparsely furnished with rugs and cushions. The walls were papered with murals of alpine lakes, and with verses from the Koran. Hamim introduced me to his young daughters, though not to his wife. The daughters disappeared into the family quarters, the harem, where unrelated men were forbidden to go. Hamim told me that the cloistering was as much his wife's choice as his. I believed him. Within the extremes of a hard desert, it made a certain amount of sense. Had Malika truly cloistered herself, Ameur would never have seen her through the eyes of strangers. There are Saharans, women as well as men, who would call that freedom.

Hamim's friends arrived—a shy postal clerk, a date farmer, and a cynical commerce inspector in a three-piece suit. Work was over until evening. Hamim's daughters served us. We shared a bowl of couscous, followed by oranges and tea. The men did not know the desert beyond the M'Zab. They wanted to talk, but had little to say. They dozed. They gossiped. They said it had been years since they had seen an American. They said now even the French were staying away.

At the time the only foreigners in the M'Zab were those who had come with a Saudi prince to hunt gazelles with rifle and falcon. The prince had arrived the week before in a private airliner, and had set up camp north of town. His pilots, whores, and retainers had taken over the hotel, where they passed the nights in drink and dance. Hamim's friends disapproved. As Mozabites, they resented hedonistic displays. As Algerians, they resented claims to royalty. I sympathized. When after a polite delay, they asked what had brought me to the M'Zab, I said I was waiting for the bus.

The bus to where?

"To Tamanrasset," I said. Far to the south.

They stared. Hamim spoke for them all. "The bus is not a bus," he said. "It's a Safari."

I did not understand him. I thought he meant an exotic trip.

The date farmer said, "The Safari is not for you. It is only for Malians. It is like hell."

"I don't mind."

Hamim had seen the same movies I had. He said, "It's not what you think." He explained that the bus from the M'Zab did not go all the way. The Safari was the name of the hard-sprung truck to which eventually I would have to transfer to cross mountainous central desert. He said, "Why don't you fly?"

"Because I want to see the desert up close."

"Buy a postcard."

"But I want to feel the desert."

"It feels bad."

In the evening Hamim took me to his movie theater. We entered by a side door, and stood near the screen, watching the show. It was a steamy Los Angeles mystery dubbed into Arabic. I forget the title and plot, but remember bared breasts and love scenes, an audience entirely of men, an atmosphere thick with sexual frustration. Hamim told me he had seen the movie before; but I noticed now that he intended to see it again. I wanted to leave, but Hamim was his own good customer. We stayed to the end.

In the morning we strolled through town. Shrouded Mozabite women scurried close to the walls, like nervous one-eyed ghosts. One of them came toward us. At first she seemed like just another figure, as anonymous and uninteresting as she was meant to be. But then we exchanged glances, she and I, and I discovered an eye of the most exquisite beauty—oval, almond-colored, lightly made up, with long lashes and flawless skin. The eye was warm, lively, and inviting. I didn't need to see more.

I asked Hamim if he had noticed. He smiled and said, "But she is married."

"You know her?"

He shook his head. "That's why she veils herself."

"And your wife, does she wear a veil?"

"Of course!" I had gone too far. He was offended that I had asked.

Later I pointed to an unveiled woman crossing the street in a tailored suit. "And who is she?"

"A whore."

"You know her?"

He shook his head.

I said, "Maybe she works in an office." I thought of Malika's sister Zora, and of women workers I had seen in other oases.

Hamim was emphatic. "She is a whore."

It was like talking to someone about his faith. I said, "Okay, but why?"

"These are loose women who become known. They screw for the pleasure of it. Afterward, no one will marry them."

About that, he was probably right. Oases are the smallest kinds of towns. People are stained indelibly by their reputations. There is little mercy. A girl who succumbs too easily to love may become a woman who knows no love at all.

Once at the outskirts of an oasis, around midnight, I was sitting with a group of men by a campfire when two women appeared in the firelight. They were unveiled and unescorted, and they wore tight jeans. One was a schoolteacher, the other

her best friend. I saw in their brazenness that they were out-
casts. The men, my friends, despised them openly. They
introduced them to me as "bad women, hungry for men."
When the women did not leave, the language escalated. In
their presence my friends called them dogs in heat. They said
I would not have to pay them, then said the women would
pay me. And still the women would not leave.

When later they allowed two of the men to take them into
the desert, it was not for love or pleasure, but for self-loathing.
The men were done quickly. The women came back to invite
the hatred of the others. They did not take money. They had
acquired the defensive habit of submission.

On another occasion, in West Africa at a riverbank market, I saw a young woman with crippled, twisted legs, who
swung along by walking on her hands. She wore a torn dress
hiked up around her hips, and had a sweet and lively face,
and matted hair. A band of market boys began to taunt her,
calling her a "goat," reaching down to fondle her breasts. She
did not seem afraid or angry. She even smiled. Then one of
the boys put his foot against her shoulder and kicked hard.
The girl rolled sideways into a puddle of fetid mud. I started
toward her, but stopped when she came up coated with filth,
and laughing with her tormentors. Walking on her hands,
swinging her twisted hips, she disappeared into the market
crowd with a final backward look, not of horror but of satisfaction. She seemed to feel she had won something. People
everywhere are confused by the oases they inhabit.

Hamim was not in the movie business by chance. He was a
good Muslim, but had a vicarious fascination with sin. One
evening he took me to dinner at the hotel, which stood on a
hill above the M'Zab like a mud-walled citadel of forbidden
pleasure. The Saudis had come in from the hunt, and had

begun a long night of drinking. They were not good Muslims. They sat at tables heaped with food and wine and were entertained by musicians with drums and horns.

Hamim and I sat in a corner with two of his acquaintances—a former farmer employed by a German company to collect scrap metal in the desert, and a wiry architect in a beard and sports jacket, more grandly employed in the study of traditional Saharan houses.

During a pause in the music, the architect told me that the houses of the M'Zab are renowned for their starkness and practicality. The French modernist Le Corbusier had come here to learn, to confirm his theories, to find a connection to the past.

I was interested, and asked the architect if he liked Le Corbusier's work.

He said, no, and changed the conversation to women.

The women with the Saudis were young Italians, starker and more beautiful than any building. The architect said something lewd about them, which rang hollow.

Hamim forced a worldly smile. But I could see by the stiffness of his expression that the women bothered him. They were lively and vain, and openly sexual; they were entirely unveiled. And it was obvious that natives like Hamim hardly existed for them.

Wine flowed heavily. Eventually the Saudi men rose from the table, and danced among themselves. The women urged them on. Then from the back reaches of the restaurant a young, lithe, curly-haired man, a stranger, leapt forward and joined the dance. He was like a woman himself. He danced the dance of a loose-limbed satyr with his arms upraised and delight on his face. He was decadent, anarchistic, and entirely sober. Hamim had to look away.

The women laughed. The Saudis were unamused. One of

their bodyguards, a huge man in a turban who had been standing with his arms folded, now shooed the satyr away. The satyr got around him and kept dancing. The bodyguard moved on him more firmly, and blocked his attempts to return. The women laughed. The Saudis were amused. The satyr slinked past our table looking aggrieved. The architect remarked wryly, "He's unemployed, but manages to live here at the hotel." He did not know how.

There was more drinking upstairs. Hamim and I went to the room of an Air Algeria captain spending the night because his Boeing had broken down. He was a tight-tempered, sinewy mustang of a man, sitting in an undershirt sharing whiskey from airline bottles with his flight crew. He liked Buffalo, New York, where he had taken his flight training. He bragged to me about being a real Saharan, the descendant of nomads. But he did not romanticize the desert. He talked about the oasis airports, and said, "V.I.P.s, there are always V.I.P.s. They make the entire airplane wait for them. I feel like telling them, 'Me—my father was killed by the French! I throw you to the dogs!'"

The pilot did not need to be a Muslim. He was a natural moralist. He drank a lot of whiskey. He curled his lips and snarled, "If I had my way, I would stand all those kinds against a wall and shoot them. Like that! And have no second thoughts about it."

He included the Saudis downstairs in his plans.

Hamim was heartened. We left the hotel. By the certainty of his stride, I saw that he felt again like a man. The Air Algeria captain had been a fighter pilot. Saudis dance, but Saharans are soldiers.

Hamim's best friend was a Mozabite named Moustafa Oukal, who was as blustery as Hamim was timid. Oukal had driven once for Texan oilmen, and had admired them, and was thereafter known as "L'Américain." When we met he grinned and said in French, "We Americans are not afraid to get our hands dirty!" He was bald and beefy, and had muttonchop sideburns, a tweed cap, and rough outdoor clothes. He told me he had given up an earlier career as a photographer. He still had a little photo shop near the market, but said he could not find film, and in any case no longer had time for such small pursuits. No matter who won the civil war, he was certain that ordinary Mozabites would continue to suffer. But he himself would prosper—he pretended to be certain of that, too.

Oukal was a Saharan survivalist. His hope lay in a patch of desert about twenty miles out of town, where he had dug a well and planted the first palms. He called it his ranch, and promised to take me there, but first wanted to do a little drinking.

We drove in his Volkswagen van, tools rattling in the back, to buy wine at the end of an alley. The wine was Algerian, originally intended for export to Europe. It was sold unlabeled from a doorway by a woman in a veil, doing a steady and furtive business. As we clattered up in the Volkswagen, an old man slipped down the alley, tucking a bottle into his robes. But Oukal was never bashful. He greeted the woman loudly, introduced me to her as his dear friend, and loaded up with two dozen bottles. He wanted to throw a party in honor of America.

He held the party that night, in the concrete courtyard of his house. Already I recognized most of the men there—the architect, the scrap-metal farmer, the commerce inspector, the clerk from the hotel, the rug merchant from the market, the policeman, the sly, hooded plumber, good for a wink and a smile, and of course Hamim, ever the voyeur of sin. Oukal was in a fine humor. He apologized for the clutter in his house and made excuses for a wife overwhelmed by two young children. I guessed she might disapprove of her husband's friends.

It was all very American. Oukal cooked. He built a big fire directly on the concrete patio, and after it had settled into a glowing heap, he roasted skewered lamb over the coals. The night air became chilly. We huddled close to the fire, chewed the meat, and set to drinking. At first the mood was jovial. When the concrete below the fire exploded, shooting embers across the courtyard, the policeman somersaulted backward in surprise, and we laughed. But the wine was strong, and the conversation flagged. I wanted to talk about the oasis, but the others had done their complaining and their bragging, and had exhausted the easy things to say. The drinking grew humorless and isolating. Only Hamim, the good Muslim, remained sure of his future. Hamim could dream. He wanted to keep the evening going. But for the others, the party had turned sour.

On a bright afternoon, Oukal drove me to his homestead south of town. It lay in a desert depression, on land available to anyone willing to work it. Oukal had claimed ten acres of level ground, and an equal amount of hill. He had drilled a well and hired two nomads to clear the rocks for him. The nomads were illegal immigrants, Tuaregs from the high-land deserts of Niger, to the south. The Tuaregs are Berber nomads, fierce camel riders who controlled the Sahara's mountainous core for thousands of years. These two were typically tall and gaunt, and wore the *chèche* of the hard desert, a long cotton turban wrapped first around the head, then forward across the nose and mouth and neck. The *chèche* protects against the dryness and dust of the hard desert, but more important still, it gives its wearers the power of anonymity.

Tuareg society was built on raiding and war. Tuareg men were so convinced of the *chèche*'s advantages that until recently they never showed their faces to strangers. Tuareg women, by contrast, do not veil themselves. Europeans excited by this apparent liberation have misunderstood the *chèche* and its context. The bareness of the women's faces is in fact an expression of their vulnerability. The men's *chèche* is not a veil but a mask.

Oukal's Tuaregs were the losers in a war against modern times. They lived in a roofless straw enclosure equipped with a wooden front door. Oukal had provided them with one shovel, one bucket, and a wheelbarrow. Today he brought them a week's groceries, with which they retreated hungrily into their dwelling. Oukal chuckled and said they had found their door out in the desert. Smoke from a cooking fire soon rose above the enclosure.

Oukal took me across the property to the well, which was 120 feet deep and sheathed in concrete. He started the diesel pump and offered me water from a gushing hose. I praised the water as sweet. He showed me the first date palms, tender chest-high infants planted in rows at the base of a hill. He explained where he would grow his vegetables. He said he would have chickens, goats, sheep, and maybe a horse for taking Texas-style rides in the hills. The water would make it all possible. He walked me over to where his house would be, and predicted that his wife would be less distracted here than in town. He predicted success for his children. He said they were young, and would learn to love the open horizons away from the oasis. He vowed to give them that freedom. Like a good American, he even paced the outline of a swimming pool.

But his enthusiasms could not endure the drive home. We both felt the change—the suspicion of defeat that overcame him like a slow fatigue, the thought that already his history could be written. He was not a young man anymore. He stopped the Volkswagen where the dirt road overlooked the valley of M'Zab, and sat silently behind the wheel. I waited for him to speak. Gazing out over the roofs of the oasis, he swore that he had no respect for the people who lived there. He called them lazy, and fearful. He called them Africans, although he was one, too. He looked into the distance. He brooded.

Hamim had told me already that Oukal's ranch would fail, as his other ventures had. His well was sweet but weak, and could be pumped only an hour a day. He implied that Oukal was a dreamer.

But Oukal was not a dreamer. Faced with the frustrations of a life in the M'Zab, he had simply refused to surrender. If this made him foolish, I admired his strength and his courage nonetheless.

Hamim had said, "Oukal's life is like this: he has a dog and a goat. The dog chases the goat. The goat chases the dog. They stir the dust."

But Hamim's life was like this: he went to the movies.

The Mechanics of Escape

If you're lucky, you just take a bus. Mine was an old oily Nissan with bald tires, heading south from the M'Zab one sunny morning. I crowded up to the door, waved a ticket, fought my way on board. The other passengers were silent, watchful men in turbans and *chèches*. I made my way past their unsmiling stares, and found a broken seat in the back. The driver climbed on looking unshaven, unalert, overweight, surly.

His assistant, the conductor, surveyed the passengers sternly. He was a small and self-important man, infused with the drama of his mission. We were headed for a town called In Salah, 400 miles deeper into the desert, down the disintegrating Trans-Saharan, in a decrepit bus, with a driver who didn't give a damn, in a time of revolution. The conductor's job was to keep the passengers under control. He seemed to look forward to the possibility of dissent.

For most of the day the Trans-Saharan resembled a road—a rough but drivable strip of black pavement stretching into the distance across gravelly plains. On level ground, the bus gathered speed, but hills threatened to defeat it. I write "hills," and remember hummocks; they were in fact mere ripples on the surface of a vast and level desert. But for our feeble engine they rose like mountains.

The steepest climb was a contest so difficult that the driver leaned forward sympathetically over his wheel. Blue smoke rose through the floorboards. The conductor scowled, daring the passengers to notice. We crept over the crest and began to accelerate down the far side. Somehow, the engine had endured. Now speed threatened to shake the bus apart. The passengers remained impassive. Windows popped open. The breeze purged the smoke.

In an oasis called El Golea more passengers boarded, and crowded the aisles. Among them was a veiled woman accompanied by children. The conductor shouldered his way into the back, and with obvious satisfaction ordered two men to give up their places. Then he shoved his way back to the front, and went outside to slam the popped windows.

The sun set, and the night turned sharply cold. The bus was unheated. I huddled on my broken seat above the engine, absorbing the warmth and fumes, listening to the driver grind the gears. A crescent moon rose among the stars. Dunes forced the bus to slow to a crawl. Once we braked so hard for a herd of camels that the luggage on the overhead racks slid forward in a cloud of dust. The conductor glowered. The driver lit a cigarette.

We came then to the first roadblock—a line of stones beyond which the pavement had disintegrated into rubble. The driver shifted down and swung over the shoulder, out into the open desert. But for the rest of the night we seldom touched pavement. Stopping, considering, backing, we traveled out in the sand and rock flanking the road, at times quite far from it. The windows popped open again. The air swirled with dirt. Breathing was difficult, sleep impossible.

I passed the hours watching the driver work. He had wrapped his face in a *chèche*, and was like a new man out here, guiding his unwieldy beast with concentration and skill. He was superb. He was proud. He was temperamental. When one of the passengers leaned forward and questioned the route he had taken, he braked to a stop, opened the door, and switched off the headlights. He wanted the moon to illuminate the horizons.

The driver said nothing.

The passenger hesitated.

The conductor looked triumphant. He said, "You can walk if you prefer." He would have stranded the man with pleasure.

The passenger retreated into his seat. We set off again. The moon set.

We came to the end of the line, In Salah, in the bitter blackness before dawn. I went into the ruined cinder-block station, where groups of men stood in the gloom. Melancholic Arabic music drifted through the air. A baby cried quietly. From far away came an early call to prayer. Huddled forms slept in blankets against the wall: it was so cold that a bucket of drinking water had iced over. I crouched with robed strangers around a paper fire. The smoke floated against the ceiling. I spread my hands to the feeble flames. Beyond In

Salah the land rises into the Sahara's wild and mountainous center. No one knew when the Safari, the passenger truck for Tamanrasset, would leave. The schedule called for one trip a week, God willing. I waited at the station because others waited.

The Inferno

I once went to the Sahara during the high heat of summer to write about water in a provincial capital named Adrar, which lies west of In Salah and is a place known even here for the severity of its climate. In Adrar, out of some 4,100 hours of possible annual daylight an average of 3,978 hours are filled with direct sun. This is steep-angle sunlight, powerful stuff. In the winter, when the air temperatures drop to freezing at night and rise to 90 degrees by noon, soil temperatures fluctuate so brutally that rocks split apart. In the summer, the Sahara is the hottest place on earth. The world record is held by El Azizia, Libya, where on September 13, 1922, the air temperature was measured at 136 degrees. Death Valley claims a close second, with 134 degrees in 1910. More recently, in 1994, the temperature in Death Valley hit 131 degrees, and the *New York Times* wrote: "An observer reported that even in the shade he could not hold out his open hand against a strong wind because the burning sensation was too painful." In Adrar this would not have made the paper. Death Valley is just one little heat trap. The Sahara is a heat trap on the scale of a continent; its air will burn your hands from one ocean to another, across plains too large even to imagine.

I could have gone to Adrar in the spring or waited until fall, but I chose July for its intensity. My only compromise was to fly. I sat in the cockpit behind the pilots. The airplane was a stodgy turboprop, a forty-passenger Fokker droning at

18,000 feet on a roundabout three-day run from Algiers to the oases. It was midday, and the Sahara stretched in naked folds to the horizon, brilliant, and utterly still. The land was blanketed by a haze of dust, suspended not by winds but by heat. The Trans-Saharan had appeared as a fading scar. Below us, a canyon had cut through the downslope of the central highlands. Now we passed across featureless plains along the northern edge of the vast and terrible Tanezrouft, where for hundreds of miles nothing lives.

The captain, who was not a desert man, had pasty skin and the look of an experienced pilot: bored, dissatisfied, underexercised. He flew with sloppy control motions, as if he could barely endure the job. For him the Sahara was a tough assignment. He said he suffered at night in the oasis hotels. "There is nothing out here," he complained. "You let a sheet of paper fall, and it takes forever to hit the ground. It's the heat."

He tried to be polite. He asked me where I had been and where I was going, and why. He seemed worried that I had a one-way ticket only, and would have to find my way out on the ground. He called Adrar hell.

The heat at the airport was brutal and disorienting. Somehow I caught a ride into town and checked into the hotel on the main square. The square was barren concrete. The hotel room was unbearably hot. I went down to the lobby, sat under a ceiling fan, and like the rest of Adrar, waited for night. It was so hot that even that did not help. After dark, people came onto the streets more out of necessity than relief.

I had the phone number of a local man who had volunteered to show me around. He was a young merchant named Moulay Miloud. Moulay is a title of respect, indicating descent from the Prophet. The family, if it can be called that, has been extraordinarily prolific. I have heard the Sahara called, only half-jokingly, The United States of Moulay.

This particular Moulay, Miloud, was stuck in Adrar for the summer because, as it was explained to me, he was still too poor to escape. However, he had wealthy cousins in Tamanrasset, whom I had met and knew to be generous men; I thought they might have given Moulay Miloud an air conditioner. I dialed his number in hope.

The man who answered said his name was Ali, and that I had the wrong number. He would not let me hang up. He said he had heard of a Moulay Miloud, and would help me to find him. He wanted to meet me immediately at the hotel. I felt too hot to refuse. He asked how he would recognize me. I told him without getting into details that it wouldn't be hard.

Minutes later, Ali pulled up to the hotel in a decrepit four-wheel drive Lada. He was a middle-aged man with a brisk manner. He loaded me into the car, clattered through the dark streets of Adrar, and within a few stops found Moulay Miloud's apartment, in a sprawl of ground-level duplexes. A neighbor told us that he had gone into the desert, to an outlying village, to visit a brother who had returned from Mecca. He would be back in the morning. Ali insisted that I leave a message on the door. He was the rare Saharan who left nothing to chance.

Ali invited me home, to the oldest part of town, for late-night coffee. We sat on rugs under a bare bulb in a high-ceilinged room. The room's walls were painted in two tones, in green and white. Ali's young son brought in an electric fan, but the air that it stirred was stale and hot, and sweat streamed down our faces. We drank the coffee strong and sweet, and sat mostly in silence. It occurred to me only toward the end that Ali expected nothing from me.

At dawn a haze of dust and heat veiled the central square.

Moulay Miloud sent word that he would meet me there at noon. He turned out to be a thin, fastidious bachelor, in a pressed white robe and sandals. We went to his apartment to talk. He did not have an air conditioner, but had a fan and an evaporative cooler that lowered the temperature in his apartment to, say, 100 degrees Fahrenheit. We sat on the floor of his living room, and waited out the midday hours, drinking brown water from a plastic jug.

The water was brown because Miloud had mixed in cade oil, which smelled of pine sap and tasted of clay. The cade is an evergreen bush that grows far to the north in the Atlas Mountains. Saharan nomads value its oil, which they use to seal the insides of their goatskin waterbags. Miloud did not have a goatskin, but he came from a long line of desert travelers, and cade oil was his heritage. He bought the oil at the market in small bottles and added it to his water for flavor and good health. He was pleased that I liked it. But I would have drunk anything, because in the morning I had gone for a walk.

During the walk the air was still, the sky nearly white. There was no shade. The streets were deserted. The heat had sharp edges that cut at my skin, eyes, and lungs. An hour was all I could endure. I felt threatened, weakened, overwhelmed. I retreated to the hotel lobby and sat very still, questioning my judgment for having come to Adrar.

Now Miloud said, "It's raining less. And every year it's hotter. Nomads can no longer survive in this climate."

I believed him.

The living room, like Miloud, was immaculate and small. It was furnished Saharan style, with mattresses, pillows, and colorful rugs. Black-and-white enlargements of nomads hung on the stucco walls, and a guitar stood in one corner. *The Cosby Show* played soundlessly on television. Miloud put on a

cassette of screechy Saharan music. In the hallway by a portrait of Bob Marley was a postcard of three naked women.
They were grotesquely fat. I did not understand why Miloud
had put them there, if this was humor or hatred or both.

Maybe it was cabin fever. Miloud said, "In the summer
even the mind shuts down. You get tired of television, music,
and books. There is no stimulation. There is little to say. You
are too much indoors."

Late one afternoon, with the air temperature settling below
128 degrees, Miloud and I drove a borrowed Renault to an
outlying oasis, south along the ancient caravan route that
leads eventually to distant Gao and Timbuktu. The road left
Adrar across a rolling plain of sand and dirt, past neglected
palm groves. The western horizon was lined by the dunes of
the Erg Chech, an uninhabited sand sea extending 600 miles
into Mali and Mauritania.

Miloud was thinking closer to home. He said, "In the winter all this is green."

Translation: In the winter a bit of moisture may sneak in
from the Mediterranean, and if some of it falls from the sky, a
few translucent grasses may sprout. But the average annual
rainfall in Adrar is less than an inch.

Still, there is water underground. Adrar's two dozen oases
sit at the receiving end of the largest dry watercourse in the
Sahara, an ancient riverbed called the Messaoud. It is a long,
shallow depression where water still collects close to the surface. The water lies on gradients, sloping with the land. To tap
into it, the people of Adrar centuries ago borrowed a tech-
nique from ancient Persia: they built their palm groves and
villages at the low points, then dug their wells uphill.

Known locally as *foggaras*, these upward-sloping tunnels
are self-filling aqueducts, designed not only to find water but

to deliver it in a constant and effortless flow. They extend for miles into the higher terrain, and are marked by regularly spaced excavation mounds like the diggings of giant moles. Although they are marvels of ingenuity, most are slipping into disrepair. One reason is the danger and difficulty of maintaining them: they clog up and cave in, and require constant shoring, and ever since the abolition of slavery—in the nineteenth century, under the French—there has been no ready supply of volunteers to do the work.

Our destination appeared as a green line against the dusty sky. The line became a palm grove and a medieval fortified village of about a thousand people. In searing heat, we walked through the streets—a warren of baked mud, and dark, built-over passages just wide enough for a loaded camel to pass. The inhabitants were Haratin blacks, the descendants of the slaves who had once maintained the *foggaras*. A band of dusty children followed us out into the desert to examine a decaying tunnel. They were surprised by my interest in it, as if the collective memories of digging were still too fresh to allow any Haratin to appreciate the engineering.

The Haratins had their own slaves now, electric pumps housed in cheap concrete shacks, requiring little companionship. The electric pumps drew water stupidly, vertically, from drilled wells. The modern world had arrived, and no one but a visitor could complain.

Still, the system of distribution was the traditional one. We followed the ditches that carried the water back through the village. Upstream the water was drawn for drinking; downstream it was used for washing and sewage. There was no treatment plant, and no need for one. The water that finally flowed into the palm grove was rich in nutrients. It was also precious. Water rights in the oases are inherited, bought, and sold, and are more valuable than the land itself. Within this grove, the water was divided and metered through finger-width gateways into an intricate branching of channels. In the end it spread into individual plots, separated by dikes and protected against wind and sand by adobe walls. There the date palms grew.

Date palms are well adapted to the Sahara. They thrive on sun and heat, and will produce fruit in water that is ten times as salty as that which humans can tolerate. Though they require copious irrigation for the first few years, they sink deep roots into the groundwater and become self-supporting. They become, in a sense, their own *foggaras*. They also shade the irrigated vegetable crops, mostly of corn and tomatoes.

The grove was small by Algerian standards—about a half-square mile of junglelike vegetation. Miloud and I strolled through it on dirt paths between the plots. The shade was dense, as was the heat. Dead fronds draped from the trees and littered the ground. Miloud pointed to them and said that when he was young the farmers would have been ashamed. Yellow butterflies flitted about. Ants carried oversized trophies. A turbaned man hacked at the earth. A ditch gurgled with polluted water. I stopped to list the other sounds: the distant music of Arab horns, a dove cooing, a donkey braying, a cricket, birds trilling, children laughing, the *thunk* of a woodchopper, a sharper hammering, a rooster, flies buzzing, a chanted prayer.

There is a limit to the insulating qualities of adobe construction, a temperature extreme beyond which the walls go critical and begin to magnify the heat. Airborne dust makes things worse because it traps the heat radiated by the soil, and does not allow it to escape on summer nights. I have studied this: the walls do not cool down at night; at dawn the inside surfaces are hot to the touch; the next day they are hotter still.

The houses become solar ovens. Concrete is worse—it gets hotter than adobe in sunlight, and no less hot after dark. In the big concrete buildings built with the help of the Soviets you can burn bare feet on upper floors.

During the peak months of summer, people move outdoors. In the morning and late afternoon they sit in the shade cast by the walls. At midday they hide as best they can, under an awning or a tree. Strangers flock to the hotels, where the lobbies have fans and high ceilings. Secret police flock there, too, for the same reasons, and to investigate the strangers. Everyone waits. At night, while hotel guests lie trapped in their rooms, the Saharans eat and sleep in the gardens.

Miloud and I went to dinner in Adrar at the house of Nouari, a bookish construction engineer. He had also invited a tall, shy hydrologist who the next day was to guide me through an irrigated "experimental farm" north of town. The four of us sat on carpets in the sand behind the house. It was a sweltering night, with the temperature still over 100 degrees. The stars were blackened by dust. The meal was lit by kerosene lanterns on a barrel. Nouari's wife and mother cooked for us, but did not appear. I made no mention of them. Nouari poured water from a pitcher, and we washed our hands.

We started the meal with warm milk and dates. Nouari said, "The Prophet recommended dates."

Miloud added, "Milk and dates make a complete meal. They are all a person needs to eat."

Nonetheless we also had tripe, couscous, and melon. Afterward we drank tea brewed by Nouari on a butane burner. The discussion returned to dates.

Saharans eat dates directly off the branch; they dry them and eat them; they bake, boil, and fry them and eat them. They are date gourmets and can distinguish hundreds of varieties by taste, texture, and color. They know date facts: that a thousand dates grow in a single cluster, that half the weight of a dried date is sugar, and that dates are rich in minerals and vitamins. Nouari listed them, taking care that I note every one: "Vitamins A, B, C, D, E."

He described the yearly pollination performed by the farmers. He recited the line from the Koran that is read while this is done. "In the name of God, mild and merciful."

The hydrologist added, "Dates help against cancer. Research is being done in the United States at a big university."

Miloud observed that the tree itself is a wonderful resource. With help from the others, he went through its uses. They are too many to list here, but they can be summarized as follows: things that can be made from palm wood and fronds.

The hydrologist finished by saying, "The Prophet loved the tree too." It is not surprising that the neglect of the groves in the Sahara has added to sympathy for the Islamic revolution.

The hydrologist's name was Sollah. In the morning he took me to see the irrigated farm, which he called a model. It sprawled across 800 unshaded acres in virgin desert—an American-style operation, privately owned, with a bright green tractor and a crew of Haratin workers. Circular irrigation systems stood over wheat stubble. There were greenhouses, and plots of tomatoes, peppers, pimentos, cucumbers, melons, and cantaloupes. There was plenty of mud. This was modern agriculture—energetic, productive, and perhaps wasteful. I told Sollah that it reminded me of the farming in California. He looked pleased, and asked why. I answered, "Cheap water." This pleased him even more, because it was *his* water. He had directed the government crew that had drilled the first well.

We went to drink the results. Two pumps drove a heavy flow into a holding tank. The water was sweet and cool. Sollah and his crew had struck it with an Oklahoman rig at a depth of 450 feet. The well had run brown with sand and mud for two days, and afterward had turned clear. The project had taken a month to complete, which was average. There were several crews like Sollah's in that part of the Sahara. Between them they were drilling forty-five wells a year. Every well had produced.

Most of the Sahara is too dry for drilling. If you do hit water, either there is too little, or it is too salty, or too expensive to pump out. Although it might sustain a few settlers, or people passing by, it is not worth the cost of getting to. But here in the northern third of the desert, large reserves of fresh water lie under the parched surface.

The shallowest reserves are the ones that for centuries have irrigated the oases. They are immediately susceptible to drought and overuse: the water table falls, crops fail, and the oases must be abandoned. But if rain falls, even far away, eventually the shallow reserves are replenished.

Of greater importance for the near future are the deep reserves, whose discovery was a by-product of the search for oil. The mere knowledge of their existence has had a profound effect on life in the Sahara. Known as confined aquifers, they are pools of fresh water trapped in permeable rock strata at depths of 300 to 6,000 feet. They hold as much water, according to one estimate, as the Amazon River discharges in two years. That is a lot of water. What's better, much of it is under pressure. Once tapped, it rises to the surface and forms artesian wells. Geysers have shot hundreds of feet into the air. Wells have been capped to keep villages from flooding.

The new water works powerfully on the souls of Saharans. Muammar Qaddafi launched an agricultural revolution in

Libya, and began building gigantic irrigation projects. He spoke of transforming the sands. If for no other reason, he was respected for this. Other Saharans have equally grandiose dreams: miles of tomatoes, famous potatoes, rice paddies, fish farms, horizons of grain—the United States of Moulay. If there is water in the desert, anything is possible. Sollah, by nature a quiet and rational man, was suffused with the glory of his mission. He spoke then not as a hydrologist, but as a Saharan. Even the taxi driver who took us out to the farm had an opinion. He believed that irrigation would eventually bring rain. Call it reverse desertification, the trickle-up theory.

But there is a problem. If you measure a desert by the amount of heat at the surface versus the amount that would be necessary to evaporate the annual rainfall, the excess evaporative power of the Sahara ranges from a factor of ten to infinity. Of course these so-called dryness ratios are high partly because there is so little rain—in places no rain at all. You might reasonably expect some level of man-made rainfall to fill the need. But even in the wettest parts of the Sahara the air is so dry that regardless of the heat, evaporation rates are the highest in the world—twice those of the Californian and Australian deserts. The average relative humidity is 30 percent, and it has been recorded as low as 2.5 percent. In the Sahara it is not only the ground but also the sky that is thirsty.

In any case, the deep aquifers are being recharged very slowly, if at all. They contain mostly fossil water, deposited long ago when the Sahara was not a desert. The water that Sollah and I were drinking was perhaps 5,000 years old. In western Egypt, well water may be five or ten times older. My comparison to California was only partly accurate, because so much of the irrigation water in the American desert comes from rivers and reservoirs—short-term, renewable surface supplies. Some waste is therefore affordable: you suffer drought, you change your laws, you wait, you drink again. But the deep water of the Sahara is different: you pump it here for keeps. Like oil, it is not renewable.

Another problem is that, despite the large reserves, only a fraction of the stored water can be extracted economically. There are many reasons for this, including lowering water tables, loss of artesian pressure, expense of drilling, expense of pumping, and increasing salinity. Thoughtful people caution that new wells should be drilled sparingly, and the water used wisely. They use terms like "practical sustained yield"— meaning you take out no more than is going in. They say an aquifer is like a bank account—if you must draw it down, the reason should be to build a return in the long run. They warn about unchecked exploitation, and talk about the end coming as soon as 2025.

But their advice passes unheeded. Saharans are as greedy as anyone. They dream of green. It is the color of Islam. In Algeria now, the revolutionaries have vowed to make a garden of the desert, though of course they never will.

The Safari

The safari rolled into In Salah after dawn, when the chill was off the air. It was a high-clearance truck, a tough three-ton Mercedes that had been modified for passengers by the addition of a narrow door at the front of the cargo box, and a row of small windows along each side. The windows were opaque with dirt. A ladder climbed the rear to an overhead luggage rack. Up front in the cab, the driver and his assistant sat smoking in self-important isolation, as sober and concentrated as pilots headed into a storm. The condition of the truck—its crumpled fenders, cracked windshields, and wired-on hood— hinted at the rigors ahead. Oil dripped from under the engine.

Twenty-five of us boarded, a full load. The air inside was stifling. We sat shoulder-to-shoulder on metal benches and looked each other over—the typical collection of tight-lipped and dusty men. The only woman was an unveiled Malian cradling a baby who, over the grueling trip to come, uttered hardly a whimper. The mother and child were accompanied by two men in filthy robes and *chèches*. I later learned that they came from somewhere near Timbuktu, had been working for years in Libya, and were struggling home. Other passengers were laborers and traders, black Africans returning south across the Sahara to the nations of Niger, Burkina Faso, and the Ivory Coast. Only the poor traveled this way. The driver's assistant made a quick count, then locked us in from the outside.

There was no road now, only the scarred and rutted desert. The first bump threw us from our seats, and some of the passengers laughed. The next bump threw us hard against the ceiling, and the fun was over. One of the young men landed badly, taking a seat corner in the ribs; he shouted in anger and pain, but shouted in vain. The driver could not hear him, and would not have cared anyway. His driving was unflinching. Because from the back we could not see the ground ahead, we never knew when the next blow would fall. Crouching to protect ourselves from serious injury, we hung grimly to the seatbacks and endured the passage of time. Imagine being blindfolded, baked, and beaten.

Every few hours, when we stopped for a rest, the driver's assistant would unlock the door. The woman and child would remain inside. Emerging into the brilliant sunlight, the men would spread into the desert, turn their backs to the truck, and kneel modestly to urinate. Sand and rock then extended with brutal clarity to the horizons. But the real Sahara was a tangle of Africans on the inside of a long-distance truck, the stink of their unwashed bodies, the poison of diesel exhaust.

The day passed in a haze of sweat and injury. The open side windows, high above eye level, let in clouds of·dust. Once, as I floated above my seat, I spotted a Mercedes sedan laboriously picking its way south. The land climbed. In the afternoon we urinated on an upsloping desert of a mountain.

The roughness of the ride forced temporary friendship on the passengers. We first shared our hatred of the driver, then shared our bread. We stopped for the night in a gorge called Arāk, a funnel through which all Trans-Saharan traffic passed. Arāk had a roadhouse—a café and a few of the traditional straw huts known as *zeribas*. The establishment was run by a wizened Frenchman, emaciated and deeply tanned, who draped a scarf around his neck. He said he had lived in Algeria for thirty-five years, as a teacher, and later here in Arāk, and he didn't give a damn about the first Algerian revolution or the second.

He took me for an adventurer and a fool. "You'd better get yourself a *zeriba*," he said. "It'll freeze tonight. These Africans, they can sleep anywhere. I've lived here long enough so I can too." He squinted at me critically. "But you—you might not survive the night."

Resisting the impulse to prove him wrong, I rented a *zeriba*. I paid him the equivalent of three dollars, six times the normal rate. He pocketed the money, and afterward left me alone. We did not speak again.

I borrowed a greasy blanket from his help, an Algerian hustler with a permanent smirk. "Keep an eye on your suitcase," he said. "These niggers will steal everything." He wanted me to change French francs with him, or sell him my razor, or my watch, or give him batteries—he was alert to any possibility. I said I had nothing for him. He lost interest and moved away.

One of the Malians warned me against eating the couscous. It had been cooked days before, he said. The café at

Arāk was known throughout the desert to make people sick. The Malians shared their tea with me. I gave them the last of my food, two oranges, and ducked into the *zeriba*. Wrapped in the blanket, I lay in the dirt and listened to the wind rustling the walls.

The next morning, I saw the Trans-Saharan from a hillside. We had stopped for a brief rest. It was eight o'clock, rush hour on the desert highway. An empty basin stretched below, twenty miles from rim to rim, crisscrossed by tracks. Far in the distance, a cargo truck inched northward raising dust.

In the afternoon we came to a sudden halt. The engine revved. The assistant did not emerge to free us. We stood on our seats and peered outside. A tractor-trailer crossing an *oued* ahead had mired to the top of its wheels in mud. Rare autumn rains had fallen on the mountains; the *oued* looked dry, but was not. The truckers now were trying to dig out.

I thought we should stop to help them, or offer a ride, or check their water supply. But not a word was exchanged. Having surveyed the trucksters' misfortune, we chose another crossing point, and with brutal speed rocked and slithered through the mud. On solid ground again, we hesitated for just a moment before hurrying on to the south. The stranded truckers, who had put down their shovels to watch, seemed not to mind.

Postscript: William Langewiesche never gave a reason for going to the Sahara, only saying, "The Sahara is not a natural destination and never will be. A writer writes about it, a reader reads about it, to satisfy his curiosity about an unseen part of the world."

Graham Mackintosh set out to walk the 3,000-mile-long coast of Baja, California, in spite of having no experience in either hiking or exposure to deserts. To survive, he ate rattlesnakes and cactus, drank distilled seawater, and hoped for the best.

INTO A DESERT PLACE

*A 3,000 Mile Walk Around
the Coast of Baja California*

GRAHAM MACKINTOSH

I *stepped into the boat just as the* sun was peeking over the horizon. Its warmth was immediate. Before long it would be glaring down in red-hot anger. I looked at the three gallons of water Guillermo had given me and felt reassured.

The new motor burst into life and whisked us beyond the awkward point. My mind was a whirl of excitement, apprehension and uncertainty as the boat weaved between the rocks guarding the narrow stone beach on the other side. I advised caution, not wanting to be responsible for damaging the new engine. It sounded beautiful compared to its predecessor, a purring kitten in place of a growling old tom cat.

Looking and feeling a bit like a spy landing on a hostile shore, I leapt out of the boat and onto the beach. Victor handed me my equipment and one final piece of advice.

"Remember, in twenty or thirty kilometres you will find the palms and possibly water."

"I won't forget! Adiós, amigos. Good luck! I'll see you in two or three days; perhaps at the palms. Thanks for everything."

Their panga disappeared into the rising fireball, leaving me alone and insignificant beneath the cliffs. Full of adrenalin, I had to force myself to keep still long enough to swallow an orange, get in my contact lenses, cover myself in sunscreen and repack my equipment. Then there was no holding me. To the crash, bash of boots on pebbles I was underway again.

In spite of the weight of the pack and the awkwardness of the water containers, I was flying along over the narrowest of pathways between the sea and the cliffs. Ribbon-like stony beaches were interspersed with steep tumbled piles of fallen boulders and great spurs of smooth rock cutting into deep water like the bows of a ship.

There was no obvious way around one such point which loomed up sheer before me. In no mood to stop and think, I turned to my right and scrambled up a dam-like slope of loose debris. I was hoping I could climb high enough to traverse the ridge and make it down the other side.

Near the top, an outcrop of solid rock defied me to pass. The only way was an inches-wide, downward-angled ledge of crumbling granite. I stared at it for several minutes. If I fell, I'd have a ten-foot sheer drop before hitting the hundred foot face of the "dam." At its base was the sea and an assortment of skull-cracking rocks.

With my feet slowly sinking into the loose material of the slope, I tied the canteen to the pack, tightened up all the straps, then, holding the water bag in my left hand, I shuffled nervously on to the ledge.

Half-way across I stepped on a loose slab of stone. Without warning it crumbled from the ledge taking me with it. I found

myself kicking and grasping air before my boots crashed into
the rubble below. The water bag went flying as I flipped into
a rocket-like, head first, belly-dragging descent. Riding on a
sliding mass of debris I accelerated like a toboggan out of control. A large rounded rock raced towards me. My arms shot
forward to protect my head; somehow they took the blow
without fracture and I skidded off into a spin before sliding to
a halt a few feet from the sea. Cradling my head I waited for
the noise to die and the dust to settle.

I was lying awkwardly, head down and half buried.
Although I couldn't feel any pain, I knew I'd been hurt; the
question was how badly.

When I tried to get up, nothing happened. I couldn't
move. The shock sent me wriggling furiously till I'd overcome
the weight of the pack and thrown off the rocks that had come
down on top of me. I scrambled to my feet to inspect the
damage.

Predictably my hands, chin, knees and elbows had suffered most. Blood flowed freely from a dozen cuts and
scrapes. Having satisfied myself that they were all superficial,
I turned my attention to that equally important liquid—water!

The aluminium belt bottle had been bashed in on one side,
but otherwise it was still intact and full. The water canteen
had remained tied to the pack and had suffered nothing worse
than the loss of some of its felt covering. But where was the
water bag? After several anxious minutes searching I found
it wedged under a boulder half-way down the slope. Miraculously, it was still full and apparently undamaged.

I had been incredibly lucky. Water aside, I could have easily broken my back in the initial fall or fractured my skull at
the bottom of the slope. As it was, I felt perky enough not to
want to waste a good photographic opportunity. I pulled out
the camera and set it up for a self-timer shot of me washing off

the blood and writhing in agony. My posing was to no avail. The camera was dead! Suddenly the pained expression was deep and genuine.

Camera or no camera, I still had to find a way out of my predicament. Reconsidering the possibility of getting by in the sea, I strangely became optimistic and enthusiastic about what was, to any sane person, a very dubious prospect. Not wanting to start a shark-feeding frenzy, I washed off most of the blood in a rock pool before wading into the sea with the pack balanced above my head. Keeping on a thick pair of socks for protection against the submerged rocks and stones, I waded as far out as I dared but couldn't see any way of climbing up the smooth wet rock. Standing shoulder deep and slipping, I came to my senses and struggled out of the water before I dropped the pack.

My first instinct had been sounder. There was only one way I was going to get both myself and my pack out of there—and that was up the slope, along the ledge and over the ridge.

Mindful of another fall, I put on a pair of jeans instead of shorts. My legs began trembling, no doubt due to the combined effects of injury, delayed shock and fear. Feeling a bit like Sisyphus, I struggled back to the top of the steep wall of rubble. The trembling grew worse as I stood by the ledge and tied both the water bag and the canteen to the pack. Having both hands free will make a big difference, I reasoned. A pity they were shaking so much. I needed those big, strong adventurers' hands noted by Chris Bonington.

For several minutes I alternated between gazing hopefully ahead and looking despondently down. Then, knowing I had no option, I shuffled across again. My toes were digging instinctively into the soles of my boots. Twice I slipped and hung on desperately while bits of rock cracked their way down to the sea. It was real B-movie stuff.

Overcoming the panic urge to run the last few feet, I kept

whatever cool I possessed to make it safely to the ridge. But I should have guessed what was on the other side; another dam-like descent of loose rock. If anything, it was steeper!

Well, I certainly wasn't going back. So, I took the water bag in my hand again, went through my customary hesitation, then stepped from more or less solid rock on to loose scree. Straightaway I found myself sliding alarmingly fast with half the slope avalanching down with me. I made a vain effort to keep feet first. The weight of the pack threw me into an uncontrollable tumble. The water bag, once again, went its own way as I concentrated on avoiding breaking my neck. When the sliding and the racket had stopped, I'd added a few more superficial injuries to my collection and virtually ruined a good shirt and an irreplaceable pair of jeans. Otherwise my luck had held once again.

With adrenalin to burn, I picked up everything and pushed on. There were more ups and downs, thrills and spills. Having been cooped up in the fishcamp for so long all I could think of was . . . go . . . go . . . go! It was crazy. Just like those flat-out, rat-race mornings driving to work—usually late—when every red light was a disaster. Then, all I could do was rant and rave. Now the energy had somewhere to go, pent up muscles had something to do.

However, Erle Stanley Gardner had wisely said, "It is almost axiomatic in Baja, California, that haste not only makes waste, but completes destruction." He was talking about driving conditions, but it wasn't just a lesson for Baja's roads. It was one I learned just in time along that rugged stretch of coast. I forced myself to stop and think; to try difficult moves first without the equipment; to split the load and make two or three journeys if necessary.

In spite of the low tide, one point was only passable up to my chest in the sea. After trying it unburdened, I took the pack forty yards over and then waded forty yards back for the boots and water. In total, I had to make five bare-footed, chest deep journeys over the same rough rocks. After that I sat out the day's high tide in a hollow beneath the cliffs. The two miles I'd put behind me had been horrendous. I hoped the next eighty would be better.

After tending to my wounds and repairing the damaged clothing, I pulled out the camera. What a disaster! I could see no alternative but to return to the United States and somehow procure another one. It would be just my luck to get bitten by a rattler and have my leg balloon up purple, green and gangrenous, and be unable to get a photo. More as a gesture than anything else, I tried changing the batteries, and that did the trick. The camera hadn't been damaged at all!

Overjoyed, I packed everything away, laced up my boots and bounced over the rocks as pleased as a porpoise.

On the beach I came across a large shark, one of the biggest I had ever seen. It was tempting to knock out some of his wicked looking teeth for souvenirs, but he was going off a bit, so I pushed on with my usual escort of seals and dolphins. It was a great afternoon's work. I kept going as long as I could. Just before sunset, the rising tide forced me to halt and make camp on a narrow little stony beach under a high cliff. I wrote in my diary:

> Probably finished the day with ten miles under my belt. Couldn't pass deep water so camped under cliff on stone. Not very comfy but slept well. Beautiful calm evening, sea flat, almost tangible silence. Red, pink and orange sunset. Pelicans active, coasting wingtips on water, diving for fish, splashing clearly heard over remarkable distance. I slept in optimum position above rising tide and away from rockfall danger. Heard some rubble falling as I entered tent (never erected, just crawled in). Before sleeping sat with head out listening to

country music and watching stars and moon shadows above.
INJURY REPORT: Palms cut and skin removed (lemon
juice and sea water sting). Left palm, base of thumb swollen
and bruised, problem when rock climbing. Other cuts and
scrapes, no problem. Soles of feet bruised and tender from
wading and all day pounding on rocks.

Next morning, I got by with the low tide and raced as fast
as I dared. I was surprised and delighted to see a panga ahead.
Whatever the two fishermen were doing they weren't shark
fishing. They were in relatively shallow water only fifty yards
from shore.

I shouted out, excitedly stringing together a whole bunch of
fairly basic, comically ungrammatical, mispronounced Spanish. One of the fishermen could stand it no longer. He called
back in perfect English.

"Say what you want to say in English, I can speak it as well
as you."

A little embarrassed, I asked, "Where are you from?"

"Alphonsinas," he replied. "We know all about you."

"What's the coast like ahead?"

"Terrible. There's nothing ahead. You won't make it.
Come back with us."

"Thanks for the offer, but I've got to try."

"There's no water."

"Some of the fishermen from Calamajué will be bringing
me water in a couple of days."

"Don't depend on anyone out here. Anything could happen. Are you sure you won't come back with us?"

"No thanks. I must try."

"You won't make it," he repeated. "If your friends show, go
back with them."

"Perhaps I will. How far ahead are the palms?"

"About eighty kilometres!"

"I was told they were just a few kilometres from here and I might find water there."

"They're eighty kilometres—may be fifty miles—and you won't find any water."

He gave a dismissive wave as if to say, be it on your own head, then started his motor and speeded back to Alphonsinas.

I was forced to climb high over huge rounded boulders to get by one headland the size of a football stadium. Approaching the point I heard what at first appeared to be mocking laughter. I had become used to the apparent laughter of the gulls but this was different.

My suspicions were confirmed. Looking down, I saw a sea lion colony. About thirty of them lolled on top of a little rocky island while another twenty rested on their backs in the water with flippers up as if about to clap: "Well done, gringo, you've made it this far, only another 2,800 miles to go . . . ar, ar, ar."

The smug-looking sea lions floating on the surface looked totally vulnerable, but from my vantage point I could see other sea lions swimming beneath their colleagues, perhaps on watch for sharks.

I thought of an incident that the ex-Royal Navy officer Lieutenant Robert Hardy had witnessed while exploring the Gulf on behalf of The General Pearl and Coral Fishery Association of London between the years 1825–8:

> My attention was suddenly diverted . . . by a splashing in the water below. . . . It was a combat between a seal and two monstrously large sharks. . . . Never did I witness anything half so terrific . . . the long tails of the sharks were four or five feet out of the water . . . and flouncing with ferocious energy to keep the seal from rising to the surface. Presently their tails entirely disappeared, and in an instant more, the ruffled surface of the water . . . was discoloured with blood, bubbling up from below!

The scene below looked so peaceful I had no wish to witness a sea lion being bitten in two amidst a billowing cloud of crimson.

A very big bull sea lion—he looked capable of biting a shark in two—spotted me on the rocks, leapt into the sea and swam beside me, head up and barking furiously. I had the feeling I was being escorted off the premises.

The coast ahead seemed to be a succession of "impossible" looking stretches; but one by one I got by them. The sun was sinking, yet there was no sign of a suitable campsite. I pushed on, hopeful to the end, telling myself that just ahead, just around the next point, there'd be a beach, or a fishcamp, or the elusive palms.

I took off my shirt and stuffed it under the shoulder straps of the backpack for added comfort as I leapt from boulder to boulder along the water's edge. Suddenly . . . Shisssh! I froze in my tracks. A yard to my right a rattlesnake was coiled, hissing and rattling. What a racket! It was a four-foot long, perfectly camouflaged, greyish coloured diamondback. If he hadn't drawn attention to himself, I would have walked right by him. He looked and sounded like the incarnation of evil.

So much for all the photographs and sleepy zoo specimens I'd seen; this guy was real, viciously alive and determined to stay that way.

Like a cat caught between caution and curiosity I remained frozen, unsure what to do. When the snake was convinced that I wasn't going to back away, he slowly uncoiled and slid into a crevice.

Emboldened by his retreat, and realizing that all I had to eat were limes and cornflakes, I found myself reaching down for a rock. The snake spotted me and struck out so quickly, I dropped the rock and got away as fast as I could. Suddenly, marinated cornflakes sounded very appetising.

I dashed on with a fresh burst of energy. The rustle of scattering "crusties" and the crunch of boots on crisp, dry seaweed had me hearing rattlers everywhere.

Just before dark I reached a broad valley, and made camp on a cracked, sun-baked river bed. Several cacti rose from the valley floor. They were more in evidence as I travelled south.

Inside the tent I was content to rest on top of the sleeping bag and listen to the silence. The moon was big and bright. I was reflecting on the fact that I was probably days from the nearest road or person when a nearby coyote sent his chilling yelp rising into the still night air.

On a ridge above the valley a lone coyote stood dramatically silhouetted against the moon-lit sky. He looked down on me long and hard before baying the moon again in fine Hammer film style. That started off a whole chorus of his unseen comrades.

I slid the machete beneath my pillow and, to help drown out the disturbing cacophony, slipped on the earphones. I heard that Texas was being battered by storms and tornadoes. In my little corner of the Mexican desert, all was quiet and peaceful, coyotes apart.

I woke with water on the brain. I had just two pints left, barely enough to get me through the morning. Beyond that, only my stills or the boat from Calamajué could save me from death by dehydration. So breakfast was just a symbolic mouthful of cornflakes and a couple of tiny limes. The terrors of thirst were putting my hunger in perspective.

Before long my way was decisively blocked by a little steep-sided salient of rock. It probably wasn't more than thirty yards from beach to point, or much higher than a truck, but it was too smooth to climb and wading around was no easy option. Sliding off my pack, I stripped and slowly edged into the sea. There wasn't a ripple or a wave. The bottom dropped away alarmingly fast but, thanks to an underwater ledge, I managed to claw my way out to the point and pull myself up to stand lord of all I surveyed. The northern tip of the forty-mile-long Guardian Angel Island floated between the blues of the sea and the sky. The island would be my constant companion all the way to the Bay of LA (assuming I got that far). The coast immediately ahead was invitingly flat. If I could just get my pack past that awkward little spur, I'd have a comparatively easy run.

The climb down the other side wasn't easy. I had to lower myself off the rock into waist deep water and wade up to the beach. Well, it was certainly possible, if a bit risky. I swam back around formulating my plan. My main fear was dropping the pack.

The tide was rising. I had to act fast. I slipped the camera, tape-recorder and such-like inside a slightly torn black plastic bag, and buried it deep inside the rucksack.

Balancing the pack on my head, I sidled out to the point without too much trouble. The problem was to lift it high enough to wedge it on the rocks. My arms were aching and there wasn't much of a foothold. I gritted my teeth and gambled. Like a snatching weight-lifter, I pushed up hard with both hands. As I did so, my feet slipped and the weight of the pack bowled me over backwards. The water crashing over my head cut short my curses.

I was underwater, hanging on desperately to the pack. I daren't open my eyes for fear of losing my contact lenses. All I could do was push up from the bottom to take a breath and my bearings, and then half-swim and half-claw my way back to the shallows.

As soon as I reached a sunny spot I pulled everything out as fast as I could. It was nearly all wet—the diary, first-aid kit, passport, cornflakes, tent and sleeping bag. My main worry was the camera and tape-recorder, but luckily the water hadn't penetrated.

Thirty minutes later, with almost everything dry, I heard a motor, looked up and saw a panga cruising down the coast. Guessing it was from Calamajué, I picked up my mirror and flashed it towards them. Sure enough, it was Victor, Victor Manuel and Loco Diez, three of the most beautiful, weather-beaten faces in the world. They had brought the food and water, and, thoughtful to the end, a breakfast of three hard-boiled eggs.

While they surveyed all the equipment spread out in the sun, we laughed and joked and discussed my adventures. I showed them the solar still and the radio distress beacon, and explained their use. These men who live and die on the sea immediately appreciated such items.

I asked them to ferry my equipment round the rocky point and drop it on the beach. They agreed, but insisted on taking me as well. At first I declined, explaining that I had to walk; then I thought, what the heck, I've already climbed and swum around; so I threw my stuff into the *Crazy Pirate* and in a moment was on the other side.

They still insisted that the palms were just ahead. Thanking my friends and congratulating them on their timing, I waved goodbye and sadly watched them tear out into the Gulf. I wondered if I'd ever see them again.

Carrying my possessions to a suitably shady spot, I burst into song, "Thank you for giving me this morning. Thank you for giving me this day. Thank you for every new day dawning. I'll be thanking you."

My needs were simple. I had food, water, shade and stacks of driftwood. The way ahead was clear. I had much to be thankful for.

After making a fire and a cup of tea, I opened up the food box and made a valiant effort to put back some of the weight

I'd lost—you can't beat carrying a heavy pack all day under a blazing sun for losing weight.

What a difference shade makes! I took a renewed interest in everything around me: the little fly that landed on my hand and obstinately refused to depart; the hummingbird that momentarily startled and delighted; the ever-present circling, soaring sea birds; the contented crows and vultures clinging to their shady nooks; and the far-off whale sending up its plumes of spray.

It was about 4:00 P.M. before I felt capable of moving again. The pack seemed ridiculously heavy. All my water containers were full and I still had a couple of pints that I couldn't drink. Reluctantly, I left it behind, buried in a heap of rocks beside the blackened remains of my fire. I fixed the location in my mind, just in case. . . .

The coast ahead loomed jagged, tumbling and defiant. It was going to make me pay dearly for every mile. In one hand I had the water bag. In the other, the canteen and a plastic bag full of food. I daren't fall with both hands full. Time after time I had to split the load, carrying one part over some awkward obstruction, then returning maybe fifty or a hundred yards for the rest. I felt I was walking Baja twice!

Guardian Angel Island appeared stark red and mountainous as I drew level with its northernmost point. The sea between was doldrum flat. Every splash and ripple could be seen and heard for miles. A shark fin rose and sliced ominously through the oily blue water. A large moray eel writhed and frolicked noisily in the rocky shallows. Like a stuttering machine-gun, a huge shoal of fish shot from the sea and curved back in again. The distant throb of a ship's engine carried from the middle of the channel.

The cliffs gave way to a stretch of flat coast where a vast wash came down from the mountains. Several cacti rose from its barren course, but no palm trees. A few miles in from the beach, the mountains leapt up beautiful in layers of salmon pink and cream, and hues of pastel green. I wondered if this was the mouth of La Asamblea canyon that Erle Stanley Gardner had explored and written about.

> Behind . . . [the rugged beach] . . . was a stretch of some five miles of deep sand running up a barren wash where some of the most colourful mountains I have ever seen were spread haphazardly on each side of the wash. Striated in a variety of colours—red, pink, green and various pastel shades—they were for the most part completely devoid of vegetation.

I recalled that he wrote about a spring of water in La Asamblea about twelve miles up from the ocean, of people who had reached it, and of others who lost their lives trying. He also described how two prospectors had landed on the beach and slogged up the sandy wash to the mouth of the canyons. One man agreed to take the food and water and to prospect. His companion returned to the boat to collect further supplies:

> On returning to the place selected as a rendezvous, the man who was laden with provisions and all the water he could carry found no trace of his companion. He waited patiently with time rapidly running out, then started exploring trying to find the tracks of his companion. Eventually he found his partner. He had been bitten by a rattlesnake and had died a horrible death. The story was pathetically told by the man's rolled-up trouser leg, the tourniquet he had contrived above the bite, and the knife slashes he had made in his leg . . . round the man's shoulder was a sack containing ore. Stories vary as to the richness of the ore. Some people say simply that it was very rich; others say that it was almost pure gold.

Just before sunset, I found my passage along the shore frustrated by a rounded pink headland which fell undercut into the sea. Walking on top was extremely dangerous. The smooth rock cracked and crumbled as if bursting from its skin. After sliding alarmingly close to one sheer drop, I back-tracked to find a place to sleep on the beach below.

It was almost dark. I hated to make camp without knowing there was an obvious way ahead. My mood became as black as the once colourful mountains silhouetted against the linger-ing redness of the sunset. However, the peace and stillness slowly revived my spirits. Conditions were perfect for the run into Bahía de los Angeles. The full moon was approaching with the promise of extreme low tides. Perhaps the morning's low would enable me to bypass the point. Perhaps . . .

The spectacular sunrise tempted me to use one of my pre-cious remaining photographs, but unfortunately the tide hadn't fallen sufficiently. The water was still much too deep beneath the smooth rocks. I climbed back on to the treacher-ously crumbling headland and reconfirmed my earlier assess-ment that it was too dangerous.

I walked back along the coast till I found a climbable gul-ley. With snakes uppermost in my mind, I ventured up to explore the possibilities. The contrast between the coal-black boulders and the bright pink soil between them, coupled with the complete absence of vegetation, produced a lunar or mar-tian effect. Bouncing little green men wouldn't have looked too out of place. On top I was greeted by a series of barren, apparently walkable hills and ridges. The time had come to cut inland. I hurried back down for my equipment.

I kept off the ridges, while the deep valleys offered early morning shade which I would never have found on the coast. Glimpses of the sparkling sea reassured me from time to time that I hadn't wandered too far from its relative security.

I found a trail. It was only a few inches wide but well worn. I followed it with increasing admiration. Taking the line of least resistance, it marked the perfect pathway paralleling the coast, guiding me safely around rocky outcrops, across dangerous little gorges and through seemingly impenetrable brush. Every time I thought I knew better I got into trouble. Clearly it was the work of some cartographic genius who knew exactly where he was going and how to get there. But who could have made it and still be keeping it open? I bent down to examine the evidence. In several places it bore the unmistakable impression of paw prints. Coyotes! It could only be a coyote trail. Without quite realizing it, I had made one of the most important discoveries of the trip. The coyote expressway led me safely back to a relatively easy section of the coast.

Unfortunately, "easy" meant little shade. And without shade there was no point in stopping; it always seemed twice as hot when I stood still. Like a figure in a nightmare, I dashed from one shadowy refuge to another. To anyone who couldn't imagine the difference between exposure to the blistering sun and the relief of a shady crevice, my antics must have looked ridiculous.

The water bag was almost empty. The bulk of its three gallons had been sweated through a myriad overworked pores. Tension rose in direct proportion to the lightening of the bag. I imagined the cool rustling shade of the palms and the prospect of unlimited supplies of water.

Ahead, rising from the heat haze, I could see what appeared to be the remains of a wood on some well-shelled sector of a First World War battlefield. What were they? Certainly not cacti. Can't be telegraph poles.

Bewilderment gave way to disappointment. I was staring at the leafless trunks of palm trees. Scattered around was the junk from a once thriving fishcamp—the usual assortment of shark heads, turtle shells, rusting cans, empty bottles and bits and pieces of metal and rope. So this was "the palms." It was such a far cry from the shady oasis of my imagination that I had to laugh.

The bare trunks offered no shade at all. Drawing short anxious breaths in the hot dry air, I searched around for a well or a source of water but found nothing. A broad, vegetation-choked valley stretched back into the mountains. That and the presence of the palm trees made it probable that there was water underground. But how far? I could easily sweat my way through the water I had left digging down two feet . . . four feet . . . who knows? Perhaps I'd find nothing.

Better to push on and find some shade. The air temperature must have been between 90°F and 100°F in the shade. Out in the mid-day sun it was hot enough to fry an egg.

Picking myself up and dusting off my disappointment, I thought back to the Desert of the Chinamen and those unfortunate Chinese labourers who wandered from one empty water hole to another. Beside each one, another group would despair and die. Again I sensed the truth behind Alain Bombard's dictum that "despair was the greatest killer of all."

As I raced ahead to find a place to rest, I felt that the entire journey so far had just been a preparation for what was to come. If ever I needed faith in my survival skills, my stills and myself, it was then as I turned my back on the palms that had promised so much.

Survival

I managed to find a sliver of shade in a coffin-sized hollow beneath a large rock. Lying down as comfortably as possible, I pulled out my maps and estimated my position. I was probably midway between the settlements in Gonzaga Bay and Los Angeles Bay, right in the heart of no-man's-land. Looking on the bright side, that meant I was no longer dashing ever further into the wilds. I could now see myself heading back towards safety.

The drawback, and the exhilaration, lay in not knowing what was ahead or whether I could make it. My maps only gave the general contour of the land and told me where the main roads and settlements were. Between Punta Final and Los Angeles Bay both maps echoed the opinions of Ed Wills and so many others—there was "nothing."

To reach safety, I would have to get as much mileage as possible from my half a gallon of water. I decided to ignore my thirst for as long as I dared. My rapidly darkening urine revealed that my kidneys had got the message—from now on every drop counted.

And every drop of sunscreen was going to have to count as well. I had just two tubes left. To save on sunscreen for my legs, I exchanged my shorts for a pair of jeans. According to the desert survival experts this would also help combat dehydration: "On hot deserts it is a big temptation to take off a shirt and wear only shorts . . . this will do nothing but make you dehydrate faster. Clothing helps ration your sweat by not letting it evaporate so fast that you get only part of its cooling effect." But I certainly didn't feel any cooling effect as I shouldered my pack and went in search of a more substantial piece of shade.

The backpack wasn't going to last much longer either. It had been badly mauled by the scraping rocks and tearing vegetation. The sun, the salt, the cactus, the granite and the baking sand had also made surprisingly short work of my boots. Both of the Vibram soles were coming adrift. Thinking of all the climbing and rock work ahead, the seriousness of that sank in ever deeper with each step I took along the pebbly beach. I was just hoping that I could make everything last long enough to get me to Bahía de los Angeles.

To save on drinking water, as much of my food as possible would have to come from the juicy flesh of likely looking plants and cacti.

My first victim was a five-foot tall, base-branching cactus that rose up like a confused candelabra. Each of the almost square bright green "candles" was as thick as a man's arm and crowned with a tuft of spiny hair. A line of sharp spiny clusters ran down each corner. In between the spines the naked walls sagged inwards as if enclosing a vacuum. Obviously it hadn't rained for a while. After a downpour the cactus would gorge itself and swell dramatically. It might have to store a year's supply of water in a few hours.

I cut hopefully into the avocado green flesh. It looked discouragingly firm and dry, and had the taste and texture of a hard, sharp, unripe peach. So much for the sumptuous juiciness I had imagined. I didn't eat much, just a nibble and a swallow.

The poorly protected plant showed little sign of bird or animal damage, only a few reddish-brown scars. Perhaps its defence was its very unpalatability? Perhaps it was poisonous?

Some time later, having suffered no ill-effects, I wandered up to a *cardón* cactus taller than myself but a mere baby of its species. Some *cardóns* grow to more than fifty feet.

I could just have linked my hands around the tree-like trunk. Not that I wanted to; rows of sharp spines ran along each of its many pleated edges. The *cardón* also was designed for considerable expansion when there was water to be had.

I cut off a piece of a spine-covered pleat. Again the supposedly water-bearing flesh was a disappointment. There was nothing thirst quenching about the *cardón*; its flesh was firm and gritty and left an unpleasant aftertaste. I had to drink more water than I could spare just to wash the taste from my mouth.

On a rocky slope I spied a small barrel cactus. It was reputed to be the best source of cactus food and water. Predictably, it was also the best protected, being covered with a densely woven network of curved orange-red spines so tough that only the most determined machete blows could break through. But having sliced off the top like an egg, it was easy to remove the spines and the dark green skin by chopping down and leaving a heart of white cactus tissue. Although bland and a bit like a rubbery apple, its taste wasn't objectionable. Nevertheless, I sampled it cautiously, chewing it to extract the liquid and spitting out the rest. Unfortunately, barrel cacti were few and far between along that stretch of coast, and more likely to be found on the higher slopes further inland where they might grow as tall as a man. In that baking heat, where one soon learns to curtail any unnecessary movement, I knew I didn't have the energy or motivation to do all the chopping and chewing, never mind the searching. Better to push on and find a shady spot to set up the solar still.

As cactus nibbling became a part of my routine, my conscience became filled with the imagined disapproving comments of nature-lovers and environmentalists: "growing there for decades, centuries . . . part of a unique and fragile ecosystem . . . endangered species."

At first I felt guilty, but my guilt gradually gave way to resentment: "I'm the most endangered species around here," I protested angrily. There in my "desert cathedral" I didn't need anyone to tell me what was right and wrong. The land was sacred to me. I was a part of it. I wasn't one of a million careless tourists with their trucks, bikes and polluting toys. I was one in a million. The desert was special and my needs were special. There was no conflict. Besides, even if I'd deliberately set about to destroy everything in sight, I couldn't have made much impact on those vast, rugged, rolling vistas of cactus, mountain and desert.

The sense of being special to a special place was very much part of the exhilaration and the experience. The desert seemed to be saying to me, "Take what you need. All my grandeur is as nothing except that it be available for you." Yet, to put it into words was to distort it. The feeling was the reality and the mystery. It saddened me to think that I might never be able to share it with another person. "In what concerns you much," wrote Thoreau, "know that you are alone in the world."

In my loneliness I could almost hear a voice whispering in the sea breeze, "This is your land, your home, your destiny." Why me? Why here of all places? Why am I doing this? Why? Why? Why?

I was convinced I was going off my rocker. Too much time alone. Too much time in the sun. . . . The sun! I needed shade quickly.

The worst of the mountains had retreated a mile or two inland, leaving a long, low, curving, shadowless bay. Before attempting to walk around, I thought it wise to take refuge in a sea-gouged shady hollow. There was room for both myself and the pack, but I tried not to move around too much as the abrasive rock had the texture of coarse sand-paper.

Feeling that every second was precious, I dug out the solar still, removed it from its plastic bag, re-read the instructions and, after sorting out the various tubes and cords, huffed and puffed till I'd blown it up. I almost fainted from the effort needed to inflate the main cone. After pouring in the recommended gallon of seawater, I placed the still on a rock and angled it towards the sun. As the still needed the greatest possible exposure to the sun, and I needed the least, I prepared myself for a long stay.

Ten miles across the barely ruffled sea the outline of Guardian Angel Island seemed to rise up and float in the air. A small island off the northern tip slowly became two islands, then three, then disappeared altogether. Steinbeck had recorded the same phenomenon in his *Log From the Sea of Cortez*:

> As we moved up the Gulf, the mirage we had heard about began to distort the land. As you pass a headland it suddenly splits off and becomes an island and then the water seems to stretch inward and pinch it to a mushroom shaped cliff and finally to liberate it from the earth entirely so that it hangs in the air over the water. Even a short distance off-shore one cannot tell what the land really looks like. The very air here is miraculous and outlines of reality change with the moment. The sky sucks up the land and disgorges it. A kind of dream hangs over the whole region, a brooding kind of hallucination.

As neither brooding nor hallucinating would be the best way to pass the next four or five hours, I rummaged through my pack looking for something to do.

The torch! The batteries had become rather dim, and I had carried a spare pair since Puertecitos. Anticipating the saving in weight, I rolled out into the sun and threw the spent batteries as far out to sea as I could. It was as if I wanted to check my beleaguered sense of distance and reality. Half-expecting them to sail right over the island or pass through its ethereal solidity, I was almost relieved to see them plop into the water only fifty yards away.

I dropped the new batteries into the torch, screwed on the base and switched it on. Nothing! I opened it again to check they were in right. Still nothing. The new batteries were dead. There was a sinking feeling in my stomach as I thought of the consequences of not having a torch. Above all, I would need to make sure I took my contact lenses out before it got dark.

After directing a half-hearted tirade against all things Mexican, and vowing always to check my batteries in future, I began to see the funny side of it. It was just as well. The sea was rising fast. As it swirled and foamed along the sand, it became all too clear I was going to be forced out of my shady hollow.

With nowhere else to go, I took my pack to higher ground and then walked fully clothed into the warm water and made myself comfortable between two seaweed-covered boulders. As seaweed was supposed to be "a godsend for the survivor," I began nibbling on all the various types floating around. I laughed as I pictured myself munching mouthfuls of the stuff. Absurdity aside, I was keeping cool and getting some nourishment while the beads of condensation were running down the inner wall of the still.

I thought about rigging up the kettle to boil seawater and condense the steam—there was plenty of driftwood—but I suspected that the plastic tubing would perish rapidly in use, possibly limiting me to just a few hours' production. I preferred to save it as a last resort.

It also seemed too much trouble to set up the hole-in-the-ground solar still. Digging a four-foot-deep hole in the blazing heat would be tantamount to digging my own grave. The yield wouldn't justify the effort unless I was going to stay put and do the digging at night. When the chips were really down, that would be the time to make a permanent "survival camp" and get all my stills going full steam.

Not wanting to miss out on the rising tide, I put rod and reel together and enjoyed a spell of "laid back" fishing. I managed to land a big fat bass. Getting my hands on him threw me into a dilemma. My hunger told me to enjoy my fish dinner. My thirst advised me not to. Convincing myself that I was going to need one last good meal for the trials ahead, my hunger won.

I soon had the victim cleaned, skewered and baking over a fire; but the fish wasn't the only thing cooking. Caught between the sun and the flames I was roasting myself too.

By the time I sat down to eat, my clothes were as dry as my mouth. I only managed to chew my way through so much fish with the aid of several long drinks of water. I had a feeling I was going to pay dearly for my protein treat.

Late in the afternoon, with the tide having fallen several feet, I left the sea for the last time to pack away my things.

Crouching down to inspect the yield from the still, I heard a rip! My jeans, the victim of continual immersion in salt water, had split up one leg from ankle to waist. But it hardly seemed to matter. If anything, the flapping leg brought back a feeling of comfort and coolness and was perhaps the perfect compromise between cover and freedom.

I paid more attention to the fact that Baja's relentless sunshine had, thanks to the still, given me over a pint of drinking water in just over four hours. It was warm, tasted disgustingly of plastic, and left a burning sensation in my throat; but it would be nothing compared to the sensation of having no water at all.

In the twenty-five minutes it took me to pack, I was totally dry. My watery "siesta" was over. After smearing sunscreen on my grateful flesh, I resumed my cactus-nibbling progress, and for two days consumed my physical, mental and material resources.

I could delay setting up a "survival camp" no longer. Looking for a sandy, sheltered, shady spot, I peered around yet another rocky headland, and my eyes popped in disbelief. Pangas! Three boats at anchor in a little sandy bay. Fishermen! My mind had to readjust. Becoming self-conscious again, I decided to take off and throw away my ripped and flapping jeans. After putting on a pair of shorts and consulting a mirror, I wandered up to the large canvas shelter the fishermen had constructed on the beach. I could tell by their blank stares and gaping mouths that passing gringos were not a common sight.

Six Mexicans sat on boxes and barrels outside their tent. The beds inside were covered with wet-suits and other diving gear. I bade them a cheerful "Good evening" and managed to recall sufficient Spanish to provide a more or less coherent explanation of my presence. As I laughed and joked about my own absurdity, the tension eased and the Mexicans slowly reverted to their usual response of frontier hospitality. I was invited to share their evening meal of tortillas, beans, fish and coffee.

When I inquired what they were doing there, one of the Mexicans searched out the eyes of his comrades as if seeking permission to reply. "We dive for oysters," he said in English. Speculating that they were probably diving for pearls, I deemed it wise to inquire no further. If they had a horde of priceless pearls, I didn't want to know and they, understandably enough, wouldn't want to tell me.

The blue of the sea and the sky faded and became tinted with pink. It was as if the purple-pink mountains of Guardian Angel Island were radiating warmth and colour. The shimmering mid-day mirages had gone leaving just the soft pastel solidity of the desert evening.

As the fishermen slowly began to talk about their work and the trials of their way of life, they insisted I try another hot drink. It was made from a candle-like lump of brown-sugar candy called panocha. "If ever there was an 'industry' in Lower California," Ann Zwinger has written, "the making of panocha must have been it, for every town had its own panocha factory. Sugar cane harvested in the spring was cut into pieces and rolled to express the juice, which was boiled down until it reached syrup stage, then poured into moulds to harden." The sweet drink was delicious by itself—if you have a sweet tooth—and even better with a little stick of cinnamon or a squeeze of lime juice. I tried it every way. My belly was distending like a rain-soaked cactus.

My hosts explained that they came from the old French mining town of Santa Rosalia, nearly two hundred miles to the south. They came out to fish and dive for a month or two every year. Except for brief supply runs to Bahía de los Angeles, they remained there in the wilderness out of touch with everything including their families. It must have been hard on them. Their faces all bore the same sad, resigned expression. I wondered if mine was beginning to develop the same look.

The English speaker joined the thumb and index finger of his left hand and bounced them on his lips. "Do you have any pot?" he inquired hopefully.

"Well actually," I replied, "I'm British, and we're not really into that kind of thing."

All hope disappeared from his countenance and the subject of conversation changed. I began to understand what they were trying to escape from when they started talking about the rattlesnakes they'd killed, the sharks they'd encountered and the scorpion stings they'd endured. When I commented on the precariousness of their existence and their inspiring courage, a finger pointed ominously towards a small hill. In mournful tones I was asked, "Can you see the three crosses?"

As my eyes strained to pick out the silhouettes against the

moon-bright sky, a surge of uneasy emotion rushed through me. I asked what had happened.

"A few years ago they were caught in a storm and drowned. We buried them on that hill. Now we call this place Campo Muertito—The Little Place of the Dead."

Suddenly my eyes were heavy. The coffee couldn't keep me awake any longer. I said my goodnights and wandered off down the beach to make camp almost beneath the crosses.

Shark heads in various stages of decay were liberally scattered along the shore. A trickle of maggots wriggled rapidly away from each one as if determined to escape the stench.

Maggots and smell apart, the sand was clean, soft and inviting. Inside the tent I stretched out in the moonlight, but in spite of my exhaustion something kept me from sleeping. The distance I'd pitched my tent from the fishermen was a measure of my uneasiness. Pearls, graves, maggots—there was a vague sense of threat about it all.

About 10.30 P.M.—late by my standards—I fell into a shallow sleep, waking several times in the night and glancing in the direction of my wilderness companions. The incredibly bright moon and the piercing quiet combined eerily.

Breakfast was a real treat, a hot spicy mix of sausage and eggs, fish and tortillas; I stuffed myself shamelessly. On top of that, I was given some batteries for my torch, enough food for a day or two, as much water as I could carry, and the usual warnings about the cliffs and mountains ahead.

After expressing my heartfelt thanks, I exchanged goodbyes and dragged my bloated frame past the three lonely crosses. I was moved enough to make the Sign of the Cross on myself. I didn't know who they were and I didn't know their names, but I felt a strange kinship with them as if I, too, were heading for a little cross on some lonely Baja shore. It was a later than usual start. With the sun high and my stomach full, the extra weight of all the food and water seemed almost unbearable. Only a massive dose of self-discipline kept me from stopping around the corner and returning to the relative security of my new found friends. As I resumed my battle with the rocks and boulders, I couldn't believe how much I was drinking. And no matter how much I drank, I couldn't escape the clutches of thirst. The foolishness of forcing down such a rich and spicy breakfast was becoming all too apparent.

I had walked over six miles before my conscience allowed me to call my mid-day halt. Making myself as comfortable as possible beneath some cliffs, I tried to sleep, but the ground was too rugged and stony, and a continual shower of clattering debris had me wondering if the background rumbling owed more to minor earth tremors than the pounding of the waves. A big earthquake would probably bring down the whole cliff on top of me. There always seemed to be something to worry about.

After eating lunch from the pack, I made a hot drink from a block of the panocha given to me by the fishermen. It was irresistible cut with the juice of a lime, and I had to fight the urge to have a refill. That would have been an unwarranted waste of water. Discipline! Discipline!

Ten miles across the sea, the 4,315-foot peak of Guardian Angel's tallest mountain shone majestically in the afternoon sun. If there was something mysterious and compelling about the coast of Baja, the island was even more so. I recalled its impact on Steinbeck:

> The long snake-like coast of Guardian Angel lay to the east of us; a desolate and fascinating coast. It is forty-two miles long, ten miles wide in some places, waterless and uninhabited. It is said to be crawling with rattlesnakes and iguanas, and a

persistent rumor of gold comes from it. Few people have explored it or even gone more than a few steps from the shore . . . but there is a drawing power about its very forbidding aspect—a Golden Fleece, and the inevitable dragon, in this case rattlesnakes, to guard it.

I had enough to worry about on my side of the channel. The dragon which stood between me and the Golden Fleece of Bahía de los Angeles was Punta Remedios. Nearly all the coast ahead would be rugged, but judging by the way the contours of my map huddled menacingly around Punta Remedios, it looked as though I'd have to tackle a stretch of huge cliffs and massive mountains. But at least it would surely be the last barrier separating me from achieving the "impossible"?

Underway again, the sullen, unfriendly shore tried every trick to thwart my progress. Every arm of every mountain seemed to fall barrier-like into the sea. Scrambling over one such wall of rock I slipped and crashed head-first to the boulders below. My arms shot forward to take the blow which, when it came, sent a painful jolt deep into my chest. I crumpled to the ground and lay there winded, bleeding profusely. The fall had opened several old wounds including a large gash on my wrist. I had an anxious time trying to stem the flow of blood.

Caked in blood, I warily edged towards another of the foothills of Remedios. It too seemed to have maliciously crashed down before me. I approached with a heavy heart. There seemed to be no way around. Then I noticed a black hollow just above the water line. My first thought was shade, but seeing it was quite a deep cave, my mind conjured up images of abandoned treasure and primitive artefacts. It's easy to do that in Baja where whole stretches of the country haven't heard the sound of human footsteps for generations. Then, seeing a shaft of light coming from deep inside, my mind turned to another possibility. Perhaps there was a way through to the other side.

For several minutes I stood at the entrance, asking myself, "Is there danger?" "Dare I go inside?" The answers didn't just come from analysing the information gleaned by my senses. Something seemingly irrational was creeping into my decision-making. It was a feeling, a knowing without necessarily knowing why. Call it intuition. Whatever it was, I had learned to trust it.

As I stood at the entrance of the cave there was no one impatiently pushing me to make a decision. I didn't have to explain myself. I would enter the cave because it "felt" right. It was the same when I was about to dive off a rock into the sea, I would often stand and stare till it felt right to take the plunge. Of course, I'd be looking for sharks and jellyfish, and listening for anything unusual; but it was more than that . . . a sort of sixth sense I had discovered through being on my own. The certainty of my feelings intrigued me. It had been so ever since my first dramatic reaction to Baja. My thoughts were a fumbling rationalization of something I failed to understand, perhaps a futile attempt to make sense of something a little more mysterious than we can sanely acknowledge. Unfortunately, justifying your actions in terms of feelings doesn't normally go down too well. All the time we demand answers and reasons that make sense. But supposing intuition is a valid way of thinking? Perhaps being in tune with that sixth sense helps to explain why some people are "lucky" and others go— for the best reasons—from one disaster to another. Perhaps Napoleon was right when he claimed that the most important quality for a general was luck.

And maybe prayer before any big decision isn't such a

quaint absurdity. Perhaps one of the tragedies of modern life is our failure to find the time for such things.

Grabbing the torch and leaving behind the pack and the sunshine, I stepped cautiously into the blackness. Suddenly the myriad noises of the shore were muffled or cut out altogether. The stillness was both calming and threatening. The sweeping torch beam convinced me there wasn't a colony of rabid bats overhead or a nest of vipers at my feet. The floor of the cavern was about the size of a tennis court. Its roof was ridge-like, running in a line roughly from entrance to entrance. Both entrances seemed tiny when viewed from the centre of the cave. Stepping carefully over the boulders on the floor, I slowly worked my way towards the distant shaft of sunlight.

Daylight was streaming in from a "porthole" halfway up the far wall. I was going to have to climb to reach it. All the walls of the cave appeared to be made up of a conglomerate of boulders embedded in mortar. Providing nothing came adrift it would afford a good climbing surface. I was able to pull myself up and peer out into the blinding glare; and I was elated to see that I was through to the beaches and cliffs beyond. It didn't matter that this might only be a temporary breakthrough. I was taking one step at a time and each successful step was a triumph. Climbing out, I saw I could get down easily and be on my way again. As ever, all that remained was to go back and do it all again with my pack.

I pushed on energetically. Amazed by my own stamina, I found myself almost running to meet my fate. Whether I conquered Punta Remedios or it conquered me, I had to find out and get it over with. The suspense was terrific. Remedios had become the focus of my existence. All that mattered was to get beyond it, to do the "impossible" and walk my way to safety.

Zig-zagging and stumbling along the cliff-shaded rocky

shore, I got my first glimpse of the point. It stood massive, brooding and contemptuous like an ill-tempered Goliath impatiently watching the laborious approach of his David. The most thunderous, blood-curdling roar could hardly have deepened my concern. In spite of my apprehension, I stood, stared and savoured the scene before me. "Please, there must be a way," I said, "I must get by. I must."

With diminishing assurance, I crashed along a narrow stony beach, my eyes firmly on Remedios. Then Baja itself suddenly shouted in its own peculiar language: "Ssschhh."

I skidded to a halt. My boots dug into the pebbles. My darting eyes picked out the coiled, hissing and spitting rattle-snake. My heart was pounding almost in unison with his vibrating tail. He was just two yards to my left and perfectly camouflaged among the yellowish stones; I would never have seen him except for his giving himself away with so much racket.

Recovering my poise and ignoring the "I've had enough, I want to go home, let me out" thumping inside my chest, I stepped back and picked up a large stone. Hurling the missile as hard as I could, it narrowly missed the serpent and shattered on a rock behind. I was astounded at the lightning speed with which the snake struck at the shattering impact. I reached down for more stones and threw them in rapid succession. The rattler, his heart probably pounding as fast as mine, decided to beat a hasty retreat. He had only half-way disappeared beneath a large boulder when a plum-shaped pebble caught the unfortunate creature full on the belly. Even so, it managed to drag its shattered body out of sight, leaving just its erratically buzzing tail. I thought of grabbing the tail, pulling him out and whipping his head down on a rock; but common sense, and my injunction about not taking unnecessary risks, prevailed. I decided to get away and resign myself to another mundane meal.

As I did so my conscience dug in its fangs. I felt a curious sympathy for the rattlesnake. I should have left it alone or killed it cleanly and eaten it. Having condemned the unfortunate creature to a lingering death, I felt lower than a snake's belly myself.

Still, I didn't escape entirely unscathed; having been sensitized again to every scrape and rustle, the final stretch of the journey to Remedios exacted a terrible toll on my nerves. I approached the point more by the light of the rising moon than by the fading light of day. Its massive cliffs, silhouetted against the last colours of the evening sky, looked even more awesome and hypnotic than ever.

With the sea coming right up to the base of the cliffs, there was very little room to get by. My weary legs were called upon to make even greater exertion. I should have called it a day and waited for the morrow's dawn and falling tide, but now that I was so close, I had to get up to Remedios and see if there was a way around.

It was hard to be sure in the moonlight. I walked right to the water's edge, to where a towering wall of black rock slipped with an awful finality beneath the waveless sea. The barrier of rock shot out undercut and unscalable into deep water. There was no way around. The race was over. Standing there in the semi-darkness, I felt painfully alone and drained of everything except disappointment. As if to underline my despair, a large shark cruised menacingly just off shore, its dorsal fin slicing through the moon-lit water.

I sat on a rock in the warm evening air and wondered what on earth I was doing there. Why wasn't I at home, in the pub, downing a pint with the boys, talking about football or politics? Instead, I was hemmed in by so much danger and insecurity I had no idea what I was going to do next.

If ever I needed someone, it was then. The descending peace of the night fell gently around me. There was no friend or lover to hold me, but the universe itself seemed to put a comforting arm around my shoulder. I would feel better after a good night's sleep.

Unfortunately there was nowhere really safe to put up the tent. It was the usual choice—do I prefer to be crushed by falling rocks or washed away by the tide? The cliffs were so tall, there was no escaping the rockfall danger, so I satisfied myself with a tiny patch of stony beach which seemed to be one of the few not destined to be totally submerged. A pair of flanking fallen boulders served as both protection and a reminder of what I needed protecting from.

With the occasional slab of debris clattering down, I was, for once, in no great hurry to get inside the tent. When finally I retired, I placed the bulky backpack beside my head. It made me feel just a little more secure.

Every evening, I'd been estimating my position on the map, marking it with a little X. From San Felipe the X's had run regularly down the coast, about an inch apart. There were four at Punta Bufeo, seven at Calamajué. Down the coast they went with a kind of inexorable inevitability. As I put my X at Punta Remedios, I wondered if I was destined to mark my final campsite with the kind of cross I'd seen on the hill at El Muertito, or would the X's on my map completely ring the coastline? If my vision and my faith meant anything, I had nothing to worry about. I was going to write that book about Baja, and presumably I would do so from this side of the grave.

Total Commitment

At the first hint of light, I was up and out to assess the situation. Cutting inland was no easy option: I'd have to backtrack a mile or more to find a relatively safe place to climb, and wandering into the mountains with just over a gallon of water wasn't a particularly attractive proposition.

Noticing that the tide was much lower than that of the night before, I reconsidered the possibility of getting by under the cliffs. The problem was a grey, boot-shaped headland that seemed to have crunched down across the narrow pebble beach. The "foot" was made up of a mass of huge, fallen boulders. They formed a potentially walkable platform, but they were all smooth, slippery and undercut; there was no way I could climb up.

A quick glance at my tide calendar revealed that I had arrived at Punta Remedios together with the lowest tide of the month. Feeling it might be an opportunity not to be missed, I stripped off and hurried down to the water's edge for an exploratory swim. In my enthusiasm, my foot slipped on a wet rock. Crash! Blood poured from a two-inch gash in my right shin.

Having spotted that shark the previous evening, I should have waited for the bleeding to stop but, more concerned about not missing the chance offered by the tide, I picked myself up and hobbled into the sea. Wading slowly out in the warm water, I studied each of the crannies between the boulders. Seeing no possibility of a way up, I breast-stroked around the point.

Just as I was thinking it was a long way back to the beach, a sudden, nearby splash and swirl of water had me trying to claw my way up a six-foot wall of wet slimy rock. Much to my surprise, I almost made it before calming down enough to slide slowly back into the sea. The swirl proved to be nothing more than the hasty retreat of a surprised fish.

I had to swim another fifty yards before finding a place to pull myself from the water. Leaping from rock to rock, I made a quick reconnaissance down the coast. The cliffs continued as far as I could see, but there was nothing as blatantly "impassable" as the barrier I'd just swum around. Encouraged, I made my way back along the platform of boulders, racking my brains for a fast and certain solution to the problem of how to get my equipment up there with me. Again it was the pack that was frustrating my progress.

Back at the point, I noticed that, up against the cliffs, there was a two-foot-wide gap between two of the less massive rocks. Peering down into the semi-blackness, I could just make out water rushing over pebbles a few feet below. Suddenly I had an idea. Plucking up the courage, I jumped into the sea, and squeezed my way into a grey-black world of claustrophobic tunnels. Every squashy thing I trod on conjured up images of giant eels and grasping tentacles.

One of my most important disqualifications for the task I had chosen was my over-active imagination. It definitely belonged with the list of major problems I drew up back in England—no money, unfit, no knowledge of desert survival, no Spanish, fair skin. The solution to those problems had been easily stated, but what was the solution, if any, to the problem of an over-active imagination? Tranquillizers? As I had felt from the start, I was the last person in the world who should be doing this; but if I could, anybody could.

Like a wading potholer I followed the cool, curving walls of stone towards the base of the cliff. It was a tighter and tighter squeeze until I splashed into a more sizeable "cavern" and there, six feet above, was the two-foot-wide gap through which I had looked down. The walls were too wet and smooth to enable me to climb out, but it would be enough if I could get my pack out.

I struggled back to the beach, tied my boots and water containers securely to the pack, wrapped the usual items in waterproof bags and stepped back into the watery semi-blackness.

Alternately cradling the pack in my arms, and carrying it over my head, I struggled back towards the "cavern" with its promising skylight. As expected, I was able to squeeze the pack out and roll it on to the platform of rock.

Five minutes later, after swimming my way around, I too was safely on top, getting dressed and pulling on my boots. To make ten yards progress, I'd had to swim twice around the point, claw my way twice in and out of a dark, water-filled network of tunnels, and, even then, I only got by because of an exceptionally low tide. Walking around Baja wasn't going to be quite as straightforward as I'd imagined.

The sun was up. The tide was swinging from one extreme to another, going in one mad rush from the lowest to the highest of the month. I swung the rucksack on to my back, pulled its straps tight and dashed on to see what else fate had in store.

My elation was short-lived. Apart from the fact that the sole of one of my boots was threatening to come off altogether, Punta Remedios and its problems seemed to go on and on, a never-ending round of climbing, wading, crawling and leaping. One rising wall of grey rock offered a single possibility: a cliff-hugging, knee-knocking sidestep along a ledge forty feet above the swirling sea and the rocks. Death or serious injury would follow any miscalculation, but it was a risk I had to take despite the unbalancing pack and the wayward sole. Luckily the rock was solid and not crumbling.

Feet back on the ground, and with the coast opening before me, I had, at last, good reason to be ecstatic. Ahead I could see one of the familiar sights of the Bay of Los Angeles, the dramatic volcanic outline of Smith Island. It looked so close. Ten relatively easy miles, I guessed. An afternoon's stroll with a light pack and I'd have achieved the "impossible."

I made a cheerful, relaxed mid-day camp beneath the shade of a low line of friendly cliffs. My gallon of water suddenly appeared extravagantly generous, so I proceeded to dispose of half of it washing down all the food I could find in my pack with cup after cup of that delicious bitter-sweet drink made from panocha and lime juice. As I washed myself and my clothes in the sea, all I could think about were the joys of company and the comforts of town.

"The one cardinal rule in desert travel is to rest quietly during the day and hike only during the night, early morning or evening." Guided by such sound common sense, I'd been typically taking four-hour mid-day breaks. However I was in no mood now to idle for so long. After halting barely an hour, I packed everything away, smeared myself with the last of my sunscreen and stepped out into the early afternoon heat.

At first, it didn't seem too bad. There was a pleasantly cooling sea breeze. But then the wind died, and before long it was blowing hot off the land.

A long narrow strip of stony beach separating the sea from a lagoon was an unpleasant surprise. I dashed along the thirty-yard wide pile of stones, dreading to think that up ahead the sea might be entering and leaving the lagoon through an unwadably deep channel. I didn't relish the prospect of going all the way back and along the inland edge of the lagoon, or having to sit for hours in the sun waiting for the tide to fall.

However, the level of the sea was clearly higher than that of the water in the lagoon. So they couldn't be connected; at least not through a single entrance. Rather, water was steadily seeping through the pebble causeway, much as it was seeping through the countless overworked pores of my skin.

My half gallon of water was disappearing alarmingly fast. I began to have my first doubts about contravening "the one cardinal rule in desert travel." I had even more doubts when, after two hours of hot and hard walking, Smith Island seemed as far away as ever.

After passing the usual assortment of dolphin, sea lion and pelican skeletons, I reached a deserted fishcamp. It was a relief to see a stack of rusting cans, broken bottles and sun-baked fish heads. I took a long gulp from my water flask. Civilization couldn't be far away, and the dusty track winding away from the camp would, no doubt, lead me to it.

The track ran along the flat monotonous bed of a dry lagoon, midway between a wall of stones holding back the sea and a forest of haze-distorted cacti apparently holding back the range of barren red mountains.

As I dropped down to the sun-cracked bed of the lagoon, I was convinced this was Baja's version of Death Valley. The wind picked up, blasting viciously hot down from the mountains. My tired legs buckled as the shock took my breath away and set my head in a spin. It was like walking in a tumble dryer.

With thirst tightening its grip on my throat, I was now anything but complacent. But at least I had the road. It would surely lead me to town, and conceivably someone might appear. Those recurring cans of cold beer seemed to float before me to lighten my step and encourage me to keep going, by moonlight if necessary.

But, suddenly, the road did the unexpected. It cut inland away from the coast, almost in the opposite direction to Bahía de los Angeles. According to my map it wasn't going anywhere, and I didn't dare head inland with just over a pint of water. It would have been a struggle to make that last through the night, and if the sun rose on me without water, my life expectancy could be measured in terms of hours. An agonizing, tragic end to my trip was all too plain to see.

As I headed back to the safety of the shore, more cliffs and mountains rose ominously before me. I had clearly greatly underestimated the distance to the town. All the rules of the survival game were back in force. Eating was out of the question, and every drop of water would have to count.

The sinking sun brought no relief. The west wind blew as if from a furnace. The need to drink was constant. I agonized over whether I should stop and set up the stills, or whether I should push on in the hope of finding fishermen or reaching the town.

An extensive lagoon of black mud and long, probably snake-infested, grass forced me inland. Mosquitoes added their nuisance value to the dank odours and the oppressive heat. It was the last place I'd want to stop. Trying to escape the clutches of its many muddy arms, I was forced to take a wide arc around the edge of the lagoon. As it grew dark, my desiccated imagination saw mountain lions behind every cactus and rattlesnakes under every bush.

Columns of cacti seemed to be holding up the star-spangled sky as I followed a craggy U-shaped valley down to the shore. Just as I reached the beach, the moon peeped over the horizon sending a glittering torpedo trail through the water towards me. I might have appreciated the beauty and peace of it all a little more fully if I hadn't been so keen on getting my tent up and imbibing some liquid.

I had never been so thirsty in my life. My body hurt. My lips were cracked and sore and I could hardly swallow. As I looked at the moon, it was frightening to think that if I made the wrong move, death itself could be the next thing peeping over that horizon. I wanted desperately to down the single cup of water I had left, but I knew I had to string out the sips as long as possible.

Inside the tent I continued to debate the respective merits of "running" for town or setting up the stills. Every instinct encouraged me to make one final headlong charge to safety. I croaked into my tape-recorder: "If I set up my stills, I could be stranded. I may not be able to make sufficient water to carry on in this heat. So I'd just be getting weaker and more dehydrated. There's a ridge running to the sea in front of me. The Bay of LA is probably on the other side. My best bet is to go for it tomorrow. I'll try to snatch some sleep and get away before dawn." When I played it back, I was amazed at how feeble I sounded; like I was mumbling in a drunken stupor.

Sleep was a welcome refuge from the agony and anxiety of thirst. I felt better on waking, though I was annoyed at myself for having left both ends of the tent wide open to the scorpions and rattlesnakes. The moon had marched some way across the sky. I guessed that dawn was an hour or two away. A breakfast of a couple of brittle, brown-skinned limes about the size of walnuts and a mouthful of water gave me the energy to take down the tent and pack everything away. Convincing myself that all I had to do was walk a mile or two and I'd be safe, I set off into the predawn silence.

The first part of the journey was the easiest, on the beach, around the curving bay and up a gently rising sandy arroyo to the steep rocky foothills of the ridge I had to cross. My imagination again ran riot with all the moonlit shapes and shadows. In the condition I was in, I wouldn't have stood a chance of surviving a rattlesnake bite.

Stepping over cactus and brush, with eyes and nerves strained to the full, I felt a sudden jab of pain in the back of my leg. I jumped and swivelled in instinctive horror. The pain intensified. Something was sunk deep into my calf. Looking down and seeing a snake-like shape, I shuddered and kicked wildly. A dead *ocotillo* branch flew through the air—my right boot must have kicked the wickedly spined stem into the back of my left leg.

Suitably spurred on, I dashed as fast as I dared towards the sanctuary of the hopefully nearby Bay of LA. According to my map, La Gringa (feminine of gringo) would be the first outpost of town. It was named, so the story goes, after a beautiful American widow who used to live there on the beach. Almost certainly there'd be tourists at La Gringa. Any one of them would look beautiful to me if they had water!

I made it to the top of the ridge in time to admire the first glow of dawn. The spreading light revealed the coast to be the usual assortment of beaches, boulders and jutting masses of rock, but there was no sign of a town. Back at the water's edge, I watched the sky fill with light and colour. Then a burst of liquid gold appeared along the edge of the world. As the rising fireball assumed a mushroom shape I stood staring, as I might at the first exchange at Armageddon.

Sun or no sun, I made up my mind to carry on till I was out of water. The few sips I had left were strangely reassuring. I was convinced that salvation was just around the corner. When it wasn't, that could only mean it was around the next one. I became so wrapped up in my desire to reach safety that I wondered if I was being foolishly single-minded in pressing on. A voice inside me protested: "Stop! For Christ's sake stop and set up your stills."

There was a rocky headland a mile in front. I couldn't see beyond it. "No more water till you get there," I vowed. "I mean it." With the sun beating down from the brilliant blue, I worked myself into a trance-like determination to reach the headland and "earn" my next drink of water.

When I got there, I peered around. Brutal disappointment. Another empty bay, more stony beaches, more awkward cliffs. I took the promised drink—taste would be more accurate—then closed my mouth firmly. A single breath in the hot, dry air was enough to undo the all too fleeting feeling of relief. Again I vowed, "The next sip at the next point."

My word had become the most important thing in the universe; the one power greater than the torment of my thirst. If I said I was going to reach an objective, I knew I was going to do it. The phrase, "I mean it," was a signal to my brain that my word, my judgement and everything I held dear was on the line. I was playing a game with myself, a game I had learned to resort to when extraordinary effort was called for and there was every chance of giving way to weakness. Having been lazy and laid-back most of my life, I was amazed at my ability to set an objective and totally commit myself to it. Having switched on to such a way of thinking, I knew I must not weaken. No matter what the pain or the exhaustion, I must not give in, I had to reach that point. . . .

I later confided to my diary: "If I could give one piece of advice to anyone believing the world to be dull, it would be this—if you have the ability to set goals and value your word, then you'll never be bored. When you're absolutely determined to accomplish something you've committed yourself to, life suddenly becomes exciting and exhilarating. Look at the importance some people attach to sport, and how excited they get at such things as getting a ball over a line or down a hole. But what is a sport but some agreed upon goal and a set of players totally dedicated to its achievement? Yet, if you're able to set your own goals and go for them with everything you've got, then you're no longer a spectator. You're living out your own intense drama; you're the one playing in the Cup Final or the Super Bowl. How can life ever be dull if you know where you're going and want desperately to get there?"

I wanted desperately to get to the Bay of LA, but I suspected that I had reached the stage when stopping itself would have been dangerous. I would just have collapsed and died before getting a worthwhile drink from the stills.

Not daring to down my final thimble-full of water, I cut open the last of the small, sad limes I'd carried since Calamajué.

They stung my cracked and raw lips, and there was nothing to wash away the sharp, burning taste. After eating all six in quick succession, my teeth were aching as if acid washed to the roots. Even so, I would have eaten a thousand rather than endure the awfulness of my thirst.

There was no more sunscreen for my skin; no more balm for my lips; and both soles on my boots were now flapping at the toes. The pack had never been lighter but it cut cruelly into my sunburnt shoulders. Some corner of reason left inside my throbbing head watched in disbelief as I kept going.

Under the mid-day sun, I came to another long stony beach stretching between the sea and a lagoon. It beckoned like a trap. There was no shade if I was forced to stop and try to operate the stills, and I wouldn't have had the energy to plod back again. Instinctively I hesitated—thinking was no longer an accurate description of what was going on inside my head—before deciding to crunch my way along the shingle beach.

I was beginning to feel strangely detached from my decisions and my suffering. I remembered, with almost academic interest, the comments of a U.S. serviceman who had experienced extreme dehydration: "Something changes when your last water is gone. Things just seem to happen to you, and you don't feel responsible. You aren't in your right mind. Whether you decide to walk on for one more night, or lay down to die, it isn't you who plans any longer. You are only watching from somewhere outside." Escaping into a kind of intoxication, I stumbled on, becoming increasingly oblivious to everything except my rapid nasal breathing and the pebble-bashing rhythm of my boots.

Suddenly, I was conscious of another sound. Looking up, I saw a small, open fishing boat coming straight towards me, right beside the beach. Mexicans! Water! Rescue! From somewhere I found the energy to jump up and down and wave frantically. The two young fishermen looked doubtfully at one another before steering into the shore.

"Good morning, amigos," I said, shocked at my own feeble croakings. "I'm walking to Bahía de los Angeles and I need water. Do you have any to spare?"

The elder of the two held up a full half-gallon jug. "We can spare some but we must keep a little as we're going out fishing."

"*Gracias, gracias,*" I said impatiently as they poured about two pints into my empty canteen. I drank half of it immediately–closing my eyes to savour the experience–then forced myself to stop and keep the other pint to get me to town.

"How far is it to La Gringa?" I asked.

"Two or three miles, more or less."

"No problems?" I inquired hopefully.

"No problems, amigo. An easy walk, and you will find many tourists between La Gringa and Bahía de los Angeles. Good luck."

"Many thanks," I said. "Go with God."

Unfortunately, they couldn't go anywhere. Their outboard motor refused to start. For fifteen minutes the confounded good samaritans sweated and cursed under the blistering sun. I couldn't just walk away and leave them, though they probably wished I would. At last, the knackered engine burst into life, allowing us to go our separate ways with more exchanges of "Good luck" and "Go with God." As I staggered onwards along the beach, and their sorry sounding motor whisked them out to sea, I suspected that God was in quite a dilemma about which way to go.

As the water percolated into my brain and clarified my thoughts, I wondered how I could still be two or three miles from La Gringa. I had already walked ten or fifteen miles since the day began; obviously I had badly mis-read my map. Then again, why hadn't I played it safe and set up a three-stilled survival camp? The questions were many, but there was time for the post-mortem (hopefully not a real one) later.

I was noticing the world around me again. I gazed out across a three-mile wide channel which now separated the Baja mainland from the precipitous volcanic slopes of Smith Island. Dolphins were leaping and a large whale was cruising a hundred yards from the shore. Judging by its size, it was probably a finback.

"While humpback and sperm whales are often sighted, the commonest species in the central gulf are the finbacks," W. W. Johnson has written. "Finbacks are streamlined monsters, second only to the great blue whale in size. They range up to 75 feet in length, up to 80 tons in weight. . . . They seem to prefer to stay in the gulf rather than to roam the oceans of the world as other whales do. Specialists have estimated that there are perhaps 250 of these nonmigratory whales. Some believe that, in times past, finbacks found their way into the gulf and never found their way out. Others think that the richness of the food resources of the central gulf makes it too attractive for them to leave."

I decided to take a quick, cooling swim. If anything, the water was too cool. As the tide raced up and down the gulf through the deeper channels it tended to produce great upwellings of cold water from the bottom. It was all this agitation and turnover that maximized the oxygen content of the water and supported the rich crop of plankton which, in turn, supported such a variety of marine life so close to one of the most barren deserts in the world.

To protect my lips, I wandered into the desert and sliced off the stem from a lomboy—a common, sprawling, spineless plant with large, luxuriously green, heart-shaped leaves. The cut stem immediately began exuding sap. I dabbed it on my lips, and as it dried, it formed a protective skin. "The astringent sap is reputed to have medicinal properties. Some Baja California travellers swear by it as a preventive (or cure) for sun-cracked lips," says the *Baja California Handbook*.

The breeze was still sweeping hot from the desert and my pint of water was disappearing alarmingly fast. It seemed a long two or three miles. By the time I reckoned I had done twice that distance, I started to feel angry. "Where the hell is La Gringa?" I asked myself. Mumbling resentfully, I added. "Why say two or three miles when you mean ten. " '*No problema*.' Like hell, *no problema*! You should try walking it!"

Still ranting away, and almost out of water again, I rounded yet another headland and forced my weary, sun-strained eyes to look up. After all the let-downs, I couldn't believe it. Motor homes, sunshades, swimmers. Just half a mile away. La Gringa!

A party of tourists from San Diego was surprised to see a heavily burdened, red-headed Englishman staggering towards them. I asked for water, drank nearly half a gallon, and needed little encouragement to follow that with four cold beers. That brought the smile back to my face and more sense back to my brain. When my appetite returned, I put away a ham sandwich and a bag of pretzels. As I told my story, I enjoyed the astonishment written on the faces of my hosts. One of them did his best to repair my boots with tape and glue. The warmth and hospitality were heartening. My strength and enthusiasm bounced right back. I was soon able to face the last few miles to Bahía de los Angeles. With more "thank yous" flying around than seagulls, I was given water and fruit, and pointed in the right direction.

I passed several other campers as I made my way around the bay. I looked a sight: boots taped together; clothes blood-stained, sweat-soaked and tattered; lips cracked; wild carrot-coloured hair; unshaven; face as red as a beetroot and beaming elation; not the kind of thing you'd want to bump into with the sun going down. No wonder most of the other Americans I met treated me with cold suspicion.

As darkness fell, I left the shore and stuck to the dirt road heading towards town. For over an hour my way was lit only by my fading torch and the occasional, often blinding, car headlight.

The moon was rising over Guardian Angel Island as I wandered into the lights and the dusty streets of Bahía de los Angeles. Finding the bakery still open, I treated myself to some sugary cakes and a delicious cold Pepsi. The proprietor found it hard to believe that I'd just walked along the coast from San Felipe, but my appearance helped convince him.

Exhausted, half-asleep, and wanting to be alone, I hurried through the town and headed towards a deserted beach a mile on the other side. The repaired boots hadn't lasted long—both soles were doubling over again—but they had made it and so had I.

Postscript: Graham Mackintosh spent five hundred days in Baja and along the way became inexplicably entranced by its harsh realities, to which he often returns.

Justin Marozzi was attracted to the old slave routes of the Sahara, and so he set out on a camel trek across the great desert to see it for himself. He had the rare privilege of experiencing the last days of camel culture in this most unforgiving of environments.

SOUTH FROM BARBARY
Along the Slave Routes of the Libyan Sahara

JUSTIN MAROZZI

Buzeima

The night was heavy with foreboding. The rain, which had been spitting down on us during the late afternoon, grew heavier. It hurled into our faces, borne by a wind that was now gusting between the dunes at full force. Deep drifts of sand streamed down from the heights into our beleaguered camp and shrouded everything in sight with a gritty blanket. Visibility fell rapidly. The air was a blur of stinging sand and rain. It was the worst storm we had encountered and Ned was out in it alone.

For half an hour Mohammed and I sat without talking, mulling over the sudden and inauspicious change that had befallen us. In the drama of the storm I wondered whether I would ever see Ned alive again and started imagining the dreadful telephone call to his family informing them of the disaster. I had not stopped him setting out on his own. Although I had attempted to persuade him to stay, I had also stood by helplessly as he left. A better mediator might have prevented his departure. Reaching Buzeima, the last oasis before Kufra, was critical. The camels were deteriorating by the day and now needed fresh supplies of food and water to keep them going. In these conditions, Ned could easily miss the oasis.

The camels reflected the bad omens of the storm. Separated from his two fellow whites, Lebead was inconsolable. He swung around to see where they had gone and roared piteously, filling our camp with a terrible chorus of lament that continued deep into the night. Commiserating with him, Asfar added his own plaintive cries. Both were restless and kept trying to get up. Mohammed and I struggled to control them, tying an extra rope around each of their front knees to prevent them escaping. Only Gobber appeared unconcerned, tucking in to the tiny hillock of barley that Mohammed had put down to calm the distraught animals. He had never been greatly loved or well treated by the whites.

"The other camels never liked him," Mohammed said quietly, looking at Gobber. "He doesn't mind them leaving at all." Wrapped against the storm in his black burnous, he looked a crumpled old man, dispirited and exhausted. I had never seen him like this. "The desert is a dangerous place," he said. "It is never good to travel alone like that. You must always have a companion with you."

At least Ned was a hardy man. If anyone could make it to Kufra alone, he could. He had taken some of the maps with him and still had his own GPS by which to navigate. As far as reaching Buzeima was concerned, if he did not get there tonight, surely he would find it tomorrow. Discovering the source of fresh water was another matter. From afar, Buzeima looked a large, sprawling oasis. The great lake, which had so entranced Rosita Forbes in 1921, contained only brackish water, which the camels would not drink. How would Ned find the solitary well?

The storm grew fiercer still, burying our bags and ruining a vegetarian pasta—the grittiest yet. We erected a barricade of bags, *bidouns*, and saddles, our only protection against the invading sand. As Richardson had advised long before, "the first thing on encamping is to look for the direction of the wind, and so to arrange bales of goods, panniers, and camel-gear, as to protect the head from the wind. In this way one often lies very snug whilst the tempest howls through The Desert."

I had a fitful night, with uneasy, dozing thoughts of Ned. Would he try to make Buzeima tonight, in these terrible conditions, or set up camp and hunt for the oasis the next morning? And what about his camels? If they had reacted like Lebead and Asfar, would he, alone, be able to control them in their blind panic? I drifted in and out of sleep, woken constantly by the roaring of the camels and the piles of sand that rushed through the barricade and swept in from all sides, pouring into my sleeping bag and streaming into my eyes, ears, nose, and mouth.

We woke early. The wind had dropped and all was quiet. There was no rain, nor any signs of damp. Overhead, the sky was cool and cloudless. Apart from our submerged bags and the sand that caked our clothes and hair and faces, the storm might never have happened. Impatient to reach Buzeima, neither of us bothered with breakfast and we pressed on towards the stirring mass of rock that hung over us like a shadow. Morale was still low. I wondered how Ned had passed the night. Where was he now and was he all right? Would we be able to find him?

We walked for an hour or so and passed into a savage arena of dark mountain ridges. Towering cliffs of Nubian sandstone, dark despite the dazzle of the sun, lay in disorder for several miles around. There was something both awful and uplifting about these shattered cathedrals of rich purple rock, streaked black with iron and manganese, which rose so starkly from the sandy, flint-strewn plain. From such close quarters it was difficult to see how far they stretched. Rosita Forbes estimated the range as a little less than ten miles in length. Moved by the terrible beauty of the place, she described it as "a veritable inferno of desolation . . . it looked as if all the old slates in the world had been flung in careless piles in this dreary region." There was not a trace of life here, but somewhere among this straggling wasteland of rock there was water and food for the camels. Dwarfed by these ragged cliffs—perhaps 500 feet at their highest—we filed along, pathetically insignificant, searching for the oasis that must be buried somewhere at their feet. Mohammed, who had never been to Buzeima, confessed he did not know where to go. I suggested we penetrate farther into the range. For a quarter of an hour we trod uncertainly over cracking slabs of flint and sank into drifts of sand. I looked around in vain for the tracks of Ned and his two camels. Nothing stirred.

"Over there, look, there it is!" said Mohammed suddenly. "That's the oasis." I followed the line of his outstretched finger. Perhaps a mile away on our right, at the most extreme edge of the mountains, was the unmistakable shadow, tinged with green, of a line of date palms. We changed our path and headed towards them, watching the oasis grow larger, opening up with each step we took until we could see a semicircle of trees and, beyond them, a disc of water, shining like a coin in the fury of the sun. As soon as the three camels saw the oasis, they roused themselves to a smarter pace and soon we were passing into its fringes.

Having heard from the tattooed policeman in Tizirbu that Buzeima was now deserted, we did not fear the sort of hostile reception Rosita Forbes's caravan had anticipated eighty years before us. The emptiness of the place, however, was disconcerting. We stopped next to a cluster of palms to pick some of these dates, which for at least a century have been considered the best in Libya. Unharvested, they lay on the ground in thick piles. Those on the trees were large and fleshy, slightly soft and pleasantly sweet. The camels joined in the impromptu fruit-picking, brushing them up from the floor rather than risking a confrontation with the sharp points of the leaves that guarded the dates and made picking them a bloody experience.

Signs of life increased as we went in. Through the layers of date palms we saw occasional wells that had once served small farmsteads. We checked each one, but all were empty and abandoned. At the north-eastern end of the lake, which stretched away on lower ground, was a collection of derelict houses, in much better condition than the deserted old city of Tmissah. Buzeima, it appeared, had been evacuated more recently. We picked our way around solid stone houses, looking for a water source. There were circular stone animal pens, more single-storey houses that would once have been handsome dwelling-places and another disused well. I felt like a time-traveller walking through this forgotten village. The outlines were all here. Everything was ready, poised for action. It just lacked life. The screams of children, the babble of gossip, and the chorus of animals had all passed away. All that remained were these solid testaments to times past. And soon, presumably, to judge by the deterioration we had seen everywhere else—from Ghadames to Idri, Germa, Murzuk, Zuweila, Tmissah, and now here—these too would crumble away and the village of Buzeima would disappear forever.

"What do you want to do?" asked Mohammed. "I think we must keep looking for water for the camels and once we have found it, *inshallah*, they can feed later." His plan was to feed and water them for several hours while we had lunch and then continue later in the day towards Kufra. After we had exhausted all possibilities of water in the empty village, we made our way around the lake, descending onto a rim of sand that bordered it. The water lay to our left, partially obscured by thick banks of bulrushes with their feathery caps shifting in the breeze. In one place, a path had been trodden between them and I followed it down to the lake, taking the plastic bowl with me to test the brackish water on the camels. "I don't think the camels will drink it, but you can try," said Mohammed doubtfully.

A thick white scum floated on the surface, bobbing about as I filled the container. The water itself was cool and clear. When I returned, Asfar was couched on the grass nibbling on some stems. I set the bowl in front of him. He sank his muzzle into the water and sucked down a deep draught. He rose instantly with a start, coughed, and spat it out in disgust. It was no good. We would have to find the well. We continued without success for another hour, making our way around the lake and looking around the deserted farmsteads. In one, there was a well with a trace of water in it but heaps of rubbish had been thrown in and it looked rank. Eventually, with obvious dissatisfaction, Mohammed suggested we call off the search. "I don't know where we can find water here," he admitted, "but we should let them feed now or they'll have no food either. You make lunch and I'll collect dates to take with us for the camels."

It was not ideal but there was nothing else for it. We could carry on wandering around the oasis, with no guarantee of finding the well, or stop to let the camels graze properly before we pressed on. We halted at a patch of grass fifty yards from the edge of the lake, unloaded the camels, and hobbled their forelegs. Taking a bucket with him, Mohammed disappeared up a hillock studded with date palms, while I scrounged for wood and lit a fire. Of the three camels, Gobber ate with obvious relish and Lebead with little interest. Asfar ignored the green grazing entirely and devoted himself instead to ridding the ground of dates. Down they went, swallowed whole and in great numbers.

Like Rosita Forbes's camels when they arrived in Buzeima after their long trek from the coastal town of Ajdabiya, ours were much thinner now. Not finding sweet water for them here was a blow. This was our fourth day out of Tizirbu and we were still a hundred miles or so north of Kufra. Since Tmissah, it had been slim pickings, and they had already had to travel eight waterless days from Wau an Namus to Tizirbu. They were still holding out, but as Muhammad Ali would have said, they were no longer in "good condition." Where was the famous Ain Nasrani (Christian Well), named after the probable camp spot of the pioneering German explorer Gerhard Rohlfs, who "discovered" Buzeima in 1879? According to Rosita Forbes, there was only one fresh spring along the lake, but as this continued for several miles—she estimated it as five miles long, today it was much less—finding it was a thankless task. And what about Ned? Where was he now, and had he managed to find food and water for his camels? If Mohammed and I together had failed to find the spring, the chances of him doing it alone with two frightened camels was even more remote. What state would they all be in now? Had they got lost?

To distract ourselves from these grim thoughts, we turned to lunch, a spicy pasta soup and several glasses of tea. We sweated silently in the sun and beat off the hordes of flies that swarmed all over us. The camels finished their lunch and stood idly by. Behind them, the view was spectacularly beautiful. The lightly swaying bulrushes with their bright green stems and soft grey tufts jostled with the overhanging branches of dipping date palms. Behind them lay the cool blue flatness of the coin-bright lake, brilliantly reflecting in its waters the great ramparts of warm stone that rose beyond them in sweeping concaves. There was no sign of man here. Nothing disturbed the silence of the desert. There had been something ghostly about the village of Buzeima. Not here. On this side of the lake, all was serenity.

Lunch came to an end and we rounded up the camels. Asfar had returned to his deep-pile carpet of dates and was guzzling them down with a comic urgency. The sun was fierce and filled me with lassitude. Ned's departure and our failure to water the camels had dented our spirits. I took a south-easterly bearing and we set off into the dunes.

"Look! What's that?" asked Mohammed, as we made our way through the fringes of the oasis. He was pointing to something on our left. Several hundred metres away, I could barely make out a flicker of white in front of a cluster of date palms.

"I can't make it out. It's too far away," I replied. We walked towards the bright shape. After a few more minutes, I could see it was a white camel feeding on palms, apparently alone. I thought nothing of it. Perhaps a farmer had brought his camels here to feed and water them.

"It's your friend," said Mohammed suddenly. A *jalabiya*-clad figure was moving to and fro in front of the camel, poking the upper reaches of a palm tree with a branch to bring down the hanging parcels of dates. Whoever it was noticed us approaching but continued with his job. It was Ned.

"Please don't say anything to him," I asked Mohammed, as we continued walking towards them. "Let me do the talking."

"I'm not going to say a single word," he said calmly. "But it is better for the three of us to travel together to Kufra from here."

Diplomatically, he stopped twenty yards short of Ned, allowing me to go on alone. Ned had a studied air of independence. Once he had travelled in a small caravan with guide and companion. Those days were long gone. Now, he was the self-contained solitary desert explorer. I approached him and made some small talk about date-picking to break the ice of our estrangement. Mohammed and I had failed to find any water in the oasis, I told him.

"There's some over there," he replied casually, pointing to the edge of the lake ten yards away. "I've already watered the camels and had a swim."

We compared notes on the eighteen hours we had spent apart. He had continued for about three miles last night, he said, and arrived in Buzeima shortly before us this morning. Here, he had been invited to a breakfast of tea and nougat by a couple of men he met, who had driven in from Kufra to collect dates. Perhaps they had pointed out the well to him.

"*Maya kwayis*" (Good water), he said pointedly to Mohammed, gesturing towards the elusive source of fresh water. Mohammed walked off down the slope of sand to investigate it, leaving me to embark upon a second round of diplomacy. Ned and I stumbled across several embarrassed silences until I asked him directly.

"Why don't you come with us? We may as well go on together, now that we've met here. It would be stupid to separate again. You and Mohammed don't even have to talk to each other."

"You know, I'm really quite enjoying travelling on my own," he replied.

"It's only for a few more days then we're in Kufra and Mohammed goes home."

"I really think you should have a swim," came the reply. "The water's fantastic." He recommended a good half-hour floating on the lake.

"I couldn't care less about swimming, Ned."

Nor could he. He only wanted me to swim so he could then make his getaway alone.

"Listen, you and Mohammed can walk miles apart and you hardly have to see each other, let alone talk."

He hesitated. It was in the balance. And then, after what felt like an age, he relented. "Of course, I'll come with you," he said. "It would be silly not to. Anyway, now that I've pointed out the well to him, I feel much better."

I walked over to Mohammed, who was watering all five camels from the plastic basin. "We're going together," I said.

"Come on then, let's go," he replied, and we were off once again, Ned bringing up the rear at a discreet distance. He still felt angry about the argument with Mohammed and felt no great urge to speak to him for the time being. After the drama of the separation, I felt huge relief the caravan was back to its full complement. It did not matter that we had not spotted Buzeima's only inhabitant, the eccentric donkey mentioned by the policeman in Tizirbu.

The dunes here were the largest we had come across. Frequently, I arrived at the crest of one to see Mohammed several steps down from me on the steep face, trying to encourage Lebead down with a few words and then pulling him hard by the nosering when that failed. His camel, frightened by the severity of the gradient, would dig in for as long as possible until it seemed that surely his nose would give way. And then, the giant would lumber into action, roaring, sliding, and skidding his way down in deep swathes of sand,

making a path of sorts for the others to follow. From the summits of the highest dunes, we caught glimpses of two great
stacks of black rock that rose from this milky white sand sea
like floundering shipwrecks—apart from the retreating features
of Buzeima, the only landmarks to disturb this sun-bleached
monotony. These were the outlying ridges of the Buzeima
Gara. Their names, Rosita Forbes was told, were Gor Sibb al
Abid and Saar al Khaddama.

Crossing these dunes was a tiring business. It was unsatisfactory to ride because the camels descended so painstakingly
and the slopes were usually far too steep for them to carry a
man without collapsing. Riding through this sort of terrain
required repeated mounting and dismounting, which would
only slow us down. Occasionally, the dunes subsided into less
vertiginous stretches and then the three of us would clamber
onto our tiring beasts. In the early evening, I swung on to
Asfar and waited for him to lurch up on first two, then four
legs. Usually, it was automatic. As soon as you hit the saddle,
he would be up with a roar. Now, he did not move. Suddenly,
with a pitiful whimper that was intended as a roar, he flopped
heavily onto his side, still kneeling, trapping my leg underneath him for a few seconds until I wriggled free. After I had
got up, I looked at him. The eyes were losing their lustre and
he was the weakest I had ever seen him. He did not look in
good sorts at all. The worst thing about it was that we could
do nothing to help him, apart from remove his load and feed
him a few dates. There was nothing else we could give him.

"He's very tired now," said Mohammed. "He needs a long
rest. When we get to Kufra, *inshallah*, you must rest all of them
for a week and feed them properly."

"Do you think he'll die before we reach Kufra?" I asked.

"*Inshallah*, he will be all right, but now he has lost his
strength."

That night we had one of our quietest dinners. Ned and Mohammed maintained a civilized chilliness towards each other. Passing a bar of (kerosene-flavoured) chocolate or a glass of tea was allowed, perhaps a muttered "*shukran*" (thank you) in return, but no conversation of greater length. Instead, they competed persistently for my attention, not because I was more entertaining than usual, but to demonstrate they could manage quite happily without each other. Some of this was amusing, but it was also irritating. Neither of them was prepared to unload the same camel together, for example, since this required the exchange of a few words. Instead, they both insisted on working with me and me alone, which meant I did double the work and things took much longer than usual. I began to understand why middlemen get paid so well.

The next day was 4 February, two months to the day since we had left Ghadames. We woke to a strange milky landscape in which sky and dunes almost merged. The sun, usually so strong and naked, was a veiled disc, pale beneath a bed of cloud. It cast a wan, ethereal light over the sand sea and made the dunes, newly naked after another night of sweeping winds, appear softer still. Not a single car track or a camel trail disturbed this unearthly kingdom that stretched out in cream curves as far as the eye could see for 360°. In mid-morning, the dark silhouette of a ragged mountain range jutted out of the froth, and Mohammed said we were approaching the end of the Rabiana Sand Sea, which meant that Kufra was close. The range in front offered little clues as to its distance from us. It could have been a matter of several hours, or a day and a half away. It was impossible to tell, but it did not matter. We were almost there. I felt a deep thrill, mounting with every step we took, as we closed in on our longed-for goal: Kufra, the fabled oasis deep in the Libyan Sahara. Ghadames, where we had started the journey, felt a world away, both in time and space.

The sun roused itself from this misty stupor, frazzling the massed clouds around it and shining relentlessly once again. By mid-afternoon we passed into a range of rocks, here crowded together haphazardly, there tapering off into the plain in layers like a neatly arranged row of giant's boots, each one a paler shade than the last. Rocks to the north-east and south-west framed our departure from the sand sea. Some rose to sharp points, others were decapitated to the same level, and were dappled in shadow. Others were blown a gritty gold with sand. Through this gravelly corridor we marched, filled with awe at the grandeur of this new scenery. Where water had once flowed, lazy *s* shapes etched into the plain meandered prettily around us. The dunes gathered themselves for a final assault on their old adversary, surging forward in waves, and then sputtered out into spitting dribbles of sand that faded first and finally disappeared altogether from the barren grey of the plain. We droned on through the plateau and came to the foot of a pass that slanted away from us towards Kufra. At the top, we turned and gazed back on the roiling rocks and dunes and said farewell to the sand sea for the last time. It was a picture I would never forget.

Postscript: Justin Marozzi completed the 1,500-mile journey from Tripoli to Kurfa, one of the last Saharan oases to be discovered by Westerners.

Six straight months of trekking in the Sahara has a way of
changing a person forever, and that was certainly the case
for Geoffrey Moorhouse, who found that no amount of training
can prepare one for this harsh reality. Debilitating dehydration, starvation, sunburn, and lice infestation are among the
routine challenges, though a far more formidable danger is
the unpredictable encounters with the locals.

THE FEARFUL VOID

GEOFFREY MOORHOUSE

We were marching our beasts
down the village, towards the edge of the gravel plain, when
Mohamed asked me to carry on for a little while alone: he
and Sidi Mahmoud had some business in one of the houses,
they would catch up with me soon. I walked on placidly,
enjoying the declining heat of the day and the sharp angular
shadows falling from the escarpment, the gentle tug of the
leading camel's headrope upon my shoulder, the rhythmic
pad of our feet upon the hard and gritty ground. Above all,
I enjoyed the solitude of the moment. I would give much, I
thought, to be able to go on like this. But I wondered whether
I would have the courage to do so.

This was something quite apart from the practical considerations of travelling alone, which I was beginning to recog-

nise as a possibly insurmountable obstacle: it took so long, even with two men, to find the camels each morning. Though their forelegs were always tightly hobbled together, they could move extraordinary distances with unexpected speed in their search for food, proceeding with the determined shuffle of a sand dancer or a series of comical bunny hops. I had watched one shift three hundred yards in a few minutes. The other morning we had been delayed for two and a half hours in looking for them, and I had not known it to take less than half an hour to bring them in. A solitary rider's energy could be dangerously dissipated by this perpetual need to ramble round the desert without advancing his position, just as it would be heavily taxed by the need to load or unload the baggage of two beasts four times each day.

But even if I could find and afford the single-handed energy for these tasks over a matter of weeks and months, could I also muster the plain gut courage to go on alone in the desert? I was not sure yet, but I had begun to doubt it. Thrice now, sitting in an oasis just before departure, I had experienced a deep primeval fear of the void around. Not quite a quaking sensation; no more than an uneasy, feathery turning of the stomach. But there, distinctly there, as a warning and as a question mark that I could not ignore. Wilfred Thesiger had told me that he would most certainly be crushed by the immensity of the desert if he found himself in it alone. I could see very well what he meant now, as I walked wonderingly between the hard impregnable outline of the escarpment and the blank, blank anonymity of the endless dunes. I was a caterpillar wriggling hopefully across an eternal nothingness from which all other life had been apparently extinguished.

I turned to see if my companions had left the oasis yet. They were about half a mile behind, two tiny dots striding vigorously to catch up. A third figure was with them. I slackened my pace and they joined me without a word, Mohamed immediately taking the headrope and handing it to the newcomer. He was a gap-toothed young man, stockily built as the shepherd lad, Mahomed ould Ely, had been, and he paid no attention to me at all.

"Where's the boy going?" I asked.

"Just down there," said Mohamed, nodding straight ahead. "He's joining some friends in an encampment."

It wasn't until three days later, in the middle of nowhere, that I decided this encampment was a long time in appearing, and broached the subject again. Calmly, Mohamed announced that the lad's destination was near Néma. A week before, I would have blown up in his face. As it was, I simply turned away wearily, shaking my head in bewilderment. I certainly couldn't abandon the youth where we were. At the same time, I seriously wondered whether our supplies would see four of us through the next ten days, or so. The only solution was to push on as hard as possible and get this growing nightmare of a passage over.

By then, however, it had become clear that our movement would be retarded by this latest recruit to the caravan. Although for a few hours each day young Erbah rode bareback behind Sidi Mahmoud, whose camel carried little baggage, we spent ourselves much more than we would otherwise have done in marching on foot, and even when we rode, it was impossible for a camel to trot very far with two men up. We plodded on through bitterly cold mornings that had no warmth in them at all until past ten o'clock, though by noon the wind that had been storming with sub-Arctic penetration was transformed into a scorching torrent that flushed the bare skin even where it had tanned deeply after weeks of exposure. We left the wide corridor of gravel. We crossed more dunes. We came to the well of Touijinit, and paused to water our beasts.

Touijinit was a much more ambitious affair than anything I had yet seen outside an oasis, with a deep shaft and a high concrete rim that prevented the muck from flowing back into the water, and troughs running fanwise from the shafthead so that many camels could drink simultaneously. A mob of perhaps twenty beasts was there before us, brought down from the pastures above the escarpment by two herdsmen, and we exchanged news and information with them. There was, they said, a little *ghudda* for beasts up there. But down here there was nothing, nothing at all, for as far as a man might ride strongly in a week. A few yards from the well lay the withered carcass of a camel, bearing witness to the desperate aridity of this area.

We climbed the escarpment again, so that our camels might find their precious *ghudda*, into a region scarcely less impoverished, for we were once more hemmed in tightly by the sands of El Mreyye. But between the sands and the rocks, a narrow strip of ground that was a mixture of both bore a scattering of yellowed grasses and even, from time to time, a tree on which the animals could browse.

This was the setting for my Christmas, which barely existed outside my imagination. By the half light of dawn I was attempting to delouse my garments, appalled by the numbers which had now attached themselves to me: they were secreted in scores within the huge ingathering at the waist of my *serwal*, and they infested the sweater which I had started to pull on at night and during the early cold of the day. The string vest which I habitually wore under my boubou might be a useful insulation against both cold and heat, but it also, I noted with dismay, provided an excellent refuge for these creatures in almost every one of its many joints.

It was so cold, this morning, that I had difficulty in getting the others on the move before nine-thirty. They seemed to be even wearier than I was, inquiring more than once during the morning whether we might not ride now. There was no question of doing so, for we were in dunes again, all of them steep and soft enough to have the camels in trouble without the added burden of riders. Mohamed's five-year-old jibbed so fiercely at one prolonged descent that, tethered as he was to the saddle of the big bull in front, he had his nose ring yanked out, which tore his nostril and left him with a very bloody face. For four hours we kept up a floundering, scrambling pace before our midday halt; then we went on as before until sunset. We had picked up a few small twigs during these hours for our evening fire, but in the end we had to augment them with camel dung. On this I managed to heat the small Christmas pudding I had brought from England. It would have just about capped a solid meal for two men, as I had originally assumed. Four of us enjoyed no more than a mouthful apiece, although the other three, after their initial suspicions were allayed, expressed great satisfaction.

Periodically during the day, I took flight to J and the children, and the ritual whose measured steps I knew so well and loved so much. In spite of my resolve to banish all thoughts of home, I had for days past followed the rising Christmas tide of tree-planting, decorating, cooking and hubbub in that house, which I had always shared so far, and it was strangely a comfort rather than a sadness—some promise of continuity, I supposed. As I paused in my lice-hunting at dawn, I visualised the opening of the presents I had left behind me, a series of cameos that were so vivid I could have reached out and touched them. They were rehearsed throughout the day, when I was not concentrated upon some purely tactical struggle up and down the dunes, for I was loath to leave them behind. In the darkness, with the pudding at last gone, I wondered whether it had been wise or upsetting to leave for the family my tape-recorded reading of *A Child's Christmas in Wales*, for my elder daughter Jane, I knew, had gone through spasms of worrying whether I would safely return. But I had wanted to share their Christmas, and it had seemed gentlest to do it by way of Dylan Thomas. Sentimentality could the better be passed off as fun and games that way.

Sentimentality was rudely interrupted by Mohamed, who rolled over in his blanket and addressed himself to our future together. Perhaps the best way out of the financial difficulties that awaited us in Néma, he said—and I marked well the "us"—would be for me to give him a camel, instead of buying him a plane ticket back to Tidjikja. If I were prepared to do this, Sidi Mahmoud would continue beyond Oualata to Néma and ride his camel home with Mohamed for company.

As a disinterested proposition, it would have had much to commend it. But nothing that Mohamed did, particularly in relation to me, was remotely disinterested. He gave away his true intent by telling me that the cost of a flight from Néma would be about 60,000 francs, which I knew to be rubbish; I could have flown from Nouakchott to London for that. What Mohamed was after, my nerve ends immediately said, was a camel on top of his wages. I did not doubt that he would pursue this objective with all the guile and determination of which he was capable. The rest of our journey, I foresaw, was going to be a wearing one. I must try to counter his strategy with opaque noncommitments of my own.

"It's a possibility," I told him, and indicated that I wished to sleep. But in my notebook next morning, I added a postscript to the entry for the day: "Woke after midnight, worrying about it all, while Orion swivelled overhead and the lice crawled across my belly and up my spine. Happy Christmas to all our readers."

As we worked our way slowly towards the eastern limit of the escarpment before turning south, I wrestled almost step by step with the financial permutations that might be possible at Néma. At least once every day Mohamed again brought up the subject of the camel, and Sidi Mahmoud now joined in the effort to press this course upon me. Only Erbah, the young man, stood outside my dilemma; indeed, he had very little to say to anyone, and I realised very well by now why he had become attached to my party. He had been recruited by the other two simply to take as much of the drudgery off their hands as was possible, in exchange for our food and our company. Whenever we camped it was Erbah who was told by Mohamed to start looking for firewood or dung; in the mornings it was he who was expected to go searching for the camels first. Mohamed and Sidi Mahmoud, meanwhile, would lie like dead things until he returned, while I wrote up my notes.

I found it curious that both seemed to be tiring much more than I was. Mentally I often felt played out, but my body seemed now to have taken a second wind, so that for the first two hours of our daily march I would stride on ahead while they trailed far behind, walking slowly as though to execution, their bodies bent against the furious head winds, the camels hanging heavily on the ropes. It occurred to me that I had much greater reserves of energy than they, doubtless the result of forty years' consistently high nourishment. And they felt the cold cruelly, wrapping their headcloths tightly around their faces, so that only their eyes were visible between the swathes. Halfway through one night I awoke to see Mohamed stoking up the embers of our fire, huddling over its wretched glow, then scraping the warm sand under his blanket before lying down again. Even in a sleeping bag, the cold continually wakened me at night. If it were not the cold that interrupted sleep, it would be the lice, or the moon shining stridently into my face. I doubt whether I had enjoyed more than two hours' unbroken repose since Tidjikja.

We traversed more dunes, and again I felt the deepest fears nudging me. In the hollows between the dunes, it was as though one were very close to the edge of the earth. There was no vista beyond that undulating ridge just ahead, nothing but flawlessly blue sky; gain it, and one would drop off into eternal space. But at the crest of the ridge a vista did appear, and it was even more intimidating than the illusion of space. Move off alone into the endless sequence of sandy hills that now stretched ahead, across the khaki colours of the foreground and into the whiteness that glared forever from afar, and one would become dazed by the sameness of those beautiful elliptical shapes, become mindless, lose the power of concentration, ultimately lose all the senses one by one. How could anyone navigate with certainty for long across such a barrier, when the compass bearing swept through 20 degrees every five minutes, the sun first burning the left shoulder, then the right shoulder, then appearing dead ahead, before turning to the left again?

We came out of the dunes and started to move across a flat pancake of pulverised gravel, maybe a mile and a half in diameter, encircled by sandy scrub. In the middle of it was a huge circle made up of stones, and in the centre of the circle, again with stones, the large lettering of the words "Bou Zib." It was an old French airfield, abandoned for some twenty years, with not the slightest trace of any buildings that might have been raised during its construction. Had I paused there, had we camped for the night on its perimeter, it might have seemed spooky in its absolute dereliction, for apart from those carefully laid stones and the fact that the ground had obviously been cleared meticulously of boulders, possibly being levelled mechanically as well, there was nothing to suggest that man had ever visited this spot before. We had seen no one for three full days. Yet there it mysteriously was, shimmering with mirage, stamped with the hallmark of ultimate civilisation. It was indicated, interestingly, on my American military chart, but not on the French maps I had brought from Paris. As we tramped across its surface, I wondered what colonial strategy had been responsible for its appearance in the first place, and whether, in due course, another one might find some aggressive use for it. And this was, for a moment in time, the justification of Bou Zib's existence: to provide me with a tiny mental exercise in the clogging tedium of my journey—that and a navigational beacon from which I might plot my further course.

I went back to take my turn on the camel ropes. As Mohamed handed them over, he announced that in two days we should pass the end of the wadi which eventually led to Oualata. What were we going to do about Sidi Mahmoud? He, I said, should return home as planned. As for Mohamed himself, when we reached Néma I would put him on a plane for Nouakchott with some traveller's cheques; he would take these to Ahmed ould Die, who would settle his account and give him a plane ticket to Tidjikja. I regretted that I would not be able to present him with a camel, but there would be so little money to spare after I had reprovisioned for the next stage of the journey, and paid an advance to whoever would accompany me to Tombouctou, that this was the only solution I could manage, and, indeed, I believed that it was. Though I was now quite capable of bloody-mindedness in my dealings with Mohamed, I exonerated myself on this occasion, while I had the malicious satisfaction of knowing that his disappointment would be essentially of his own making, for it was he who had induced the financial crisis by involving me in much greater expenditure than I had bargained for when I deployed my monies before leaving the capital.

When I told him my decision, he broke into an aggrieved bickering. It would take him a long time to get home by flying this roundabout way, he shouted, and his wife was pregnant. I don't think I managed to avoid a grin when I pointed out that it would take him a lot longer to ride home by camel, if that was what he'd had in mind.

Then something in the tone of his response—"You have decided, then?"—wiped the grin from my face. I watched him join Sidi Mahmoud, speaking quietly and sourly, and uneasily wondered what might happen next. I couldn't imagine that Mohamed would turn to violence, for he had a healthy respect for the law, and I doubted whether he would have the guts to risk falling foul of it. But would he possibly dare to leave me in the lurch here, trusting, in his huge contempt for European navigation, that I would never find my way to either Oualata or Néma? I suddenly recalled the room in Nouakchott where I had imagined him, whom I had not then met, abandoning me in some such wilderness as this one. It was probably just as well, I concluded, that I was sleeping very lightly these days.

We started riding a little later, and Mohamed began officiously to correct my mannerisms. I should place my foot thus, when mounting, and hold the headrope so when in the saddle, and on no account rest both legs on the same side of the animal's neck, as one did from time to time to relieve stiffness in the limbs. The fellow invariably turned pompous teacher whenever he felt put down. As often as not, he made mealtimes the excuse for a lecture on how to roll rice into a ball with one hand before eating it, a trick which I never tidily performed. On other occasions he had fussily rebuked me for my habit of leaving empty eating bowls the right way up on the ground. They should be turned over, he advised, or the Devil would come and sup from them. I was in no mood for his patronage now, though, and irritably waved him away.

We jogged on slowly, with a great space between us.

Somewhere behind, Sidi Mahmoud followed, with young Erbah clinging to his camel's rump. For maybe half an hour not a word was exchanged by any of us, Mohamed moodily watching the ground just ahead of his beast, chewing a piece of stick as he so often did. Then he drifted over to me, one arm arrogantly resting on his hip, the headrope dangling casually from his other fingers. He looked up at me, with a wicked half grin on his face.

"Why won't you," he demanded, and there was no mistaking the truculence of his tone or his manner, "why won't you buy me a camel, then?"

It was an ultimatum, a challenge, and in a fury I rose to it, heedless of the consequences. My riding stick came up and I levelled it at his head menacingly; had he been a foot or so nearer, I believe I might have slugged him with it on the spot.

"Listen," I shouted, "and listen well, little corporal. The subject is closed. Do you understand? It's closed. Finished!" And I brought the stick down with a thump on the wing of his saddle. I was shaking with a rage which obliterated everything but a desire to smash this source of torment.

He glared at me for an instant, openmouthed with shock. Then he uttered something between a grunt and a sneer, grinned again secretly to himself, and dragged his camel away from mine, to resume his moody passage across the sands.

Mohamed did not mention the camel again, but next day he pursued a new tactic. We had descended the escarpment now, moving due south across a gravel plain, almost as though we were coasting down the English Channel close inshore to the cliffs. At our midday camp, Mohamed very deliberately made tea, cut up some meat and put it into the cooking pot, then lay back as though nothing else would happen till this food was ready. Up to now, our drill had always been to break open the dates and share them as soon as the fire was made up, while waiting for the first glass of tea. As Mohamed lay down, he said something to the other two, and Erbah giggled.

I waited a few moments, then said, "Dates?"

Uproarious laughter from Sidi Mahmoud and Erbah, and a sly grin from Mohamed. I took no notice, but repeated my question, and Mohamed languidly brought them from the *tassoufra*, then dished them out. The tension passed. We finished our meal and rode on.

That afternoon my camel stumbled four times, always as his left foreleg went down. I wondered whether he was going lame. But Mohamed said that it was no matter, just a tripping over larger stones, and I could see nothing wrong with the beast's leg myself.

Our food situation was, as I had expected, becoming poor. Our flour had been finished three or four days ago, and there was little left of either dates, rice or meat. On December 30 it became serious. We had trekked to refill our almost empty *guerbas* at Hassi Fouini, a miserable hole flush with the ground, whose water contained much camel dung and was sour with diluted piss. In the hour or two before our arrival, Mohamed had started to lobby me on behalf of his comrade-in-chief. The entrance of the wadi leading to Oualata stretched wide open to the east of us. Sidi Mahmoud, said Mohamed, was prepared to continue to Néma, but there I would have to provision him for his return journey; otherwise he would now ride to Oualata, but would need money to buy food there. I said that I had no wish for Sidi Mahmoud to prolong his journey with us, that I would give him 1,000 francs, which was all that I had left apart from small change, if he desired to make for Oualata.

We had idled by the water hole for an hour or so when Sidi Mahmoud got up and announced that he was going home now. I handed him 1,000 francs and wished him well. Then Mohamed turned to the *tassoufra* and began to divide the contents. It appeared that Sidi Mahmoud was not going to Oualata after all, but had decided to return home direct, without making a detour to the oasis above the escarpment.

I was beyond arguing about the small deception which had winkled more money out of me; I was too content to be rid of Sidi Mahmoud. His presence had never been satisfactory after the first few days, for he had been too ready to lie around and leave others to do the work, his idleness occasionally causing Mohamed to chastise him resentfully. Above all, from my point of view, he had been an accomplice, essentially a weak yes-man to Mohamed's various ploys, and thus some threat to my security. But as he turned away and mounted his camel without a word to any of us, without a backward glance, I could not help being moved by the bravery of his going back alone, even though he would have our tracks to follow. It would be three weeks before he regained his own tent across some of the most awful travelling country in the world. I recognised that I could not have done what he was undertaking.

His departure was a relief to me, but it left us with little to eat before Néma, which was still three days away. On impulse, I had decided to ride directly there. We had enough rice for two meals, and thirty-three dates—all of them withered, some of them so hard and dessicated as to be virtually inedible. On New Year's Day, we used the last of our precious, restorative tea and sugar, which was a far greater blow than the lack of meat, flour or rice. We were moving now, as we had been ever since Tichit, across ground that was unpeopled by nomads who might give us food if we could find their tents at the end of the day. Had one felt fit and well, the landscape would have been exciting here, for the plain now and then erupted into huge rocky hills that reminded me of photographs I had seen of the buttes of Arizona, gaunt and stratified and lonely, with half a day's journey in between each. We came past four upstanding slabs of rock, too carefully arranged in a rectangle to have happened naturally, which Mohamed said were graves, and which, if that were so, must have been as ancient as the four arrowheads I had now collected; for many centuries would have passed since there was enough life in this ground to support a family long enough for them to have settled and died there.

One took scant notice of such things, however, for hunger was beginning to deaden all the senses. I had long since become accustomed to its daily advance, to those tentacles of discomfort that slowly crawled up the belly and into the mind. On the march I had habitually been less aware of them than when lying inert at an oasis, for the preoccupying sensations of travel were those of pain and physical exhaustion; a conscious weakness as the moment approached for more food was almost the only signal that one needed food. In an oasis, where there was small pain and no exhaustion, attention shifted to the stomach, to the windy emptiness within, to the growing ache. At all times, food had been reduced to a necessity, quite devoid of its emotional pleasure. One devoured the gritty evening couscous avidly, as an animal among others. One stuffed down the plain boiled rice at midday, no longer caring much, scarcely realising that it had no taste at all. Emotion attended only the meat, rationing the amount one consumed quite as much as the sheer common sense that warned of potential disease, ranging from dreadful hydatids to wasting dysentery, which could reside in this half-cooked flesh.

But now, with no food to revive the body, the body's failures became the focal points of existence. One noted much less the perpetually bitter taste in the mouth than the increasing stupor of giddiness. I began to weave uncertainly when I was walking. It became difficult to climb into the saddle for riding. I found that my chin tended to loll on my chest, my shoulders sagging, when I mounted, and I rolled around the saddle inertly as a sack of potatoes. At noon on that first day of 1973, we drank water, ate nothing and collapsed into sleep. I was astonished that such a transformation had overtaken me in such a short time; only a few days before, I had been surging ahead of my party on the march, feeling much the strongest person in it. Now a curious detachment had set in. Lying there on the ground, nothing mattered but sleep. I wanted nothing but the peace that would let me sink into sleep and forget.

We dragged ourselves on slowly, taking turns to share the two camels between the three of us. Though we exchanged no words on the subject, spoke scarcely at all, it was implicit in our situation when dusk came that we would not stop to make camp, but would continue our sluggish movement through the darkness. By then we should normally have been fed and ready for sleep, but now we had no food. For the first time I was peering ahead and around as keenly as my companions had always done, in the hope of finding a sign of other human life on this desolate plain, which might mean sanctuary and a chance to fill our bellies on someone else's good nature. Instinct said that there must be people in the country just ahead; there always were nomads camped in country immediately around an oasis, and Néma was not too far off now.

It was young Erbah on foot who spotted the faint flicker in the black night. Then Mohamed, then I focused it in our blurring vision from the superior heights of our camels. A campfire was burning in the distance. There was no commanding gallop towards our prey this time. We just stumbled on quietly through the darkness. It took us half an hour to draw close enough to see, in the occulting glow of several fires, that here were no tents, but the mud walls of houses. We got down drunkenly beside the nearest dwelling and began to unhitch our gear. Faces appeared, but no one stepped forward to help until Mohamed burst out angrily at a man who stood watching. He started to berate the fellow for lack of welcome and, as the man listened stolidly, Mohamed addressed his words to include a gathering audience of half a dozen or so. Grudgingly they moved to our assistance when we had done all but hobble the beasts, grudgingly they put down mats in the lee of a wall. Then they left us.

"*Ma marhaba*—Not welcome," I said to Mohamed wearily.

He did not reply, and for the first time in several weeks I warmed to the man. He was, I realised, ashamed of these people and their failure to offer hospitality to a Nasrani.

It was an hour before anyone visited us, while we lay slumped upon the mats. A woman then brought a bowl of milk, which we sucked noisily in turn. That was all we received from this settlement. It was very strange, I reflected next morning, that the wealthiest group of people we had met outside an oasis—people who had fowls and the first cattle I had seen, as well as sheep, goats and houses—should also be the stingiest.

The bowl of milk, little though it was, had put some life in us again. It kept us going through a hot and windless morning, until we came to a small encampment of tents among trees. There, with the last few coins in my possession, we bought a piece of sugar and some tea, the leaves being carefully measured out and handed over in a small drinking glass. So many times on this journey, we had given tea in this fashion to satisfy the perpetual craving of nomads. But now, for once, I found myself the supplicant. We moved on a little, to camp alone and brew a pot of this blessed infusion. It revived us enough to face the last few miles to Néma in good heart. The plain, which since the previous night had been thickly garnished with trees, now became positively fertile. There were more cattle here, corn was being grown in quantity, and many rough fences had been constructed out of thorny branches; the ground was also increasingly strewn with the wretched cram-cram grass and its scratching, hooked burrs.

We overtook a small family, a man, his wife and their son, and they were the most attractive people I had seen since returning to Africa. The parents laughed and joked together, amiably and affectionately, and looked as if they cared to be in each other's company. There was not a hint of dominance in him, or of subservience in her. I had not before seen a nomad man and woman who appeared to be living together on the basis of what I could recognise as friendship and equality. They shared some food with us and we pottered on comfortably together towards the last range of hills before the oasis. These were no more than 500 feet high, but my coming to them was both healing and unforgettable. A field of corn was being worked by some women underneath these hills, a warm and declining light glowed upon everything, and the earth's stillness was only heightened by the distant shouts of people across fields, by the movement of some women on donkeys, by the trilling of a few birds.

I remembered those beautiful opening lines of Alan Paton's: "There is a lovely road that runs from Ixopo into the hills. These hills are grass-covered and rolling, and they are lovely beyond any singing of it . . . and from there, if there is no mist, you look down on one of the fairest valleys of Africa." For the first time in my life, I felt touched by the magic of Africa.

It was long after nightfall when we came to Néma and

found lodgings with some kinsmen of young Erbah. Next morning, disconsolately, I discovered at the post office that there had been no word from Ahmed onld Die in Nouakchott, though it was now nearly a fortnight since I had dispatched my cheques to him from Tichit, with the urgent plea for cash to be awaiting me here.

Once more I turned to the official residence for help, seeking the provincial Governor who controlled Mauritania's southeastern boundaries with Mali from this place. The Governor himself was away, but I secured an interview with his deputy, a formidable-looking man whose headcloth concealed much of his face, giving what was visible a slightly forbidding air. He questioned me sharply about the purpose of my arrival in Néma and asked me some detailed questions about my journey as a whole, revealing rather more knowledge than I had expected of the geography of Egypt.

All this time he had been doodling moodily on a pad in front of him and now, without looking up, he uttered a sigh and said, "Well, you've a long way still to go, haven't you?"

I gaped with amazement, for he had just spoken impeccable English, the first words I had heard in my own language for the best part of two months. He put his head back, his headcloth slipping down to his chin, and laughed marvellously at my surprise. We swung our hands into a delighted clasp of greeting. We were friends at once.

This man, Abdellahi ould Erebih, was to offer me much comfort as well as kindness over the next few days. He had been his country's ambassador in Cairo and Bonn, as well as a member of its delegation to the United Nations, and I found it very odd indeed that someone of his experience, intelligence and sophistication should now be dumped somewhat less than grandly in an insignificant township on the edge of the Sahara desert. He was about my own age, and in the West he would most certainly have occupied some senior post in the capital or in one of its most prestigious embassies abroad; or, in some countries, he might have been banished to some obscure and remote place as a potential threat to the ambitions of the leadership.

I did not once detect in Abdellahi a trace of bitterness at this apparent waste of his considerable talents. He had much natural dignity, a piety that he wore very lightly, and he seemed totally at peace with himself in this environment. There was something splendidly innocent and wondering about him as he showed me some curious stones he had found a little while before, during a visit to another oasis. What was the meaning of those whorling marks on them, clearly man-made? His brow furrowed with perplexity as we bent over them together—the look of a small boy who thinks he may have found his first fossil, but still isn't quite sure. Yet he had the gentle wit of the man who is poised enough to be at ease in any world. Once, he told me, he had officially visited Luxembourg, to be shown some steel mill by people who were anxious that this man of Africa should be impressed. What did he think of the tremendous power at work in the building, of this astonishing spectacle of molten metal, they asked?

"I just told them, 'It seems very hot to me'"; and he shrugged apologetically, with a comedian's twinkle, at the memory of it.

Abdellahi did three things at once to raise my spirits even more. He promised to telegraph a message directly to Nouakchott about my money, he asked an assistant to find someone to travel to Tombouctou with me, and he suggested that I might like to move into what was euphemistically called the Government rest house, across the road from his administrative offices. It was rather ramshackle, he said, and more than a little grubby, but at least it would give me peace and quiet.

The rest house was all these things, but it enabled me, after

a rusty water tank had been laboriously filled from the well
outside, to wash for the first time since Nouakchott; and that
alone was good enough. I found a mirror and was dismayed
at my appearance. My face was scorched and windblasted, the
nose cracked wide open along the bone, the lips badly swollen
and blistered, and there were an old man's wrinkles puckering
the skin around bloodshot eyes. The eyes themselves held
me, much more than the rest of my bedraggled, whiskery
Rumpelstiltskin of a face. They were staring, too strained by
far, the eyes of someone who looked as if he felt hunted and
on the run. This was not the passable Moorhouse of England,
home and beauty, but some decrepit saddle tramp discovered
in desolation. Would I return to Europe looking as I had done
when I left? Would my own people recognise and own me?
Could my body survive this elemental treatment intact? The
nervous questions tumbled after each other as I gazed upon
this relic of myself. "Read next week's instalment of . . . Dick
Barton, Special Agent," a boyhood memory mocked me.

Next day I returned from some errand to find Mohamed
sharing tea on the floor of our room with a newcomer. He was
introduced as Sid' Ahmed ould Eli ould Simmad, and the man
who would travel with me beyond Néma. He was of much the
same build as Mohamed, but he had a wider face which
flashed its teeth frequently, and an ingratiating manner which I
did not take to. Sid' Ahmed, I noticed, tipped his head on one
side when requesting something, rather like a cocker spaniel
attending to master's whistle. I was not at all pleased that the
two had struck up an acquaintance, for I could imagine that
Mohamed would conceive it as at least a tribal loyalty to
inform his successor of every detectable weakness in the Nasrani, particularly those which laid me open to exploitation.

I was very sharp with both, in my attempt to convey the
message that the easy meat Mohamed had discovered in
Nouakchott was no longer being served up on a platter in

Néma. I was not gratified, in these few days, to find Sid' Ahmed
lying in wait for me near the post office on my frequent excur-
sions to see if my money had arrived; he, too, wanted a substantial advance of cash before we set out. A couple of times I
was stopped by strangers, who promptly burst into eulogies
about the fellow, telling me how lucky I was to secure his services, how I must be sure to buy him some cartridges, for he was
one of the best shots in Mauritania, and many other praise-
worthy things. At which point Sid' Ahmed himself would
invariably appear like a genie from the crowd, beaming with
pleasure and cocking his head in emphatic expectation.

I found myself with another crisis on my hands, apart from
the one involving money. My camels had been taken to some
pasture a couple of miles outside the oasis on the morning
after our arrival, and in the afternoon young Erbah was told
by Mohamed to go and check on their safety. On the second
evening he returned to our room when it had been dark for
several hours, looking very gloomy and sullen. The animals,
he announced, were nowhere to be found. Mohamed became
agitated and said that someone must have stolen them, that
we must report the matter to the Governor at once.

Unwillingly, for it was late, I went over to Abdellahi, feeling sick at heart in the face of this new reverse. I had already
noticed that there were scarcely any beasts about Néma, none
apparently for sale. If my camels had indeed been taken, my
journey was in jeopardy. Although part of me would by now
have been very happy to board the next weekly flight to
Nouakchott and have done with the thing at last, the prize of
Tombouctou was so very nearly in my grasp, no more than
another fortnight away. Reach Tombouctou, I told myself,
and I could retire from this awful endurance test with at least a
smattering of self-respect.

Abdellahi, when I told him, was inclined to agree with

Mohamed that the beasts must have been stolen. Indeed, after questioning both men closely, he took me aside and suggested that Erbah might not be above suspicion of abetting the theft. This I found hard to believe, for the young fellow had never shown me the slightest ill will, and had seemed to me a trifle dull-witted into the bargain. I doubted very much whether he would have had the initiative to take part in such a coup. But once I realised the deputy Governor's suspicions were pointed at Erbah, the thought crossed my mind that, in view of all that had happened before, Mohamed was a much more likely candidate for camel-rustling. I would, by now, have been surprised at such boldness on his part; but I wondered, for he surely had the cunning to appear concerned about a matter for which he was responsible.

Next day, the two were dispatched very early in the morning to accompany a pair of trackers in a Land Rover. In addition, Abdellahi commandeered a couple of Army *goumiers* mounted on camels themselves, to follow the party in the Land Rover. Their orders were not to return to Néma without my camels and the men who had stolen them.

"I will not have this happening round here," he said. "Particularly to a stranger. It would be a disgrace to our people."

Then, swiftly, all the crises dissolved. That afternoon the camels were found, and they had not been stolen. They had merely wandered off in search of forage much farther than we had known them to go before. At almost the same moment, I found myself embarrassed by a superabundance of money. Abdellahi, impatient for a reply from Nouakchott, had privately arranged for a wealthy trader to give me cash in exchange for some traveller's cheques. No sooner had this transaction been completed than a man came running from the post office to announce that Ahmed's money had arrived. I now had just about twice as much as I had hoped for.

In this glow of affluence I summoned Mohamed into my confidence for the last time. I explained what had just happened and said I was now in a position to let him choose how our contract should end. Either I would buy his air ticket to Tidjikja and give him in cash what I owed him, or else, in addition to his outstanding wages, I would simply hand him the 20,000 francs of the fare, and he could use it as he pleased. I had no doubt at all, beforehand, which course he would fancy most. He could cheaply buy himself a place in a truck that would go down the dirt road linking Mauritania's southern villages below the desert until he came to Kiffa, and there he could doubtless board another vehicle that would take him on to Tidjikja and his coveted camel.

That night I awoke to see him doing something secretively by the shaded light of a flashlight. He had his back turned to both Erbah and me, and he was murmuring quietly to himself, over and over again, "*Ilbamdu Lillab*—In the name of God." He was counting out the notes of the 56,000 francs I had given him. He could never have handled so much money in his life before. If he was careful, he might just be able to buy two camels with it. Even though I disliked the man intensely by now, I could not for the life of me begrudge him this fortune. He was, after all, very poor and I was very rich.

Next morning we parted, and it was a shame that two men who had travelled so far together left each other with so much relief on both sides.

"Well," I said, "buy yourself a good camel, Mohamed."

He barely touched my outstretched hand, muttered a tight-lipped "Good luck," and turned quickly away, scurrying down the street with Erbah like a small boy heading for the sweet shop with his new spending money.

In better spirits than I could remember for a long time, I led the way up the steep hill behind Néma. The little town spread

out below, doped with heat, dusty, lying between the throbbing gravel plain to the north and the parched scrublands to
the south, had given me great relief in the past three days.
Much of this had been Abdellahi's doing, but I had also been
conscious of more concerted warmth flowing towards me
than ever before in Africa. After Mohamed and Erbah had
returned with the vagrant camels, men had hailed me in the
streets with cries of "They've been found!" nodding their
heads and smiling broadly with genuine pleasure. A youth in
the shop where I reprovisioned informed me cheerfully that
he had heard about my coming on the radio and wished me
good luck and safe journey ahead. My morale was enor-
mously raised by this feeling that I had been surrounded by
friends; so many people had shown so much concern for my
well-being that it was as though I had become an adopted
kinsman of the community. All this, and solvency again, set
me on my last stage to Tombouctou eagerly and in good
heart.

The one setback I had received in Néma was doubtless no
more than a passing nuisance. For the first time I was in the
throes of chronic diarrhoea and acute stomach cramps whenever I took food. I was, if anything, merely astonished that I
had not been attacked by such a tummy bug much earlier,
considering what I had been eating and drinking since mid-
November.

I was also coming to the conclusion that in Sid' Ahmed I
might have a companion more suited to my temperament and
needs. True, he had cadged a little from me over and above
his agreed wages and the advances I had given him. Watching
me rearranging my kit in the room one evening, he had
dropped a heavy hint that the weather was sometimes cold in
the desert and that he would welcome a shirt I kept against
the day of my return to civilisation. "*Ana meskeen*—I'm a poor
thing," he had declared, with that awful, wheedling tilt of his

head. And I'd handed the garment over brusquely, rich man morally trapped by the irresistible blackmail of poverty. After much more than one heavy hint, I had given him another 1,000 francs so that he could buy ten cartridges with which, he said, he would shoot us some meat.

We were to travel armed, then, and I wondered whether this was entirely in order to supply our cooking pots. Mohamed had been full of foreboding about the tribesmen I might meet once I was over the border and into Mali; they were, he said, rapacious and vicious, unlike the Moors of his own country. But Mohamed, I well knew, besides being patriotic, was also alarmist, either born that way or bent by trying when he saw some opportunity to gain from it.

Yet in spite of those mannerisms which had put me on my guard and the cadging that followed them up, one thing in Sid' Ahmed had already impressed me a lot. Alone with me after our contract had been made, he had asked what exactly it was that I required of him on this journey. My reply was that essentially I wanted him to do the heavy physical work of handling the camels and baggage, for I had become worn out by the hard riding and marching across Mauritania, whereas he would be fresh. The route-finding, I said, I was prepared to tackle myself.

"Ah, good," said Sid' Ahmed, "for I can lead you to Nbeiket el Ouahch"—a well almost on the border with Mali— "but after that I don't know the way to Tombouctou."

If the man could be as open and straightforward as that before we set off, I thought, he had something that I prized and had missed badly in Mohamed ould Moctar ould Hmeida. Sid' Ahmed, I discovered, had been to Tombouctou just once, many years before, when he was a soldier with the French, but on that occasion he had come to it from Araouane in the north, and had travelled to Néma in a truck by a dirt road far to the south of the direct route across the desert.

So although, as we crested the hill, we walked straight into a fiercely hot head wind that swept across clinging soft sand thickly carpeted with cram-cram, the worst possible combination of conditions, I was buoyant. One year ago to the day, almost to the hour, A and I had been sitting in a café in dear old Harrogate, surrounded by tweedy landladies discussing their winter holidays in the Canaries and Majorca; and then we had gone up Wharfedale, walking from Buckden to Hubberholme on a misty and very still winter's morning. Strange that this blistering season should be called winter, too; without the thermometer I could not be sure of the heat, but my body told me it was probably over 100 degrees F. I could not imagine how any human being might endure the superheat of a summer in the Sahara, yet thousands always did, and even Europeans had been known to travel through the worst of it. When René Caillié joined a caravan of six hundred camels moving north from Tombouctou in 1828, it was May; and when they reached Morocco across the desperate Tanezrouft it had become September. How softened, how enfeebled, I wondered, had Western man been made by his civilisation in the meantime? A European would be thought a suicidal maniac to attempt such a journey today; even great Thesiger and glorious Monod had said as much to me bluntly, when I had canvassed them about crossing Libya after March.

We were moving almost due north ourselves for a couple of days, heading for the tent of Sid' Ahmed, where he could deposit his advanced wages and collect his own camel for the return journey. At the midday halt, two men rode up to share our food and afterwards asked if they might continue with us, for they were travelling to an encampment near Oualata and would need to turn aside from our track only a little way before Sid' Ahmed's tent. We all remounted and rode on at a spanking trot, unbroken for three hours, which left me numb from knees to navel, but fairly shifted some ground beneath our camels' pads.

That night we made a huge fire, for there were many trees and bushes around; and, though it seemed to me much less cold than sometimes on the passage to Néma, I woke once or twice to see somebody or other crouched round the embers, blowing them up into leaping flames, with a blanket round his shoulders to hold the warmth. For a little while I would lie awake before slipping into sleep again, aware of a contentment that had been scarce before. It seemed to me just possible that I might actually enjoy the road to Tombouctou, if this day was something to go by. I had dared eat nothing but a couple of potatoes, part of a few kilos I had bought in Néma to vary the diet of dreary rice, for my bowels had been churning madly. But otherwise there had been little but pleasure so far.

Sid' Ahmed had shown eagerness in everything he did, and that, too, had been foreign to Mohamed's nature. The moment we stopped at midday, my new companion had scrambled like a monkey up the nearest tree with an axe, to chop down the tastiest high branches for the camels. He had been anxious to get going again after the break; it was the shortest halt for food I could remember. He had, most importantly, not attempted to belittle things European in general and me in particular. When the others joined us he clearly did not try to raise a laugh at my still stumbling effort to speak Hassaniya.

In the evening, before we slept, he had asked me if my charts marked all the wells he knew in the region. I reeled off the names one by one . . . Achmim, Tingarn, Tiferguig and the rest. And he, looking concentrated as my finger traced the place of each, replied, "Yes, yes, yes—no, don't know that one—yes, yes—no; ah, yes, but we call it . . ." This was an excellent beginning. If we continued together like this, it should be a good journey.

We rode hard and fast again next day, bade farewell to our

fellow travellers at the midday camp, and reached Sid' Ahmed's tent as the heat was going out of the afternoon. It stood with half a dozen others in a gently rolling landscape of sand and occasional scrub perhaps a day's ride southeast of Oualata, which I had now almost circumnavigated but never seen.

No sooner had we taken tea than Sid' Ahmed lay down, complaining of pain in his back. He had done this twice already since leaving Néma and I had been very cool in my sympathy, fearing that once again I might have picked up a man who made hypochondria the excuse for laziness. I had, in any case, nothing but codeine left to offer him, for the embrocation had long since been rubbed away upon a variety of nomadic aches and pains from one end of Mauritania to the other. Here, however, it was evidently not in demand. Sid' Ahmed summoned his young son, who massaged the father's back with fat. He then took two of the small tea glasses, lit a match in each, and smartly upturned them upon Sid' Ahmed's spine, pressing the rims hard into the flesh. As the flames swiftly died, the vacuum inside each glass clamped it strongly to the body. The boy then moved them up and down the greasy skin, while Sid' Ahmed groaned and winced histrionically; but afterwards he declared that his pain had been much relieved.

Later, in the lambent glow that followed sunset, the people of the encampment said prayers together outside their tents, the men shoulder to shoulder, the women standing a little to one side, the small boys behind their fathers and elder brothers, the girls mixed in with the womenfolk. In that brief space when the lingering blue of the desert sky is swiftly overtaken by shadow and then by darkness, lending every shape a softness and substance that it never knows by the harsh outlining light of day, the people gradually went through the motions of their worship. They bowed deeply, then knelt and submitted their heads to the dust; then rose again for an interval before kneeling once more and kissing the earth.

All this time the senior man at each tent intoned the words of adoration and obeisance . . . *"Bismelleh er Rahman er 'aDheem*—In the name of Allah, the compassionate and merciful . . . *Mahlik yaw medeen*—King of the Day of Judgement . . . *er Deen esseraht el mustaqeem*—lead us into the straight way . . . *walla Dahleen*—and not those who have gone astray . . . *Ahmeen."* But when these people knelt for the last time, it was in silence, and silently they sat there for a while, their faces turned to the eastern darkness, blankly wondering. I had watched this expression on the faces of Italian peasants kneeling before gimcrack statues of the Virgin Mary, and I had seen it stamped upon Mongolian comrades as they stood for hours contemplating the marble blockhouse that shelters Lenin's corpse in Moscow.

I had never known any of my companions in the desert to miss a prayer time, in the morning, at midday, in late afternoon or at nightfall. On such occasions I would wait quietly on one side until they had done, and I had never failed to be moved by their piety and their devotion, which was something far removed from raging fanaticism. Even the truculent Mohamed had been transformed at these moments into a helplessly obedient child-man, who kissed the earth with the same greedy noise that I had once heard from the lips of an old woman after she had crawled with very clumsy dignity to lower her face upon the gaudy star which marks the birthplace of Christ in Bethlehem. There was a verse which A had found for me in the Hebrew of her prayer book among the Psalms that said something of what these people and I together sensed in the tranquillity of the desert prayer times: *"Lo tira mippahad lay'lah, mehetz ya-uf yoman.* . . . You shall not fear the terror of the night, nor the arrow that flies by day:

Because you have made the Lord your refuge, the Most High your habitation. . . ."

I could see very well how the devotion of simple Moslems had turned Charles de Foucauld back to the Catholicism of his youth after years of separation from any faith at all. However repugnant some of Islam's philosophies might seem, like some of Christianity and others of Judaism, the devotion itself was clearly so central to the life of these people and so fortifying in circumstances that were otherwise almost wholly bleak as to incite whatever form of imitation one might manage in good conscience.

I had known the same feeling myself when staying in Christian monasteries, much of whose life was quite intolerable to me, yet containing a central activity and mood with which part of me very strongly wished to identify. Christian monks and Moslem nomads alike were in these postures sharing that proximity to vitality, to truth, to holiness, which I had fleetingly experienced on my visits to the Russian Orthodox in Paris. A prolonged encounter with this mood in the Sahara had made de Foucauld into a hermit-monk himself in the end, a not improbable translation after a swashbuckling life in the cavalry. God alone knew what it would do to me. But on this journey so far, I had found myself frequently wondering a great deal about de Foucauld and about that other deeply faithful but unorthodox Frenchman, Pierre Teilhard de Chardin.

In the months before leaving England, it had occurred to me that I might have to take refuge in fantasies in order to survive moments of impending crisis, or even the merely uncomfortable humdrum of the almost day-to-day. I might have to pretend that I was a second El Aurens (in reality, of course, a second Peter O'Toole portraying Lawrence of Arabia) or another Sir Richard Burton, who had long stood higher than most heroes in my private and wistful pantheon. It would not have been foreign to the nature of someone who, at the age of fourteen, had fondly imagined himself into the position of Nat Lofthouse, centre forward of Bolton and England, and who, in his mid-thirties, was to be found filing dispatches from Czechoslovakia, blissfully aware that he was now as much of a foreign correspondent as any of the fictionalised figures who had so frequently before swirled attractively in the fore-ground of his ambitions.

I had not, so far in the desert, caught myself wearing such fanciful camouflage as might have been provided by the images of Lawrence or Burton. But my attention had become fixed from time to time upon de Foucauld and Teilhard de Chardin. If I was identifying with them at all, it was because they were both men who had made long interior journeys of their own, as well as travelling the hard way across rough parts of the world, as I was myself. I was eager to see civilisa-tion again at the end of my travels for many reasons: one of the smaller, but gradually more pressing, reasons was my desire to reread Teilhard's letters from China and to discover what I could for the first time in de Foucauld's journals of that period when he wandered the northern Sahara before at last finding his anchor-hold near Tamanrasset. Could either of them possibly have experienced within themselves any of the things I felt out here? How did they submit, in what terms precisely, to what they and their Church called the will of God?

And then, with a furtive genuflection towards the greatest traveller of them all, I wondered whether, if Isabel had not made that wretched bonfire of diaries, I might have found that Burton, too, could descend to the trivia which constantly adorned my own notebooks: "As I write that, I watch a louse, drugged with my blood, lumber slowly up the leg of my

infested *serwal*. I am not outraged any longer, merely interested; maybe I'll squash him, maybe not (What's the point
when there are so many more where he came from?). Is this
the beginning of surrender to *Inshallah*?"

At the end of the family worship, with the light now almost
vanished from the sky, Sid' Ahmed ould Eli ould Simmad laid
a hand upon the outermost pole of his tent and fairly bellowed into the night the information that prayers had just
been said in this household, in the name of Allah, the compassionate and merciful. I liked this man. He was upstanding and
he had gusto.

In the morning, he half hinted that we might stay another
night in his tent, and my very firm no made me feel guilty for
a moment. But he seemed to accept the decision as though he
expected no other, and dispatched his two sons to find his
camel out in the pastures. They were gone for hours, for so
long that I began to wonder suspiciously if they had been told
to lose themselves and the beasts until it was too late to start
the day. Sid' Ahmed himself rubbed his face with the contents
of a tin labelled Tarzan's Mustard Ointment (Made in Ghana)
and then disappeared to gossip with the men of the other
tents. His wife and another woman bent over pieces of hide
with knives in their hands, fashioning a fresh pair of sandals
for him. I examined his aged and double-barrelled shotgun,
and the cartridges that went with it. In Néma he had implied
that unless I provided some, he would have no ammunition at
all, but here in his tent was a bag containing about fifty cartridges, a remarkable assortment of colours and balls, manu-
factured variously in Mali, France, Italy and Poland. I hoped
that he would be carrying the new ones I had bought, for
some of these looked very old and insecure.

By the time the boys returned it was past noon and, a lamb
having been slaughtered for our journey, everyone gobbled at

its entrails almost steaming from the carcass. I picked cautiously at a small piece of liver and wondered how long it
would be before my ailment cleared up. I was loath to use the
drugs I was carrying except in case of dire need, but, the way
things were shaping, that point might not be far off.

We got away at three o'clock, and I had not known such
warmth in a desert farewell. At Mafud's camp and throughout
my time with Mohamed, I had often reflected how curious it
was that, although people fairly flocked to greet someone
arriving, they paid scarcely any attention when he departed. It
was not so here, however. As I led the camels away from the
tents, Sid' Ahmed walked slowly some distance behind, surrounded by his kinsmen and their women. The men pressed
their hands upon his and put their arms round him. A
woman, walking alongside, carefully made signs across the
palm of his hand with her rosary. Children danced and
waved, shouting his name over and over. Sid' Ahmed himself
responded to all this affection with wide-eyed pleasure, flashing his smile like a boy after collecting his prize at the school
speech day. Yes, I did like this man. I was very glad to be travelling with him.

We rode for two hours and then, seeing a tent just ahead,
Sid' Ahmed suggested that we might camp here for the night.
His style was much different from Mohamed's. There was no
riding arrogantly up to this dwelling, as of right. We stopped
two hundred yards away and unloaded our baggage. After a
while a woman and a small boy appeared, bringing a mat and
some milk. We arranged our possessions round the mat for a
windbreak, made a fire and, while the teapot was brewing, I
medicated a baby which the woman brought from her tent, its
crotch badly chafed and blistered. Later a man joined us for
our evening meal. The other day, he said, not far away, a
"lion" had killed seven goats in one night. Certainly it could

not have been a proper lion, and the presence of any predatory cat in this part of the world, so far north of the Niger
River system, seemed most unlikely to me. But just before we
slept, Sid' Ahmed vowed that he had himself shot a "lion"
only a month before. He described it as a brown creature
about four feet long and maybe two and a half feet high, with
a smooth and unruffled fur, which made it sound like some
puma or cougar. I had no idea whether it was theoretically
possible to find such animals even in the scrub which grows
profusely on this southern edge of the Sahara. This was so
thick in the area of our camp as to put me in mind of an everlasting and abandoned golf course, devoid of greens and fair-
ways, but overendowed with thousands of sandy bunkers.

The next day was unpleasant. I had never really shaken
off the bronchial cold that had attacked me on leaving
Chinguetti, and we now found ourselves riding directly into a
strong wind from the east, which seemed to drive straight
through my nostrils, setting them aflame. My inability to eat
much was beginning to take the stuffing out of me, so that I
was riding like a sack of potatoes again, barely able to sit
straight in the saddle after an hour or so. Walking, too, was a
penance, for the cram-cram was thick upon the ground and
the burrs were a perpetual irritation upon the legs. By the time
we were ready to mount, both in the morning and the afternoon, we spent about twenty minutes picking them from our
garments, taking anything up to fifty from my *serwal* alone.

We had one mishap after another. First, a tin mug, which
I had inadequately secured, disappeared. Then a bag, tied on
by Sid' Ahmed, plunged to the ground, smashing more ciga-
rettes and leaving an awful mess of bits and pieces inside its
battered canvas. Finally, and much worse, there was a sudden
gusher below the left flank of my camel, and as I struggled
to control the startled beast, I looked down to see the water

pouring out of a *guerba* and onto the sand. It was the only skin we had jointly heaved up into place, and we exchanged exasperated looks without a word. With three others still well filled, the loss was not serious, for Nbeiket el Ouahch was no more than three days ahead. But I made a decisive mental note that such a thing must never happen again.

We camped again with nomads, and I was glad to crawl into someone's tent without the need to set up our own refuge for the night. I was somewhere beyond mere weariness and approaching real exhaustion, for several parts of my body were not functioning as they ought to. I found myself blinking rapidly to bring things into focus, and my limbs were trembling with excessive fatigue. As I lay limply on a mat I fervently hoped that the weakening of my flesh would not seep into my spirit, enfeebling it so much that I would give up and go home at the next opportunity. That evening and night was one of intermittent sleep, sporadic awareness, haphazard thoughts. I emerged from a doze to perceive the movements of people eating food which I had refused, to avoid the scalding pains which would instantly have followed digestion. In my hunger, I had dwelt much on my stomach during the day, my imagination floundering towards oases of European cooking. Once, before Néma, I had been dazzled by a vision of gooseberry pie; now I began seriously to consider the respective merits of bread and cheese, rich French stews and sticky Danish pastries (I knew the very shop in Hampstead where I would buy some the moment I reached home).

Sleep again, then consciousness once more at 11 P.M. As I looked at my watch, with its tiny calendar, I reflected on the different time scales of existence. At home it was based upon the hour: "In an hour I must be . . . a couple of hours ago I was . . ." Everything was immediate there. Here, one went by the month: "It is now ten days past the beginning of

January ... at twenty-three days towards the end of the month I shall be ..." The immensity of everything here, including time. Sleep yet again until just after two o'clock. The sound, unmistakably, of an owl hunting. Well, why not? There were other birds about. There were hares, too, for we had started three or four from their hiding places during the day. As always, there had also been small khaki lizards scuttling over the ground, leaving their foot-dappled, tail-trailing marks in the sand. Plenty of food for an owl.

Halfway through the next morning, we were jogging gently along when an enormous bird rose cumbersomely into the air from behind a nearby bush. It was brown, white and black, and its wingspan looked greater than the distance I could have stretched with both arms extended. Sid' Ahmed shouted "Bustard!" and reached for the gun lodged in the wing of his saddle. The bird had cruised through the air a little way and gone to ground again, though just where I could not see. Still riding, we began to circle the area, and I was searching the bushes as keenly as my companion. In Europe I would have been horrified at the idea of killing a wild bird, but now I was beginning to smack my lips at the prospect of roasting over a fire something that resembled a large turkey; it was yet another small fall from civilisation. Suddenly, Sid' Ahmed threw the gun to his shoulder and fired—and the bustard rose from the ground, unhurt, no more than ten yards in front of us, and flapped heavily away over the trees. Without question, I was disappointed, and Sid' Ahmed was sucking his teeth ruefully. Only the camels were unmoved by the encounter. Not one of them had shown the slightest reaction to the gunshot.

By the time we reached Nbeiket el Ouahch, the drugs seemed to have taken some effect, stanching a little the flow of my bowels. But I was still feeling so wasted that an hour or

two of riding had me reeling in the saddle, and I almost fell
over when I dismounted. We had pushed on east through a
succession of mornings more bitterly cold than any I could
remember, the wind howling into our faces till almost midday,
freezing and slashing even through the headcloths we wound
tightly round everything but our eyes. We had suffered
another mishap. Twice in one day, when riding too close
together, the legs of the cooking pot lashed behind Sid'
Ahmed's saddle had snagged in my baggage, threatening to
tear something adrift, and I had warned him to keep a distance. When we stopped for his afternoon prayers, I found
that one of my sandals had vanished from where the pair normally dangled when riding; almost certainly it had been
wrenched off in one of our collisions. I groaned at the loss but
could not be angry, for Sid' Ahmed immediately volunteered
to ride back the way we had come, to look for it—a pointless
exercise in that scrubby ground, like searching for the needle
in the haystack.

The well itself was much more sophisticated than any I
had seen so far, including Touijinit. It not only had a deep
concrete shaft, with four outlying troughs for watering many
beasts, but was equipped with a wooden pulley at the angle of
each trough. A camel was hitched to the rope running over
each pulley and driven away from the well to haul the bucket
up. Judging by the distance each went before the bucket
reached the surface and the animal was turned and brought
back to the shaft head, the well must have been about 150 feet
deep. It had been bored, what's more, through the top of a
hillock, so that the liquefied muck which surrounded any
watering place would tend to drain away and reduce the
chances of pollution almost to nil. As we came up to it, half a
dozen men were drawing water for a herd of camels, the ones
standing by the shaft shouting loudly to those leading the
haulage beasts as the buckets surfaced, squirting jets in all

directions from their leaky leather sides. As well as warning their mates to turn back again, they seemed to be enjoying the shrieking echoes they were producing from deep inside the shaft.

We made camp with these men, and once more I found myself warming to Sid' Ahmed for his attitude towards me in front of others. Far from inflicting the petty humiliations that I had occasionally experienced before, he seemed actually to be proud of his relationship with me.

"When this Nasrani," he told them, "flew from England to Africa he was sitting in the sky for six hours!"

And they all shook their heads and clicked their tongues at the fantastic nature of this feat; aeroplanes they seemed to understand, but to stay in the sky for six whole hours was obviously regarded as some unconnected form of the miraculous.

I then heard my companion extolling my excellence as a navigator, which at that stage was more than a large assumption on his part, for I had done nothing but keep a compass check over ground that he knew well enough by heart. "Tell them," he said with massive confidence, "tell them which way it is to Tombouctou."

I drew the chart from its case, fiddled with the protractor, found the bearing with my compass and flung an arm out decisively across the sand and scrub that surrounded us monotonously.

"Eeehhh!" they all said, with definite approval.

Sid' Ahmed beamed like a man whose favourite poodle has just won the dog show against most of the popular odds. I seemed, *Ilhamdu Lillah*, to have got it right. I noticed, nonetheless, that before, we moved away, Sid' Ahmed was careful to inquire about the route to the well of In Kerchouf, two days over the border.

We probably crossed the frontier sometime during the next morning, January 12, two men and three camels simply

moving from one arbitrary longitude to another with an
uncertainty that mocked territorial possessions and international politics. There was nothing at all to tell us at any
given hour whether we were still in Mauritania's share of the
wilderness or Mali's. Yet some things were beginning to
change. The camels we had seen at Nbeiket el Ouahch
seemed stockier than those I had encountered in the past two
months. Their humps were indisputably firmer and more
upright with fat; they looked better fed than most I had seen
so far.

At the well I had also discovered a different kind of saddle
for the first time. The Mauritanian *rahhla* was large and rather
cumbersome, with high side wings and a backpiece to match,
as well as a sturdy pommel in front, the whole usually much
decorated on a basically yellow ground. Riding in one of these
was a bit like sitting in a bucket. The saddle used in southern
Mali, on the other hand, was comparatively light, without
sides, with a very slender piece of wood to hold onto in
front and an equally high panel to rest against at the back.
Without the pommel it was basically a legless chair mounted
on the camel's back, quite without decoration. I was later to
see that it involved a different method of mounting, the rider
invariably twisting the beast's head round so that he could
hold it firmly by its lower lip, while he cocked his leg into the
saddle without the acrobatic leap that the Mauritanian *rahhla*
demanded. And because of the structural difference, as much
as anything, men in this part of the Sahara tended to ride with
their feet resting on the nape of the camel's neck, which consequently acquired a bald patch there as often as not.

The days now telescoped into a sequence of pain, of
hunger and of blinding exhaustion. Only thirst was missing
from the perpetual agonies of travel, for our supply of water
was secure. From Nbeiket el Ouahch we dragged on to In

Kerchouf, then to El Basriye, then to Tin Fata, and there were never more than a couple of days between any of these wells. One never suffered more than the bitter and gummy dryness of the mouth that invariably began within half an hour or so of drinking deeply from the canteen I had slung from my saddle. Otherwise, I was rapidly sinking into something close to a physical wreck, compared with the lusty individual who had left Nouakchott in the middle of November. There were raw and weeping patches of flesh spreading everywhere from my ribs to my thighs. A network of sores had broken out upon my face. Curious blisters had started to appear upon the backs of my fingers and hands, oozing pus instead of fluid.

Resentfully I scrutinised this damage, contemplating my body with growing distaste. The anticipated, dramatic nightmares about this journey had not so far materialised, but now all manner of sublimated fears rose to the surface. Not only were precious possessions slowly falling to bits—the kit bags worn into holes through constant friction, the map case unstitched and coming apart, the books badly tattered and torn—but my body, cared for and enjoyed so much over the years, was becoming unrecognisable as a source of vanity. Oh, yes, one feared these things very much: the loss of possessions and the loss of beauty.

The drugs no longer seemed capable of holding my sickness in check. When I had gone without food for a day before Néma, I had realised how slender my resources of energy had become. Unless the body could receive some nourishment every few hours, it wilted alarmingly in these conditions. Now, nothing that I ate remained in the body for more than a quarter of an hour or so; it was evacuated long before it could do me any good. I was existing on liquids alone and the almost wholly emotional comfort of masticating a few dates, a boiled potato, a handful of rice or a fragment of meat. I could only guess what my condition would have been without the invigorating refreshment of highly sweetened tea and coffee. As it was, by the time we were half way to Tombouctou, I knew that I was in deep trouble.

A succession of brief but vivid cameos lodged in my consciousness during these days. There was a night when we camped with nomads whose tents had been pitched in a deep basin of sand. A great fire had been built up in the ground between them. Every time I woke, a group of sheep was huddled motionless, sitting or standing, around this fire, their glass-eyed, slightly anxious faces glowing in the yellow light. There was something instantly recognisable in the posture of the sheep, in the light upon their bodies, in the tranquillity of the moment. Dozily my mind groped for the origin of the painting in which I had seen it all before, but I drifted away again before deciding whether it was something in the National Gallery at home, or one of the Le Nains in the Louvre.

There was an afternoon when we rode up to a small camp where three men lounged and a woman sat apart, nursing a baby so new that it was still pink. We paused to exchange a greeting before riding on, but the men seemed anxious that we should stay and talk. Supposing that they wanted tea and sugar, we dismounted, Sid' Ahmed murmuring that it would be a good chance to obtain information about the lie of the land ahead. One of the men was wearing a European coat over his boubou, and this strangeness made me uneasy. All three continued to stare at me, while they talked with Sid' Ahmed about the lack of *ghudda* to the north, the plenty to the south. As Sid' Ahmed handed the first glass to the man in the coat, asking him to pass it to his mate, the fellow made an insolent gesture to my companion with his mouth, which Sid' Ahmed appeared not to notice. But as the third round of glasses was being poured out, I sensed that he was suddenly intent on getting away quickly. We had done nothing but remove the kettle and tea things from our baggage, leaving the camels couched and loaded, so we were off with little delay. As we mounted, out of earshot, Sid' Ahmed muttered that it was dangerous to stay; one of the men had asked him whether the Nasrani was carrying much money. We must ride fast, to get away from this camp, he said. And we did ride fast, at an appalling gallop for the best part of two hours, until the sun was almost set and I all but unconscious in the saddle.

There was another evening when we rested with some friendly people who put up a small tent of hides for our bene-fit, and then produced a great stream of children and old men, all suffering from eye infections. I was squeezing tetracycline across the lids of the prettiest child I had seen for months, a slim and delicate girl with pigtails hanging to her waist, when I suddenly fell over, half swooning away. Dizzily, I staggered behind some bushes to be ill again. It was the first time since reaching the desert that I could remember being drenched with sweat, which sprang out of every pore in my body in an almighty rush.

Then my camel, the twelve-year-old bull I had ridden down from Tidjikja, started to founder. After stumbling a little one day before Néma, he had carried on as well as before. But since leaving Sid' Ahmed's tent, he had begun to show signs of growing tiredness. Once or twice, after being unloaded, he had seemed reluctant to rise again and start browsing. After our furious gallop away from the camp of the sinister three, he had been limping in the left foreleg, which had troubled him before Néma. Sid' Ahmed suggested cutting the leg above or below the knee joint and letting out some blood, which, he said, was a well-known remedy for lameness. I had refused to allow this at first. Next day, we travelled very softly, but even so my bull and I were trailing badly. Sid' Ahmed, leading the spare camel by its headrope, kept looking back anxiously to see how the two sick creatures behind were doing. When he asked my permission to bleed the bull, I agreed, telling myself that perhaps there was pus on the leg that ought to be drained.

We couched the beast and I held down its lower lip with one hand, covering its right eye with the other, hauling its head round parallel with its neck so that it would be unable to see out of the other eye, too. Sid' Ahmed slashed it above both knee caps, then cut it deeply at the shoulder of its right fore-leg. The poor creature scarcely struggled at all when this happened; it really had very little energy left. But it got to its feet without much trouble, blood streaming everywhere. There was no question of riding it now; the question seemed to be whether we could get it to Tombouctou, which was at least five days away.

An hour later the bull fell down, his forelegs giving way beneath him. With Sid' Ahmed hauling on his headrope and with me kicking him hard behind, we got him up. We put him between the other two camels, fastened headropes to saddles, and led them in line ahead for half an hour. Then the rope which Sid' Ahmed was hauling pulled taut with sudden strain, the rope behind broke in two, and the sick bull was down on his knees again before settling on all fours. We got him up once more, spliced the broken headrope and started off. Almost immediately, the same thing happened again. Again we got him moving, and this time he kept going until we made camp for the night.

I was badly spent myself by now. I had drunk a mug of coffee before starting the day's march, I had eaten a boiled potato at noon, which had gone straight through me, and I had sipped a round of tea. Sid' Ahmed ordered me to lie down while he unloaded and hobbled the camels singlehanded. I lay like a log while this splendid, bandy-legged fellow arranged our camp, collected wood for a fire, made it up, brewed tea, did everything himself.

I raised myself on an elbow as he offered me the first glass. "You're a good man, Sid' Ahmed," I said.

His head tilted to one side in that mannerism I had associated with wheedling. I realised now that essentially it betrayed embarrassment. "You're a good man yourself, *sayyid*," he replied.

Quickly, I turned my head away from him. I could feel the tears springing into my eyes, starting to roll down my scarecrow cheeks. There had been something terrible but very beautiful in that gesture of his. It was as though the thought that he was a decent human being had never crossed his mind before.

The next day, January 16, we marched for almost two hours, much longer than usual, having some vague intention of sparing the sick bull with a reduced pace. After a mile or so I stumbled and fell. For a fraction of a moment, as I collected my breath on hands and knees, I was of two minds whether to get to my feet again or lie down properly and rest for a little while. I hauled myself up and carried on walking. Some time later I fell again. This happened two or three times, until Sid' Ahmed insisted that I mount his own stocky bull, on which he would return to his camp from Tombouctou, while he walked with the other two. I scarcely noticed the relief from marching, for the pain from my body sores was now intensified by the rubbing jerks of the saddle. I realised, in a moment of coherence between the blurring waves of torment, that I was holding onto the pommel, as I had not done since my prentice days of riding, in an effort to reduce the strain upon my body. My hands were clutching it as fiercely, as weakly, as an infant

holds onto a security when it is learning the first spastic movements of walking.

I tried to think of my children setting off to school, of J
dashing round the house to get them away on time, of A walking down a hill to catch a bus for work. Normally, the vacuum
hours of a day's journey were much relieved by such
thoughts. I would linger over them fondly to make them last,
and sometimes I would start talking audibly, asking these two
women in my life what they were doing this day, explaining to
the children something that I was seeing for them and wished
to convey at once. It was my lifeline, without which I would
be lost, and it was a promise that the dreariness and discomfort of this journey would not go on forever, that one day I
would have done with it and return, that what I cared for
most deeply went on without me and would be there awaiting
me at the end. It was assurance and insurance, both.

But now I could not even focus the images of home for
more than a split second. They flicked into my consciousness
and were gone again, and I had neither the strength nor the
will to hold them to me, to retrieve them from the blankness
that encircled me. They seemed to have lost their power and
their hold upon me. They had no meaning in this blinding
struggle to go on. They were irrelevant. Even food was irrelevant now. I could no longer identify my stomach-empty pain.
Body was pain and it had no separate parts. I wanted release,
nothing more. I wanted to sleep, nothing beyond.

I reined in the bull and made him couch. I got myself out
of the saddle and began my tottering walk forward again. If
I stumbled and fell now, I would go to sleep. I knew it. I
desired it. I think I almost willed it. But we then walked over a
low dune and saw two tents in the hollow beneath. It was
hardly past midmorning but Sid' Ahmed, I saw, was already
couching the other two beasts and removing their gear. We

stayed there all day and I lay without moving for hours at a time, with my boubou billowed about me like a tent to ward off the great heat that had now overcome the days of glacial cold. This was the only distinct advantage in what was otherwise a quite impossible garment. The people in the camp gave me some milk, and towards the evening I was revived a little, though otherwise I ate nothing.

On January 17 we marched again. I fell down once, the sick bull twice. At some stage in the day we reached the well of Tin Fata and I, sitting dazed under a tree, could hear Sid' Ahmed asking three men if they had a camel they could sell. But he returned from the wellhead without a word, and we marched on to the southeast.

Next day, we lost the sick bull. We had walked for three hours when, without warning, he fell down again. This time we couldn't get him up. After we had hauled on his nose ring, as always, and offered him kicks from behind, as we had done before, Sid' Ahmed unhitched a *guerba* and brought it over to the beast. Then he poured water into its nostrils in a rushing jet, while the bull strained laboriously to get its head out of the way. More hauling and kicking, and still he wouldn't budge. Sid' Ahmed drew his knife and, before I realised what he intended, he had jabbed it into the animal's side. I sharply ordered him to stop, as the blood began to flow, the bull having merely uttered a grunt and twitched along the flank. Sid' Ahmed turned away and began to cast around the area for wood. I supposed he had decided that we should make camp, to see if a rest might revive the camel enough to go on. But when he returned with an armful of firewood, he dumped it alongside the sitting beast and asked me for the matches. What, I asked, was he going to do? Sid' Ahmed replied that sometimes a fire would make an exhausted animal rise when everything else failed; it hurt more than a knife.

I shook my head. "No," I said, "we're not going to do that."

Sid' Ahmed gestured impatiently. "Then he's finished," he said.

"Then we must leave him," I replied. I was remembering the two camels I had seen—how long ago it seemed—which had been abandoned on the brink of the well of Chig.

Sid' Ahmed removed the animal's headrope and the few small things it had been carrying. I could see that he was very cross with me. How long would it be, I asked, before the bull died? Sid' Ahmed shrugged. Perhaps the bull would sit there for two days, manage to get up and browse a bit, then slowly regain his strength. But probably not. "He's finished, that one," he said.

We mounted the other two camels and slowly rode away. I did not look back. I was blank about this, too.

We were now heading for the northern shore of Lac Faguibine, which had seemed in prospect a pretty implausible thing to find anywhere within the limits of the Sahara Desert. But every chart clearly marked this wedge-shaped sheet of water, about fifty miles long and ten miles across at its wider end. I knew it to be of comparatively recent origin, for the German explorer Heinrich Barth, who travelled in this area in the 1850s, observed only that the village of Ras-el-Ma lay at the head of a creek connected to the Niger River system; and Ras-el-Ma now evidently looked down the full extent of the lake from its westernmost end. The question in my mind had been whether the lake would be dried up when I reached it, but the men Sid' Ahmed had talked to at Tin Fata said that this was not so. They called it "the sea."

Almost as soon as we left the dying bull, we entered a region quite unlike anything I had seen before. The ground was still basically one of extremely shallow, undulating sand dunes. But now it became thickly forested with thorn trees.

They were set so close together that, mounted, we found ourselves swerving sharply to avoid being swept off by the branches. They were pitifully poor in green leaves, but it seemed to me that, given a week's heavy rain in these parts, they would have had something as lush as the Forest of Arden here. As it was, the place was eery with a blessed gloom which protected us from the sun's burning. I was but dimly aware of gratitude, for my mind was clamped ferociously on the twenty yards immediately ahead of my camel and the need to hang onto my seat.

We had almost trampled into a small encampment before we knew it lay there in a clearing. Here were dwellings which spoke of Black Africa, not the desert: tipsy hutments made of rattan sheets and bundles of thorn. A girl stood naked to the waist, motionless after she had turned her back on us. Sid' Ahmed ignored her completely, but addressed the hutments with *"Selebmoo alaikum,"* though there was no one else in sight. Nothing stirred, and there was no response. We rode on, twisting and turning around the trees again, the thorny branches scratching our arms and plucking at our garments.

Then it lay before us, this miracle of water. We trotted towards a dense belt of shade, like many we had already passed, but on the farther side, instead of dappled light, there was dazzling, glinting glare. Immediately ahead was a flat, white, sandy shore, maybe 500 yards deep. Beyond that, utterly smooth, the water. Here and there were tiny islands, covered in green vegetation. Two dugouts were fishing a few hundred yards offshore. To the west, the lake evaporated in a shimmering haze of heat. To the east, a few miles away, was a ridge of low rocky hills, and the lake at that end so much reminded me of a Scottish loch that I wanted to embrace everything I could see in one great enveloping hug.

Slowly our camels walked up the shore towards those hills,

and there we came upon a marvellous thing. At the foot of the hills was a tiny bay, fringed with green trees and rushes. On its farther shore some children were bathing, scuttering the water up into each other's faces and squealing with laughter. A heron was standing up to his knees, peering steadily at the surface. An egret stood quietly some way off, on the edge of the rushes.

Sid' Ahmed wanted to refill the *guerbas*, but we already had enough water to last us four or five days at a pinch, and Tombouctou should be only a couple of days away now, so I forbade him to. I suspected that Lac Faguibine might breed the flukes of bilharzia; otherwise I would have stripped off and bathed myself. So we sat there for a little while, while the camels drank deeply, and then we walked quietly past the hills to make our camp for the night among the lushest trees I had seen since Europe.

That night I wrote in my notebook; "'I will lift up mine eyes unto the hills, from whence cometh my help.' It's always been one of the loveliest Psalms. Tonight it perfectly expresses what I've felt this past hour or two. The last few days have been so awful, we're not out of the wood yet, I'm a half wreck of an exhausted man but, by God, my spirits have come up off the deck again. My thanks."

I wrote that too soon. I should not have been so enthusiastic about the hills. Next morning I decided that we must cross them, to shorten the time to Tombouctou, though Sid' Ahmed was in favour of taking a longer but easier way round the back. At a distance I had thought them to consist of nothing but rock. Now, on their flank, it was obvious that we were facing a 600-foot dune of sand extending between two proper cliffs of stone. Almost as soon as we started, the incline became something like one in three. The sand was soft, the beasts were in difficulty from the beginning and, though we were not really hauling them up the slope, the strain on the headropes felt like it most of the time. Sid' Ahmed, reaching the top before I was even halfway up, came slithering down to help me bring my camel up to his.

We mounted for the descent down the other side, which was hardly less steep, but the flaming agony of my sores with the rub, rub, rub of the saddle and the jolting of the gait was such that I couched my camel and dismounted before reaching the bottom. I had walked no more than a few hundred yards when I pitched forward and lay there, shaken, without the energy to rise again, not even wanting to make the effort. I raised my head. Sid' Ahmed was some distance away, riding slowly, waiting for me to catch up. Foolish man, he didn't know that I wasn't going to this time. Sleep was what I wanted, what I would have now. My head went down on my arms again and I could feel my body relaxing beautifully. Then a voice somewhere above me was curtly saying that I must get up and move on. I paid no attention. I was supremely uninterested. The voice insisted and began to irritate me. It would not stop haranguing me; it was breaking my wonderful peace.

I heard Sid' Ahmed hissing his camel to couch. Murderously my head came up. How dare this little shit take it upon himself to disturb me when I wished to be left alone? Then I was on all fours, hurling obscenities at him in English, hauling myself to my feet in mid-flow of my shrieking invective. The little bastard now had a half grin of superiority on his rotten wheedling face; he was in the saddle again, waving his arms forward imperiously and shouting, "Come on, advance, advance!" as though he were talking to a dog. Still shouting my oaths, I dragged my camel up so that I could mount and pursue this appalling little tick to tell him what I really thought of him and his God-awful self-inflated image of himself.

At midday, camped beside some bushes, I wondered whether I would have lain in the sand for good if I had been travelling alone. Sid' Ahmed, who had conceivably just saved my life, paused before downing the third glass of tea. "Tomorrow night, *Inshallah*, Tombouctou." Then he grinned at me with God's face.

We had just crossed a desolate plain, which had followed the steep ridge of rock and sand, in a high wind that was laced with dust from the open desert. There were blackened stalks of corn standing in long files, the useless remnant of a crop which either drought or ·disease had wiped out. There were humpy tents made of grasses bundled across sapling frameworks and, as we rode past one of them, three small boys looked up from a game they were playing. The largest urchin, his black and naked body almost whitened by the dust, rose and laughed at us. Then he broke into a loose-limbed dance on the spot, his legs dangling from side to side like a marionette's, perfectly mimicking the swinging and lopsided gait of the camels.

Occasionally we passed men riding beasts which were much more richly decorated than those of Mauritania; they were geared with halters tricked out with woolly tufts, tiny bells and brasswork. The men themselves wore broadswords at their belts, their scabbards gaudily coloured green and scarlet. Two or three carried long spears as well. We passed one man on foot who had a bow and some arrows slung across his back. There was not a flicker of hostility from these people, but there was almost complete indifference to our presence. No one altered course to come and speak with us, which was the unvarying rule in the open desert; if we met by chance, we exchanged a *"Selebmoo alaikum"* and nothing more, without stopping. Sid' Ahmed, I noticed, had no inclination to converse with them. I sensed that he, wholly of the desert, was ill at ease among these people who lived on its edge and who belonged, even more, to the Black Africa of the savannah away to the south.

We left the plain and people behind, we made our midday camp alone and we continued our way across shallow sand dunes well covered in scrub. At first we walked for a while, Sid' Ahmed soon outstripping my pedestrian meander, which had become so slow that the camel I was supposed to be leading was padding close behind me, his neck looming over my head. In an effort to jerk some morale into my fading spirit and some vitality into my tired body, I began to hum "The British Grenadier."

It was exactly the wrong choice of music. Among other things, it had been the regimental marching tune of the old Lancashire Fusiliers, in which my grandfather had been an undistinguished but very proud lance-corporal long before I was born. More times than I could remember, when I was a child and the tune had been played on the radio, Grandad would stiffen a little at the sound and announce, with a gleam in his damp old eyes, "I've marched thousands of miles across the desert to that tune," by which he probably meant a number of ceremonial parades upon the South African veldt in the Boer War. As I hummed the first few bars, I remembered all this again and burst into tears, weeping uncontrollably for several minutes, very thankful for once that Sid' Ahmed was so far ahead that he couldn't possibly see what was going on. I was crying for so many things. For my present abysmal state, for my loneliness, for the memory of that gentle old man, with his obvious jokes and his dogged loyalty to the Fusiliers and the six VCs which, I must never forget, they had won before breakfast in the assault on Gallipoli.

I was crying, too, I think, from a sense of shame, for he had come home from two wars to support a blind wife, a divorced daughter and a small grandson and had not failed one of them at any time, while I, who had not been to any war, had failed so many people. I wished, through this mixture of tears, that Grandad were still alive to know that I was slogging through the desert; I wanted to be told that he might have been proud of that, too.

We made camp that night in the sandy scrub. Sid' Ahmed sniffed the air and said that there were people camping nearby, but we saw no one. In the desert, he said, a man could smell a campfire anything up to three miles away. He began to put henna on the fingertips of his left hand, to restore the red stain that was almost faded away. It was his preparation for our arrival in Tombouctou. He was the only man I had seen decorating himself thus, and when I asked him why he painted his left hand, but not his right, he said it was because he was left-handed.

We cooked our last piece of meat in the embers of the fire, such a gritty, dried-up lump of gristle as I would not have thrown to a pet animal in England—it looked like something dropped behind the stove while cooking, to be discovered weeks later and pitched rapidly, with much distaste, into the rubbish bin. But I was very hungry, I needed anything that would nourish and I wolfed it down greedily, hoping that the after-effects would not be more than usually unpleasant.

Next day, January 20, we rode into thorn trees again. They were not as close-set as in the forest before Lac Faguibine, but they reduced the visibility ahead to no more than a few hundred yards. After the midday camp, we came upon the first wheel tracks since Néma and began to watch eagerly for the first sign of habitation. Tombouctou, one of the world's fabulous place-names, was close at hand, and I ought to have been tingling with the excitement of this landfall. But my eagerness had nothing to do with the fable; I was looking hard for a refuge from the desert, a place where I could rest and repair my body. It could have borne the dullest name on earth and I would have ridden into it with boundless gratitude.

Uncharacteristically, I was the first to spot it. A pale flash above the treeline caught my eye, and I realised I was looking at a tall cylinder of corrugated iron, possibly a water tower, maybe a mile away. It was probably part of the local airstrip, for we rode another hour along the wheel tracks before we saw anything else. Then gradually the trees around us parted and Tombouctou came into full view. In the diminishing light of late afternoon it seemed to be a grey place, not white as I had somehow imagined it. Nor was it walled, as I had expected, though the strong horizontal lines of the buildings suggested something of fortification. Only the conical tower of the mosque stood vertically above this lateral sweep. In the foreground, before the buildings began, was a great hollow in the sand, and here many men were busy making stacks of muddy grey bricks.

We reined in our camels and paused a moment before dismounting. I looked across at my companion, who was studying the walls beyond the brickworkers. "Well," I said, "we got there."

"*Inshallah*," said Sid' Ahmed, still looking to his front. He tilted his head, more dramatically than usual. "*Ilhamdu Lillah! Ilhamdu Lillah!*"

Postscript: Six months after he began, Geoffrey Moorhouse arrived at the Trans-Saharan Highway in Libya, many miles short of his original goal of the Nile River but grateful to be alive.

John Wesley Powell's epic 1869 expedition down the Colorado
River through the Grand Canyon is one of the greatest stories
of the American West. With nine men and four wooden boats,
Major Powell set out from Green River, Wyoming, to explore
territory and rapids never before viewed by human eyes. This
is adventure on a grand scale.

THE EXPLORATION
OF THE COLORADO RIVER
AND ITS CANYONS

J. W. POWELL

August 13.—*We are now ready*
to start on our way down the Great Unknown. Our boats,
tied to a common stake, chafe each other as they are tossed by
the fretful river. They ride high and buoyant, for their loads
are lighter than we could desire. We have but a month's
rations remaining. The flour has been resifted through the
mosquito-net sieve; the spoiled bacon has been dried and the
worst of it boiled; the few pounds of dried apples have been
spread in the sun and reshrunken to their normal bulk. The
sugar has all melted and gone on its way down the river. But
we have a large sack of coffee. The lightening of the boats has
this advantage; they will ride the waves better and we shall
have but little to carry when we make a portage.

We are three quarters of a mile in the depths of the earth, and the great river shrinks into insignificance as it dashes its angry waves against the walls and cliffs that rise to the world above; the waves are but puny ripples, and we but pigmies, running up and down the sands or lost among the boulders.

We have an unknown distance yet to run, an unknown river to explore. What falls there are, we know not; what rocks beset the channel, we know not; what walls rise over the river, we know not. Ah, well! we may conjecture many things. The men talk as cheerfully as ever; jests are bandied about freely this morning; but to me the cheer is somber and the jests are ghastly.

With some eagerness and some anxiety and some misgiving we enter the canyon below and are carried along by the swift water through walls which rise from its very edge. They have the same structure that we noticed yesterday—tiers of irregular shelves below, and, above these, steep slopes to the foot of marble cliffs. We run six miles in a little more than half an hour and emerge into a more open portion of the canyon, where high hills and ledges of rock intervene between the river and the distant walls. Just at the head of this open place the river runs across a dike; that is, a fissure in the rocks, open to depths below, was filled with eruptive matter, and this on cooling was harder than the rocks through which the crevice was made, and when these were washed away the harder volcanic matter remained as a wall, and the river has cut a gateway through it several hundred feet high and as many wide. As it crosses the wall, there is a fall below and a bad rapid, filled with boulders of trap; so we stop to make a portage. Then on we go, gliding by hills and ledges, with distant walls in view; sweeping past sharp angles of rock; stopping at a few points to examine rapids, which we find can be run, until we have made another five miles, when we land for dinner.

Then we let down with lines over a long rapid and start

again. Once more the walls close in, and we find ourselves in a narrow gorge, the water again filling the channel and being very swift. With great care and constant watchfulness we proceed, making about four miles this afternoon, and camp in a cave.

August 14.—At daybreak we walk down the bank of the river, on a little sandy beach, to take a view of a new feature in the canyon. Heretofore hard rocks have given us bad river; soft rocks, smooth water; and a series of rocks harder than any we have experienced sets in. The river enters the gneiss! We can see but a little way into the granite gorge, but it looks threatening.

After breakfast we enter on the waves. At the very introduction it inspires awe. The canyon is narrower than we have ever before seen it; the water is swifter; there are but few broken rocks in the channel; but the walls are set, on either side, with pinnacles and crags; and sharp, angular buttresses, bristling with wind and wave polished spires, extend far out into the river.

Ledges of rock jut into the stream, their tops sometimes just below the surface, sometimes rising a few or many feet above; and island ledges and island pinnacles and island towers break the swift course of the stream into chutes and eddies and whirlpools. We soon reach a place where a creek comes in from the left, and, just below, the channel is choked with boulders, which have washed down this lateral canyon and formed a dam, over which there is a fall of 30 or 40 feet; but on the boulders foothold can be had, and we make a portage. Three more such dams are found. Over one we make a portage; at the other two are chutes through which we can run.

As we proceed the granite rises higher, until nearly 1,000 feet of the lower part of the walls are composed of rock.

About eleven o'clock we hear a great roar ahead, and

approach it very cautiously. The sound grows louder and louder as we run, and at last we find ourselves above a long, broken fall, with ledges and pinnacles of rock obstructing the river. There is a descent of perhaps 75 or 80 feet in a third of a mile, and the rushing waters break into great waves on the rocks, and lash themselves into a mad, white foam. We can land just above, but there is no foothold on either side by which we can make a portage. It is nearly 1,000 feet to the top of the granite; so it will be impossible to carry our boats around, though we can climb to the summit up a side gulch and, passing along a mile or two, descend to the river. This we find on examination; but such a portage would be impracticable for us, and we must run the rapid or abandon the river. There is no hesitation. We step into our boats, push off, and away we go, first on smooth but swift water, then we strike a glassy wave and ride to its top, down again into the trough, up again on a higher wave, and down and up on waves higher and still higher until we strike one just as it curls back, and a breaker rolls over our little boat. Still on we speed, shooting past projecting rocks, till the little boat is caught in a whirlpool and spun round several times. At last we pull out again into the stream. And now the other boats have passed us. The open compartment of the *Emma Dean* is filled with water and every breaker rolls over us. Hurled back from a rock, now on this side, now on that, we are carried into an eddy, in which we struggle for a few minutes, and are then out again, the breakers still rolling over us. Our boat is unmanageable, but she cannot sink, and we drift down another hundred yards through breakers—how, we scarcely know. We find the other boats have turned into an eddy at the foot of the fall and are waiting to catch us as we come, for the men have seen that our boat is swamped. They push out as we come near and pull us in against the wall. Our boat bailed, on we go again.

The walls now are more than a mile in height—a vertical distance difficult to appreciate. Stand on the south steps of the Treasury building in Washington and look down Pennsylvania Avenue to the Capitol; measure this distance overhead, and imagine cliffs to extend to that altitude, and you will understand what is meant; or stand at Canal Street in New York and look up Broadway to Grace Church, and you have about the distance; or stand at Lake Street bridge in Chicago and look down to the Central Depot, and you have it again.

A thousand feet of this is up through granite crags; then steep slopes and perpendicular cliffs rise one above another to the summit. The gorge is black and narrow below, red and gray and flaring above, with crags and angular projections on the walls, which, cut in many places by side canyons, seem to be a vast wilderness of rocks. Down in these grand, gloomy depths we glide, ever listening, for the mad waters keep up their roar; ever watching, ever peering ahead, for the narrow canyon is winding and the river is closed in so that we can see but a few hundred yards, and what there may be below we know not; so we listen for falls and watch for rocks, stopping now and then in the bay of a recess to admire the gigantic scenery; and ever as we go there is some new pinnacle or tower, some crag or peak, some distant view of the upper plateau, some strangely shaped rock, or some deep, narrow side canyon.

Then we come to another broken fall, which appears more difficult than the one we ran this morning. A small creek comes in on the right, and the first fall of the water is over boulders, which have been carried down by this lateral stream. We land at its mouth and stop for an hour or two to examine the fall. It seems possible to let down with lines, at least a part of the way, from point to point, along the right hand wall. So we make a portage over the first rocks and find footing on some boulders below. Then we let down one of the boats to the end of her line, when she reaches a corner of the projecting rock, to which one of the men clings and steadies her while I examine an eddy below. I think we can pass the other boats down by us and catch them in the eddy. This is soon done, and the men in the boats in the eddy pull us to their side. On the shore of this little eddy there is about two feet of gravel beach above the water. Standing on this beach, some of the men take the line of the little boat and let it drift down against another projecting angle. Here is a little shelf, on which a man from my boat climbs, and a shorter line is passed to him, and he fastens the boat to the side of the cliff; then the second one is let down, bringing the line of the third. When the second boat is tied up, the two men standing on the beach above spring into the last boat, which is pulled up alongside of ours; then we let down the boats for 25 or 30 yards by walking along the shelf, landing them again in the mouth of a side canyon. Just below this there is another pile of boulders, over which we make another portage. From the foot of these rocks we can climb to another shelf, 40 or 50 feet above the water.

On this bench we camp for the night. It is raining hard, and we have no shelter, but find a few sticks which have lodged in the rocks, and kindle a fire and have supper. We sit on the rocks all night, wrapped in our *ponchos*, getting what sleep we can.

August 15.—This morning we find we can let down for 300 or 400 yards, and it is managed in this way: we pass along the wall by climbing from projecting point to point, sometimes near the water's edge, at other places 50 or 60 feet above, and hold the boat with a line while two men remain aboard and prevent her from being dashed against the rocks and keep the line from getting caught on the wall. In two hours we have brought them all down, as far as it is possible, in this way. A few yards below, the river strikes with great violence against a projecting rock and our boats are pulled up in a little bay above. We must now manage to pull out of this and clear the point below. The little boat is held by the bow obliquely up the stream. We jump in and pull out only a few strokes, and sweep clear of the dangerous rock. The other boats follow in the same manner and the rapid is passed.

It is not easy to describe the labor of such navigation. We must prevent the waves from dashing the boats against the cliffs. Sometimes, where the river is swift, we must put a bight of rope about a rock, to prevent the boat from being snatched from us by a wave; but where the plunge is too great or the chute too swift, we must let her leap and catch her below or the undertow will drag her under the falling water and sink her. Where we wish to run her out a little way from shore through a channel between rocks, we first throw in little sticks of driftwood and watch their course, to see where we must steer so that she will pass the channel in safety. And so we hold, and let go, and pull, and lift, and ward—among rocks, around rocks, and over rocks.

And now we go on through this solemn, mysterious way. The river is very deep, the canyon very narrow, and still obstructed, so that there is no steady flow of the stream; but the waters reel and roll and boil, and we are scarcely able to determine where we can go. Now the boat is carried to the right, perhaps close to the wall; again, she is shot into the stream, and perhaps is dragged over to the other side, where, caught in a whirlpool, she spins about. We can neither land nor run as we please. The boats are entirely unmanageable; no order in their running can be preserved; now one, now another, is ahead, each crew laboring for its own preservation. In such a place we come to another rapid. Two of the boats run it perforce. One succeeds in landing, but there is no foothold by which to make a portage and she is pushed out again into the stream. The next minute a great reflex wave fills the open compartment; she is water-logged, and drifts unmanageable. Breaker after breaker rolls over her and cue capsizes her. The men are thrown out; but they cling to the boat, and she drifts down some distance alongside of us and we are able to catch her. She is soon bailed out and the men are aboard once more; but the oars are lost, and so a pair from the *Emma Dean* is spared. Then for two miles we find smooth water.

Clouds are playing in the canyon to-day. Sometimes they roll down in great masses, filling the gorge with gloom; sometimes they hang aloft from wall to wall and cover the canyon with a roof of impending storm, and we can peer long distances up and down this canyon corridor, with its cloud-roof overhead, its walls of black granite, and its river bright with the sheen of broken waters. Then a gust of wind sweeps down a side gulch and, making a rift in the clouds, reveals the blue heavens, and a stream of sunlight pours in. Then the clouds drift away into the distance, and hang around crags and peaks and pinnacles and towers and walls, and cover them with a mantle that lifts from time to time and sets them all in sharp relief. Then baby clouds creep out of side canyons, glide around points, and creep back again into more distant gorges. Then clouds arrange in strata across the canyon, with intervening vista views to cliffs and rocks beyond. The clouds are children of the heavens, and when they play among the rocks they lift them to the region above.

It rains! Rapidly little rills are formed above, and these soon grow into brooks, and the brooks grow into creeks and tumble over the walls in innumerable cascades, adding their wild music to the roar of the river. When the rain ceases the rills, brooks, and creeks run dry. The waters that fall during a rain on these steep rocks are gathered at once into the river;

they could scarcely be poured in more suddenly if some vast spout ran from the clouds to the stream itself. When a storm bursts over the canyon a side gulch is dangerous, for a sudden flood may come, and the inpouring waters will raise the river so as to hide the rocks.

Early in the afternoon we discover a stream entering from the north—a clear, beautiful creek, coming down through a gorgeous red canyon. We land and camp on a sand beach above its mouth, under a great, overspreading tree with willow-shaped leaves.

August 16.—We must dry our rations again to-day and make oars.

The Colorado is never a clear stream, but for the past three or four days it has been raining much of the time, and the floods poured over the walls have brought down great quantities of mud, making it exceedingly turbid now. The little affluent which we have discovered here is a clear, beautiful creek, or river, as it would be termed in this western country, where streams are not abundant. We have named one stream, away above, in honor of the great chief of the "Bad Angels," and as this is in beautiful contrast to that, we conclude to name it "Bright Angel."

Early in the morning the whole party starts up to explore the Bright Angel River, with the special purpose of seeking timber from which to make oars. A couple of miles above we find a large pine log, which has been floated down from the plateau, probably from an altitude of more than 6,000 feet, but not many miles back. On its way it must have passed over many cataracts and falls, for it bears scars in evidence of the rough usage which it has received. The men roll it on skids, and the work of sawing oars is commenced.

This stream heads away back under a line of abrupt cliffs that terminates the plateau, and tumbles down more than

4,000 feet in the first mile or two of its course; then runs through a deep, narrow canyon until it reaches the river.

Late in the afternoon I return and go up a little gulch just above this creek, about 200 yards from camp, and discover the ruins of two or three old houses, which were originally of stone laid in mortar. Only the foundations are left, but irregular blocks, of which the houses were constructed, lie scattered about. In one room I find an old mealing-stone, deeply worn, as if it had been much used. A great deal of pottery is strewn around, and old trails, which in some places are deeply worn into the rocks, are seen.

It is ever a source of wonder to us why these ancient people sought such inaccessible places for their homes. They were, doubtless, an agricultural race, but there are no lands here of any considerable extent that they could have cultivated. To the west of Oraibi, one of the towns in the Province of Tusayan, in northern Arizona, the inhabitants have actually built little terraces along the face of the cliff where a spring gushes out, and thus made their sites for gardens. It is possible that the ancient inhabitants of this place made their agricultural lands in the same way. But why should they seek such spots! Surely the country was not so crowded with people as to demand the utilization of so barren a region. The only solution suggested of the problem is this: We know that for a century or two after the settlement of Mexico many expeditions were sent into the country now comprising Arizona and New Mexico, for the purpose of bringing the town-building people under the dominion of the Spanish government. Many of their villages were destroyed, and the inhabitants fled to regions at that time unknown; and there are traditions among the people who inhabit the pueblos that still remain that the canyons were these unknown lands. It may be these buildings were erected at that time; sure it is that they have a much more modern appearance than the ruins scattered over Nevada, Utah, Colorado, Arizona, and New Mexico. Those old Spanish conquerors had a monstrous greed for gold and a wonderful lust for saving souls. Treasures they must have, if not on earth, why, then, in heaven; and when they failed to find heathen temples bedecked with silver, they propitiated Heaven by seizing the heathen themselves. There is yet extant a copy of a record made by a heathen artist to express his conception of the demands of the conquerors. In one part of the picture we have a lake, and near by stands a priest pouring water on the head of a native. On the other side, a poor Indian has a cord about his throat. Lines run from these two groups to a central figure, a man with beard and full Spanish panoply. The interpretation of the picture-writing is this: "Be baptized as this saved heathen, or be hanged as that damned heathen." Doubtless, some of these people preferred another alternative, and rather than be baptized or hanged they chose to imprison themselves within these canyon walls.

August 17.—Our rations are still spoiling; the bacon is so badly injured that we are compelled to throw it away. By an accident, this morning, the saleratus was lost overboard. We have now only musty flour sufficient for ten days and a few dried apples, but plenty of coffee. We must make all haste possible. If we meet with difficulties such as we have encountered in the canyon above, we may be compelled to give up the expedition and try to reach the Mormon settlements to the north. Our hopes are that the worst places are passed, but our barometers are all so much injured as to be useless, and so we have lost our reckoning in altitude, and know not how much descent the river has yet to make.

The stream is still wild and rapid and rolls through a narrow channel.

We make but slow progress, often landing against a wall

and climbing around some point to see the river below. Although very anxious to advance, we are determined to run with great caution, lest by another accident we lose our remaining supplies. How precious that little flour has become! We divide it among the boats and carefully store it away, so that it can be lost only by the loss of the boat itself.

We make ten miles and a half, and camp among the rocks on the right. We have had rain from time to time all day, and have been thoroughly drenched and chilled; but between showers the sun shines with great power and the mercury in our thermometers stands at 115°, so that we have rapid changes from great extremes, which are very disagreeable. It is especially cold in the rain to-night. The little canvas we have is rotten and useless; the rubber *ponchos* with which we started from Green River City have all been lost; more than half the party are without hats, not one of us has an entire suit of clothes, and we have not a blanket apiece. So we gather drift-wood and build a fire; but after supper the rain, coming down in torrents, extinguishes it, and we sit up all night on the rocks, shivering, and are more exhausted by the night's discomfort than by the day's toil.

August 18.—The day is employed in making portages and we advance but two miles on our journey. Still it rains.

While the men are at work making portages I climb up the granite to its summit and go away back over the rust-colored sandstones and greenish-yellow shales to the foot of the marble wall. I climb so high that the men and boats are lost in the black depths below and the dashing river is a rippling brook, and still there is more canyon above than below. All about me are interesting geologic records. The book is open and I can read as I run. All about me are grand views, too, for the clouds are playing again in the gorges. But somehow I think of the nine days' rations and the bad river, and the lesson of the rocks and the glory of the scene are but half conceived.

I push on to an angle, where I hope to get a view of the country beyond, to see if possible what the prospect may be of our soon running through this plateau, or at least of meeting with some geologic change that will let us out of the granite; but, arriving at the point, I can see below only a labyrinth of black gorges.

August 19.–Rain again this morning. We are in our granite prison still, and the time until noon is occupied in making a long, bad portage.

After dinner, in running a rapid the pioneer boat is upset by a wave. We are some distance in advance of the larger boats. The river is rough and swift and we are unable to land, but cling to the boat and are carried down stream over another rapid. The men in the boats above see our trouble, but they are caught in whirlpools and are spinning about in eddies, and it seems a long time before they come to our relief. At last they do come; our boat is turned right side up and bailed out; the oars, which fortunately have floated along in company with us, are gathered up, and on we go, without even landing. The clouds break away and we have sunshine again.

Soon we find a little beach with just room enough to land. Here we camp, but there is no wood. Across the river and a little way above, we see some driftwood lodged in the rocks. So we bring two boatloads over, build a huge fire, and spread everything to dry. It is the first cheerful night we have had for a week—a warm, drying fire in the midst of the camp, and a few bright stars in our patch of heavens overhead.

August 20.–The characteristics of the canyon change this morning. The river is broader, the walls more sloping, and composed of black slates that stand on edge. These nearly vertical slates are washed out in places—that is, the softer beds are washed out between the harder, which are left standing. In this way curious little alcoves are formed, in which are quiet bays of water, but on a much smaller scale than the great bays and buttresses of Marble Canyon.

The river is still rapid and we stop to let down with lines several times, but make greater progress, as we run ten miles. We camp on the right bank. Here, on a terrace of trap, we discover another group of ruins. There was evidently quite a village on this rock. Again we find mealing-stones and much broken pottery, and up on a little natural shelf in the rock back of the ruins we find a globular basket that would hold perhaps a third of a bushel. It is badly broken, and as I attempt to take it up it falls to pieces. There are many beautiful flint chips, also, as if this had been the home of an old arrow maker.

August 21.—We start early this morning, cheered by the prospect of a fine day and encouraged also by the good run made yesterday. A quarter of a mile below camp the river turns abruptly to the left, and between camp and that point is very swift, running down in a long, broken chute and piling up against the foot of the cliff, where it turns to the left. We try to pull across, so as to go down on the other side, but the waters are swift and it seems impossible for us to escape the rock below; but, in pulling across, the bow of the boat is turned to the farther shore, so that we are swept broadside down and are prevented by the rebounding waters from striking against the wall. We toss about for a few seconds in these billows and are then carried past the danger. Below, the river turns again to the right, the canyon is very narrow, and we see in advance but a short distance. The water, too, is very swift, and there is no landing-place. From around this curve there comes a mad roar, and down we are carried with a dizzying velocity to the head of another rapid. On either side high over our heads there are overhanging granite walls, and the sharp bends cut off our view, so that a few minutes will carry us into unknown waters. Away we go on one long, winding chute. I stand on deck, supporting myself with a strap fastened on either side of the gunwale. The boat glides rapidly where the water is smooth, then, striking a wave, she leaps and bounds like a thing of life, and we have a wild, exhilarating ride for ten miles, which we make in less than an hour. The excitement is so great that we forget the danger until we hear the roar of a great fall below; then we back on our oars and are carried slowly toward its head and succeed in landing just above and find that we have to make another portage. At this we are engaged until some time after dinner.

Just here we run out of the granite. Ten miles in less than half a day, and limestone walls below. Good cheer returns; we forget the storms and the gloom and the cloud-covered canyons and the black granite and the raging river, and push our boats from shore in great glee.

Though we are out of the granite, the river is still swift, and we wheel about a point again to the right, and turn, so as to head back in the direction from which we came; this brings the granite in sight again, with its narrow gorge and black crags; but we meet with no more great falls or rapids. Still, we run cautiously and stop from time to time to examine some places which look bad. Yet we make ten miles this afternoon; twenty miles in all to-day.

August 22.—We come to rapids again this morning and are occupied several hours in passing them, letting the boats down from rock to rock with lines for nearly half a mile, and then have to make a long portage. While the men are engaged in this I climb the wall on the northeast to a height of about 2,500 feet, where I can obtain a good view of a long stretch of canyon below. Its course is to the southwest. The walls seem to rise very abruptly for 2,500 or 3,000 feet, and then there is a gently sloping terrace on each side for two or three miles, when we again find cliffs, 1,500 or 2,000 feet high. From the brink of these the plateau stretches back to the north and south for a long distance. Away down the canyon on the right wall I can see a group of mountains, some of which appear to stand on the brink of the canyon. The effect of the terrace is to give the appearance of a narrow winding valley with high walls on either side and a deep, dark, meandering gorge down its middle. It is impossible from this point of view to determine whether or not we have granite at the bottom; but from geologic considerations, I conclude that we shall have marble walls below.

After my return to the boats we run another mile and camp for the night. We have made but little over seven miles to-day, and a part of our flour has been soaked in the river again.

August 23.–Our way to-day is again through marble walls. Now and then we pass for a short distance through patches of granite, like hills thrust up into the limestone. At one of these places we have to make another portage, and, taking advantage of the delay, I go up a little stream to the north, wading it all the way, sometimes having to plunge in to my neck, in other places being compelled to swim across little basins that have been excavated at the foot of the falls. Along its course are many cascades and springs, gushing out from the rocks on either side. Sometimes a cottonwood tree grows over the water. I come to one beautiful fall, of more than 150 feet, and climb around it to the right on the broken rocks. Still going up, the canyon is found to narrow very much, being but 15 or 20 feet wide; yet the walls rise on either side many hundreds of feet, perhaps thousands; I can hardly tell.

In some places the stream has not excavated its channel down vertically through the rocks, but has cut obliquely, so that one wall overhangs the other. In other places it is cut vertically above and obliquely below, or obliquely above and vertically below, so that it is impossible to see out overhead. But I can go no farther; the time which I estimated it would take to make the portage has almost expired, and I start back on a round trot, wading in the creek where I must and plunging through basins. The men are waiting for me, and away we go on the river.

Just after dinner we pass a stream on the right, which leaps into the Colorado by a direct fall of more than 100 feet, forming a beautiful cascade. There is a bed of very hard rock above, 30 or 40 feet in thickness, and there are much softer beds below. The hard beds above project many yards beyond the softer, which are washed out, forming a deep cave behind the fall, and the stream pours through a narrow crevice above into a deep pool below. Around on the rocks in the cavelike chamber are set beautiful ferns, with delicate fronds and enameled stalks. The frondlets have their points turned down to form spore cases. It has very much the appearance of the maidenhair fern, but is much larger. This delicate foliage covers the rocks all about the fountain, and gives the chamber great beauty. But we have little time to spend in admiration; so on we go.

We make fine progress this afternoon, carried along by a swift river, shooting over the rapids and finding no serious obstructions. The canyon walls for 2,500 or 3,000 feet are very regular, rising almost perpendicularly, but here and there set with narrow steps, and occasionally we can see away above the broad terrace to distant cliffs.

We camp to-night in a marble cave, and find on looking at our reckoning that we have run twenty-two miles.

August 24.–The canyon is wider to-day. The walls rise to a vertical height of nearly 3,000 feet. In many places the river runs under a cliff in great curves, forming amphitheaters half-dome shaped.

Though the river is rapid, we meet with no serious obstructions and run twenty miles. How anxious we are to make up our reckoning every time we stop, now that our diet is confined to plenty of coffee, a very little spoiled flour, and very few dried apples! It has come to be a race for a dinner. Still, we make such fine progress that all hands are in good cheer, but not a moment of daylight is lost.

August 25.–We make twelve miles this morning, when we come to monuments of lava standing in the river—low rocks mostly, but some of them shafts more than 100 feet high. Going on down three or four miles, we find them increasing in number. Great quantities of cooled lava and many cinder cones are seen on either side; and then we come to an abrupt cataract. Just over the fall on the right wall a cinder cone, or extinct volcano, with a well-defined crater, stands on the very brink of the canyon. This, doubtless, is the one we saw two or three days ago. From this volcano vast floods of lava have been poured down into the river, and a stream of molten rock has run up the canyon three or four miles and down we know not how far. Just where it poured over the canyon wall is the fall. The whole north side as far as we can see is lined with the black basalt, and high up on the opposite wall are patches of the same material, resting on the benches and filling old alcoves and caves, giving the wall a spotted appearance.

The rocks are broken in two along a line which here crosses the river, and the beds we have seen while coming down the canyon for the last thirty miles have dropped 800 feet on the lower side of the line, forming what geologists call a "fault." The volcanic cone stands directly over the fissure thus formed. On the left side of the river, opposite, mammoth springs burst out of this crevice, 100 or 200 feet above the river, pouring in a stream quite equal in volume to the Colorado Chiquito.

This stream seems to be loaded with carbonate of lime, and the water, evaporating, leaves an incrustation on the rocks; and this process has been continued for a long time, for extensive deposits are noticed in which are basins with bubbling springs. The water is salty.

We have to make a portage here, which is completed in about three hours; then on we go.

We have no difficulty as we float along, and I am able to observe the wonderful phenomena connected with this flood of lava. The canyon was doubtless filled to a height of 1,200 or 1,500 feet, perhaps by more than one flood. This would dam the water back; and in cutting through this great lava bed, a new channel has been formed, sometimes on one side, sometimes on the other. The cooled lava, being of firmer texture than the rocks of which the walls are composed, remains in some places; in others a narrow channel has been cut, leaving a line of basalt on either side. It is possible that the lava cooled faster on the sides against the walls and that the center ran out; but of this we can only conjecture. There are other places where almost the whole of the lava is gone, only patches of it being seen where it has caught on the walls. As we float down we can see that it ran out into side canyons. In some places this basalt has a fine, columnar structure, often in concentric prisms, and masses of these concentric columns have coalesced. In some places, when the flow occurred the canyon was probably about the same depth that it is now, for we can see where the basalt has rolled out on the sands, and—what seems curious to me—the sands are not melted or metamorphosed to any appreciable extent. In places the bed of the river is of sandstone or limestone, in other places of lava, showing that it has all been cut out again where the sandstones and limestones appear; but there is a little yet left where the bed is of lava.

What a conflict of water and fire there must have been here! Just imagine a river of molten rock running down into a river of melted snow. What a seething and boiling of the waters; what clouds of steam rolled into the heavens!

Thirty-five miles to-day. Hurrah!

Postscript: After three of his men deserted the expedition and were killed by Indians, Major Powell and his remaining companions successfully completed the expedition down the Colorado to the Gulf of California.

In 1847 the Englishman Bayle St. John and three of his colleagues trekked by camel deep into the Libyan Desert where few had gone before. They went in search of an oasis, as do all desert explorers, and what they discovered in the process was nothing short of astounding.

ADVENTURES IN THE LIBYAN DESERT

BAYLE ST. JOHN

We stayed about twenty-eight hours at Mudar, and, having thus refreshed ourselves, started at five o'clock on the afternoon of the 25th of September; and issuing from the narrow slip of plain land between the hills we had descended the day before and the beach, entered a broad valley, formed by a backward sweep of the high ground, which to the east and west advances far into the sea, forming two bluff promontories, and inclosing what I believe in the charts is called Port Mahada. The great patch of white sand, from which the water of the Mudar wells seems to distil, stretches a great deal to the west, occupying indeed the whole bottom of the port or bay. The part of the range of hills which we were leaving behind us was far less steep than that to our left, and directly in front, which indeed appeared at a little distance to be perfectly unbroken and precipitous. The line of its summit was level like a wall; and we began to puzzle ourselves with conjectures how we were ever to get to the top. Our impatience was not soon gratified; for we were compelled to zigzag slowly across the valley, which was cut up by a most extraordinary network of ravines and watercourses, now approaching the sea, now receding, then again facing towards it, then wheeling about, but preserving a general W.S.W. direction.

All this time our Bedawíns and the new guide—as entering on a journey of more than ordinary difficulty and danger—were occupied in saying their prayers piecemeal with unusual assiduity. There is something curious in the mode of praying adopted by these people whilst travelling in deserts where time is of consequence. Instead of stopping the *kafila*, and spreading the carpet, and sticking the spear in the sand, and fettering the camel—instead of forming a picture for Horace Vernet to paint—our uncouth companions went about the affair in a much more business-like way. Walking a little forward, they knelt down and complied with the form of mock ablution with sand—laying their hands flat on the ground, passing them along their arms, over their faces, round their necks in a fixed order, and then going through a few evolutions. By this time the camels were moving ahead, or were straying or loitering, and required direction or encouragement. So the conclusion of the ceremony was adjourned, and the necessary duties were attended to. Then the prostrations and kneelings were resumed at a more advanced spot; and so on, three or four times, until their consciences were satisfied and the sun went down.

The interval was brief between the coming on of darkness and the rising of the moon, which had just passed her full, and, shining through a wonderfully clear atmosphere, enabled us to avoid, whilst she magnified to appearance, the dangers of our road. Two hours of toil brought us at length to the foot of the range of hills at a point at which they were to all appearance inaccessible. Here we again turned towards the sea, and, having passed the mouth of a gloomy gorge, began to climb a rugged incline, covered at first with huge loose stones that gave way beneath our feet nearly at every step. As we proceeded the ascent became steeper and steeper, and our progress more and more slow. Stoppages were frequent. The camels, heavily laden, seemed unwilling to move; and paused every now and then to turn their long necks and look wistfully around, as if seeking a better path. But better path there was none. On either side, as now appeared, a deep and rugged ravine descended, sometimes in rapid slopes, sometimes in sheer precipices; and it was up a kind of spur thrown out between these, that we were to escalade this frightful mountain. For some time our progress, though slow, was sure. The camels, encouraged by the shouting, and coaxing, and whistling of old Saleh, gradually worked their way up until they came to a kind of slippery staircase of rock that led to the very brow of the range. Up this they at first refused to go, moaning and complaining at the hard task set them, and turning a deaf ear to entreaties and stubborn flanks to the stick. So, without any further experience, we had ample reason to deny that "The camel labors with the heaviest load."

Meanwhile we sat down to rest from our wearisome walk, and to contemplate the dark valley beneath, surrounded by a semicircle of frowning hills and the opaque expanse of the sea. A few points only, touched by the moonlight, relieved the sombre monotony of the scene. All around was dark, rugged, and inhospitable. No light or other sign of human habitations cheered us. The little settlement of Mudar, nestling in its own snug hollow, alone intervened between us and Abusír, whilst above our heads were the confines of a vast plain that stretched we knew not how far, for aught we knew a hundred and fifty miles without water or fixed inhabitants. Something we had heard, it is true, of a spring that had of late years bubbled up in the midst of the waste, and it was on this new-born well, that might have been stifled by the sands in its infancy, that we depended for crossing the Desert without suffering the horrors of thirst. The supply we carried with us was scarcely sufficient for three days' economical consumption, and we had to look forward to five days' travel at least before reaching that little vanguard of the oasis called Garah. But this slight uncertainty, this dash of peril, rather heightened the pleasure with which we entered on the journey; and, instead of wishing to linger in sight of the sea, we were anxious to leave it far behind, and be once for all in the midst of the Libyan Desert.

The physical obstacles, therefore, that we encountered at the outset were rather trying to our impatient tempers, and we gladly hailed the moment when we saw the tall ungainly form of the first camel, swinging its huge burden to and fro in its exertions, begin the slippery ascent. One after another, the steady brutes, not however without complaint, ventured on the dangerous ground, which had evidently been of late fatal to some of their predecessors, for several white skeletons gleamed in the moonlight on either hand. Had the leader fallen, all would inevitably have been rolled down the side of the hill, to the imminent danger of our little band, some of whom the struggling creatures would most probably have overwhelmed. Fortunately, however, the ascent was accomplished without accident, and our little *kafila*, after winding along the edge of a steep precipice that descended into the ravine on our right, entered at length on a flat stony plain. The guide now turned our head, if I may so express myself, to

the W.S.W., and, directing his course by the stars, began to
steer across this trackless expanse for the promised well. On
accordingly we went for several hours, stumbling and staggering, afraid to mount, lest our beasts should miss their footing
and fall, and yet scarcely able to pick our way amidst the loose
and pointed fragments of rock that encumbered the ground.
Both shoes and feet suffered severely that night; and though a
clearer space occasionally intervened, we were glad to stop a
little before midnight and bivouac. A sound sleep, in spite of
the cold and damp, prepared us for next morning's work,
which we began surrounded by the illusions of mirage, that is
to say, by imaginary lakes and islands breaking the otherwise
level horizon, which only by degrees revealed itself in all its
naked monotony as the sun rose higher in the heavens.

I had often heard and read descriptions of the Desert as a
"sea of sand," but we now found ourselves in what might
almost be called a "sea of stones," with, it is true, here and
there at wide intervals a patch of bushes, and the contorted
form of the ligneous plant called *shía* dotting the ground. This
plant exhales a strong odor something resembling rue, and is
cultivated in pots at Alexandria on that account. In the Desert
its more tender extremities serve as food for the gazelles, small
troops of which were now and then seen browsing out of gunshot. As we approached, they raised their heads and appeared
to listen and watch, but the result of their examination was
never, it seemed, encouraging, for off they invariably went,
cocking up their tails, at first gently trotting, but by degrees
lengthening their steps, then bounding, scudding; flashing
along, as it were, over the vast level, now huddling together,
now spreading into a long irregular line, seeming at times to
outstrip the sight, but coming again into view, flitting away
swiftly like uncertain shadows, until at length they faded into
nothing; as a prolonged echo, after quivering through the air,

subsides into a faint murmur, and dies away in the distance.
On one occasion a mother and its fawn lingered to nibble a
green shrub, and our Bedawíns began to manœuvre to get
a supply of fresh meat, one crouching down, and another
advancing obliquely; but the cautious creature took the alarm
and made away with her young charge in double-quick time. I
may here remark that the agreeable musk-like smell of the
excrements of these animals is doubtless derived from the aro-
matic plants on which they feed.

As day advanced our attention was attracted to a brilliant
speck on the horizon, glittering like the summit of a snow-clad
mountain, or a peak of silver. It turned out to be a *koom*, or
hillock of white sand, with a well in the neighborhood, called
Shenéneh. We left it some distance to our right, and made
direct for another white spot said to mark another well, and
visible at a distance of two hours, half way up a well-defined
slope in the Desert immediately ahead. This was the first
variation in level that had occurred since we ascended the
table-land, and was therefore gladly hailed as promising a
somewhat less monotonous road.

It was near mid-day before we reached what had appeared
a mere milky spot, which turned out to be a cluster of mounds
of white stone and sand. We saw a human form from a distance on the top of one of these, but when we approached it
had disappeared, and no trace of it or the well at first presented themselves. A sound from beneath the earth, however,
directing us, we discovered a little channel cut in the flat surface of the rock, and at the bottom a hole large enough to
allow passage for a man of ordinary size. It was evidently
made for the use of the inhabitants of the Desert, and not destined to admit the respectable rotundity of civilization. Some
of our party, therefore, declined to explore, and trusted to the
report of the more active.

We descended, guided by the voices below, into a dark passage which led to a spacious subterranean chamber cut out of the solid rock, and about thirty yards square. The roof was pretty even, and the walls were perfectly smooth, and covered with those rough marks and figures which, when first noticed by travellers on all the rocks and monuments of this part of the world, were thought to be the alphabet of an unknown language. They are now, I am told, known to be the distinctive marks of the various tribes of Arabs who may have sojourned a while in these regions. The floor of this chamber was covered with mounds of clayey soil, evidently allowed to gather by neglect, so as nearly to choke up the springs. Of these there are two, at the bottom of deep holes: one in a dark corner, the other in the centre, exactly underneath a square aperture in the rock made for the double purpose of admitting light, and of letting down buckets when the rains of winter have filled the whole cistern. Two boys, who seemed to be there watching for the water as it oozed up, gave us to drink from their skin bucket. The taste was muddy, but it was cool as if it had been iced. The cave itself, though at first agreeable after the burning atmosphere above, we soon found to be too chilly to stay in. It is almost unnecessary to add that this place must date at least as far back as the time of the Romans, and was probably one of the stations as now on the caravan-road to the oasis. If properly cleared out it might yield a large supply of good water, whereas when we passed there was barely sufficient for our donkeys. The others made a hole in what we had brought from Mudar, whilst the camels, of course, abstained.

On ascending from this cave we found that the party had been joined by a number of Bedawín women and children, from a neighboring encampment. No men, however, made their appearance, which fact afterwards received a probable explanation. One damsel was rather pretty, and very obliging. Seeing that there was some difficulty in setting up our tent in the hard ground, which seemed an agglomeration of particles of stone, she seized the mallet, and, with great dexterity, soon got through the work, and drove the pegs at which our two Arabs had boggled, and then went her way without waiting for *backsheesh*. The act was one of simple kindness, *sans arrière pensée*, unless we choose to suppose that the wench took a pride in showing her superiority in the arts of desert life. It appeared that this party had come for the purpose of assuaging their thirst, but, above all, of enjoying the coolness of the cave or cistern; for they all descended amidst great shouting and laughter, and stayed some time below. When they came up, we were making our meal; and, whilst looking with contempt on most of our good things, they cast covetous eyes on the precious biscuit, fragments of which that fell to the ground were snatched up and eagerly devoured. Our gallantry might have induced us to make them a present of some, but stern reason forbade.

The Arethusa of the well of Selém—she, namely, that drove the pegs—had a tame gazelle, which, though professing to be very fond of, she asked us to buy. We declined doing so, alleging our inability to carry it; but she said it would follow us like a dog, and be not so easily tired. Probably she expected it would soon return to her side. At a subsequent period we met the same gazelle and its owner in another part of the Desert, near the sea, and inquired its price. We were told ninety piasters, nearly a pound sterling. These animals, indeed, are difficult to be procured, and sell for a large sum in Alexandria, whither this one was bound. I noticed that its mistress, when tired, mounted a camel, and carried it in her lap. Perhaps it will not be out of place here to mention that a very young gazelle, that unfortunately had its leg broken, was once given to me by Lamport, and that I have succeeded in rearing it in my courtyard in Alexandria. The Bedawíns who took it bandaged the injured limb so well that, though for a long time lamed, it scarcely now retains even a mark to reveal the accident it encountered.

The well of Selém, which supplies water to a tribe of seventeen guns, is distant twelve hours' journey, or about thirty miles, from Mudar, as nearly as we could make out, in a W.S.W. direction by compass. There is at first neither track nor bold landmark on this vast expanse; but by night our guide shaped his course by the stars, whilst in the morning he had the assistance of the glittering Koom of Shenéneh. The country, when once we reached the table-land, had no remarkable feature, except its extreme flatness, and the circumstance that it is strewn over, and in many places encumbered, with loose pieces of sandstone resting on a clayey soil mixed with sand. The vegetation is similar in character to that on the coast, except that it is more scanty and stunted, and that the *shía* is in greater abundance.

We were in the saddle again at half-past three; and, rising over the ridge, got into a country covered with low hills. Whilst quietly jogging along over them, we suddenly became aware that something out of the way was the matter by the shouts and gestures of our Bedawíns. Looking in the direction they indicated, we saw a party of eight men, seven of whom were armed with guns, advancing at a short run over the hills to our left, and a little in our rear, from the direction, in fact, of the encampment to which the women and children I have mentioned belonged. They were instantly pronounced to be robbers; and their mode of approach was certainly most suspicious. The very fact of their lying close whilst we were so many hours in their neighborhood without paying a visit, and then suddenly showing themselves in this manner, was judged, apparently with reason, to be a sufficient proof of their evil intentions. At any rate, especially when we saw them getting their weapons ready, there was ample justification for the word which immediately passed round to load with ball; after which the camels, which had been slightly scattered at the first alarm, were again collected and put in motion, whilst we followed, prepared to face about before the pursuers overtook us, and summon them to halt and reveal their intentions. These preparations did not escape their notice, and they visibly slackened their pace, so that it was some time before they came sufficiently near to answer the hail of old Yúnus, who had been meanwhile making great show of his weapons, fresh priming and examining the lock of his gun, and seeing that his pistols were in fighting order. Saleh also pulled his meagre beard with considerable energy, begged a pinch of Frank powder for his single but large pistol, and loosened his poniard in its sheath. As for Wahsa, our new guide, who had a camel at stake, he also made war-like demonstrations; whilst our poor Arabs looked very peaceable and woeful. They evidently expected to have their throats cut in a few minutes, and wore visages corresponding.

Matters, however, were not quite so bad as all that. Whether we showed too good a countenance, or whether our Bedawíns had libelled those "who drank at the well of Selém," I cannot determine. Certain it is that the so-called hostile party halted at speaking distance; a parley ensued, and, after some time, we were favored with the information that this armed detachment had come out to offer for sale a single *ihram* or blanket, price seventeen piasters. We were glad to accept this pacific interpretation of their movements, and Yúnus made the purchase. A capital bargain it was, too. The piece had evidently been woven in the tents, of Desert wool, and was striped tastefully with black. We should have been very glad to procure a similar one all round to protect us against the cold of the night.

This little adventure being over, we pursued our journey, not however without many broad hints of approaching assassination from our still frightened Arab lads, who inferred, from the ambiguous direction taken by the Selémites at parting, that, finding us at present well prepared, it was their intention to fall upon us at night. Their idea under the circumstances did not appear unreasonable, as we saw these doubtful characters at intervals until nightfall keeping nearly in a line with us, though at a gradually increasing distance.

At a quarter past four we descended from the ridge of hills we had been crossing in a S.W. direction from Selém, into a remarkably flat valley that lay athwart our road, forming a trench, as it were, called Wady Färagh, or the Empty Valley. Its sides resemble the steep banks of a river, with a level line of summit, and here and there in its centre rise hills with precipitous sides, exactly the same height as the surrounding land, and looking like islands left dry by the receding waters. This valley evidently extends a great distance S.E. and N.W. We crossed it again on our return more to the east; and on neither occasion could we detect any change in its character.

We had now entered upon a tract of country somewhat different from that which we had hitherto traversed—a series namely, of small, level, stony plains, ending, as in the Wady Färagh, in steep descents, and divided by smooth valleys interspersed with isolated hills or islands as I have called them. By moonlight especially, these hills, with their scarped sides and regular forms, reminded one strongly of a vast system of fortifications, like those of Alexandria; and even by day there seemed no comparison so apt for many of the crumbling eminences amidst which we passed as bastions and earthworks. Some of the sharpness of their forms, however, was taken off by the detritus accumulated at their base, which suggested the idea that the soil of the valley was entirely formed of contributions washed down by the rains. Much of the substance of the hills seemed to consist of hardened mud, and it is to be supposed that large masses of this have yielded to the influence of time, and been gradually spread over the valleys, raising their level and leaving the more solid sandstone in its present extraordinarily denuded state. The soil thus formed has, in many instances, been turned to account by the Bedawíns. Some time after sunset we halted to wait for the moon in a valley called Wady Ed-Delma, amidst the stubble of a field that had been sown with barley the previous winter; and both camels and donkeys found some occupation for their teeth.

It will be difficult to convey an idea of the pleasure with which I look back to these little halts, affording as they did a most welcome interruption to the monotony of a ride of several hours at *kafila* pace. On this occasion we found ourselves, though beneath a brilliant canopy of stars, in almost total darkness, at the bottom of a shallow basin, of which we could scarcely distinguish the dim outline; and, sitting down here and there upon the ground, proceeded to enjoy the luxury of a pipe, whilst anxiously watching the eastern quarter of the heavens for the coming luminary that was to light our path through the labyrinth of hills and passes in which we were engaged. Perhaps the slight sentiment of the probable neighborhood of danger, in the shape of prowling Bedawíns, contributed to heighten the enjoyment of our halt, which was not, however, of long duration, for, soon after the moon had risen, and enabled us dimly to distinguish objects near at hand, we were again in motion, journeying nearly in a south direction up a valley flanked as usual by apparent fortifications, which led to another stony table-land. We were now near the proposed place of stoppage, and, having made a sharp descent, came upon a flock of sheep and goats. After a few words with the shepherds, we proceeded about a quarter of a mile in search of the well of Haldeh. We only found, however, the traps of some Bedawíns covered with a blanket, and abandoned to the honesty of passers-by. Here we spread our mat, and lay down to sleep, with our firearms, as in duty bound, within reach in case of a surprise.

Early dawn found us in a broad shallow valley, with openings on several sides. A few tents appeared to our right, and directly in front the customary white patch that announced the presence of a well. On reaching this we were surprised to find the place strewed with ruins, evidently belonging to some structure, once of importance. The only European traveller who had preceded us on this road, our countryman Browne, says nothing about them, and must have passed them at night. In his time, probably, the spring that now bubbles up and supplies the great cistern did not exist. Indeed we learned from the Bedawíns that Haldeh had only recently become a fixed station, as formerly it depended on the rains of winter; whereas now one of the thin veins of water that trickle beneath the surface even of the Desert had broken into it. Very likely the feeble current had only been checked for a time by an overwhelming weight of sand, and, accidentally bursting forth, had been assisted by the removal of the obstruction, and coaxed into regularly supplying a few dozen *kúrbehs* a day even in summer. Three hundred people, with their flocks, are said regularly to drink from this well, not to speak of the *kafilas* that may resort thither on their way to or from the coast.

The ruins were manifestly those of a fort built in ancient times to protect the waters, and to a certain extent command the return to the oasis. I did not examine the cistern, as there is no regular descent, as at Selém; but it is evidently very spacious. Over the mouth, which is cut in the rock, there was formerly a great round tower, built of massive stones, and standing at the northwest angle of a considerable solidly constructed square building, from the corners and sides of which there radiated to some distance irregular walls, thrown out evidently for the purpose of preventing an enemy from bringing too great a front to bear upon the garrison. There were no traces of a moat: the precautions taken being sufficient against the Desert tribes, to overawe whom the fortress was intended. The whole structure is overthrown almost to the ground; many of the fine large squared stones are honeycombed by the atmosphere, and others have been used to form the Bedawín tombs which crown one of the two white mounds that rise near the well.

I believe that there existed in ancient times, both Greek and Roman, a regular series of strong places, extending from the confines of Egypt to the oasis, and possibly beyond, wherever water could be procured, in order to protect and assist the caravans. At what period they were erected I know not. Those along the coast may seem to have been superfluous whilst the country was an inhabited province filled with towns; but it was probable that there was always some danger from the wandering tribes that hung upon the flanks of the narrow strip of cultivated land: at any rate, that there was a line of wells protected by forts appears indubitable. Our guides had a sort of theory that every permanent station on the coast had a corresponding castle with a cistern some miles inland, as Munchúrah, Kasr el-Amaïd, Shemainéh, Gobísa, and Gemaima. Kassaba is a common name to give to the ruins at such places, because they generally consist of four bare walls.

The water in the well of Haldeh has a cold stony taste and a milky look. It does not rise immediately under the mouth of the cistern, so that it is necessary for one man to scramble down in order to fill the bucket, which another hauls up. This bucket was simply a piece of sheepskin, with the edges roughly sewed to a kind of hoop. It belonged to a sheikh, who has the superintendence of the well, and whose person and flocks are protected by the sanctity of his character. He was a stout, well-made, dark-skinned fellow, with a simple, good-humored expression of countenance, and worked cheerfully to water our camels and donkeys. He entertained us, as did every one we met in this road, with the exploits of the *Manser*, which means a band of sand-troopers, if I may use the expression, engaged in a foray. A party of fifty horsemen from the West were, he told us, to be met with on our road, and would most probably relieve us of some portion at least of our luggage. They had been last heard of in the neighborhood of Garah, and were said to have been guilty of considerable familiarity with the flocks and herds of the Waled Ali. He admitted, however, that the country was up in arms against them, and that by this time they might have beaten a retreat. For himself he felt no fear, belonging as he did to the class of Marâbuts, and being venerated by both sides. How often do civilized invaders respect the temples and altars of their foes?

We had now before us, we were told, a very arduous march of several days, during which we should meet neither well nor encampment, and be entirely dependent for subsistence on the water we carried in our *kúrbehs*. It was necessary, therefore, to take a good supply; to be very economical; and to push on with increased energy. The slightest delay might be productive of suffering; whilst any considerable impediment thrown in the way of our uninterrupted progress would certainly lead to very disastrous consequences. It was to insure the *kafila* against accidents of this sort that the new guide had been procured at Mudar: for were we once to deviate from the road, we might wander about in search of it until our water and provisions were exhausted. Wahsa had been, according to his own account, twenty—that is to say, a great many times—to Síwah; and we committed ourselves unhesitatingly to his guidance.

Having well filled the skins with the cold white water—that looked as if mixed with lime—we left Haldeh and its ruins after an hour's halt. The Europeans of the party, buoyed up by their excitement, were high in spirits and pressed cheerfully on; but Derweesh and Saād followed with hanging heads, and gloomy, dissatisfied countenances, looking like sheep going to the slaughter, whilst even the Bedawíns seemed not at all confident of their safety. The alarm of robbers, which had been raised the evening before—the unsatisfactory accounts of the Sheikh of the Well—the difficulties and dangers of the road itself—combined to fill them with anxiety. However, on we went at a rapid pace, nearly southward, up a long valley, or furrow, in the Desert, with many openings to the left filled with Moyet-Eblis, or the Devil's Water, which is the name given by the Arabs to mirage illusions. Heaps of stones at very short intervals marked the road, which it would otherwise have been impossible to keep, so utterly devoid of character were the low hills, or rather undulations, among which we soon found ourselves. Having continued ascending and descending until near noon, we were right glad to encamp in a little copse and seek the shelter of our little tent, where the thermometer stood at 96°.

It is difficult to convey an idea of the pleasure which these mid-day halts afforded us, especially in a tract of country consisting of a monotonous expanse without the grandeur of a

level plain—exhibiting always a limited, undefined horizon—
and covered for the most part with loose stones. Here and
there a small patch of stunted shrubs springs up from a spot to
which the winter rains have washed down a little soil; but
although the camels browsed willingly on the tender green
extremities, our donkeys went snuffing about in vain for
something to suit their palates. On the coast, they greedily
devoured the gray lichens, I remember, that covered the
ground at some places; but here this resource failed them:
and, as not a single blade of grass ever showed itself, they
were always obliged to wait for their periodical supply of
beans and chopped straw. This was given them by the boys in
nosebags immediately on our arrival at a camping ground;
whilst we four set to work merrily to put up the tent. No true
traveller expects to have all this done for him. Half the enjoyment would have been destroyed if other hands had labored
whilst we sat lazily by. When the tent was up with the door to
the north, each procured his carpet-bag and his cloak to form
a temporary divan—a tin of preserved meat was opened—the
biscuit-bag was visited—a few raw onions, bought at Mudar,
were added as a relish—a single bottle of porter, to be diluted
with water into four good tumblers, was got ready—the tin-
plates were cleaned; and the frugal meal commenced. Lucul-
lus never relished his innumerable dishes as we did this
humble fare. Though we had no picturesque prospect before
us, every accessory of the scene was romantic. The very fact
of our having created for ourselves, for a moment, a home in
the midst of the Desert, gave a zest to all our comforts. No living creature was near that did not belong to us. Our beasts of
burden were dispersed here and there. The Bedawíns sat in a
group apart; our donkey boys enjoyed the shade of the tent
on the outside. It was as if we had landed on a little uninhabited island in the midst of the ocean, and had covered it for the

first time with life. But the signal for departure is given. The hours have flown rapidly by. Down with the tent—out again into the blazing sun—gather the camels—pile up their burdens—and away!

We again started, this time late in the afternoon, and having rounded a hill on the left and crossed the bed of a winter's lake—a broad level expanse of hard-baked white mud—proceeded in a general southerly direction until dark. The road is here marked by little heaps of stones placed at tolerably regular distances; so that Wahsa thought he could advance without danger by the help of a lantern. He might as well have attempted to steer across the Atlantic with the same assistance. Presently there was an uncertainty in our movements: sometimes we went to the right, sometimes to the left; then came a pause; and another hurried move; a halt; and then a confession that we had lost the track, and had, perhaps, entered the wrong valley. This was not at all a pleasant announcement. True we could not be very distant from the right path; but each step might take us farther away, and every hour lost now, promised an hour of privation to come. We sat down accordingly; and watched with some anxiety the motions of the lantern as it flitted here and there over the country. At length the Bedawíns returned, and, without saying a word, collected the camels and began driving them on in a westerly direction. We were soon climbing a steep declivity, at the top of which we once more came to a stand-still, and found that the proper course had at length been determined on, namely, to wait for the rising of the moon. Our reflections during this halt could not be very satisfactory. There we were crowded together on a little barren, waterless spot, in the midst of darkness, with nothing but silent hills repeating one another in an endless succession of resemblances around, ignorant in what direction to move, with every chance of choosing the wrong one, far removed both from the coast, and from the little speck of verdure towards which we were steering. What if we could not regain the road; and, attempting still to proceed, were to get entangled in an inextricable labyrinth? Alexander the Great, it is true, when he lost his way in the same region, was rescued by miraculous interposition. Was there any likelihood that we should be equally favored? As to making a disgraceful retreat, guided by the compass toward the sea, it was abhorrent to our thoughts, involving as it would have done the total failure of the expedition. So we sat silently down, and managing, under cover of our cloaks, to light pipes or cigars in spite of the strong northeast wind that went roaring by over hill and dale, waited with patience for the result.

At length the moon rose above the black, undulating horizon, and cast its pale deceitful light upon us. The word was now given to drive on the camels; but it was evident no new discovery had been made. The Bedawíns spread themselves on either side hailing each other, or rather barking now and then in imitation of the jackal to communicate their whereabouts. It was difficult to prevent a feeling of awe from stealing into the mind. These strange sounds struggling with the furious blast—dim forms flitting here and there—the solemn motions of the groups of camels—the beams of the moon revealing no distant object—a world of unsubstantial shadows—the known and possible danger—all united to act powerfully on the imagination. The conduct of the Bedawíns was by no means reassuring. Our inquiries as to the result of their endeavors were met by brief, evasive answers, or sulky silence. They evidently attached more importance to the accident that had happened than we at first did, probably from having some traditions in their minds, more fresh and palpable than our classical ones, of how *kafilas* that have strayed as we had done, have perished of starvation in the howling wilderness. After wandering about for some time, we were once again compelled to give up the search and halt on a bleak stony ridge for the night. Here we huddled together on our mats, endeavoring to keep off the cutting wind by a line of *zembils* and carpet-bags; and suffering intensely from the cold. Fatigue, however, caused us to sleep, and we woke in the morning drenched by a heavy fall of dew, and shivering like aspen leaves.

Wahsa now went back in search of the road, whilst Saleh and Yúnus, after leading us some distance ahead, each took a separate direction. We remained on a slope, at the foot of which the skeletons of several camels told that the place had been a disastrous one to former travellers. I noticed here the excessive clearness of the atmosphere, showing the forms of our Bedawíns as they gained the summits of distant hills, and making them appear almost close at hand. The sound of their footsteps too, as they came running back to announce the fruitlessness of their search, and compare notes, resounded afar over the Desert.

Whilst in this state of suspense we saw two crows wheeling in the air for some time, and then taking a southwest direction. Had we been in an age of superstition, we should have considered this a suffent indication, and have followed these kind guides, the descendants possibly of the birds which, on a similar occasion, and very near, says tradition, the point at which we had arrived, extricated Alexander the Great from the horrors of the pathless wilderness. Had we obeyed the augury we should not have gone wrong; but we did not yield to the suggestions of our imaginations, and waited for the return of Wahsa, who had certainly taken the best method of repairing his mistake. The stupid obstinacy of our Bedawíns, however, had nearly made matters worse. Instead of remaining where they were, or choosing some conspicuous spot for a halt, they drove their camels down into a little patch of vegetation to browse, and, as I have said, each went his way, giving us full leisure to reflect on the utter sterility of this country, in which neither tent nor well is to be found, and which is probably never trodden by the foot of man, except on the line marked out for the caravans, in the course of ages.

At our suggestion a gun was at length fired for Wahsa's information, but the sound did not reach him. As time wore on, I became impatient, not to say uneasy, and ascending an eminence, at length discovered a human form moving rapidly to and fro at an immense distance; so I constituted myself into a landmark, and soon had the satisfaction of seeing the guide make straight in my direction. On arriving, he seemed exhausted with fatigue, blessed my eyes (*"Salâm ala eynak!"*), and abused old Saleh, who he said ought to have guessed that, unless some one of the party showed himself, he should never have been able to rejoin us.

He now took us in the direction the crows had indicated, and it was not long before we fell into a well-defined track along a broad shallow valley. From this point onwards we were rarely out of sight of a double row of piles of stones, raised by the industry of successive caravans. Without their assistance indeed it would be impossible to keep the road, amidst the labyrinth of hills through or rather over which it passes, making no account scarcely of natural difficulties, up and down the steepest slopes in a direct line as nearly as possible as the bird flies. Some of these marks consist of five or six large flat stones, placed on one another so as to form a rickety column; others are great heaps, in some instances six or seven feet high. I believe that in most of the deserts which are traversed by caravans, and where materials are to be found, this benevolent practice of marking the road for future travellers exists. It is a tradition, however, mentioned in the Kitâb el Gemân of Shehab-ed-din, that the Berber race was always unwilling to adopt it; and I believe that the people of Siwah— an offshoot from this stock—have never contributed to render the road to their oasis obvious and easy. The Arabs, on the contrary, are very particular in performing this sacred duty.

All this region is covered with low flat hills, rising like islands out of a level plain, and scattered in front of long ranges, with occasional breaks, allowing one to see on either hand other expanses of country, with isolated hills of the same monotonous character, rarely differing in height, and, like those between Selêm and Haldeh, bearing a great resemblance to fortifications. At about half-past ten we issued into a plain, at the entrance of which the termination of the right-hand range, although not remarkable in appearance, bears the name of Húsbain el Gäoud, or "The Camel's Mouth." Beyond this we halted, among some of the stunted shrubs, that afforded a welcome opportunity for our camels to browse, and the existence or absence of which in this generally barren wilderness often determined us to abridge or prolong our morning's ride. During the halt we were reminded that our course lay now southward, for the thermometer rose to 100° in the tent. The air, however, was occasionally stirred by cool puffs of wind that lasted about five minutes, and somewhat revived us. Our poor donkeys were the worst off, and came hobbling, in spite of their fettered legs, to get under the scanty shade of our tent, in the cords of which they perpetually entangled themselves, to the great peril of its stability. They were now necessarily on short allowance of bad water, and were visibly knocking up.

All the bushes in this part of the Desert were covered with a white snail. I noticed several dozens on a plant not more than a foot high. The earth is thickly strewed with their shells, which have the peculiarity of a peak over the opening, divided from the rest of the shell by a ridge raised about an eighth of an inch. It is said that some of the inferior Bedawíns, who are generally unburdened with the scruples of the civilized Muslim, eat these snails. The Egyptians make fun of them on this account, and quote similar facts to prove that they are an accursed race. They tell a story to the effect that two hungry Bedawíns once found a cow that had died of disease, and, having been long without tasting flesh, made a hearty meal on the best parts. The period of digestion became the period of doubt and repentance, and, going to a holy Marâbut, they laid the case before him, expecting to get their consciences eased. "My sons," said the saint, "you have committed a great sin—" They would not allow him to proceed further, but exclaimed, "If it be a sin, we have eaten; and if it be not a sin, we have eaten. *Duffer fee eynak!* (An ass's hoof in your eye!)" and went their way in high dudgeon.

At this encampment we were covered with an immense number of gray lady-birds; and on the way from Haldeh, a few brown butterflies had fluttered across our path. A gray snake also, of the species common at Garah and Siwah, and reported to be extremely venomous, wriggled along the sand in the neighborhood of a little extempore tent, which the Bedawíns had rigged, with their guns for poles, their blankets for coverings, and our bags of beans and other traps to keep down the corners. This reptile I believe emerged from our provision basket, into which I was about to put my hand.

In the afternoon of this day I believe we reached the highest point of the great range of hills and series of table-lands along which we had been travelling from Mudar. For a time we could catch a wider glimpse than before of the surrounding country; but the line of stone-heaps we had hitherto faithfully followed soon led us into a valley surrounded with precipices of calcareous formation. The sides generally descended sheer down, and along the base were scattered fragments that had gradually given way from above. On either side opened glens and passes, obstructed by mounds and hills, which sometimes wore the appearance of tents, at others of houses, at others of ruined forts. The cliffs were generally of a reddish hue, but intersected with long white bands. As we advanced, with the sun ahead, this valley assumed an extraordinary appearance. All the ground began sparkling, as if strewed with a profusion of precious stones; and I easily understood how such a sight might have suggested to an imaginative Arab the gorgeous idea of that valley of Diamonds, where Sinbad once found himself pining to death amidst inestimable treasures. Here, as there, not a vestige of vegetation presented itself; but the ground was covered with innumerable fragments of talc, as well as pieces of oyster and other shells that glittered and twinkled, and blazed with a silver light over a vast expanse as they caught the sloping beams of the sun.

I may as well mention here that a little further on, at a place we passed during the night, and noticed only on our return, the road had been cut or worn through an immense bed of gigantic oyster shells, which seemed to form three fourths at least of the substance of the lofty banks on either side. These fossils are to be met within greater or less quantities all the way to Síwah, where many of the rocks are nothing but buge agglomerations of shells. I was the more particularly interested in noticing the fact, because Strabo quotes a passage from the geographer Eratosthenes, in which it is stated that near the temple of Jupiter Ammon and along the road to it, vast quantities of oyster and other shells are found, from which the inference is drawn that the Mediterranean Sea formerly extended so far inland.

All the points of the hills overlooking the road were marked by the little columns of flat stones I have mentioned: and by their assistance we managed to keep the direction along the centre of the series of basins of which the valley is formed. We now learned that we were descending toward the plain by what is called the Nugb el Ghrâb, or The Pass of the Crow, a name which may possibly have some connection with the story of the journey of Alexander, and his miraculous extrication from difficulties. The names of places in the Desert are not often changed; and if we wish to give a reasonable explanation of a poetical legend we may, without difficulty, suppose that when the illustrious traveller lost his way it was because he missed this Pass, which appears to be the only one by which a descent can be effected to the plain. When at length his guides hit upon the right valley, and mentioned it as The Pass of the Crow, we can easily imagine how the tradition took its rise. Peter Pindar has explained the whole philosophy of the thing.

A little after sunset we came to a steep declivity, down which it was necessary to force the camels into a lower part of the Pass. At the bottom we halted three or four hours to wait for the moon, in a position sufficiently romantic and uncomfortable. A northeast wind, cold and cutting, came whistling over the tops of the hills and seemed to be sucked down into the hollow, where we sat on the chilly stones wrapped in our cloaks, or lay prostrate to snatch a brief spell of sleep. On all sides perpendicular masses of rock reared themselves, black and frowning, looking like a vast ruined wall encircling us; whilst overhead the Milky Way spanned the heavens, and all the constellations shone with a brilliancy, known only in the East, and, I may, add, in the Desert. At about ten the moon lifted up its slightly depressed orb over the vast pile of rocks, and we were soon again in motion, right glad to escape from so bleak a spot. A few hundred yards ahead, after passing a narrow defile, an extraordinary scene burst upon us. Whilst the irregular line of rocks continued close on our left, we suddenly beheld to the right a great chasm; and beyond, glittering in the moonlight, and clothed by it, no doubt, with yet stranger forms and more gigantic proportions than nature had afforded, a huge pile of white rocks, looking like the fortifications of some vast fabulous city, such as Martin would choose to paint, or Beckford to describe. There were yawning gateways flanked by bastions of tremendous altitude; there were towers and pyramids, and crescents, and domes and dizzy pinnacles, and majestic castellated heights, all invested with unearthly grandeur by the magic beams of the moon, yet exhibiting—in wide breaches and indescribable ruin—evident proofs that, during a long course of ages, they had been battered and undermined by the hurricane, the rain-shower, the thunderbolt, the winter-torrent, and all the mighty artillery of time. Piled one upon another, and repeated over and over again, these strangely contorted rocks stretched away as far as the eye could reach, sinking, however, as they receded, and leading the mind, though not the eye, down to the distant plain below. In vain did our eager glances endeavor to ascertain the limit of the descent to which we had so abruptly come. The horizon was dissolved in a misty light; but stars twinkling low down, as if beneath our feet, showed that we were about to abandon, once for all, the great range along the summit of which we had toiled during so many nights and days.

A gorge, black as Erebus, lay directly across our path; and we had to make a detour to the left in order to reach the place where it is practicable for camels. Here there was a pause; for again the generally patient beasts hesitated, and moaned and backed, and drew up their long necks and huddled together;

as well, indeed, they might. The declivity was steep, and filled with heavy shadows. Precipices hemmed it in on every side; and here and there we could distinguish a huge fragment of rock standing, like a petrified giant, in the way, and catching perchance on its bare scalp some stray beams of sickly light. But down we did go; the camels, when once the impetus was given, carried forward by the weight of their burdens, yet keeping their footing with admirable sagacity; we, almost in the same manner, each leading by the halter his long-eared monture. In truth it was a picturesque scene—partly lighted by the slanting rays of the moon, partly buried in broad masses of shade, and only requiring a few Bedawín heads appearing from behind the jagged rocks, and the flash of a gun or two, to make it worthy of the pencil of Salvator Rosa. According to our guides some probability existed of such an illumination taking place; and our imaginations were thus supplied with materials to work on, as in the solemn hush of that romantic night was scrambled, slid, staggered, almost rolled down.

A series of sloping plains and rapid descents, with an occasional rise, led to the bottom of the Pass; where we bivouacked for the night. To our left the range of hills had receded out of sight; whilst that to our right, which here and there exhibited the most fantastic shapes, sometimes of fortresses, sometimes of pyramids surmounted by sphinxes' heads, stretched away in rugged grandeur to the southwest. In every other direction opened a plain, above which the dim forms of detached hills showed themselves at intervals.

Postscript: Bayle St. John successfully finished his excursion into the Libyan Desert and then in 1849 published his account of the journey.

When he first set foot on his journey across the Moroccan Sahara, Jeffrey Tayler wanted to personally experience the life of the Bedouin nomads who accompanied him. The horrible conditions assaulted him: intense heat, blinding dust storms, and overwhelming filth and poverty. His account of the ordeal is a riveting one.

GLORY IN A CAMEL'S EYE
Trekking Through the Moroccan Sahara

JEFFREY TAYLER

Assa and Houris in the Mists

Hassan and Mmbari were spirited conversationalists. It was a rare moment indeed when they weren't praising the virtues of a prominent 'Arib sheikh, debating the vices of a controversial cameleer, or disputing the lay of the land ahead. I often found myself enraptured by the guttural music of their Hassaniya Arabic. I reveled in its rich interdental consonants, which, thanks to the isolation imposed on the Saharawis by the desert, had mostly retained their classical pronunciation (in contrast to the degraded consonants of the Moroccan dialect). I was intrigued by its vocabulary, which contained words (*witta* for "car," *dashra* for "city," *shidda* for "drought," for example) that existed in no other dialect I had heard. And I relished the throaty 'ain and ghain sounds common to all forms of Arabic, dialectal and classical.

No other language enchants me the way Arabic does. *Sihr halal* (lawful magic) is what the Arabs call the effect their poetry produces on its hearers. The magic was born in the desert, among the Bedouin of pre-Islamic Arabia, who, though illiterate, were among the most accomplished poets of any age. Poor denizens of denuded earth, they had nothing but their tongues with which to make art; in a world where a cup of water and a handful of dates made for luxury, extravagant language took on heightened importance. The odes the Bedouin composed before the advent of Islam remain some of the greatest in Arabic literature. Even the words of simple orators like my Ruhhal companions held something of the poetic and worked *sihr halal* on me. Their talk, pealing with locutions from the Qur'an and invocations of God, its Hassaniya inflections conjuring up the vast burning wastes of their homeland, made a description of camel fodder or sand dunes sound dramatic and grand. This was a matter of sound more than sense, to be sure, but here among the rocks sound was all we had.

Yet no enchantment with language could compensate for the physical and spiritual deterioration we suffered as we marched farther and farther down the valley. After we left Foum al-Hisn the rigors of the trip began wearing on all of us in ominous ways. We felt with each new day a fatigue more penetrating, and, at times, disorienting; we suffered more and more stress-related ailments. Hassan's back now pained him as much as his knees; Mbari complained of spasms in his calves that turned each step into agony for hours on end; and the sun, growing stronger as summer came on, kept me lightheaded, fever-stricken, and nauseated for most of the day. Mbari and I tried to resign ourselves to silence about our growing infirmity: we knew it would not outlast the trip. But Hassan was volubly humbled. "In the old days our ancestors walked twelve hours at a stretch without drinking water. They died strong. But look at us. We live weak."

Could the desert defeat us, cripple us, prevent us from making it to the Atlantic? The closer we came to our goal, the weaker we became, and the more anxious I grew.

But good times were just ahead, Hassan kept saying. Refreshing blue mists would fill the air in Assa, which was just a couple of hundred kilometers from the Atlantic. As summer drew on and the heat increased, we thought only of the mists of Assa.

The next day, in the distance, between Jbel Ouarkziz and the Anti-Atlas, the twin minarets of Assa's two main mosques wobbled rubbery in the heat under a fiery noon sky. There were no mists. We staggered, weakened from the sun, toward a pair of acacias that were more bushes than trees, the scrawniest acacias we had seen so far. We couched the camels beside them and unloaded, moving slowly to conserve our strength.

I tossed my mattress under a square yard of acacian shade and collapsed—on thorns that stabbed through two inches of foam and punctured my back and elbows. I bounced back up in pain and impaled my straw hat on the branches. Smarting, for a moment I sat still and composed myself. After extracting the thorns I carefully cleared the ground and repositioned the mattress. This time I lay back slowly. Next to me was a hole in the ground, a burrow of some sort a few inches wide. Finally relaxing a bit, I peered into it, wondering what sort of animal would dig it. Not the palm rat, I hoped, whose bite was said to be fatal. I began to doze off.

From out of the rippling mercurial mirages in the east

whence we had come materialized three hourilike creatures
swathed in robes of black, blue, and purple. At first I disbe-
lieved my eyes and strained to refocus them. But there *were*
three women gliding toward us through the blaze, their dark
milhafas fluttering with the hot drafts rising from the stony
earth.

"As-salam 'alaykum!" they intoned, making demure gestures
of salutation and pulling up their *milhafas* to cover their chins.

We answered their greetings. Right away I noticed the
striking beauty of the youngest one: oval-faced, she had pale
sea-green eyes, a regal arched nose, and round lips; tufts of
unkempt hennaed hair were struggling free of her shroud.
Beauty was beauty. She had power, and I found myself
staring.

"Shhalkum?" (How are you?) I asked them.

"Shi bes ma kain" (Nothing to complain of), the oldest one
replied in a lilting voice; the other two kept silent, smiling and
bashfully averting their eyes.

Hassan, who was starting a fire to make lunch, made a
space for them on one of the rugs he had spread out. Mbari, I
noticed, looked away, too modest to confront them. But only
the eldest one sat down. She had a row of crooked teeth; the
skin on her face was crinkled white paper; her hands were
hennaed leather; her sandaled feet were hennaed in elaborate
geometric designs, as were the feet of the others, who walked
off a little ways and examined us, holding their *milhafas* over
their mouths. Hassan offered them tea, but only the eldest
accepted.

She addressed me. Did I have medicine for the itch? For
the eyes? For the joints? I was sorry to tell her that I had no
medicine for any of these things. She was suffering from
rheumatism. Had I rheumatism pills? I hadn't. "I'm just too
old to live!" she said with a chuckle.

She and Hassan began exchanging news. She and her daughters lived in the white tent we had passed in the wadi an hour ago; her husband and sons were off tending their camels. Their talk ranged over the price of oats in Tata, the cost of flour in Fez, the flocks we had seen, the rain that, this year, was now certain not to fall. Her manners contrasted with those of Ruhhal men: she didn't slurp her tea, pick her nose, or shout at the top of her voice to those sitting a foot or two away; as she spoke she made graceful gestures with her hennaed hands. I could have watched her and listened to her lilting voice for hours. Lawful magic, if of another form.

The heat grew unbearable, the shade even scarcer. Hassan finished baking bread, and stew bubbled in our pot. They declined to lunch with us. The eldest got up and they all ambled away, their shrouds fluttering in the heat. The minarets of Assa had disappeared in noontime haze, and we sat down to eat.

"In Assa it's cool," Hassan kept saying. In Assa it felt like it was 150 degrees.

By any measure, however, Assa was modern. Unfortunately, "modern" in the Moroccan Sahara equates with concrete row houses where the plumbing backs up until people prefer to "go" in the streets, where temperatures inside exceed those outside by a factor of ten, and where the screaming of one child echoes from house to house until it kicks off a crying jag among all the tots in the neighborhood. Modern also means soldiers in sandals peddling bicycles, plainclothes policemen, recognizable by their crewcuts and urban dress, and a walled-off palace with crenelated roof and white-trimmed windows for the royally appointed governor. And modern of course means electricity, much of which goes to illuminating the governor's residence.

All this modernity impressed my companions. Assa had become modern in the decade since they last saw it; in those benighted times it had been a tranquil scattering of adobe houses built around a mosque under swaying palms. Yet there is still no hotel in Assa, and there are only a couple of store-front dives serving grilled chicken and french fries. This makes sense, for many of the Ruhhal who live here do so only for part of the year (they spend the rest of their time with their flocks) and have no tradition of eating out, unless you count eating out in the desert as eating out. I invited Hassan and Mbari to have lunch in one of the restaurants, but they said no. Food from the common pot was all they knew and all they wanted.

We pitched camp on the *hamada* a mile away from the walls of the governor's palace. After doing our laundry and hanging our clothes on thorns to dry, Hassan and I sat and watched the sun go down and the palace lights come on. The wind was at our backs, wafting the latrine stench of the nearby wadi away from us and into the cement lanes. As in Akka, the outskirts of the town were used as a dump.

"How beautiful," Hassan said. "The people here are all Saharawis, all from one tribe. Their ancestry is grand. I'm proud to see the city they've built. Before the drought it was just a few mud houses. The sheikhs have planned this city with the government."

"Where do nomads get the money to buy houses?"

"Oh, money is no problem. A nomad will sell ten of his camels at ten thousand rials apiece"—about five hundred dollars—"and he can buy a house. A house with a floor and ceilings, made of concrete. If he wants, he'll buy a fan to make a breeze in the house."

"And what happens to his camels?"

"He gets a cousin to look after them. Some of the people of

Assa have three hundred camels. These are rich people. With ancestry. But living in a town like this changes people."

"How?"

"I have relatives here. I saw them today, but they didn't even invite me for tea. Their manners are becoming those of city people. There are even drunks here."

There was no reason to stay in Assa. We bought supplies, rested for two days, and prepared to move on. But by now we were too worn out to recover in so little time. Only the proximity of the Atlantic—the end of the trip—gave us the energy to get going.

Around dawn the next day, baby blue mists rolled in and cooled the valley. Nothing could have raised my spirits more, and I spent several minutes standing outside my tent taking deep breaths of the wet air—and listening to Hassan say, "I *told* you so! By God, I *told* you so!"

But soon the sight of blood and gore and a bellowing beast spoiled my cheer. Hassan and Mbari decided that Hanan was still too young to be led with an *aghaba*. So, using a knitting needle, they tore him a new nostril and ran a rough nylon rope through the hole (his *khurs*, or nostril ring, having been lost along the way). The rope not only stretched the hole, it abraded it and added to the animal's misery. From then on, every morning, despite Hanan's protestations, they would rotate the rope in the hole (and rip apart the scab) to make sure his flesh did not grow into it.

Hanan, thus punctured, was the most obedient he had ever been. By now we knew the character of all three camels, which had developed to meet the challenges of the trip. Hanan had been a complainer who cried out whenever any of us approached him; now he was docile and stoic. As ever, his lower lip drooped and gave him a doltish look. However, he took his revenge on Hassan and Mbari by defecating whenever they passed by his rear end, wherefrom green pellets would tumble out and bounce onto their sandals. Na'im was still petulant, but he had matured a bit and come to understand his job; I couldn't remember the last time he had couched without permission. Still, he had a ways to go. He was a frequent belcher and avid urinator, taking advantage of any pause in our progress to spread his legs and pee. (In this he differed from Hanan, who dribbled as he walked.) Mabruk no longer stole vegetables, so we changed his nickname from Sinbay (thief) to Biyyid (the white one, on account of his color). He was as cheerful as ever and carried the heaviest loads without complaining. I humored him and often brought him orange peelings on the sly or gave him a carrot or two from the couscous pot.

None of the camels ever bit, kicked, or otherwise threatened us, though they were powerful animals, and my Ruhhal cautioned me never to let my guard down around them. I grew dearly fond of all of them. They worked hard on this trip, harder than they had ever worked, and they suffered much—pulled muscles, stomach upsets, hunger, and, most of all, debilitating fatigue, which was evident in their grunting gaits and belabored, oft-aborted rises when loaded.

So we left Assa and headed into the mists, following a piste that led up a slope, with Jbel Ouarkziz and the Drâa somewhere to the south, the Anti-Atlas as ever a wall to the north. Our destination was the village of Âouïnet-Torkoz, a two days' walk away. Torkoz was our last supply stop before we would enter the Anti-Atlas and face what my Ruhhal warned me would be our toughest trial yet—a week of trekking up steep mountain trails under a pitiless sun. This was a necessary detour. For a stretch the Drâa lacked wells, so we would cross the mountains and pick up the valley on the other side.

Given our weakened state, I preferred not to contemplate entering the mountains.

Not an acacia or a tamarisk intruded upon the emptiness—there were only vistas of sweeping *hamada* ending in mist between the two mountain ranges. We breathed in the cool and walked. By midmorning we reached the zenith of the slope and began a descent, passing a dead jackal, who resembled a long-snouted dog, but with sharp ears, tawny fur, and vicious slit-opal eyes.

Âouïnet-Torkoz

By noon the mists had evaporated. After lunch, Hassan grew oddly quiet. I asked him what was wrong.

He stood up. "I cannot lie." He stretched out his arms and shook his head; he closed his eyes, as if prepared to reveal the painful truths of a tormented soul. "No, I can't say it'll take only two days to get to Âouïnet-Torkoz. God knows how long it will take. God knows."

I got out the map and spread it on the ground. It showed that fifty kilometers separated Assa and Âouïnet-Torkoz—a two-day trip, given that we usually covered twenty-seven to twenty-nine kilometers a day.

"But—"

"Don't tell me what's on that map," he said. "Looking at paper isn't the same as walking."

"Hassan, excuse me, but this map is accurate. We've seen that. I don't know what you're talking about. You just told me in Assa it would take two days to get to Âouïnet-Torkoz. You and Mbari *both* told me."

"We never said that. I cannot lie. God alone knows—"

"Mbari?"

"Hassan said that, not I."

This was not true.

"You *did* say that, both of you did. And why do you keep saying God knows and you can't lie? There're a finite number of kilometers between the two villages. The map shows it. It's not a question of words."

He spread his arms again. "I cannot lie. I swear by God on High, we're three days away. At least. Maybe more."

"That's absurd! We've walked half a day, and now we've got less than one and a half to go! It can't be otherwise! Think of how many kilometers we cover in an hour, and look at the map!"

Raising his forefinger and placing a hand on his heart, Hassan swore to God that he was truthful to a fault, a hater of liars, a straight talker renowned throughout the valley, nay, across the Sahara for his honesty. His greatest fault was—it so happened and he would dare just this once to admit it—an overly zealous respect for the truth. In making such theater of his honesty, he convinced me that he was trying to deceive me—in order to lengthen the trip and increase his fee. In other circumstances this might not have been a big deal: I knew he was poor, with many mouths to feed at home, and I sympathized with him. But we were all exhausted, our camels were weak, and the heat now spoiled meat and vegetables so quickly that a delay would entail the risk that we might be caught out for several days or more with only rice to eat. I had no desire to slow our pace.

Seeking support, I turned to Mbari. "Well, what do you think?"

"By God, Hassan speaks the truth."

"Mbari, *you* are the one who knows this part of the route, remember?"

He muttered something inaudible and looked away.

That was it: they were conspiring against me. I told them

to pack up—we were going to make Âouïnet-Torkoz by the next evening, and I would talk no more about it.

The heat returned and intensified: the next day at lunch it was 110 degrees in the shade. Late that afternoon, after entering upon a stretch of valley rich with limestone and strewn with marble-colored slag, we crossed Wadi Talh (Wadi Acacia) and dragged ourselves panting and bleary-eyed up a stony rise. From its height we saw, beneath a sun that burned straight into our faces, the village of Âouïnet-Torkoz (Little Spring of the Torkoz Tribe). Little more than a few dozen stone houses and a mosque beside a grove of stunted palms, Torkoz promised meager provisions. Beyond it, following the base of Jbel Ouarkziz, the Drâa wandered away to the southwest, without wells, untrammeled by Ruhhal. Above the village towered the Anti-Atlas: crag after jagged crag cut into the sky, separating us from the Atlantic.

We made our way down to the village, with Mbari stumbling along sunstruck in the final half-mile.

We set up camp beneath the palms as the sun went down. After filling our jerry cans halfway at the well (we could not burden the camels with full cans in the mountains), Mbari and I walked into the village, needing a sack of oats or dates for camel feed, plus couscous, meat, and vegetables. It was deserted (its inhabitants were out grazing their herds, or drought had driven them away, we didn't know) except for a few Saharawi elders crouched in the long evening shade of stone walls near the tiny central square. They set suspicious eyes on me; perhaps I was the only Nasrani to visit this remote settlement in years. In the one open shop there was no meat to be had, and no couscous. The vegetables were scrawny and expensive, but we bought them. There were no oats or dates for the camels. Worse, Mbari said the camels might be squeamish about eating in the mountains, where the vegetation differed from that of the desert.

We returned to camp, ate dinner, and assessed our situation. Between here and the Atlantic there were two small villages, but they would have few supplies, being basically Ruhhal settlements and therefore probably as deserted as Âouïnet-Torkoz. We had only rice and flour, plus three days' worth of vegetables, along with tea and some sugar. According to the map, and as the crow flies, Tiglite, the first village we would come across, was fifty kilometers away, but this was fifty kilometers through mountains, which led me to think that if we followed a trail, we could expect three days of strenuous travel, at least. I asked them if they knew the trail; yes, they did, roughly. My map showed that we could pick up some sort of piste (winding down from the north) about halfway to Tiglite, but neither Hassan nor Mbari had ever heard of it. Did they know where the wells were? Not exactly, but there *should* be wells, and there should be Ruhhal to ask— or at least there *could* be: maybe the drought would have forced them north, to the Sous. In consideration of how much water we were going to lose in sweat hiking uphill in this heat, and given that the higher altitudes would make the sun harder to bear, increasing the likelihood of dehydration, their uncertainty about the wells made me nervous.

We stared at the map. Hassan and Mbari exchanged subtle glances. Mbari stood up. His voice shook with anger. "It is not fifty kilometers to Tiglite but seventy! Or eighty! By God, with these mountains it could be more. Maybe a hundred. God alone knows. The mountains are very hard. I'll not kill these camels with a breakneck pace! No, I will *not*!"

We had not talked of traveling at a breakneck pace. I sensed a continuation of their ruse.

"Mbari, *what* are you talking about?"

Hassan arose next. "The camels must live! We must go slowly—*slooowly*—in the mountains!"

I stood up and looked at them. We were all tired, but they had strength enough for more acts in their drama. I didn't. I said good night and walked back to my tent.

Mbari shouted after me. "By God! I won't let these camels drop in the mountains! I swear it! I—"

Hassan asked him to calm down.

With the heat, which was not abating with the night, and with my nerves, which were growing tauter, I couldn't sleep, so I came out an hour or so later to sit with Hassan and Mbari by the fire. Soon after, strangers approached us. Two were young men in white djellabas, whose cheeks sported three-day beards (worn by some pious Muslims as a sign of humility; such beards cannot be groomed, and thus show a disregard for personal appearance); the third, who was older, wore the chocolate-brown *'abaya* robes of the Saharawis who live in the Western Sahara. They were all from the village.

After the greeting ritual ended, the older one asked us if we had come for the magic of the cave.

No, we answered. What was that?

"You leave flour in the cave up there and pray to the jinn. In the morning you find it changed into whatever you want, money or gold or silver. But it's deep in the mountains and many don't find it. You want to know the way there?"

We thanked him but said no, and asked him about wells. He explained where the first one was, but his directions were complicated, and I doubted whether a stranger to the region could follow them.

After that he looked up at the village. "We're right on the border with the Western Sahara, you know. The Spanish were there"—he pointed to the south—"the French here. When the

Moroccans took over we built the village. We were all just Ruhhal till then. Anyway, good travels!"

He walked on. The others sat down with us. They were teachers at the school, and pleased to meet me; they got no foreign visitors here. After introductions we started chatting. They had never traveled to Tiglite and so couldn't help us plot a route there.

During our talk, one of them, Omar, called me a Nasrani. He meant no offense, but it rankled me. It was unpleasant being labeled, and it vaguely smacked of racism. Past experience had made me sensitive: while I was living in Marrakesh, no one called me anything but Nasrani until I adopted my Arabic name.

"You know," I said, "I'm not sure calling me a Nasrani is polite. I just told you my name."

"Oh, I didn't mean any harm," he said. "But you *are* a Nasrani, a believer in Jesus."

"How do you know? You have no idea what religion I am."

His friend Samir cut in. "To us Nasrani means foreigner. Just like *gaouri*." *Gaouri* was even less flattering: it derived from an old Turkish word for infidel and was now often used in Morocco in place of Nasrani. "Even some Moroccans call themselves *gaouri* now. Those who adopt Western ways are proud to say they're *gaouri*. It's not such an insult anymore."

"*Gaouri* reminds me of religious discrimination, of how in the Umayyad Empire and Ottoman Turkey non-Muslims had to cut their hair in a weird way, weren't allowed to ride horses, wear hats, or build churches or synagogues. In the Abbasid Empire they even had to attach wooden statues of devils to their houses and had to step aside when Muslims passed. So why don't we just call each other by name."

Omar said, "Well, it *is* natural that Christians were not allowed to do everything Muslims could do. There had to be some discrimination. After all, Islam is true, and privileges have to be given to those who follow the truth. We respect your religion, but it isn't true. Christianity is incomplete, after all. Only Islam is complete. Isn't that so?"

Samir nudged him. "Don't talk like that."

"This Nasrani speaks Arabic. He should have read the Qur'an. Have you?"

"I don't ask you whether you've read the Bible. Religion is a personal matter. I respect that you're Muslim and I respect Islam, or I wouldn't be here. I don't ask you to explain why you believe in Islam."

"I'll be happy to tell you."

"There's no need to. All I'm saying is that religion is a personal affair. Even in the Qur'an it says this. And it says there should be no compulsion in religion."

This kind of talk would only prompt him to lecture me about Islam, to do his sacred duty and try to convert me, so I changed the subject to language. The gendarmes who had questioned us recently had noted down all our details in French. When I was a Peace Corps volunteer in the 1980s, the Moroccan government was Arabizing its schools, phasing out French. This was a major shift, even though education had been in both Arabic and French during the colonial days. After independence government affairs and business still tended to be conducted in French; the educated middle class wanted to retain French, which allowed them to lord it over the Arabic-educated masses and the illiterate (more than half the population), who knew only their dialects. Many of Morocco's best-known authors write in French (and live in France, where they are free to write what they want). The Moroccan independence movement, led mostly by French-educated Moroccan intellectuals, issued its first demands in a French-language document. French politicians at times still

praise Morocco's Francophone heritage, which certain nation-
alistic Moroccan politicians answer with anti-French rhetoric—
in French. Morocco is Arab and Islamic, they tell them—in
French. So what had happened to Arabization? Why was
there still so much French in official circles?

"Arabization failed," Samir said. "The schools are Arabi-
cized but not the universities, except in literature and history,
which were in Arabic anyway. This makes it tough on the stu-
dents who go to college because they have to study French
hard to catch up. All the university textbooks in sciences and
philosophy are in French, and it costs too much to translate
them. This is bad. We're still stuck with the colonial mindset,
even though our constitution says we're an Arab and Islamic
state. What we really are is a Muslim state made up of two
peoples. We have three Berber dialects in this country and a
third of Moroccans speak them. Should Berber speakers be
forced to use Arabic? A lot of them prefer French because
they don't like the Arabs."

He was right, but there was more to the language question
than failed government programs or the Berber-Arab divide.
Perhaps more than any other country in the Arab world,
Morocco has developed a national identity that exceeds in
strength the pan-Arab nationalism that has so many adherents
elsewhere in North Africa and the Middle East. The simplest
explanation for this lies in Morocco's geography and in its history of isolation: the Turks, who unified most of the Arab
world under the Ottoman banner, never managed to conquer
Morocco, thanks in part to the Atlas Mountains. Later, com-
peting Great Power designs on Morocco resulted in a stale-
mate that kept the country nominally independent until 1912.
In recent decades, tension with Algeria (especially over the
Western Sahara) and a perceived threat to the Moroccan
monarchy from Islamic fundamentalism and radical Arab

ideologies, along with simple economics, have prompted the Moroccan elite to look to Europe for alliances, cultural exchange, and trade: France remains Morocco's chief creditor, investor, source of tourists, and host of guest workers. In 1984 the French-educated King Hassan II even officially requested membership in the European Union.

We discussed all this until midnight. Then the teachers told us that they had to get up early in the morning, and we had to rest before heading into the Anti-Atlas, so we all said good night.

I crawled into my tent, worrying about the Anti-Atlas. The antics Hassan and Mbari had performed to convince me that God alone knew how long it would take to reach Tiglite made me wonder if they might not know the route. They knew the desert, but how could they know the mountains?

A wind began stirring. I hoped it would bring cool, which would greatly ease our travels. But it was coming from the east. Blowing in from the Sahara, the wind carried only more heat, more dust. It was a Shirgi, the same broiling, sand-laden gale that had once nearly cost me my life.

Crossing the Anti-Atlas

To our relief, the Shirgi died at sunrise, but it left behind stagnant, ninety-degree air that so early in the day boded ill for hiking. At eight in the morning we trekked out of Âouïnet-Torkoz in an effulgent bath of sunlight, passing around the rear of the village and up into a meandering valley formed by several abutting mountains. Sluggish from the heat, we walked slowly, saying nothing, dreading the terrain ahead.

We had begun the day in foul humor. I had deposited my gear in Hanan's saddlebag. Hassan came over and started working the nylon rope back and forth through Hanan's new nostril, abrading the hole and bloodying the rope. Hanan hollered and shook his head and tried to rise, spilling his load; Hassan cursed and pushed him down. I flinched at all this pain. Hassan saw my reaction and yanked the rope harder. He must be holding a grudge from our argument the day before, I thought, and he's taking it out on the camel. I glared at him, and thought of protesting. But an argument was the last thing we needed now, so I turned away. Soon we were packed and on our way.

An hour after leaving Torkoz, we came upon a piste, much degraded, here and there blocked by fallen rocks, but passable. Wanting to face the rigors of the land alone, I walked ahead of the group, but, step by step, to my surprise and increasing delight, I found that we were entering a new world. Argan trees replaced acacias and clustered in low groves, their thick, holly-green foliage hiding acorn-sized fruit and sheltering squirrels. Manic butterflies and lazy bees attended rafts of crimson, purple, and pale blue flowers. Patches of thyme began proliferating over the earth, which was turning from dust-brown to a pale limestone-green.

We were leaving the Sahara! I walked faster and faster up the piste, breathing in air that was growing cooler, an unexpected elation rushing over me. Grasshoppers jumped about in thickening brush. Beetles with opalescent shells scuttled at the base of rocks. Red-rumped swallows darted against slopes of shale tinged with delicate mossy green. Martins and swifts cut through the pure morning light. Ahead a falcon dipped low and then ascended to an aerie on a cliff shaded by a crag. The thick argan trees chased away any hint of drought, the dry, or the dead.

We climbed higher and higher, sticking to the serpentine piste. The sun beat down but, breathing in the ever cooler air,

I jumped ahead, quickening my pace and leaving my Ruhhal behind, feeling for the first time that I was nearing the end of my trip. I suddenly wanted nothing more than the caress of Atlantic breezes on my face. I yearned to forget about the Sahara. The Atlantic, the Atlantic! I pictured myself crashing into the cold, thrashing surf, as "Uqba bin Nafi" is reputed to have done after leading the first Arab campaign of conquest into Morocco more than thirteen centuries ago.

At noon we stopped in a high valley and rested under a canopy of argans. The camels turned their heads away from the unfamiliar leaves and fruit, and they refused to eat the grass. This worried Hassan and Mbari, but they were pleased with the change in climate, if somewhat apprehensive: it was new to them, as were the mountain environs. We ate a salad and slept until three, and then moved on.

Nothing could dampen my joy at what I was seeing. The trail wound and rose and looped upward, until finally we were trekking single file atop a ridge, bathed in cool wind and light and the scent of wildflowers. But we didn't know where to find a well, and we needed water, having only half-filled our jerry cans in Âouïnet-Torkoz. Just as we realized our predicament, we spotted a nomad tent. A skinny youth in a blue-gold *dara'a* and an indigo *firwal* emerged and, calling out a greeting, waved for us to approach. After prolonged salams and inquiries about our health and provenance, he agreed to walk us to a nearby well, and we set out behind him. His long feet were jammed into kid-sized sandals; his toes appeared ready to burst like ripe grapes, and he walked with a limp.

We passed along a windy, slag-littered escarpment, with the sun hanging straight ahead of us. I shielded my eyes, but the light burned into my brain, and something went wrong with me. My steps became tottery; a cold sweat ran over my.

forearms and dripped down my palms; I felt hot and then cold; the rock- and argan-covered slopes of the Anti-Atlas flashed with pinpoint stars before my eyes. Mbari was staggering along, also sunstruck, keeping himself from falling by holding on to one of Mabruk's saddlebags. We followed a footpath down into an explosion of pink-blossomed reeds and sprouting palms set amid a tiny canyon of black rock. There was a well there. Two women, young and fleshy and pink-cheeked, wearing djellabas but no veils, were doing laundry in plastic tubs. I took wobbly steps to a sofa-shaped rock and collapsed thereupon. Mbari did the same. Hassan alone remained unaffected. The thin air of the mountains and the sun were getting to us, I thought: *need to drink more water.* I started dozing off.

"*Hak!*" a female voice said to me. "*Hak, khud!*"

I opened my eyes. One of the women was offering me a glass of tea. I sat up and took it and opened my mouth to thank her, but no words came out; my hands trembled as I raised the glass to my lips. But she kept smiling at me, in a motherly way. She was squatting over her tub, her djellaba pulled up, her floral-patterned *sirwal* covering her legs to her ankles. Her kohl-blackened eyes and aquiline nose, her dark hair glinting with tints of henna, her high-arched, dainty feet all marked her as a beauty. I sipped the tea and recovered. Hassan filled our jerry cans and watered the camels.

"The camels must eat," Hassan told the boy, "but they won't eat all these strange plants you have around here."

"There is a wadi," the boy replied. "I'll show you."

We thanked the women for the tea. Too weak to walk yet, I climbed aboard Na'im. Led by the boy, we left the oasis and traveled higher and higher, ascending the rumplike mountains into a realm of sea breezes and whirling mists that moistened my skin and brought on a delirium of pleasure. The

Anti-Atlas spread to every horizon, wild and pristine, like the surface of a forgotten planet.

We left the heights and descended into a valley, Wadi Mhijjiba, still led by the boy. A wind from the west ripped through the palm- and argan-studded slopes, bringing billowing mists, and even, now and then, drops of water large enough to be called rain, but the sun was shining, slanting toward the horizon, turning the mists red-gold. I found myself shivering as we reached the spot where we were to camp: it was cold enough that I almost needed a sweater. There were many herds of camels there. The valley resounded with the bellowing of adult males, the nasal complaints of children, and the groans of pregnant females. Their Ruhhal masters, all in brown Saharawi 'abayas, greeted us; they were heading for the Sous. The boy said goodbye and left.

We pitched camp. Incredulous of the change in climate, I sat down with Hassan and Mbari as Mbari made tea.

Hassan was grinning: he was happy with the cool. Our mood lightened. "That girl at the well invited us to spend the night in her tent with her and her friend."

"Are you serious?"

"I'm not joking. But I wasn't sure if you would permit it, so I said no. After all, we want to stick to our schedule. We can't take any extra days to fool around with houris."

I looked at Mbari. "He's joking, right?"

"By God, I don't know."

"I'm not joking. Not at all. By God!"

He had to be joking about the woman: we had been together at the well and I had heard no such talk. Still, it was odd to hear him speak of sex in this lighthearted way, after he (and Mbari) had shown themselves so reticent on the subject. I could only ascribe it to the intoxicating effect the cool was having on us all.

———

The night was cold. I slept with my sleeping bag zipped to my neck, waking up now and then to wonder at the sound of the wind soughing in the trees. Around dawn a raucous chirping of birds awoke me for good. The temperature hovered at fifty degrees. The sun shone through crystalline air; the breezes carried the scents of pomegranates, grasses, and other vegetation—the scents of life. The Ruhhal were already on the move, herding their camels north into the mountains.

Hassan and Mbari had thrown on every piece of clothing they owned and were already packing when I came out. We picked up a piste that wandered out of the valley, climbed up and around a succession of low ridges, and then led onto a mesa where the wind played and sheep grazed—there was grass enough here for livestock. Now round, leafy shrubs dominated the land, increasingly mixed with low, round cacti. Even at noon it was only sixty-eight degrees here (I kept checking my thermometer), but the wind made it seem colder. With a feeling of newfound gratitude I pulled my sweater out of my pack, shook off two months of Saharan dust, and put it on. I walked, hugging the wool to my body, enjoying the comfort of wearing a warm sweater in cool air. We stopped for lunch beneath a bower of argans. I grabbed my foam mattress and threw it down in the sun. Luxuriating in the warmth, I slept until the food was ready.

By late afternoon, the piste had left the mesa and led us into rolling mountains. We would not make Tiglite that evening, that was clear, but Mbari said it was close. We stopped for the night in a valley, and I took my tent and hiked away with it to a secluded dell of argans and cacti, needing solitude. The foliage in the landscape was reminding me of something familiar, making me feel at home, and I relished this half-formed sensation. Selfishly, I did not want my companions to intrude. They seemed to understand, and took no offense.

Iron-gray clouds hung low over the valley, sifting shafts of failing sunlight over the mountains and rendering the dusk lonely and mournful, reminiscent, somehow, of death. The night fell truly dark, without stars. Bundled in my sleeping bag, cold, still somewhat weak and nauseated, I ate a cous-cous and tomato dish in my tent. The camels soon couched around me and began munching on argan leaves; they were adjusting.

In the middle of the night a pelletlike rattle awoke me, along with gusts of wind. Rain was hitting my tent. The camels, I heard, were still chomping argan, and the rain was washing the dust off their hides.

We awoke to a bizarre sight: a dawn without a visible sunrise, the first such dawn since we departed Tizgui Falls in February. I climbed out of my tent and hiked up the small mountain above us. The cactus-covered slopes, the tawny ancient earth, the sheep and goats and leaden rocks filled me with nostalgia, and I tried to think for what. As I studied the scene I felt more and more strongly that I had been here before. Then it struck me: This was the landscape of Crete, these were the hills of the southern Peloponnesus. In truth, this was once the Roman territory of Mauritania: could the ruins of Volubilis be far? This was the Morocco of classical history, not the Morocco of tribal wars and Ruhhal.

I sat down, entranced. It became February of 1984. I was riding a rusty old Icarus bus across the craggy, mist-sodden mountains of Crete, beneath Gero-Psiloritis under thunder-head skies, heading for the village of Sphakia on the island's southern coast. A raven-haired young woman sat opposite me. Her melodious wild banter in Greek with the other women aboard filled the bus. She was perhaps only five years older than I (which made her about twenty-eight) but of a different world. Her black dress, black stockings, and black scarf told me she was a widow; she would wear black for the rest of her life and never remarry.

We trundled out of the mists, and the road wound down toward the Libyan Sea, a rainbow breaking over its azure swells. After arriving in Sphakia I never saw the widow again. The next day I set out walking down a dirt road for Frango-kastello ("Castle of the Franks"), passing through mountain villages: Vouvas, Komitadhes, Agios Nektarios. Villagers on donkeys rode by and said *kalimera* to me, but others stared in silence. Some of the young women were widows in black scarves that covered their faces almost as much as a veil or *fir-wal*, a tradition that the Ottoman Turks had brought to Greece. The Mediterranean was one world.

Firwal. The word woke me up, and I was back in Morocco. It seemed newly wonderful that a country could be both on the Mediterranean and in Africa.

Hassan was ill, stricken with an upset stomach and exhaustion. This I learned as we were packing up. We hiked for three hours down the piste, with him lagging behind. Where three shale-covered mountains met, we saw white stone houses with smoking chimneys, heard the barking of dogs and the bleating of sheep. Tiglite. Berber shepherdesses in pink and black robes and tinselly headdresses stood leaning on staffs, examining the strangers walking out of the mountains. Here houses stood far apart, one to a slope; farther on, they clustered under palms.

"Hooa! *As-salam 'aaykum!* Where from?"

A tall Saharawi in a dark gray djellaba and white turban, his high-browed face handsome despite its pockmarks, was coming down the road, followed by a long-faced Berber. Hassan and

Mbari stopped for them, and I had the sense that the turbaned man was a little too direct, too effusive, to be a common resident of Tiglite.

Abundant greetings followed, along with lengthy handshakes. God have mercy on our parents, how were we? What might bring us here? Where might we be headed? By God, we were on our way to the Atlantic. For the first time Hassan admitted our destination.

"Well, all that sounds fine," the man said. "Welcome to our village. I'm the sheikh. I invite you to tea. We can take care of the formalities a bit later."

"The formalities?" I asked.

He smiled broadly. "Every visitor to our modest village is obliged to leave behind his story. Words on paper."

"Such as?"

"Passport number and date of issuance, date of birth, purpose of visit, profession, father's full name, mother's maiden name. The sort of information that lets us understand who this man is, and what he's doing in our region." His eyes hardened. "We're close to the Western Sahara, you know."

Hassan perked up and winked at me. The beauties of the police state.

"In fact, would you like to take care of business now?" the sheikh asked.

We said we would. We left our camels with some children called over by the sheikh and set out after him. He and his friend walked up the hill ahead of us, looking back to make sure we were following. Both Berbers and Saharawis lived in this village, which was nothing more than stone houses scattered around various converging slopes. They were heading for a pink concrete building that was the headquarters of the village. Hassan whispered to me. "See, no troublemaker could get away with *anything* here!"

"Hassan, we're not troublemakers."

"We could be Algerians."

"But we're not."

"They wouldn't let an Algerian get away with *anything* here. Algerians are crazy. They kill children. Listen, they're afraid here. They have to take measures. Any Moroccan passing through here would be questioned too."

We entered the headquarters. The sheikh led us to a door marked Communications Room. Next to a radio transmitter a short, beetle-browed man with mussed-up hair sat beneath a portrait of King Hassan II and the Crown Prince Mohammed; he was behind the times in his royal portraiture.

The man looked as though he'd just woken up. He took my passport. "An Englishman!" he pronounced with a smirk.

"I'm American."

He rolled his eyes. "You were colonized by the English. You speak English."

"We haven't been English since the eighteenth century."

He glared at me and shook his head. He set about writing down the information in French.

Up at the sheikh's stone house, in a chilly and Spartan stone room, we sat around a bowl of couscous piled high with vegetables and meat. It was a succulent meal, and Mbari and I enjoyed it; Hassan ate little, still feeling sick. The sheikh poured out his woes to us. It was hard getting by on a sheikh's stipend—a thousand dirhams a month, about a hundred dollars. (In the 1960s the government began appointing village sheikhs, who became state functionaries.) He reported to the president of the community, who reported to the governor, who reported to the head of the region, who reported to the king. He never said *what* all these people spent so much time reporting, but Hassan found the arrangement very reassuring, and he nodded at each mentioned rung in the ladder, repeating the ranks for me to make sure I was following.

Looking around me, I suddenly felt depressed. We were in a land of rock and shrub and sheep and poor people, sitting in a stone room that could have been a prison cell. I fleetingly sensed exile, which no doubt would be what affluent Moroccan friends of mine in Rabat and Casablanca would consider life in Tiglite. They dwelled up north in a pseudo-European country within a country, where people talked of reforms and constitutional monarchy, of winning rights for women and freedom of the press. They wanted these changes for their own reasons—for themselves, that is—but they spoke of the good of the People. But what would the People say about these rights? What would Hassan and the sheikh and all the Ruhhal and villagers we had met in the Drâa think about such changes, about democracy? Always in Morocco the People—the masses—have stood behind the king and Islamic traditions. In any case, when more than half the population is illiterate and under the age of twenty, when millions live in tin-shack slums, what would democracy lead to here? If I objected to the police-state order of which Hassan so approved, what would I replace it with?

After the meal, the sheikh and his aide led us back to our camels. We thanked our hosts for the meal and the hospitality—it had chased away my nausea and revivified Mbari and me (but not Hassan, who still looked ill). Unfortunately, the sheikh said, they could offer us nothing else. The village had no real store; for supplies people here traveled to Guelmim, a five-hour drive by four-wheeler.

They pointed out the piste winding up the mountains. We said goodbye and began the trek up and up steep switchbacks, toward the sky, which raced with clouds and now and then spattered us with chill rain. We clutched our clothes tight against the cold and wet, and climbed higher.

Late that afternoon, high on the plateau to which the piste had led us, amid the low scrubby golden hills of Wadi Ghumman, Hassan collapsed. I ran up to him. He had vomited; his cheeks were drawn and pale. He rolled over onto his back and shut his eyes, and a frigid wind blew sand over his face. We waited for Mbari and the camels to catch up. Aside from nausea, he complained that his knees and shoulders were aching so much that he could no longer sleep at night. He had pushed himself so hard that he had ruined his health; he had done his best to live up to his soldier's standards, and his strivings had taken their toll.

The camels looked worse than ever. Hanan was irritable, his jowls caked with dried blood from his new nostril; Na'im was bellowing and urinating and releasing dung at the slightest provocation; only Mabruk was holding up, but he was fatigued and walked slowly, his limp almost crippling him.

I sat by Hassan, rocking back and forth to fight the chill. Eiderdown clouds rolled swiftly across a low turquoise sky, the sky of cold climes. My wool sweater and long-sleeved shirt did not keep me warm. The change in climate, so welcome at first, was now proving hard on us all, and the cold made the fatigue tougher than ever to bear.

We would go no farther that day.

After the sun set, luminous lavender light poured from a band of sky above the horizon and filtered through gunmetal clouds marching in from the Atlantic. The wind blew in wailing gales across the golden, coarse-grained sand, over the cacti. We were somewhere around four thousand feet above sea level. Wadi Ghumman was a lonely place to stop, but we were not alone. A Saharawi shepherdess, thirteen or fourteen years old, wearing manifold robes of wool and cotton, and white wool leggings, drove a flock of goats our way, tossing stones at stragglers, uttering little sounds to keep them going. "Chit-chit, kh-kb, utch-utch, tsud-tsud, click-click, ay-ay!" Her disheveled russet hair was stuffed under a black scarf; her skin was fresh, if sunburned. We asked her where she was from. She pointed to a white tent just barely visible at the end of the wadi, and kept on her way, making her sounds. This wadi was her home.

Rocking back and forth on his haunches, Hassan watched her walk away. "We need whiskey."

"We do?" I asked.

"It would warm us up. We used to drink it in the army."

Mbari said he had never tried alcohol, and he praised God for that. He was also sick to his stomach and had curled up by the fire.

A couple of hours later, under a cold black vault bejeweled with stars, a young man came from the direction of the shepherdess's tent and sat down by our fire. He wore a heavy wool djellaba and sandals but had an imitation gold watch on his wrist. None of us had the strength to make conversation, and he seemed to understand our fatigue. We fed him some couscous. A little while later, he consulted his watch and bade us good night.

Lying in my tent that night, I reflected on what I had seen since leaving Tizgui Falls. Most of the Ruhhal I had met, like the young man and the shepherdess, possessed an innate dignity. They suffered every caprice of weather, from heat to rain to sandstorms, but did not complain. They cared for their animals and did not abuse one another: crime is unheard of among them (now that raiding belongs to the past; but then raiding was never considered a crime). The dignity of the Ruhhal was commanding. At times a regal silence seemed to hang about them, making polite inquiries—or any speech at all—sound frivolous. They led an ancient way of life that harmed no one, and they were content with it.

I thought of Omar, my old Saharawi cameleer of 1998. Looking at the dunes of Shgaga, he had told me then, "Desert life has no equal. What a pleasure it is to lie down at camp at the end of the day, your camels watered and fed next to you. They rest and you rest. You sip your tea, you eat your dates, you look at the sky. This is pure. And the children of the desert are brought up pure, with no narcotics or alcohol or brothels. In the cities children are born sick. Here you're healthy from birth and your mind is clear."

Every Ruhhal to whom I mentioned the cities of the north expressed a distaste for them. Here they differed from Moroccan villagers, who often wanted to move to the nearest town, or preferably, cross the Strait of Gibraltar and make their way to the tenement conurbations surrounding Paris or Marseilles. The Ruhhal were convinced that the nomadic way of life befitted them more than any other and saw the same humiliation that I saw in the bidonvilles in which more and more Moroccans, driven off their land by drought, are seeking refuge.

But the Ruhhal's world is changing, and the bidonvilles and other slums are spreading and becoming inevitable. In the past twenty years, the anticyclones from the Azores that once brought Morocco rain have rarely come ashore. Eight of the thirteen major droughts that have struck Morocco since 1940 have occurred since 1980. Of the 53 million hectares of land suitable for pasturage (three quarters of the surface of the country), 18 million have been severely damaged by drought. To be of use, rain must fall between planting season and the harvest. Morocco's scarce rain now often comes at the wrong times of the year and simply washes dried topsoil into rivers and reservoirs (the latter are now two thirds empty of water) and silts them up, worsening the country's chronic water shortage. Overpopulation aggravates everything: at independence in 1956 there were 8 million Moroccans; now there are 30 million, and the population keeps growing.

The climate and the earth have been altered, and the Ruhhal are suffering as a result. They are fleeing the sands, and the bidonvilles are filling up. In the tin-shack slums of the north, the ancestry of which Hassan spoke so proudly means nothing, tribal identity dissipates, and the Sons of 'Atta and the Daughters of Yahya take their place in the bread lines. Many turn to theft, smuggling, or prostitution. There are no reliable statistics, but roughly out of every hundred Ruhhal who roamed the desert a decade ago, only two or three remain. Drought, in short, is killing the Drâa and a way of life; its parching winds are eroding the casbahs, the most authentic architectural vestiges of North Africa's long, glorious Islamic history.

More rain fell during the night. I awoke shivering, my sleeping bag failing to keep me warm for the first time since the Upper Drâa. At dawn I crawled outside. Hassan and Mbari had been too fatigued to set up their tent; they awoke soggy in their 'abayas and wanted to move on quickly. The camels had feasted all night on argan fruit. I walked over to Mabruk and patted him and fed him the remnants of my couscous.

Hassan looked at him. "You like Mabruk, don't you?"

"Yes."

"Well, he's going to die, the poor fellow."

"What?"

"He's about to die."

His face was overcast and his eyes dark; he threw his gear together in an aggressive manner. I asked him how he was feeling; he was obviously much improved to be in such a bad mood.

"Oh, my brain is deranged today. I'm disturbed. Let's just get going."

I watched him finish packing. I sensed he must have been frustrated at having failed to slow the pace of our trip. He knew Mabruk was my favorite camel, and he just wanted to upset me.

After eight hours of walking we reached Âouïnet-Ait-Oussa, the last village of the Anti-Atlas before the Atlantic. It consisted of a few houses beneath a lump of rock called Jbel Guir. There was a telephone there but little else. I called Ali and we agreed that he would wait for us either at the bridge over the Drâa at nine o'clock on the morning of the twenty-third of April (in which case he would hike the last day with us to the ocean), or at the village of Foum Oued-el-Drâa (Mouth of Wadi Drâa) on the Atlantic that evening. We would rest here for two days and try to recover our strength for the last days of hiking.

I walked back to camp, sensing deliverance. The trip was ending, but I felt an emptiness coming on—the emptiness that follows the fulfillment of a cherished dream.

Postscript: Suffering from the heat and dust storms, Jeffrey Tayler finished his three-hundred-mile journey through hazards that have plagued desert travelers since the beginning of time.

Wilfred Thesiger was a renowned British explorer in the same vein as Richard Burton and T. E. Lawrence. His affection for extremely desolate places and the tribal peoples who inhabited them was obvious, and he was never fully able to adjust to the incursions of the modern world.

THE LAST NOMAD

One Man's Forty-Year Adventure in the World's Most Remote Deserts, Mountains and Marshes

---

WILFRED THESIGER

For years the Empty Quarter offered the ultimate challenge of Arabian exploration. Charles Doughty, returning from his dire wanderings in northern Arabia, wrote, "I never found any Arabian who had aught to tell, even by hearsay, of that dreadful country," and in 1929 Lawrence suggested to Trenchard that either the R 100 or R 101 should be diverted on a trial flight to India to pass over it. He wrote, "To go over the Empty Quarter will also be an enormous advertisement for them: it will mark an era in exploration. It will finish our knowledge of the earth. Nothing but an airship can do it, and I want it to be one of ours which gets the plum."

The Arabian Peninsula is as large as India without the Himalayas, and only some parts of the Yemen and Oman and various scattered areas can be cultivated. The rest is desert, covering nearly a million square miles. The southern part of this desert, a wilderness of sand dunes surrounded by feature-less gravel plains even more lifeless, extends for nine hundred miles from the foothills of the Yemen to the mountains of Oman, and for five hundred miles from the Indian Ocean to the Persian Gulf. It is a desert within a desert, which even Arabs call Rub al Khali, or the Empty Quarter.

Bertram Thomas crossed the Empty Quarter from south to north in 1930–31 and next year St. John Philby crossed it from the north. But even as late as 1945 no European had been there since Thomas and Philby, no aeroplane had ever flown over it and no car had been nearer to it than the RAF camp at Salala, on the shore of the Indian Ocean, or the town-ships on the Trucial Coast. In contrast with the Sahara, which the French had long explored, pacified and administered, vast areas of the Empty Quarter were still unexplored and it was surrounded by a no-man's land of warring tribes.

The Bedu tribes in southern Arabia were insignificant in numbers compared with those of central and northern Ara-bia, where the tents of a single tribe might number thousands. I had seen the Shamar migrating, a whole people on the move, covering the desert with their herds, and I had visited the summer camp of the Ruwalla, a veritable city of black tents. In southern Arabia families moved over great distances seeking pasture for their camels. Only the bushmen of the Kalahari and the aborigines of Australia led a life of compara-ble hardship.

I arrived in Dhaufar, on the southern coast of Arabia, in Octo-ber 1945, and stayed in the RAF staging camp near the small town of Salala, where the airmen were strictly confined to their camp to avoid incidents with the tribesmen. I had come to Arabia resolved to explore the Empty Quarter. It was one of the few places left where I could satisfy an urge to go where others had not been. I believed that the circumstances of my life had so trained me that I was qualified to travel there. The Locust Research Centre required me to go to Mughshin on the edge of the Sands and find out if it was a potential outbreak centre for desert locusts. This suited me well. I expected to be away for two or three months. I hoped this journey would give me the opportunity to accustom myself to the country and so win the confidence of the Arabs.

The Wali or Governor insisted that I should be accompanied by thirty of the Bait Kathir tribe, maintaining that where I was going there was danger from raiding parties. I was reluctant to take so many, but was in no position to argue, knowing nothing of local conditions. A fortnight later the Bait Kathir came to fetch me from the RAF camp. Most of them wore only loincloths and were bare-headed, their long hair tangled and unkempt. All were armed with rifles and daggers. My first impression was that they were little better than savages; they looked as primitive as the Danakil.

We camped that night at the foot of the Qarra mountains and sorted ourselves out. Next day we forced our camels along boulder-strewn tracks, among the tangled woods and ravines, until we came at last to the grassy slopes above. Here the Qarra, a strange folk who spoke a language of their own and never ventured far from their mountain fastness, herded small humpless cattle. In the woods were Paradise fly-catchers and brilliant butterflies. I walked to the watershed and found myself standing between two worlds. To the south were green meadows, thickets and spreading trees, to the north was empty desert, sand, rocks and a few wisps of withered grass.

During the days to come we lived crowded together in the emptiness of the desert. I was accustomed to some degree of privacy; here I had none. At first I found the Arabic of these Bedu almost incomprehensible, so there were often misunderstandings. Rain had fallen recently and some vegetation had come up. My companions dawdled along, stopping frequently to let their camels graze, and camping after a few hours of this leisurely progress. I suspected that they were deliberately lengthening the journey in order to get more money: they were paid on daily rates. When I protested that we must do proper marches they argued that their camels were in poor condition, which was evident, that they had a long journey ahead of them, and that there was no grazing further on. Next morning we would go for an hour or so, find more grazing and stop once more. Instead of enjoying this easy travel I got increasingly frustrated and irritated. I had yet to learn that Bedu will always sacrifice every consideration to the welfare of their camels. There were many Arabs in the area, attracted by the grazing. A score would collect, sit down without being invited, eat with us and make heavy inroads on our food. Some of them attached themselves to us for days. My Bedu accepted their presence with equanimity, for they would have done exactly the same themselves.

On previous journeys I had commanded respect as an Englishman, and in the Sudan I had the prestige of being a Government official. These Bedu had never heard of the English. All Europeans were known to them collectively as Christians, or more commonly as Infidels. They were prepared to tolerate my presence as a welcome source of revenue, but they never doubted my inferiority. They were Muslims and Bedu. I was neither. Anxious to prove their equal, I wanted no concessions and was irritated when pressed to ride while they still walked, or when they suggested I was thirsty and needed a drink. I wore their clothes—they would never have gone with me otherwise—and went bare-footed as they did. In camp, especially when we had visitors, I sat in the formal way that Arabs sit, and found this unaccustomed position trying. I thought many of their formalities irksome and pointless. Sometimes we shot a gazelle or oryx and then fed well, but our usual fare was unleavened bread, brick hard or soggy, depending how long it had lain in the embers of the fire. On the gravel plains the water from the infrequent wells tasted of camel's urine, but it was even worse when we reached the Sands, where it resembled a strong dose of Epsom salts, fortunately without the same effect.

After travelling across country that had suffered twenty-five years of unbroken drought we visited the small uninhabited oasis of Mughshin. Skeletons of trees, brittle powdery branches fallen and half-buried in the sand, and deposits of silt left by ancient floods marked the course of Umm al Hait, the "Mother of Life," the great wadi that leads down to Mughshin. Beyond Mughshin we wound our way among dunes that rose above us like mountains. Later we rode, hour after weary hour, across the emptiness that was the Jiddat al Harasis. It was now that I learnt to appreciate my companions and to admire their skills, their uncanny sense of direction and their skill at tracking. One day we passed some wind-blown tracks, to me just a disturbance of the sand. One of our party climbed down from his camel to look, followed them for a while, fingered some droppings and came back. "Awamir from the north, six of them. They have raided the Junuba on the southern coast and taken three camels. They came by way of Sahma, watered at Mughshin and passed here six days ago." We had seen no Arabs for seventeen days and were to meet none for another twenty-seven. When we did we heard that six Awamir had raided the Junuba, killed three of them and taken three camels. The only thing we did not already know was that they had killed anyone.

———

After ten weeks journeying we returned to Salala. I enjoyed
the days I spent there. It was agreeable to have hot baths and
eat well-cooked food, to sit at ease in a chair and talk English
for a change, but the pleasure was enhanced by the knowledge that I was going back into the desert.

I now planned to travel in company with the Rashid westward
to the Hadhramaut, through country that no European had
yet penetrated. I had encountered some of the Rashid in the
desert and arranged for them to meet me in Salala.

Many tribes lived round the Empty Quarter, or as these
Arabs call it "the Sands." Among others were the Yam and the
Dawasir, who owed allegiance to Abd al Aziz ibn Saud, King of
Saudi Arabia; the Saar and the Manahil near the Hadhramaut;
the Bait Kathir; the Duru, on the borders of Oman; and the
Manasir near the Persian Gulf; but only the Rashid and the
Awamir, and in the north the Murra, were at home in the Sands.
Some thirty Rashid had been waiting for me when I arrived
back at Salala. They were dressed in long Arab shirts and
headcloths, dyed a soft russet-brown with the juice of a desert
shrub. They wore their clothes with distinction, even when
they were in rags. They were small deft men, alert and watchful. Their bodies were lean and hard, tempered in the furnace
of the desert and trained to unbelievable endurance. Looking
at them I realised that they were very much alive, tense with a
nervous energy vigorously controlled. They had been bred
from the purest race in the world and lived in conditions where
only the hardiest and best could survive. They were as fine-
drawn and highly strung as thoroughbreds. Beside them the
Bait Kathir lacked the final polish of the inner desert.

It was on this journey that I met Salim bin Kabina. He was
to be my inseparable companion during the five years that I

travelled in southern Arabia. He turned up when we were watering thirsty camels at a well that yielded only a few gallons an hour. For two days we worked day and night in relays. Conspicuous in a vivid red loincloth he helped us with our task. On the second day he announced that he was coming with me. I told him to find himself a rifle and a camel. He grinned and said that he would find both, and did. He was sixteen years old, about five foot five in height and lightly built. He was very poor, so the hardship of his life had already marked him. His hair was long and always falling into his eyes, especially when he was cooking, and he would sweep it back impatiently with a thin hand. He had very white teeth which showed constantly, for he was always talking and laughing. His father had died years before and it had fallen on bin Kabina to provide for his mother, young brother and infant sister. I had met him at a critical time in his life. Two months earlier he had gone down to the coast for a load of sardines: on the way back his old camel had collapsed and died. "I wept as I sat there in the dark beside the body of my old grey camel. She was old, long past bearing and very thin, for there had been no rain for a long time, but she was my camel, the only one I had. That night death seemed very close to me and my family." Then he grinned at me and said, "God brought you. Now I shall have everything." Already I was fond of him. Attentive and cheerful, anticipating my wants, he eased the inevitable strain under which I lived. In the still rather impersonal atmosphere of my desert life his comradeship provided the only personal note.

We rode slowly westward. There should have been Arabs here, for rain had fallen and there was good grazing in the broad, shallow watercourses that ran down towards the Sands. But the desert was empty, full of fear. Occasionally we saw herdsmen in the distance, hurriedly driving camels across the plain. Some of the Rashid would get off their camels and throw up sand into the air, the accepted sign of peaceful intentions. Then they would ride over and get the news. Always it was of Dahm raiders from the Yemen, who had passed westward a few days before. Some said they were three hundred strong, others a hundred.

We were camped on a plain near some acacia bushes among which our scattered camels were grazing. Half a mile to the west were limestone ridges, dark against the setting sun. The Rashid were lined up for the sunset prayer. Suddenly one exclaimed, "There are men behind that ridge." They abandoned their prayers. "The camels! The camels! Get the camels!" Four or five ran off to help the herdsmen, who had already taken alarm. The rest of us took cover behind the scattered loads. A score of mounted men swung out from behind the ridge and raced towards our camels. We opened fire. Bin al Kamam, who lay near me, said, "Shoot in front of them, I don't know who they are." I got off five shots. Everyone was firing. Bin Kabina's three rounds were all duds. I could see the exasperation on his face. The raiders sought cover behind a low hill. Our camels were brought in and couched. "Who are they?" There was general uncertainty. It was agreed that they were not Dahm or Saar, their saddles were different. Some said they were Awamir, perhaps Manahil. No, they were not Mahra, their clothes were wrong. A Manahil who was with us said he would go and find out. He went forward to the low hill, situated against the glowing sky. We saw a man stand up and come towards him. They shouted to each other and then came together and embraced. They were a Manahil pursuit party following the Dahm, and had seen our camels and taken us for yet another party of Dahm raiders. We had bought a goat that morning which we meant to eat for dinner; instead we feasted the Manahil, who were now our guests.

Six weeks after leaving Salala we were in the valley of the Hadhramaut, and rode slowly up it to Tarim. I was interested to see this famous valley and its unspoilt cities with their distinctive architecture. We were lavishly entertained, sitting indoors in cushioned ease; we ate well-cooked food and drank water that did not taste of goatskin. But my companions were anxious to return to the desert. They fretted about their camels that would not eat the clover they were offered. I persuaded them to remain a few days longer, for I was desolate at the thought of parting. The privacy I had so often craved while I was with them was here, behind a door: but now was aching loneliness.

I had no inclination to return to England. I decided instead to go to Jedda and travel in the southern Hejaz mountains and the Assir. For years I had longed to visit this little-known corner of Arabia. During the next three months I travelled there, riding a thousand miles, some by camel, some by donkey, accompanied by a Sharifi boy from the Wadi al Ahsaba. Together we wandered through the Tihama, the hot coastal plain that lies between the Red Sea and the mountains, passing through villages of wattle and daub huts reminiscent of Africa. The people here were pleasantly easy and informal in their manners. We watched them, dressed in loincloths and with circlets of scented herbs upon their flowing hair; dancing in the moonlight to the quickening rhythm of the drums, at the annual festivals when the young men were circumcised. We stayed with the Bani Hilal, destitute descendants of that most famous of all Arab tribes, in their mat shelters on the lava fields near Birk, and with the nearly naked Qahtan who bear the name of that ancestor who sired the Arab race, and live today in the gorges of the Wadi Baish. We visited weekly markets, which sprang up at dawn in remote valleys in the mountains or packed for a day the streets of some small town.

We saw towns of many sorts: Qizan (or Jizan), Sabyia, Abha and Taif. We climbed steep passes where baboons barked at us from the cliffs and lammergeyer sailed out over the misty depths, and we rested beside cold streams in forests of juniper and wild olive. There were wild flowers here, jasmine and honeysuckle, roses, pinks and primulas. Sometimes we spent the night in a castle with an Amir, sometimes in a mud cabin with a slave, and everywhere we were well received. We fed well and slept in comfort, but I could not forget the desert and the challenge of the Sands.

At last I went back to London and reported to Dr. Uvarov, head of the Locust Research Centre. I was able to assure him that the floods from the coastal ranges seldom reached the Sands; that in consequence there was no permanent vegetation to afford an "outbreak centre" for locusts in the Sands between Mughshin and the Hadhramaut. Pleased with this information Dr. Uvarov said to me, "I wish you could get into the interior of Oman. That is the country that really interests us. Unfortunately the Sultan won't hear of your going there." "Get permission for me to go back to Mughshin," I replied, "but don't for God's sake mention Oman." We discussed this for a long time and at last Dr. Uvarov agreed. As I left his office I thought triumphantly, "Now I shall be able to cross the Empty Quarter."

The Bait Kathir were waiting for me in Salala when I returned in October 1946, twenty-four of them, most of whom had been with me the year before, including their head sheikh, Tamtaim, a delightful old man, still active in spite of his years; Musallim bin Tafl, who had proved a redoubtable hunter and kept us in meat; and Sultan, the dominant personality in the tribe. I found one of the Rashid in the town and sent him with

a message to bin Kabina and certain others of his people to
join me at Shisur.

We were watering at Shisur when the sentry gave the
alarm. We hurriedly couched our camels. In the distance riders were approaching. We fired two shots over their heads,
whereupon one of them dismounted and threw up sand into
the air. As they drew nearer someone said, "They are Rashid.
I can recognise bin Shuas's camel." There were seven and we
formed up in a line to receive them. They halted their camels
thirty yards away, couched them, and came forward, carrying
their rifles over their shoulders; only bin Kabina was
unarmed. When they were a few yards away Mahsin, whom I
identified by his lame leg, called out, *"Salam alaikum"* (Peace be
on you), and we answered together, *"Alaikum as salam"* (On
you be peace). Then, one behind the other, they passed along
our line greeting each of us with the triple nose kiss. They
then formed up opposite us. Tamtaim said to me, "Ask their
news," but I answered, "No, you do so. You are the oldest."
Tamtaim called out, "Your news?" Mahsin answered, "The
news is good." Again Tamtaim asked, "Is anyone dead? Is
anyone gone?" Back came the immediate answer, "No, don't
say such a thing." More questions and answers, which never
varied. Then they unsaddled their camels while we made coffee and set out dates. When they had joined us the youngest
of our party poured coffee, a few drops in the bottom of a
small cup, and handed it to Mahsin and the others in order of
their importance. Now at last we would get the real news.
They sat before us, very unhurried in their movements; quiet
and slow of speech, careful of their dignity in front of
strangers. Only their dark watchful eyes flickered to and fro,
missing nothing.

Mahsin sat with his crippled leg stiffly out in front of him.
He was a compactly built man of middle age with a square

face. His thin lips were pinched and there were deep lines round his mouth and nose. I knew that before he was wounded he had been famous as a raider and had killed many men. But Muhammad al Auf interested me most, for the Rashid had talked of him the year before. He looked about thirty-five years old. He was famous for his journeying and his knowledge of the desert. He had a fine face, skin and flesh moulded over strong bone; his eyes, set wide apart, were flecked with gold, while his nose was straight and short, his mouth generous. His hair, long and wavy, was unbraided and fell about his shoulders. When we got up bin Kabina came over and joined me. "How are you, Umbarak?" he asked, using the name by which the Arabs knew me. I was delighted to see him. He was in rags, but in my saddlebag was a new shirt, a loincloth and a dagger which I had brought him. I had six spare Service rifles with me and one of these I lent him.

We left Shisur on 9th November in the chill of dawn; the sun was on the desert's rim, a red ball without heat. We walked until it got warm, then one by one, as the inclination took us, climbed up the camels' shoulders and settled in our seats for the long hours ahead. The Arabs sang, "the full-throated roaring of the tribes," the shuffling camels quickened their pace, thrusting forward across the hard ground, for we were on the steppes which border on the Sands. We noticed the stale tracks of oryx, saw gazelle bounding stiff-legged across the plain, and flushed occasional hares from withered bushes in shallow watercourses. In the late afternoon of the second day we saw the Sands, a shimmering rose-coloured wall stretching across our front, intangible as a mirage. The Arabs, roused from the nodding torpor of weary, empty hours, pointed with their sticks, shouted and broke into a sudden spate of talk. We camped that night among some *ghaf*, large mimosa-like trees. Deep down the questing roots had found water, and their branches were heavy with flowering trailing fronds that fell to the clean sand.

I had told the Rashid that I wished to cross the Sands. Bin Kabina said at once, "Al Auf can get us across." The other Rashid agreed to accompany us, and Sultan and Musallim bin Tafl asked to come with us. We agreed that the rest of our party should go and wait for us near the coast at Bai.

Eight days after leaving Shisur we reached Mughshin. As we approached the well the camels unaccountably panicked, scattering in great plunging bounds. When I looked back Mahsin lay crumpled on the ground. We ran to him. His damaged leg was twisted under him and he was moaning faintly. We tried to straighten him, but he screamed. I fetched morphia from my saddlebag, gave him an injection and then we carried him on a blanket to the trees. We fashioned rough splints from branches and set his leg, all splintered bone. His nephew bin Shuas crouched beside him, keeping the flies off his face, while the others sat round him discussing whether he would live or die. Then we rose and set about our tasks, watering the camels and cooking food.

It now seemed that this accident would frustrate my plans, since the Rashid declared that they must all remain with Mahsin till he recovered or died, for he had many blood feuds on his hands and if his enemies heard the news they would come far to kill him. Sultan was already suggesting that instead of trying to cross the Empty Quarter we should hunt oryx to the east. However, after further discussion among themselves the Rashid agreed that al Auf and bin Kabina should go with me. I now told Sultan that I would send bin Kabina to fetch more Rashid if none of the Bait Kathir wished to cross the Sands. Eventually he agreed that provided we took eight other Bait Kathir he and Musallim would come. I argued in favour of a smaller party with only the best camels, but he was adamant. He said the Al bu Falah of Abu Dhabi and the Bin Maktum of Dubai were at war, and tribes beyond the Sands were involved, and in any case the Duru, through whose territory we must pass on our return, were hostile.

We had left Salala with ample rations, but my companions, after leaving some with their families, had with their customary improvidence used up most of what remained. We now divided what we had, between the thirteen of us crossing the Sands, the Rashid staying with Mahsin, and Tamtaim's party going to Bai. Our share was about two hundred pounds of flour, enough rice for two meals, a few handfuls of maize, some onions and a little butter, coffee, tea and sugar. This must last at least a month. It worked out at half a pound of flour a day for each of us. We were going to be very hungry. I reckoned that we could probably carry enough water for twenty days if we rationed ourselves to a quart a day. Twenty waterless days was the very most that camels could stand, travelling for long hours across the Sands, and they would only do that if we found grazing. Should we find grazing? That is the question that always faces the Bedu. They maintain that in cold weather they can survive for as long as seven days without food or water. It is the collapse of their camels that haunts them. If this happens death is certain.

We had been at Mughshin for nine days. Mahsin was better. For several days he had not eaten, but now he was feeding again and he said the pain was less. Bin Shuas would be able to shoot gazelle, of which there were a number in the vicinity, and one of the camels was in milk. That night we camped a few miles from the well. At last I had started on my journey across the Empty Quarter.

I joined al Auf, who was herding the camels, and we sat together in the twilight and talked of the journey ahead. He had crossed the eastern Sands two years before. He told me he was worried about the condition of some of the Bait Kathir camels. He doubted if they would be able to cross the Uruq al Shaiba, which he described as mountains of sand. I asked if we could avoid them, but he said they extended a week's journey to the west and ended in the east against the Umm al Samim, those legendary quicksands of which Bertram Thomas had heard the Bedu speak. Cross the Uruq al Shaiba we must, he said, if we were to reach Dhafara and the oasis of Liwa. I had heard the Bait Kathir use the expression "As far as Dhafara" to describe the limit of the world. I had never heard of Liwa where, according to al Auf, the palm groves and villages extended for two days' march. This oasis must be far bigger than Jabrin, discovered by Cheesman in 1924. There were fascinating discoveries to be made in the desert ahead if we could only get there. As I stood up to go back to camp al Auf said, "There are Bait Musan ahead of us. With them we will exchange the worst of our camels. Don't worry, Umbarak. God willing we will reach Liwa."

At first we rode through country familiar to me from the year before. Isolated dunes, two or three hundred feet high, rose in apparent confusion from the desert floor. Each dune was known individually to the Bedu, for each had its own shape that did not vary perceptibly over the years, but all had certain features in common. On the north side of each dune the sand fell away from beneath the summit in an unbroken wall, at as steep an angle as the grains of sand would lie. On either side of this face sharp-crested ridges swept down in undulating curves, and behind there were alternating ridges and troughs, smaller and more involved as they got further from the main face. The surface was marked with diminutive ripples, of which the ridges were built from the heavier and darker sand, while the hollows were of smaller paler-coloured grains. It was the blending of these colours that gave such depth and richness to the sand: gold with silver, orange with cream, brick-red with white, burnt-brown with pink, yellow with grey. There was an infinite variety of colours and shades.

Four days after leaving Mughshin we reached Khaur bin Atarit, discovered by some forgotten Bedu but still bearing his name. The well was drifted in, but we dug it out. The water, as I expected, was very brackish and would get worse the longer it remained in the goatskins. Musallim made porridge for our evening meal, the only meal of the day. From now on we should be eating gritty lumps of unleavened bread smeared with a little butter. Bin Kabina poured water over our outstretched hands. This was the last time we should wash, even our hands, until we reached the wells at Dhafara.

In the morning we gave the camels another drink. Several refused to touch the bitter-tasting water, so we held up their heads and poured it down their throats. We filled the skins and plugged the tiny dribbling holes. The others said their midday prayers; then we loaded the camels and led them away between the golden dunes. We went on foot, for the full skins were heavy on their backs. The next morning we found a little parched herbage on the flank of a high dune and let our camels graze for two hours. Where we camped the dunes were very big, whale-backed massifs rising above white plains of powdery gypsum. The scene was bleak and cheerless, curiously arctic in appearance. Twice I woke in the night and each time Sultan was brooding over the fire. We started again at sunrise and four hours later came to large red dunes, close together, covered with green plants, the result of heavy rain two years before. Fresh camel tracks showed that the Bait Musan were camped nearby: Sultan and the Bait Kathir went off to find them. Bin Kabina warned me that the Bait Kathir were going to make trouble.

When they came back Sultan informed me that, as our

camels were in poor condition and the Bait Musan said there
was no grazing ahead, it would be madness to go on. Anyway
we were short of food and water. The Bait Kathir were prepared to travel with me in the Sands to the east before rejoin-
ing the others near the coast. They would on no account try
to cross the Empty Quarter. I asked al Auf if he would come
with me and he said quietly, "We have come here to go to
Dhafara. If you want to go on I will guide you." I asked bin
Kabina and he answered that where I went he would go. I
knew Musallim was jealous of Sultan. When I asked him he
said, "I will come," whereupon his kinsman Mabkhaut volunteered to join us. The others said nothing. Once again we
divided up the food. We took our share, fifty pounds of flour,
some of the butter and coffee, what remained of the sugar and
tea, and a few dried onions. We also took four skins of water,
choosing those that did not leak. Later, after much haggling
and for an exorbitant price, we bought a spare camel from the
Bait Musan, a large, very powerful bull. Our other camels
were all females. That evening I told my four companions
that I was giving them as a present the Service rifles with
which I had armed them. I watched the disbelief slowly fade
from bin Kabina's eyes. He had confided to me that he
intended to buy a rifle with the money I would give him. No
doubt he had visualised himself the proud owner of some
ancient weapon, such as he had borrowed when he accompanied me to the Hadhramaut. Now he had one of the finest
rifles in his tribe, with fifty rounds of ammunition.

Next morning the Bait Kathir helped us load our camels;
we said goodbye, picked up our rifles and set off. The Rashid
took the lead, their faded brown clothes harmonising with the
sand: al Auf a lean, neat figure, very upright; bin Kabina more
loosely built, striding beside him. The two Bait Kathir followed close behind with the spare camel tied to Musallim's

saddle. Their clothes, which had once been white, had become neutral-coloured from long use. Mabkhaut was the same build as al Auf, whom he resembled in many ways, though he was a less forceful character. Musallim, compactly built, slightly bow-legged and physically tough, was of a different breed. The least attractive of my companions, his character had suffered from too frequent sojourns in Muscat and Salala.

The sands here were covered with yellow-flowering tribulus, heliotrope and a species of sedge. In the Sands, even in areas that have been barren for years, vegetation will spring up after rain and if the rain has been really heavy it may remain green, without even a further shower, for as long as four years. After two hours we encountered a small boy, dressed in the remnants of a loincloth, herding camels. He was from the Rashid and led us to a camp nearby. Here three men sat round the embers of a fire. They had no tent; their only possessions were saddles, ropes, bowls and empty goatskins, and their weapons. Bedu such as these, having located grazing, which is often very hard to find, move on to it in the autumn. They remain there, sometimes a hundred miles from the nearest well, for six or seven months until the weather becomes hot. They live on camel's milk, which suffices them for food and drink, the camels obtaining sufficient moisture from the green plants. On grazing such as this camels can last months without a drink of water.

These men were very cheerful and full of life. The grazing was good; their camels, several in milk, would soon be fat. Life by their standards would be easy this year, but tonight they would sleep naked on the freezing sand, covered only with their flimsy loincloths. There were other years, such as al Auf had that very morning described to me, when the exhausted men rode back to the wells, to speak through blackened, bleeding lips of desolation in the Sands, of emptiness such as I had seen on the way here from Mughshin; when the last withered plants were gone and walking skeletons of men and beasts sank down to die. I thought of the bitter wells in the furnace heat of summer when hour by reeling hour men watered thirsty, thrusting camels, till at last the wells ran dry and importunate camels moaned for water that was not there. I thought how desperately hard were the lives of the Bedu in this weary land, how gallant and enduring was their spirit. The milk they gave us at sunset was soothing, in contrast to the bitter water which had rasped our throats. In the morning they handed us a small goatskin full of milk to take with us.

I noticed, as we were preparing to leave, that bin Kabina no longer wore his loincloth under his shirt. I asked him where it was and he said, "One of them asked me for it." I told him that he could not travel without a loincloth through the inhabited country beyond the Sands, and gave him some money to give the man instead. He protested, "What use will money be to him here? He needs a loincloth." "So do you," I answered, and grumbling he retrieved it. Our hosts bade us go in peace and we wished them the safe-keeping of God. There were no more Arabs ahead of us until we reached Dhafara.

At first the dunes were separate mountains of brick-red sand, rising above ash-white gypsum flats ringed with the vivid green of salt-bushes. Later they were even higher—five hundred feet or more—and honey-coloured. At sunset al Auf doled out to each of us a pint of water mixed with milk, our ration for the day. After we had eaten the bread that Musallim cooked, bin Kabina took the small brass coffee-pot from the fire and served us with a few drops each. We piled more wood upon the fire, long snake-like roots of tribulus, warmed ourselves for a while and then lay down to sleep. A chill wind blew in gusts, charged with a spray of sand. I was happy in the company of these men who had chosen to come with me; I felt affection for them personally, and sympathy with their way of life. But though the easy equality of our relationship satisfied me, I did not delude myself that I could be one of them. Nevertheless I was their companion, and an inviolable bond united us, as sacred as the bond between host and guest, transcending loyalties of tribe and family. Because I was their companion on the road they would fight even against their own tribesmen in my defence, and would expect me to do the same. But I knew that for me the hardest test would be to live with them in harmony and not to let impatience master me; neither to withdraw into myself, nor to become critical of standards and ways of life different from my own.

Next morning we found a small patch of grazing and for an hour or two let our camels graze. Before going on we collected bundles of tribulus to feed to them in the evening. We were worried about our water: all the skins were sweating and there had been a regular ominous drip from them throughout the day. There was nothing we could do but press on, yet to push the camels too hard would founder them. They were already showing signs of thirst. After we had fed, al Auf decided we must go on again. We rode for hours along a salt flat. The dunes on either side, colourless in the moonlight, seemed higher by night than by day. Eventually we halted, and numbly I dismounted. I would have given much for a hot drink, but I knew I must wait eighteen hours for that. We lit a fire, warmed ourselves and lay down. I found it difficult to sleep. I was tired; for days I had ridden long hours upon a rough camel, my body racked by its uneven gait. I suppose I was weak from hunger, for even by Bedu standards the food we ate was a starvation ration. But my thirst troubled me most. I was always conscious of it.

The others were awake at first light, anxious to push on. In a few minutes we were ready. We plodded along in silence. My eyes watered with the cold; the jagged salt-crusts cut and stung my feet. The world was grey and dreary. Then gradually the peaks ahead stood out against a paling sky; almost imperceptibly they began to glow, borrowing the colours of the sunrise that touched their crests.

A high unbroken dune chain stretched across our front like a mountain range of peaks and connecting passes. Several of the summits seemed at least seven hundred feet above the salt flats on which we stood. The face that confronted us, being on the lee side to the prevailing wind, was very steep. Al Auf told us to wait and went forward to reconnoitre. I watched him climb up a ridge, like a mountaineer struggling upward through soft snow, the only moving thing in all that empty landscape. I thought, "God, we will never get the camels over that." Some of them had lain down, an ominous sign. Bin Kabina sat beside me, cleaning the bolt of his rifle. I asked him, "Will we ever get the camels over those dunes?" He pushed back his hair, looked at them and said, "Al Auf will find a way." Al Auf came back, said "Come on," and led us forward. It was now that he showed his skill, choosing the slopes up which the camels could climb. Very slowly, a foot at a time, we coaxed the unwilling beasts upward. Above us the rising wind was blowing streamers of sand. At last we reached the top. To my relief I saw we were on the edge of rolling dunes. I thought triumphantly, "We have made it. We have crossed the Uruq al Shaiba."

We went on, only stopping to feed at sunset. I said cheerfully to al Auf, "Thank God we are across the Uruq al Shaiba." He looked at me for a moment and answered, "If we go well tonight we shall reach them tomorrow." At first I thought he was joking. It was midnight when at last al Auf said, "Let's stop here, get some sleep and give the camels a rest. The Uruq al Shaiba are not far away." In my troubled dreams that night they towered above us, higher than the Himalayas.

Al Auf woke us while it was still dark. The morning star had risen above the dunes and formless things regained their shape in the dim light of dawn.

We were faced by a range as high as the one we had crossed the day before, perhaps even higher, but here the peaks were steeper and more pronounced, many rising to great pinnacles down which the flowing ridges swept like drapery. These sands, paler than those we had crossed, were very soft, cascading round our feet as the camels struggled up the slopes. It took us three hours to cross. From the summit we looked down to a salt flat in another great trough between the mountains. The range on the far side seemed even higher than the one on which we stood, and behind it were others. I thought, "Our camels will never get up another of these awful dunes." Yet somehow they did it. Then, utterly exhausted we collapsed. Al Auf gave us a little water to wet our mouths. He said, "We need this if we are to go on." I pointed at the ranges ahead but he said, "I can find a way between those; we need not cross them." We went on till sunset, but now we were going with the grain of the land, no longer trying to climb the dunes—we could never have crossed another. We fed, got back on our camels and only stopped long after midnight; we started again at dawn.

In the morning a hare jumped out of a bush; al Auf knocked it over with his stick. By three in the afternoon we could no longer resist stopping to cook it. Mabkhaut suggested, "Let's roast it in its skin to save water." Bin Kabina led the chorus of protest: "No, by God, we don't want Mabkhaut's charred meat. We want soup. Soup and extra bread. We will feed well today. By God, I am hungry." We were across the Uruq al Shaiba, and intended with this gift from God to celebrate the achievement.

As bin Kabina cooked the hare he looked across at me and said, "The smell of this meat, Umbarak, makes me feel faint." They divided the meat and then cast lots for the portions. Bedu generally do this; otherwise there are heated arguments, someone refusing to accept his portion, declaring he has been given more than his share. After we had taken it, bin Kabina said, "I have forgotten to divide the liver. Give it to Umbarak." After a show of protesting, I accepted it; I was too hungry to refuse. No Bedu would have done this.

Al Auf told us it would take three more days to reach Khaba well in Dhafara, but that he knew of a very brackish well, nearer; the camels might drink its water. We rode again late into the night and there was a total eclipse of the moon. Again we started very early and rode for seven hours across rolling dunes. The colours of the sands were vivid, varied and unexpected, in places the colour of ground coffee, elsewhere brick-red, purple or a curious golden green.

Here we encountered Hamad bin Hanna, one of the sheikhs of the Rashid. He was looking for a stray camel, but abandoned his search to come with us. He told us that Ibn Saud's tax collectors were in Dhafara, and advised us to avoid contact with the tribes, so that my presence would not get known. I had no desire to be arrested and taken off to explain my presence here to Ibn Jalawi, the formidable Governor of the Hassa. But we must at all costs avoid giving the impression that we were a raiding party, for honest travellers never pass an encampment without seeking news and food. It was going to be very difficult to escape detection. Two days later we were at Khaba well, on the edge of Dhafara. The water here was only slightly brackish, delicious after the filthy, evil-smelling dregs that we had drunk the night before. We had passed another well but even our thirsty camels would not drink the bitter stuff. Here they drank bucketful after leathern bucketful. I have since heard of a test when a thirsty camel drank twenty-seven gallons.

That night bin Kabina made extra coffee and Musallim increased our ration of flour by a mugful. This was wild extravagance, but even so the food he handed us was woefully inadequate to stay our hunger now that our thirst was gone. The moon was high above us when I lay down to sleep. The others talked around the fire, but I closed my mind to the meaning of their words, content to hear only the murmur of their voices, to watch their outline sharp against the moonlit sky, happily conscious that they were there, and beyond them the camels to which we owed our lives.

I had crossed the Empty Quarter. It was fourteen days since we had left the last well at Khaur bin Atarit. To others my journey would have little importance. It would produce nothing except a rather inaccurate map that no-one was ever likely to use. It was a personal experience and the reward had been a drink of clean, tasteless water. I was content with that. This journey was set in the framework of a longer journey, and my mind was already busy with the new problems which our return to Bai presented.

We went north to the outskirts of Liwa, and bin Kabina visited the settlements to buy something for us to eat; I was disappointed not to be able to go there myself. By now we had finished the last scrap of our food and for three days we starved, awaiting his return. I had hoped he would bring back a goat, but all he had been able to buy were dates and a little wheat. Al Auf said disgustedly, "Soon we shall be too weak to get on our camels." We had to get back across Arabia, travelling secretly, and we had enough food for ten days if we were economical. The Duru, through whose territory we must pass, would make trouble if they discovered I was a Christian. They owed allegiance to the Imam of Oman, a fanatical reactionary who hated all Europeans. His Governors were in all the big towns, and the Riqaishi in Ibri was reputed to be the worst of them. Yet Ibri was the only place where we could hope to buy food.

Musallim, striking the sand with his camel stick to give emphasis to his words, said, "Listen, Umbarak, don't hang about in the Duru country and don't go near Ibri. Have you not heard of the Riqaishi? By God, what do you suppose he will do if he knows there is a Christian in his territory? He hates infidels. God help you, Umbarak, if he gets hold of you." We agreed that we must pass quickly and secretly, but somehow we must get more food from Ibri. The others said, "We are bound to encounter Duru: how are you going to account for yourself?" I thought and then suggested, "I will say I am a Syrian from Damascus on my way to visit the Sultan at Muscat." "Who are the Syrians?" bin Kabina asked and I answered, "If you don't know I don't suppose the Duru will either."

Near Rabadh Musallim suddenly jumped off his camel and pulled a hare from a shallow burrow. We stopped to cook it; except for the hare which al Auf had killed, we had not eaten meat for a month. We sat in a hungry circle round the fire. Just as it was ready bin Kabina looked up and said, "God! Guests!" Three Rashid were coming towards us across the sands. We greeted them, asked the news and made coffee for them, then Musallim dished up the hare and set it before them, saying with every appearance of sincerity that they were our guests, that God had brought them, that today was a blessed day. They asked us to join them, but we refused.

When they had finished bin Kabina put a sticky lump of dates in a dish and called us over to feed. Next morning one of them invited us to come to his tent, saying he would kill a camel for us, but as there were many Arabs in the neighbourhood we reluctantly refused. Two days later we came unexpectedly on an encampment. The old Rashid to whom it belonged would brook no refusal. He slaughtered a young camel and for two days we feasted. He had heard of me as the Christian who had travelled with the Rashid to the Hadhramaut the year before, and made me very welcome.

Three days later we were on the eastern edge of the Sands; ahead of us lay Oman. At dawn I saw a great mountain to the east which Musallim told me was Jebel Kaur near Ibri. It was not marked on the map. Later the haze thickened and hid it from our sight. In the nearby Wadi al Ain we encountered a delightful old Duru called Staiyun. He accepted the account I gave of myself and invited me to stay in his encampment, while his son Ali, with al Auf and Mabkhaut, went to buy provisions in Ibri. They were pleasant, lazy days. Staiyun fed us on bread, dates and milk, spending most of his time with us. The more I saw of the old man the more I liked him. The others returned after six days and we were off again. We crossed two more great wadis, that ran down from the Oman mountains and emptied their occasional floods into the Umm al Samim. Perhaps another year I should be able to explore these quicksands; there was no time now. We must get to Bai as quickly as we could if we were to keep our rendezvous.

Each seemingly interminable day dragged on from dawn till sunset. The others ate dates before we started off, but I could no longer face their sticky sweetness and fasted till the evening meal. Hour after hour my camel shuffled forward, seeming to move always up a slight incline towards an indeterminate horizon; nowhere in all that glaring emptiness of gravel plain and colourless sky was anything my eyes could focus on. I watched the sun's slow progress and longed for evening. When at last the sun sank into the haze it was an orange disc without heat or brilliance.

On 31st January 1947 we reached Bai, where the others were waiting for us. We had parted from them at Mughshin on 24th November. We rode back towards Salala across the flatness of the Jiddat al Harasis, long marches of eight and even ten hours a day. I was as glad to be back in their friendly crowd as I had been to escape from it at Mughshin. I delighted in the surging rhythm of this mass of camels, the slapping shuffle of their feet, the shouted talk, the songs that stirred the blood of men and beasts so that they drove forward with quickening pace. Then we climbed from the void of the desert on to the crest of the Qarra range and looked once more on green trees and grass, the beauty of the mountains and the distant sea. We rode singing into Salala, and the Wali feasted us in a tent beside the sea.

A large gathering of Rashid under bin Kalut, who had taken Bertram Thomas across the Sands, were waiting to go with me to Mukalla. From them we heard that Mahsin had recovered. Among them was a boy with a face of classic beauty; rather sad and pensive in repose, it lit up when he smiled, like a pool touched by the sun. Antinous must have looked like this, I thought, when Hadrian first saw him in the Phrygian woods. Bin Kabina urged me to let him join us, saying he was the best shot in the tribe, as good a hunter as Musallim. "He is my friend. For my sake let him come with us. The two of us will go with you wherever you desire." I told him he could come, and handed him one of the spare rifles to use. His name was Salim bin Ghabaisha.

A few evenings later bin Kabina stood up to fetch his camels, walked a few paces and collapsed. He was unconscious when I reached him. His pulse was very feeble and his body nearly cold; he was breathing hoarsely. I carried him over to the fire and covered him with blankets. His breathing became easier and his body warmer, but he did not recover consciousness. I sat beside him, hour after hour, wondering miserably if he was going to die. I remembered how I first met him in the Wadi Mitan, how he had joined me at Shisur, remained with me when the Bait Kathir deserted me. I remembered his happiness when I gave him the rifle. I knew that whenever I thought of the past months I should think of him, for we had shared everything, even my doubts and difficulties. Hours later I felt him relax and knew that he was sleeping. By the following afternoon he had fully recovered.

We took a different route from the one we had followed the year before. We had plenty of food, so we fed well and travelled slowly towards our journey's end, which I had no desire to reach. Often bin Ghabaisha came back to camp with an ibex or a gazelle slung over his shoulder, and dropped it triumphantly beside the fire; then we ate the meat for which bin Kabina and I had hungered in the Sands. One evening I saw a young man sitting under a cliff near our camping place. I noticed that his wrists were shackled with a short length of heavy chain. I greeted him but he did not reply, though he turned his head and looked at me. He had a striking face but there was no intelligence in his eyes. His hair was long and matted and the rag he wore did not cover him. He stood up, yawned and walked away. Later I asked bin Kabina who he was and he said, "He is Salim bin Ghabaisha's brother, the unfortunate one. Three years ago he lost his reason. Before that he was one of the friendliest boys in our tribe." I asked why he was shackled and he answered, "Two years ago he killed a boy while he slept; battered in his skull with a rock. The boy was his greatest friend. The family accepted blood money because he was mad. God made it easy for him."

Bin Ghabaisha returned a little later carrying an ibex he had shot. Bin Kabina told him his brother had turned up; without a word he went off to find him, carrying a dish of dates. Later he came back depressed and unhappy and took me aside. "Have you any medicine, Umbarak? I beseech you, if you have, to give it to me. I loved my brother; we were inseparable. I was like his shadow. We did everything together, went everywhere together. Now he barely knows me. He wanders round like an animal. By God, today my camel is more responsive. Cure him, Umbarak, and all that I have is yours, only cure him." There were tears in his eyes as he implored me. I said sadly, "I have no medicine that will help your brother. Only God can cure him." He said resignedly, "God is merciful."

Accompanying us to Mukalla was a small man with very bright eyes. He looked, I thought, rather like an assertive sparrow, for his movements were quick and jerky. He wore a large silver-hilted dagger set with cornelians, and he was never parted from his brass-bound Martini rifle. I asked bin Kabina who he was. He looked at me in surprise. "Don't you know him? He is bin Duailan, known as 'The Cat'. A sheikh of the Manahil." I looked at him again with interest, for bin Duailan was the most famous raider in Southern Arabia. Eight months later he led a raid which was to plunge the desert into war. Even now the country through which we passed was more disturbed than it had been the year before.

We reached Mukalla on 1st May and here I parted from bin Kabina, bin Ghabaisha and the others, not knowing if I should ever see them again.

Before going back to England I returned for two months to the southern Hejaz, accompanied by bil Ghaith, a light-hearted young Harbi. I rode once more along the Tihama

coast, again watched garlanded men and boys dance throughout the breathless, moonlit night, and stayed with the Amir
in the small port of Qizan, sweltering in the heat of summer.
We dragged camels up the seemingly impassable face of the
escarpment, followed for a while the strange paved "Road of
the Elephant," and reached Najran in the country of the Yam
on the edge of the Empty Quarter. Then we returned to
Jedda.

In deserts, however arid, I have never felt homesick for green
fields and woods in spring, but now that I was back in
England I longed with an ache that was almost physical to be
back in Arabia. The Desert Locust Control offered me a job
with a good salary and the prospect of permanent employ-
ment supervising the destruction of locusts. But this was not
enough. I craved the wide emptiness of the Sands, the fascination of unknown country and the company of the Rashid.
The western Sands still offered the challenge I sought; to cross
them would complete the exploration of the Empty Quarter.

I went back to the Hadhramaut and spent the next two
months travelling among the Saar. Boscawen in 1931 had
hunted on the edge of their country, and Ingrams had paid
them a cursory visit in 1934. A large and powerful tribe, they
had been aptly described as "the wolves of the desert." They
had been the most formidable and feared raiders of southern
Arabia, but in recent years the Dahm and the Abida from the
Yemen had proved themselves more aggressive. Their raids
involved two hundred men or more, covered as much as a
thousand miles and lasted up to two months.

　　Amair, a hard-faced lad of little charm, joined me while I
was among the Saar. He had been with me on two previous
journeys. He brought news of bin Kabina, who had received a

letter from me on the edge of the Sands, taken it to the coast to have it read and foundered his camel on the way back, in all a journey of nine hundred miles. He was now on his way to meet me at Manwakh, accompanied by Muhammad, his half-brother, son of old bin Kalut. Bin Ghabaisha, Amair told me, was somewhere out of touch near Salala. I suggested sending a wireless message when we returned to Tarim, asking the RAF at Salala to contact bin Ghabaisha through the Wali and fly him to Mukalla. Amair said, "He is only a boy. I don't think he has ever seen a plane. He might get in one if you were with him; he won't on his own." However, I sent the message and ten days later bin Ghabaisha turned up in the Hadhramaut. Very erect, his head thrown back, he greeted me in a rather gruff voice, odd in a boy of his age. He wore his dagger and was neatly dressed as always. I asked him if he had minded travelling in an aeroplane. "Why should I mind? You sent for me and so I came." "Had you ever seen an aeroplane before?" "Yes, once, very high up. It made more noise than this one. Where do you wish to go?" I told him. "I shall need a rifle." "Choose one of those," I said, pointing to five Service rifles. Eventually he selected one. "This is indeed a good rifle, Umbarak." "Take it, it is yours, and one hundred rounds of ammunition." "With this rifle I can go anywhere!" he said, smiling. Armed with it he was to become in a few years' time one of the most renowned outlaws on the Trucial Coast, with half a dozen blood feuds on his hands. A skilled rider and a deadly shot, he was always graceful in everything he did. He had a quick smile and a gentle manner, but I already suspected that he could be both reckless and ruthless. Amair was equally ruthless, but had none of bin Ghabaisha's charm. He had a thin mouth, hard unsmiling eyes and a calculating spirit without warmth.

We left the Hadhramaut and rode northward to Manwakh,

one of the only two permanent wells in the Saar country, an area the size of Yorkshire; it was situated on the edge of the Empty Quarter. In the sharp cold of the winter morning we rode into the Saar camp, passing herds of fat milch camels which the boys had just driven out to graze. Small black goat's-hair tents were scattered along the valley. Naked infants romped round them and dark-clad women sat churning butter, or moved about gathering sticks or herding goats. Several families had struck their tents and loaded their camels. The small children were seated in camel litters, the first I had seen in southern Arabia, though I was familiar with them in the north. These were Maaruf Saar, who for a dozen years had pastured their herds near Najran and acknowledged King Ibn Saud as their overlord, but some of them had been implicated in the recent raids on the Yam so, fearing retribution, the Maaruf had all fled southward to seek refuge among their kinsmen.

Bin Kabina and Muhammad were waiting for me in the Saar camp. Muhammad, heavily built like his father bin Kalut, and already going bald, was an amiable if rather self-important person, the least competent of my four companions. Bin Ghabaisha was probably the most competent and bin Kabina the most endearing.

There were many Saar collected at Manwakh where the talk was all of raids and rumours of raids. A large force of Abida from the Yemen was even then raiding to the east and it was said that they had fought off a pursuit party from the Rashid after suffering some casualties. I already knew that bin Duailan, "The Cat," had recently surprised two Government posts in the Hadhramaut and captured a number of rifles and much ammunition. I now heard that he had led a large force of Manahil in another raid against the Yam. The raiders had killed ten Yam and captured many camels, but bin Duailan and eight other Manahil had been killed. Bin Duailan had remained behind to give the others time to drive off the looted camels. He had fought to the last before he was knifed. Later I met the man who killed him. He said admiringly, "By God, he was a man. I thought he would kill us all." Ibn Saud, infuriated by these raids on his tribes, had given the Yam and Dawasir permission to retaliate on the Mishqas, their collective name for the southern tribes. We now heard that advance parties of Yam were even then ravaging the country to the west of Manwakh, killing anyone they met. In consequence the Saar were preparing to abandon Manwakh. I had arrived only just in time if I was to start from there.

One of the Saar called bin Daisan was reputed to know these western Sands and I was anxious for him to accompany us. I offered him a rifle and a large sum of money, but avarice fought a losing battle with the caution that comes with old age. In the evening he would agree to come with us; in the morning he would go back on his word. We knew we must have at least one of the Saar with us, otherwise their tribe, blood enemies of the Rashid, might follow us into the Sands and kill us. Everyone at Manwakh assured us we should in any case be killed by the Yam or the Dawasir. They said contemptuously that my Rashid were too young and inexperienced to judge the risks ahead of us. Young they certainly were: Muhammad was perhaps twenty-five years old, Amair twenty, bin Kabina and bin Ghabaisha seventeen. Yet they refused to be intimidated or to desert me, though realising far better than I the dangers that faced us. I was more concerned with the physical difficulties of crossing the Sands, especially without a guide, than with the risks we ran from the tribes once we had crossed. Looking back I was to realise how greatly I had underestimated this danger, how very slight had been our chances of survival.

———

Finally we persuaded two young Saar, called Salih and Sadr, to come with us, in return for a rifle and fifty rounds each. They had watered at the Hassi the year before, and were confident of finding this well once we reached the Aradh, a limestone escarpment that jutted a long way southward into the Sands. I reckoned we had four hundred waterless miles ahead of us before we reached the Hassi. We watered our camels again in the morning and filled our skins. Muhammad invoked the protection of God and then we started our journey. We had with us four baggage camels and on them we loaded most of the water-skins and the food, of which we had a sufficiency. The water, at least at first, was clean-tasting, unlike the bitter stuff bin Kabina and I had drunk the year before. Later in the day we crossed the tracks of the Abida returning from their raid with a large herd of looted camels.

At first the weather was grey, with a bitter north-east wind. The Sands were flat, drab and desolate; day after day there was no grazing. The camels were already beginning to show signs of distress and I missed the reassuring presence of al Auf. We were travelling in the direction given us by bin Daisan which I hoped was correct. After six days we chanced on a patch of rich grazing. We could easily have missed it, for it was only two or three miles across. It was alive with larks and butterflies and the sand was patterned with the tracks of gerbils and gerboas. Here our camels gorged to repletion. In the next three months they were only to get two more such meals.

Days later we came to the extensive plain of the Jilida which bin Daisan had described, and knew that we were half-way across. Wind-polished fragments of rhyolite, porphyry, jasper and granite formed a mosaic set in hard sand above an underlying conglomerate. We had seen oryx during the pre-

ceding days; here we saw a herd of twenty-eight. Two days
after leaving the Jilida we were faced by the mountainous
dunes of the Bani Maradh. Luckily the easier slopes faced
south, but even so they imposed a severe strain on our fam-
ished camels, which by now were also very thirsty. One of
them collapsed as we struggled over the dunes; to revive her
we poured a little of our precious water down her nostrils.
These dunes were a lovely golden red; the ones behind us had
been dreary and uninspiring.

Beyond the Bani Maradh we found tracks, some less than
a week old, of many Arabs and camels. Later we learnt that
rain further north had drawn the Yam and Dawasir with their
herds out of these Sands and thereby saved our lives. From
now on two of us scouted continuously ahead, and each
evening before we stopped someone remained behind to
watch back along our tracks. We cooked our evening meal
before it was dark, put out the fire and talked in whispers.
One night bin Ghabaisha noticed that the camels were watching something. He signed to us; we got into position, and lay
with rifles handy through the night. It had begun to rain and
was very cold. In the morning we found the tracks of a wolf.
"God! Awake all night in the rain on guard because of a
wolf," Muhammad exclaimed disgustedly, and bin Ghabaisha
answered shortly, "Better than waking up with a dagger
between your ribs."

We reached the limestone escarpment of the Aradh. When
I woke at dawn the valleys were filled with eddying mist
above which the silhouettes of dunes ran eastward like fantastic mountains towards the rising sun. The world was very
still, held in a fragile bowl of silence. Standing at last on this
far threshold of the Sands, I looked back almost regretfully
the way that we had come. I had crossed the Empty Quarter
for the second time, a journey almost as testing as the first.

Two days later, as we approached the Hassi well, we
rounded a corner and came unexpectedly on eight mounted
Yam. They were only a few yards from us. I saw bin
Ghabaisha slip his safety-catch forward. No-one moved or
spoke until I said *"Salam alaikum,"* and an old man replied. A
boy whispered to him, "Are they Mishqas?" and he snarled
back, "Don't you know the Arab? Don't you know the foe?" I
could see the hatred in his eyes. We told them that our main
party was just behind and warned them to be careful. I wondered what we would have done if we had surprised them in
the Sands. Perhaps if we had taken their rifles and camels we
could have let them live. Twenty minutes later we were at the
well. It was sixteen days since we had left Manwakh.

Ibn Saud's guardian was not at the well, so Salih and Sadr
watered their camels, filled their water-skins, took all they
could carry of our rations and slipped away. A year later on
the Trucial Coast, I heard that they had arrived safely. When
the guardian returned he took us to Sulaiyil, a small oasis
town. He was very hostile when he learnt that I was a Christian, a foretaste of what lay ahead. In Sulaiyil the Amir, who
was a young slave, and the two wireless operators, were
friendly; everyone else was hostile, hating me as a Christian
and my companions because they were Mishqas. The elders
spat on the ground whenever they passed, and the children
followed me chanting derisively, "al Nasrani, al Nasrani"—the
Christian, the Christian. That evening the Amir said to us,
"By God, you were lucky. Did you not know that Ibn Saud
had given his tribes permission to raid the Mishqas? For years
raiding has been forbidden. Now they are wild with excitement. Any of them would have killed you if you had run into
them. Ten days ago the country to the south was full of our
Bedu. Nothing could have saved you, especially if they had
found out one of you was a Christian. Even here in the town
you can see how they hate you." I realised how badly I had

misjudged our chances, and this increased the responsibility I felt towards my companions who had appreciated the risks and yet come with me.

Two days later the Amir received orders from Ibn Saud that we were to be imprisoned, but the next day he received further orders that we were to be released and allowed to continue our journey. St. John Philby had fortunately been in Riyadh and been able to intervene with the King on my behalf. We left Sulaiyil next morning on our way to Laila, a hundred and fifty miles away. Abu Dhabi, our destination, was at least six hundred miles beyond that, and none of us knew the country ahead. The townsfolk at Laila were even more fanatical than at Sulaiyil. They reviled my companions for bringing the Christian to their town and made difficulties when we tried to buy food, declaring that our money must be washed. Eventually we obtained a little food, but no-one would guide us to Jabrin. "Go and die in the desert, don't come back here," they shouted as we left.

Jabrin was a further hundred and fifty miles away according to Philby's map. I believed that I could find the oasis by following a compass bearing. The others, especially Muhammad, were sceptical. "Crossing the Sands we could not miss the Aradh: a few palm trees are different." Bin Ghabaisha said, "God forbid we should stay here." Bin Kabina agreed and added, "We must trust Umbarak." All of us realised that if I went wrong we should be lost in the waterless desert. My diary shows that it took us eight days to reach Jabrin, and that our marching hours were not very long; only twice did we do more than eight hours. But my recollection is of riding interminably through glaring, haze-bound wilderness, without beginning and without end. The weariness of our camels added to my own, making it barely tolerable, especially when their bodies jerked in flinching protest as they trod with their worn soles upon the flints, which strewed alike the hollows and the ridges. After we had halted, hobbled them and turned them loose I suppose they found something to eat during those shuffling quests that took them so far afield. Bin Kabina turned from watching them and said to me, "Their patience is very wonderful; what other creature is as patient as the camel? That above all is what endears them to us Arabs."

Eventually I saw in front of us the palm groves, dark against the khaki plain, but the oasis was drought-stricken and there were no Murra here. Between Jabrin and Abu Dhabi the map showed only Dhiby, a well that Thomas had located at the end of his great journey across the Sands. It was another hundred and fifty miles away, and I had a horrid feeling that al Auf had declared its water undrinkable. Now, to add to our hardships, it rained almost continuously for three days and intermittently for the next four, especially heavily at night, the rain soaking away into the sand. We had nothing in which to catch it. Each morning we exchanged the sodden misery of the night for the cold dripping discomfort of the day. Very little food was left from the meagre supply we had secured at Laila. One evening Muhammad grumbled that we must increase our rations. I lost my temper: "Eat the lot tonight and then at least we shall know where we stand." The others intervened to quiet us. Day after day there was nothing for the camels. Each morning I expected to find some of them dead. We were in the Jaub depression which I hoped would lead us to the Dhiby well. Those were bad days.

On the eighth day after leaving Jabrin I got cross bearings on two rocky peaks, shown on the map as near the well. "We are at the well," I said. Bin Ghabaisha found it nearby. "By God, Umbarak, you *are* a guide. The very best," he said admiringly. Unfortunately the water was too brackish for us, but the camels drank enormous quantities. Amair said, "If we get desperate we shall have to push a stick down their throats and drink their vomit." I knew Bedu were sometimes reduced to doing this. The idea did not appeal to me.

Two days later we came on abundant vegetation. Bin Ghabaisha said to me as we watched the camels hasten from plant to plant and rip off great mouthfuls, "God's bounty. It has saved the camels. They were almost finished, especially those two over there." Later they lay down and belched and chewed contentedly. "God's gift," the Arabs call them.

But we were still in trouble; we had very little food and water left. We would never get direct to Abu Dhabi, it was too far. We agreed we must turn back into the Empty Quarter and hope to find Liwa. Bin Kabina thought he would recognise the big dunes where we had camped two years before, and he did. Fifteen days after leaving Jabrin and with only a gallon or so of water left we found a shallow well, brackish but drinkable, and from there bin Kabina took us to the settlements. The Manasir who lived there were the first people we had encountered since the Arabs who had cursed us as we left Laila, more than five hundred miles away. They gave us a guide to take us to Abu Dhabi, yet another hundred and fifty miles ahead. As we approached the sea we slithered across interminable blinding salt flats; we then waded across the creek which separated Abu Dhabi from the mainland, and after a further ten miles of empty desert arrived at a large castle that dominated a small dilapidated town along the seashore. Near the castle were a few palms and a shallow well, where we watered our camels. Then we sat under the castle wall waiting for the sheikhs to wake from their afternoon slumbers. It was 14th March 1948. We had left Manwakh on 6th January.

Sheikh Shakhbut received us with great kindness, especially warming after our reception at Sulaiyil and Laila. He showed us to a house on the waterfront and said, "This is your home

for as long as you will stay with us," and here we remained for
twenty happy days, thankful that for a while there was no further need for travelling. Once again we ate meat and slept
when we felt inclined. The house was always full of friendly
visitors. From them bin Kabina and the others could hear the
news for which they had craved so long. We spent a few
agreeable days with Hiza and Khalid, the Sheikh's brothers,
sailing in a small dhow among the islands. Then we rode at
leisure across the sands to visit Shakhbut's other brother
Zayid, at Muwaiqih. I had heard the Bedu speak of him with
admiration. "Zayid is a Bedu, he knows how to ride and
fight."

I hoped to return the following year and explore the interior of Oman. It was now too late in the season and I was too
tired. Wellsted had travelled in Oman in 1835. He had been
followed by Aucher-Eloy, by Colonel Miles and finally by Sir
Percy Cox in 1901. All four of them had travelled in Oman
with the approval of the Sultan of Muscat, its effective ruler.
Since then the tribes in the interior had thrown off their allegiance to the Sultan and elected an Imam. The present Imam
was bitterly opposed to the Sultan and fanatically hostile to all
Europeans. Much remained to be examined if I could get
there. Jebel Kaur was shown on no map; Jebel al Akhadar was
largely unexplored; no European had seen Umm al Samim.
As soon as I met Zayid I felt confident that he could and
would help me. When I discussed my plans with him he said,
"The tribes, the Duru in particular, will try to stop you.
Above all you must not fall into the hands of the Imam. I
don't know what he would do to you. Anyway I have friends
in Oman and will do what I can to help you."

Before leaving Muwaiqih I hunted Arabian tahr, a species
of wild goat, on a nearby mountain and secured some specimens for the British Museum. I was the first European to have

seen this tahr. Then, riding a superb Batina camel which Zayid lent me, I travelled to Dubai. Zayid sent four of his retainers with me since we would pass through the territory of the Bani Kitab who were hostile to the Rashid. In 1948 the sheikhs along the Trucial Coast relied on armed retainers to maintain their position and in time of war sought the support of the tribes. Only the year before the rulers of Abu Dhabi and Dubai had been at war.

I stayed for a while in Dubai, then still a fascinating unspoilt Arab seaport, and at the beginning of May sailed on a dhow to Bahrain. Storms drove us to seek shelter off the Persian coast where we were joined by many other *boom*, sailing home from Zanzibar. These beautiful craft were almost the last trading vessels in the world to make long voyages entirely by sail.

At the end of October 1948 I returned to Muwaiqih accompanied by bin al Kamam, the Rashid sheikh who had been seeking a truce from the Dahm at the time we crossed the western Sands. Bin Kabina and bin Ghabaisha joined us and we spent the next month exploring Liwa oasis, fifty miles of palm groves and settlements scattered among great golden dunes. Close though it was to the coast, no European had yet been there to deprive me of my discovery. Everywhere the Sands were like a garden after the recent rain. Occasional beauty such as this was all the Bedu ever knew of the gentleness of life. Generally bitter winter turned to blazing summer over a parched and lifeless land.

We were back in Muwaiqih in time to go hawking with Zayid at the opening of the season in December. Thirty of us followed him into the Sands, singing the *tagrud* to which the Bedu trot their camels. His falconers each carried on his wrist a hooded peregrine or a saker. For an unforgettable month we ranged the Sands hawking McQueen's bustard, and I watched the contests in the sky enthralled. The falcon, whether peregrine or saker, never waited on, but was flown from the fist. It often saw the bustard on the ground before the Arabs did. As the falcon, flying near the ground, approached, the bustard would take to the air, but it would often land again when overtaken. It would then try to beat off the falcon with blows of its wings, or to squirt at it an evil-smelling fluid. Meanwhile the salukis, which always accompanied us, would have raced off on seeing the falcon take wing. When they arrived, unless the falcon had already fastened to it, they would drive the bustard back into the air. The falcon appeared to fly much faster than the bustard with its slow wing beats, but I once saw a bustard outfly a peregrine after a long hard chase. The peregrine always bound to its quarry when it struck. However the most spectacular display I watched was between a peregrine and a stone-curlew, twisting and turning close over our heads. In the evenings we rode back to camp, with sometimes half a dozen bustards and some hares for our meal.

On 28th January six of us, including bin Kabina and bin al Kamam, slipped away from Muwaiqih. Bin Ghabaisha remained behind to harry the Bani Kitab with whom he had a feud. I was happy to have bin al Kamam with me; a lean middle-aged man, with a quick receptive mind and restless spirit, he was the most widely travelled of the Rashid and the most intelligent, quick to tell me anything he thought might interest me. I carried a letter from Zayid to Yasir, Sheikh of the Junuba, asking him to help me.

Detained in the Wadi al Ain by bitter weather, so cold that our camels staled blood, we were confronted by a truculently vociferous gathering of Duru declaring that they would allow no Christian in their land. More and more of them arrived, often two on a camel; fortunately among them were Staiyun and his son, who immediately came over and sat beside me, and thereby split the Duru. "Umbarak is a good man, I know him; he stayed with me two years ago," the old man asserted. "Now I will take him wherever he wishes to go, with or without your consent." His advocacy won the day. I asked him later if on my first visit he had guessed I was a European. "No. We often wondered who you were, but it never occurred to us you were a Christian."

He took me down to Umm al Samim, which bordered the Sands for nearly a hundred miles. A tawny plain blended with a dusty sky; the ground at our feet was of gypsum powder, coated with a sand-sprinkled crust of salt. Staiyun put his hand on my arm. "Don't go any nearer, it is dangerous." A few dead salt-bushes marked the edge of firm land; beyond them only some darkening of the surface betrayed the bog below. "I once watched a flock of goats disappear here," Staiyun said. "Have you not heard of the Awamir raiding party that tried to cross Umm al Samim and was swallowed up?"

Eventually we reached the southern coast near the island of Masira. I had crossed southern Arabia once again. This was the sort of journey to which I was by now accustomed. The journey from here however, back through Oman, was one which would require diplomacy rather than physical endurance.

We visited the Wahiba. A friendly tribe with the bearing of aristocrats, comparable with the Rashid, they were a striking contrast with the uncouth Duru. Two of them led bin Kabina and me northward through the Wahiba sands to the valley of the Batha Badiya, beyond which we could see the stark range of the Hajar. At my request we returned through the settled country of the Sharqiya. "When we meet Arabs keep silent," they told me. We were still on foot when we met three men and a boy, all armed with rifles, leading a string of camels. We stopped and spoke with them. I watched their dark gypsy eyes inspecting me, never dwelling on me but missing nothing. "Who is your companion?" "A Baluch from Sur; buying slaves and on his way to Nazwa." This was the first of several such encounters. Standing among them waiting for my identity to be revealed I realised that the fascination of the journey lay not only in seeing this country, but above all in seeing it under these conditions.

Several days later we rejoined the rest of my party whom we had left behind with the Wahiba. Here I met Ali bin Said, a Wahiba sheikh. Among the Bedu a sheikh's authority depended entirely on the force of his personality. First among equals, he had no retainers to enforce his orders. Ali, despite his good-natured face and quiet speech, had unmistakable authority. "So you have returned safely. You are very welcome. You must be tired for you have travelled far. Remain with us and rest. All the Wahiba are your friends." When we discussed my plans, he warned me, "The tribes from the north now know that you are here. They will be on the watch for you." I told him I had a letter from Zayid to Yasir and he said, "Yasir may be able to get you through. But I don't know whether you will be able to persuade him. Be sure and come back here if you fail. Anyway I will send my representative with you."

Yasir, a big heavy man with ill-proportioned features and a large beard streaked with grey, was embarrassed when I met him. He owed allegiance to the Imam but was under an obligation to Zayid. Apparently the Imam had given orders for my arrest. When in 1977 I visited Nazwa I was shown a deep pit inside the fort. "This is where the Imam intended to keep you," the guardian told me.

Yasir rode to Nazwa, which was nearby, and after a stormy interview persuaded the Imam to let him take me to Muwaiqih. When Yasir rejoined us, the Imam's representative was with him. I expected him to be a sour-faced fanatic, and was agreeably surprised when he proved to be a friendly old man with an obvious sense of humour.

Now I had no further cause for anxiety. I could work openly, taking bearings and photographs. Except for the outline of the Jebel al Akhadar and a few of the larger towns the map was blank. We passed close under the precipice of Jebel Kaur. In the distance I could see the Jebel al Akhadar; it stretched for fifty miles across our front, its face scarred by deep gorges, streaks of purple on a background of pale yellow and misty blue.

We reached Muwaiqih on 6th April 1949. We had ridden some eleven hundred miles since leaving Zayid's fort on 28th January.

I returned again to Muwaiqih in November, anxious to visit the Jebel al Akhadar and if possible to climb it. I believed I might succeed if I could get in touch with Sulaiman bin Hamyar, ruler of the mountain. I had heard that he was free from the narrow fanaticism of most of Oman's townsmen, and was interested in the inventions of the West. He owed allegiance to the Imam, but was anxious to establish his independence and consequently was suspect.

Bin al Kamam had left Muwaiqih when I returned but, among others, bin Kabina and bin Ghabaisha joined me. In the Wadi al Ain we were confronted once again by a crowd of hostile Duru. I had been stung twice in the night by a scorpion, and was still in pain and feeling rather sick. We argued for three days and then bin Ghabaisha said to me, "It is up to you, Umbarak, but if we stay here we shall have to fight for our lives. They are saying it is as meritorious to kill a Christian as to go on the pilgrimage."

We turned back into the Sands, made a wide detour and succeeded in getting within twenty miles of the Jebel. I had sent a message ahead to Sulaiman, and he sent word back that he would meet me and take me to Birkat at Mauz at the foot of the mountain. But the hue and cry was out, and before he arrived our camp was surrounded by a hundred or more armed townsmen sent by the Imam. Fortunately some Wahiba and Junuba had joined us, which gave them pause.

Sulaiman, a large man with a sallow complexion and long black beard, arrived next day. He was immaculately dressed and wore a cloak of the finest weave. His dagger was ornamented with gold. He took me inside a small mosque nearby, where we had a long talk. He was anxious for British recognition as the independent ruler of the Jebel al Akhadar, and hoped that I would intervene on his behalf. Extremely ambitious, he struck me as a powerful but rather uncongenial personality. On learning that I had no political standing, he was unwilling to defy the Imam by taking me to the Jebel, but he did undertake to cover my withdrawal. Ten days later, on 6th April 1950, we were back at Muwaiqih.

It was disappointing to have failed. To have climbed the Jebel al Akhadar would have crowned my exploration in Oman. I realised that my journeys in Arabia were over. There was nowhere left where I could travel. The Sultan of Muscat, the Imam, Ibn Saud, even the British officials in Aden and Bahrain, had for their differing reasons closed in on me, resolved to prevent further journeys. I had gone to Arabia just in time to know the spirit of the land and the greatness of the Arabs. Shortly afterwards the life that I had shared with the Bedu had irrevocably disappeared. There are no riding

camels in Arabia today, only cars, lorries, aeroplanes and heli-
copters.

For untold centuries the Bedu lived in the desert; they
lived there from choice. The great nomad tribes of the north
could have dispossessed at any time the cultivators of Syria or
Iraq; bin Kabina or bin Ghabaisha could have settled in the
valley of the Hadhramaut. All of them would have scorned
this easier life of lesser men. Valuing freedom above all else,
they took a fierce pride in the very hardship of their lives, forcing unwilling recognition of their superiority on the townsmen and villagers who feared, hated and affected to despise
them. Even today there is no Arab, however sophisticated,
who would not proudly claim Bedu lineage. I shall always
remember how often I was humbled by my illiterate companions, who possessed in so much greater measure generosity,
courage, endurance, patience, good temper and light-hearted
gallantry. Among no other people have I felt the same sense of
personal inferiority.

Bin Kabina and bin Ghabaisha accompanied me to Dubai,
and there we parted. "Remain in the safe-keeping of God."
"Go in peace, Umbarak," they replied. As the plane climbed
up over the town from the airport at Sharja and swung out to
sea, I knew how it felt to go into exile.

Postscript: Wilfred Thesiger lived the peripatetic life of his
dreams, and he mourned the passing of the simple and
nomadic way of life that he so artfully described.

Fascinated by the salt mines of the Sahara and the caravan routes to market, Richard Trench traveled with nomads on their way to Timbuktu. He wanted to see firsthand the dangers and difficulties that these people have for centuries taken for granted. The journey exceeded his wildest expectations.

FORBIDDEN SANDS

A Search in the Sahara

RICHARD TRENCH

T*he way ahead was sombre. The* flat landscape of sand and stones seemed to stretch to the very ends of the earth. Above our heads the sun glared down without pity, its white light blinding what faded colours there were; around the sun the two buzzards dived and circled, playing games with the force of gravity.

There was nothing orderly about Tahar Omar's caravan. Some of us walked and others rode. Men shouted and camels roared. It was hardly the "off" that I had expected. At its constant pace of two and a half miles an hour, the walking pace of a man and a camel, our caravan looked tiny and pathetic stretched out across the desert floor in its irregular and haphazard fashion.

We drifted on for several hours within vague limits halfheartedly imposed by the Half-Child at the front, Dermas the slave at the back, and the two blue-robed outriders prancing like fussy butterflies on either flank. At midday Omar beckoned me forward. I beat my camel into a disjointed trot and rode up to him.

"Today we will march thirty kilometres," he said, looking down on me from his big white bull. (Omar was always looking down at me.) "Tomorrow we will march thirty-five and the next day forty. Then, *Inshallah*, we shall be at the well of Bouir Ikrief, where we will drink water for the last time. After it will be all speed to Taoudenni, more than twelve days away."

I remembered the words of the Sous-Préfet. "Do as they do and do not express your surprise at anything." I tried to look nonchalant and at ease.

"I hope that the slow pace at the beginning is not for my benefit?" I said to Omar.

"Of course not," he replied, astonished that I should even mention such an idea. "It is not for your benefit, Nasrani. It is for the camels'."

We never travelled thirty kilometres that day, nor thirty-five the next. Omar never kept his word on distances—or anything else, for that matter, which could be delegated to the authority of *Inshallah*. An hour after he had given me his provisional timetable, he motioned the caravan to halt. I looked up at him questioningly.

"Over there," he said, pointing to a few slender shoots of grass. "There is grazing. Only God knows if there is any further on."

I will always remember that first day out. It was new and brightly painted, like the shining red fire-engine of my earliest recollection. Time has not dulled it, nor has routine blunted it, and besides, I was giddy with the novelty of everything around me. I had left behind me the common regions of universal experience, and was walking across the desert towards "a bit of one's own," to use Conrad's phrase. From now on every move, every decision, every gamble, indeed every step that took me nearer Taoudenni would be a very personal triumph.

I now realize that that day was a deceptive one. The endless hours of boredom, weariness, and dissatisfaction were yet to come. Yet that day remains dominant in my memory. It established a rhythm to the ones that followed and gave my life a pattern—and thus, a sense of security—that I was to conform to, almost without exception, until I reached the salt-mines of Taoudenni.

The days began with prayers.

"Come to prayer, come to prayer," Omar barked out amid a background chorus of coughs and hacks. "Come to success, come to success. Prayer is better than sleep." He spoke to his god in a no-nonsense manner, with the same tone of voice that he would use with any other creditor.

After Omar had called out to pray, the nomads would gather together to wash before prayer, using sand, instead of water, to cleanse themselves. After they had lined up facing the east and prayed, they gathered round the feeble beginnings of a fire, huddling together to warm themselves from the early morning cold. They sat on their haunches slowly and laboriously talking. Each time a nomad came up, the men round the fire would rise onto their feet to greet him. *"Salam alaikum." "Alaikum wa salam."* How beautiful those salutations sounded.

While Omar made early morning tea, Dermas would be cooking a spicy porridge that had been built up with the scraps from the previous night's meal. Although the hot porridge burnt the throat, it warmed the body and filled the stomach, helping me to face the journey ahead.

After breakfast the camels would be rounded up and brought into camp to be saddled and loaded. Rounding up the hobbled camels could take anything from five minutes to two hours. In spite of the tight ropes that the nomads twist around their forelegs like handcuffs, hobbled camels can hop incredible distances. In one night a camel may hop ten miles in his search for grazing. But that, fortunately, is rare.

With the exception of Omar's white bull, all the camels in the caravan were small and in poor condition. But I noticed, with a certain sinking feeling, that my camel was in the worst condition of all.

There had been a long drought in the Sahara, Omar reminded me. Except for an occasional very light shower, there had been no rain in the desert for seven years. Omar's camels, like all other desert creatures, were weak from hunger and fatigue.

The camels of the Sahara are single-humped. Unlike in Arabia where the females are ridden, only the males are used in the Sahara. Female camels, like female nomads, are kept in the encampment for milking and child-rearing.

When the camels had been brought in, the business of saddling and loading would begin. With a jerk of the head-rope and a slow hissing sound from between the teeth, the nomads would couch the camels. There was no sympathy for objectors. Troublesome camels would have their nostrils grabbed by a hooked forefinger and be hauled down by their nose.

A camel's descent from a standing to a kneeling position is a long and complicated affair. They flop down onto their forelegs, settle onto their hindknees, then sink onto their hocks. Once they are on the ground, they are tightly hobbled with ropes twisted round their doubled-up forelegs. Particularly aggressive camels would have a rope slung across them

from one foreleg to the other, pinioning down their necks.
Camels regularly try to attack their loaders. Later I was to
meet a man who lost half his right foot in a fight with a camel.

Saddling and loading were always noisy and chaotic. The
camels would roar and snarl when approached, belching half-
regurgitated curd out of their mouths. A camel's roar carries
for miles across the desert. I once asked Omar how bedouins
used to keep their camels silent in the days of tribal raids,
when surprise was so essential. He picked up a twisted piece
of rope that had been used to hobble a camel and twisted it
round my face, closing my mouth.

The actual saddling of a camel is relatively simple. A blanket is thrown across the camel's hump, and either a riding
saddle or a pack saddle is slung on top of it. The saddle that
Omar had sold me, for the ridiculously large sum of ten
pounds, was a Mauritanian saddle. If it had not been for the
dangerously large pommel in the front, it would have looked
something like an armchair with wings on it. It was made out
of a wooden structure with leather stretched over it, which
made a hollow in the centre, which was easy to sit upon.

"It is extremely hard to fall out of," Omar told me encouragingly when he sold it to me. "Perfect for a beginner."

The Mauritanian saddle is much heavier than the flimsy
Malian saddle that I was to see further south. The Malian
saddle is made of three pieces of wood, with a pommel and
backrest. It is very hard to ride on. As well as being comfortable, the Mauritanian saddle has another great advantage. Its
two wings act as sunshades, and when the sun is at its highest, it
is often possible to walk along close by your camel in the shade.

Another blanket or sheepskin rug would then be thrown
on top, and a noose tightened around the saddle's "neck."
From this we hung our entire portable world: waterskins, saddlebags, food, clothes, and cooking utensils.

The importance of correct loading cannot be over-estimated; a badly balanced load is a threat to the entire caravan, Omar told me, in his easy, patronizing way. If the load slipped the camel might panic; this might spread among the other camels and soon the entire caravan would bolt. Elaborate precautions were taken to ensure that a camel's load was evenly distributed, and on our first few days out we were constantly stopping to shift loads. The art of loading a camel is to spread and balance, making sure that there are no hard edges rubbing against the camel's sides. Omar told me that a well-loaded camel should be able to move at ease, without a girth and with a man on top, without it over-balancing.

When the loading was finished, the six goatskins that we kept our water in were distributed amongst the three strongest camels. The skins were strung on either side of the camel's hump. The outsides of the skins looked vile and dirty, covered in hair and sand, wet with the camel pee that the animals sprayed around themselves generously. Yet inside they were clean and cured. The neck and the legs had been cut off, and the legs and the anus sewn up to prevent the water splashing out. The neck, or spout, was tied together with cord and the four legs were attached to ropes that hung down from the camel's hump.

Every night Omar carefully checked these skins for leaks, treating them with rancid butter to keep the leather in good condition. Yet in spite of his care, two of them leaked profusely. The first time that I saw them I was struck with horror at the thought of our lives depending on these primitive water-holders. Now I take back that first impression. Canvas water-bags would leak, plastic ones would melt in the heat, and steel or tin ones would rub sores on the camels' flanks. No modern invention can beat the goatskin as a safe and efficient carrier of water for the desert nomad.

Saddled and loaded, the camels were ready for mounting. Mounting a camel I found was far harder than actually riding one. Standing on the left side of the camel, facing forwards, you swing your right leg over the pommel, grab it with both hands, and somehow perform a sideways vault. It is a dangerous business. Before you have begun to find your balance, the camel will have started to rise. First the camel raises its hindlegs and comes up onto its knees. This pushes you forwards onto its neck. Next it raises its forelegs with the same series of motions. This throws you backwards. Then it brings its hindlegs up to a standing position. This sends you flying forwards again, and after that it comes up on its forelegs, throwing you backwards.

With the high pommel in front of the saddle, there is a very grave risk involved in mounting. Several times I misjudged my timing and, feeling a shot of pain between my legs, feared a fate almost as bad as death.

With the exception of Omar, all the nomads could mount with ease. Poor Omar. Right up until we got to Taoudenni he had to ask Dermas to act as a mounting-block. Once mounted, however, Omar was a different man. On his camel he was supreme and all-powerful. With an utterance to God and a movement of his wrist his orders went unchallenged. None save a god, or the captain of a ship, know such power.

Few of the nomads bothered with saddles. They were quite happy perched on their camels' humps, sitting on blankets. Sometimes they sat on their haunches, sometimes cross-legged, sometimes with their legs astride. Sitting on my Mauritanian saddle I felt at a disadvantage. While it may have been hard to fall out of, it was very restricting, and I envied the other nomads the ease with which they could move around.

Only the Half-Child, who led the caravan towing Omar's

white bull, did not have a camel to ride. Nor did he have shoes for that matter. As the youngest in the caravan he was the most insignificant. On Omar's ladder, just as there had to be someone at the top, so there had to be someone at the bottom, without camel and without shoes.

Occasionally, during a particularly long march, Omar would allow the Half-Child to sit in front of him on the white bull's neck. Sitting there on the camel, Omar and the black boy would chat away as the mood took them. Don't get me wrong. Omar was not patronizing. Like so many other illiterate people he was able to talk to a child as an equal. I think it was this that made me put total trust in Tahar Omar. This ability to talk to children as equals is not, of course, dependent on illiteracy. But it is dependent on goodness. The quality of amusing and interesting children, Claud Cockburn wrote in his autobiography, "Is a sign of goodness. Many good men cannot do it very well. But no bad man can do it at all."* Tahar Omar was a good man.

In spite of the horror stories that I had heard in England about camel-riding, I found that the actual riding was simple and straightforward—a typical amateur's over-confidence. If I wanted to go right, I would tap the camel with my riding-stick on the right side of his neck. If I wanted to go left, then I would tap him on the left. If I wanted to stop him or slow him down, I would just give a gentle tug on the headrope, and if I wanted to lower him to a couch, then I just hissed. The only problem was to go faster. My camel, whom I named *Mr. Wilson*, was loath to go any faster than he had to, and it took the hardest of wallops on his behind to get him to break into a funeral march. Altogether I was astonished at the ease with which I learnt to ride a camel. Each time I learnt something

* Claud Cockburn, *I, Claud . . .* , Harmondsworth, 1967.

new, the nomads smiled encouragingly. Only Omar offered me no encouragement; he looked at my efforts at camel-riding with the same ill-disguised disgust with which he looked at my table manners.

A camel does not walk like a dog or a horse, with its four legs moving alternately. Instead it walks with the foreleg on one side followed by the hindleg on the same side, then the foreleg on the other side followed by the hindleg on that side. The result is an easy, swaying movement that swings your whole body from side to side, forcing you to surrender into its drunken, rolling gait.

I found walking to be much easier than trotting, which shook every bone in my body. This surprised me; most Europeans who have ridden camels have enthused about the joy of trotting but have had little good to say about walking. My father recalled reading the poems of Rupert Brooke on a trotting camel. Possibly it was because of the very sore bum that I quickly developed? I do not know. But I could not bear trotting. Galloping, I will admit, was great fun. It was cool, refreshing, and exhilarating. But I rarely got that chance. The caravan went no faster than walking pace, and Omar discouraged anything faster that might tire out the camels.

The camel is an ecological miracle. Unlike their cousins in the eastern Sahara who are grain-fed, these camels had no food supply save what they could grab from the land around. With sufficient grazing they can travel for fifteen days in between waterings; without grazing they are lucky to last five. The camel's rate of water elimination is one-third that of the average mammal, including the human being. Not only can he lose in liquid up to a quarter of his total weight without serious risk, but drinking at an average rate of two and a half gallons of water per minute, he can absorb that loss in a single watering.

The arrival of the camel in the Sahara did more to shape the economy and the society of the desert than any other single event, until the arrival of the motor car. Prior to the introduction of the camel into the Sahara, the desert was inhabited by a black race, troglodytes, according to Herodotus, who were swift on foot and "eat snakes and lizards and other reptiles and speak a language like nothing on earth—it could be bats screeching."*

Like the inhabitants of the Kalahari Desert today, they were bushmen. These primitive men and women left their marks on the caves that they lived in, turning their underground homes into great art galleries full of rock paintings that gave a golden portrait of the light of early day. Naked and unalienated, they painted themselves as they hunted and they painted the animals that they hunted. Their testament has been found on rocks all over the Sahara.

Archaeologists have identified five different styles in these paintings, styles that bear a remarkable resemblance to similar ones found in France, Spain, and the Kalahari Desert. Each style seems to represent a stage in primitive man's evolution. In the earliest stage man is a small creature. He is dominated by the animals around him: the elephant, the rhino, the buffalo, and its now extinct predecessor, the Bubalus Antiquus. In the second stage man has grown in stature, and he is seen hunting the animals that had previously dominated him. In the third stage domestic animals make their appearance. There are cattle and dogs. Chariots can be seen pulled by horses, but so far the horse has not been ridden. In the fourth stage man is seen on horseback. It is not until the fifth and last stage, artistically the crudest of all, that the camel makes its appearance.

* Herodotus, *The History, IV.*

The arrival of the camel opened up new routes and new water-holes to man, bringing him into contact with the most isolated quarters of the desert. With the camel came hordes of Zenata Berbers, who swept across the Sahara, pushing the black races to the south, "like a hoard of locusts," according to one chronicler. A few generations later the Arabs came, repeating the movement that pushed the black races to the south, a historic movement still in motion today.

"With these changes," wrote E. W. Bovill, "came a new man to Africa, the camel-owning nomad, turbulent, predatory, elusive, and unassailable. Thus was civilization faced with a menace from which it has never since been wholly free and one which the legionaries of Rome never knew."*

Yet sitting on my camel I felt neither turbulent, predatory, elusive, nor unassailable. My camel, I noticed as I fell further and further behind, was going far slower than the others. When I was walking I could drag him along at the same speed as the others, but the minute I got on top of him he came to a stop.

There are two types of camel in the Sahara, I recalled, as I seethed with frustration, the camel or dromedary, and the baggage camel, the everyday beast of burden. The dromedary is lightly-coloured and finely-boned, capable of averaging forty miles in a day. Graceful and imposing, he is good at short fast sprints, but lacks endurance over long distances. He is less thickly furred, more delicately built, and better tempered than his proletarian cousin, the camel of the caravan routes. Although the baggage camel is smaller, he is sturdier and can carry weights of up to five hundred pounds with ease. The dromedary will collapse suddenly and die on the trail; the baggage camel will walk out his life on the caravan routes

* Bovill, *op. cit.*

like some old soldier, until he finally fades away while pulling
up water from some dark and depressing well.

Suddenly it occurred to me, as suddenly as St Paul's con-
version on the road to Damascus, that I had been conned.
Omar told me that the camel that I was going to buy, for a
hundred and twenty of the two hundred pounds, was going to
be a dromedary. But it was plain, even to a beginner like me,
that *Mr. Wilson*, as I called my camel, was a straight working-
class baggage camel. He was no problem walking along
beside me, of course he wasn't. He was used to that. What he
was not used to was being ridden. He would tolerate me on
his back, but he would only do it with a go-slow protest. No
wonder he was so easy to ride. A cart-horse is easy to ride for
someone who has never been on a horse.

I looked at Omar with smouldering resentment. He stared
back at me like a second-hand car salesman. But I couldn't
keep my resentment up. He might have outwitted me and
made a handsome profit out of it, but there was nothing malicious in him. Omar was a sharp businessman, and he would
have expected me to play the same trick on him if I could.
Besides, I recalled with resignation, I was a *nasrani*, and that
made me fair game for such tricks. In Omar's eyes he was
doing nothing but assisting in re-distributing the wealth of the
world. He treated money as we treat love and war. All was fair.

As I thought of the consequences of *Mr. Wilson*'s resistance
to having me on his back, a sick feeling came over me. I realized
that if I was to keep up with the others and get to Taoudenni,
then I would have to walk most of the way there, pulling *Mr.
Wilson* behind me.

We drifted on, our lives governed by the scarcity of grazing
and the will of God. As we moved across the dry and empty
land we gave our camels as much freedom as possible to
stretch out their long necks and grab what shoots of grass

they could as they meandered along. At times there would be
a moment of excitement when I saw an old broken calabash
or some other relic of man. For the country that we were travelling through was one of the original homes of pre-cameline
man. Huge primitive axes of Palaeolithic age have been found
in the Erg Cherch.

It was during these long and monotonous hours that I
began to get to know my travelling companions. They were
an extraordinary combination of opposites. At one moment
proud, arrogant, and frank, at the next, grovelling, ingratiating, and dishonest. They would think nothing of walking
twenty miles to pass the time of day, but they would whimper
and complain if they had to walk twenty yards before they had
had their morning tea. They were unbelievable hypochondri-
acs, who lived in fear of the slightest pain, yet they would think
nothing of dying for a single gesture. It was strange and disqui-
eting to live among people who would cheat you of everything
you had, yet would leap to your defence if you were attacked
by strangers.

Their values were not those of a Westerner. They saw nothing degrading in either poverty or begging, yet they regarded
meanness of pocket and meanness of spirit as the greatest of
all vices. They would treat their camels far better than they
ever treated their women, but they had within them reserves of
love and chivalry that would have put Chaucer's Knight to
shame.

In spite of these virtues, however, I found the constant
cadging and curiosity overwhelming.

"What is this?"

"It is . . ."

"What is it for?"

"It is for . . ."

"Give it to me."

"No I need it."

"But you are a *nasrani*, you are rich. I am poor, I have nothing."

"Let me use it as well as you then."

It was tiresome. Every answer resulted in a loss of face.

"And what is this?"

"May I use it too?"

"No, because only one person may use this."

"Then let me use it. You are rich and I am poor."

"No, you may not use it."

"Why?"

Only Omar at the top of the social ladder and Dermas close to the bottom would not intervene in these exchanges. They left it to the *nasrani* to learn the hard way. Neither did either of them ask for anything that was not theirs. Dermas was too busy with the menial tasks of cameleering to be able to participate, and Omar clearly considered himself to be above all that. While the others were going through my belongings, asking about everything and demanding it all for themselves, Omar was greasing the waterskins, checking his goods, or simply intoning to himself verses from the Koran. Yet nothing escaped his tight, narrow little eyes. He saw everything and forgot nothing.

It was hard. The physical strain weakened my resistance and made the mental strain harder to bear. I felt isolated and self-conscious. I suspected the nomads of laughing at me. There was nothing new in this feeling. It has been felt by imperialists, missionaries, explorers, traders, and just plain vagabonds like myself. Didn't George Orwell say that the greatest fear of the Englishman in the East is the fear of being laughed at?

The blame for these moments of paranoia should fall on me. This was their country and their life-style. It was for me, not them, to make the compromises. As the name which they gave me, el Nasrani, made dear, I was nothing but an unclean stranger. And when I did try to change to their nomadic ways, I was applauded with enthusiasm and encouragement. Soon I changed from despising my fellow travellers to respecting them, from respecting them to admiring them, and from admiring them to loving them. I had come to the Sahara to find slaves. I found far more besides.

Sometimes we would travel for fourteen hours without stopping; at other times we would halt after only a couple of hours on the move. It all depended on the grazing. At first, because I insisted on seeing my journey in terms of an airport timetable, I found these continual delays infuriating. After a while, however, I just drifted along like everyone else, totally surrendering to the will of God, young and irresponsible in the freedom and the necessity of it all.

But it took time to reach that level of acceptance and resignation. At first my whole journey seemed punctuated by delays. There were times when I feared we would never reach Bouir Ikrief, let alone Taoudenni; and Timbuktu seemed several fantasies away. Like most Westerners, I had been taught to chop Time up into pieces, and after twenty-five years of urban life I found it hard to accept the fact that Time, as a definite and measured period, had stopped at Tindouf. So I clung on to the idea of it, frightened of what would happen to me if I let it go. I had come from a society that measured Time in terms of minutes, into a society that was not happy measuring it in terms of days. Time was no more. The past was dead, the future was in the hands of God, there was only the present. I thought of Stanley on his death-bed, listening to the chimes of Big Ben. "So that, that is Time," he said.

After we had unloaded and hobbled the camels, Dermas would dismiss them with a silent flick of his wrist, and they would shuffle off to find what grazing they could on that mean and barren land. With the camels taken care of, we would build a wind-break with the baggage and collect up dried roots to make a fire. I became quite good at picking out the tiny stems that protruded from the ground with an enormous cluster of thick roots underneath them spreading out under the sand to suck in every drop of moisture around.

Caillié had seen the same foliage a hundred and fifty years earlier on his journey back to Europe from Timbuktu:

These plants have short and flexible leaves; the thorn is short but very hard; by the wise providence of Nature this plant, the only resource of the animals of the desert, has the property of remaining green all the year round, in spite of the burning east winds which so frequently prevail; the camels though not very delicate would refuse the dry leaves. This plant is very tenacious of life, throws out long roots on the surface of the ground, and does not grow to a height of more than eighteen inches; it is found in sandy places, and I have generally observed that it is more abundant on the west side of hills. The roots are thick and serve for fuel; the Moors use it to cook their provisions, and at sun-set the slaves went to collect it, to boil our scanty portion of rice with water and salt, to which they added melted butter for sauce; this was our frugal supper.*

When the firewood had been collected and the fire had been lit, we would sit on our haunches waiting for tea, while a scroll of smoke slowly rose into the sky. When tea had finally been served, the sitting-around, tea-drinking, eating, and talking began. It took us far into the night.

* Caillié, *op. cit.*, Vol. II.

Usually I tried to join in these evening conversations, but after an hour of heavy mental strain I usually gave up. Although nomads are one of the most individualistic races in the world, they have absolutely no understanding of privacy. Sometimes I found the loneliness of living among alien people so crushing that I would take myself off into the desert alone, just to be by myself. But my companions were offended by this anti-social behaviour, and remembering the advice of the Sous-Préfet to "do as they do," I forced myself to give this pleasure up. After that, my sleeping-bag was the only escape that I had. I would lie in it, looking up at the stars, while the night became clear and lucid. There I would hover for a while, in the blurred regions between sleep and wakefulness, until finally I faded into another world.

The nomads camped, ate, and slept in the closest proximity to each other. It was as if my companions wanted to escape from the vast empty spaces all around by drawing into themselves, so close that it was claustrophobic. Yet in spite of the total absence of women, I never encountered one case of homosexuality among these Arabs, even though they did sleep next to each other for protection from the cold. They did not even masturbate. I think that the extremes of heat and cold made everyone totally sexless.

When I awoke on my second morning, the call of the muezzin was the only sound in the world. I tried to get up but felt so stiff I could hardly move. Thanks to his radio, Omar had heard that the English drank tea. Was *nasrani* tea different from Arab tea, he asked. I told him it was. I had brought some Indian tea with me, so I offered Omar a sample of black Indian tea, mixed with sugar and condensed milk. There is little to say about that cultural exchange except that from then on Omar regarded *nasrani* tea as a punishment inflicted on disbelievers by Allah, the exact reason for which God, in his infinite wisdom, would reveal at a later date—no doubt.

We travelled that day over the same blank landscape. It was empty and infinite, unfamiliar and featureless. We shrank beside the enormity of it all. The ever-blowing north-east wind had blown all the fine sand off the plain, or *reg* as the Arabs call it, leaving behind a bare surface of stones and gravel. It was to be this type of *reg* that was to be the dominant feature of the desert between Tindouf and Timbuktu.

About midday the *reg* was interrupted by chaotic heaps of tumbled-down boulders. Stony valleys slashed and disfigured the *reg*'s flat surface. We hopped and danced across the haphazard confusion for about a mile, and then we found ourselves back on the same monotonous *reg* that we had been travelling on all morning. Above us the sun beat down, blinding our eyes. Below us its reflection rebounded off the shining stones of the *reg*. I tried to look ahead, but the flat horizon was vague and broken up, shimmering in the heat like an airport runway in June.

There was less talking on that second day out of Chegga. The heat and the beginnings of boredom dulled the brain. During that entire day I was only asked a question once. 'Mood, shouting from one of the flanks and waving his rifle in the air to attract my attention, asked me what it was that I missed most. Was it women? I already suspected them of laughing at me and I was determined not to give them any more ammunition, so I told them—which was true—that women were the last thing on my mind. What I missed most was tobacco. 'Mood shouted back that with God's will I should have tobacco. I thought no more of it and walked on through the Saharan day in silence.

About four o'clock there was chaos. My saddlebag got loose and slipped off *Mr. Wilson*'s back, getting tangled up in his feet. *Mr. Wilson* reared up, broke free of the headrope I was holding, and galloped off, dragging a trail of my belongings behind him. A flood of Omarian abuse was hurled at me. He

shouted at me to study the way a camel was loaded more carefully. I was not only a hindrance, he went on, I was a danger.
Dermas, without a word, had caught the camel and was bringing it back. Omar shouted at him not to do the *nasrani*'s work
for him, and then the whole caravan stopped while I collected
up my belongings.

Sometime that day we crossed the frontier into Mali. The
landscape looked no different, there were no sudden changes.
I would not even have known that we had crossed the frontier
if Omar had not told me. "Another frontier crossed," I wrote
in my journal. "Theoretically my seven-day visa for Bamako
starts today!"

That night we camped in Mali. I expected to dream of the
frontier, but I dreamt of pillarboxes and Trollope instead.

We did not leave the following morning, our first morning
in Mali. According to Omar, more camels were needed to take
his merchandise to Taoudenni. Without more camels we
would have to turn round and head back to Chegga. So Dermas and el Kiad were dispatched to the south, Mohammed to
the west, 'Mood and Kahil to the east, and Lehia went north,
all looking for nomad encampments where they might buy
camels.

Omar, the Half-Child, and myself stayed behind. Omar
sent the Half-Child off to watch the grazing camels and then
set about the business of the day. He checked the waterskins,
baked bread, and made yet another inventory of his goods.
He was like a well-run family firm. If Omar was an aristocrat,
as the Sous-Préfet had told me, a lord of the desert, then he
was a very hard-working one. He threw himself into his tasks
with dedication and a sense of industry. The Protestant ethic
was deeply ingrained in his unquestioning Moslem beliefs.

Occasionally he would stop his work and let his eyes wander over the empty spaces, scanning the nothingness around

him like a guru, or a man whittling. Then, suddenly, he would catch himself doing it and return to the task in hand, annoyed at his own lack of concentration. With two wives, two houses, and a radio to support, he could not afford leisure.

At midday he called the Half-Child back and made tea. Sitting there under the inadequate shade of a crippled tree, brewing tea, there was something very benevolent about him. After tea he turned on his radio. There was news of the Spanish Saharan situation. Morocco was making fresh claims on the territory and Spain had announced that they would resist. Omar spent some of his time in "Spain," as he called the Spanish Sahara, and he feared that fighting would be bad for business. I asked him his opinions on the Moroccan claims. He spat on a patch of sand.

"No one troubles us in 'Spain.' There are no police asking questions, nor are we expected to pay any taxes. The Spanish stay in the towns. 'Spain' is the only country left where you can buy and sell slaves without being troubled. They don't want to be liberated from 'colonial oppression.' "

For the first and last time on my journey I got Omar to talk a little of politics. His politics were those of any other sensible small businessman. He went with the tide.

"When I am in Mali I am a capitalist. I like money and business and I listen to the '*Voice of America*' on the radio. When I am in Algeria I am a socialist, because the Algerians give away *dowa* (medicine) and I can have my teeth taken out when they hurt. But when I am in Morocco I am not a Moroccan, because I have my dignity. But when I am in 'Spain,' " he said with a grin, "I am a nomad because no one bothers me there."

Omar's economic opinions were interesting too. He told me that Algeria was better to live in than Morocco, but Mali

was better for business. The Algerian police and government
were honest, he told me, while the Moroccans were only out
for themselves. But in Algeria he had to pay higher taxes and
so, at tax time, he preferred to do business in Mali from his
Timbuktu house and then return to Algeria in the summer.
Tahar Omar was more than just a caravan-master. He was an
international tax-dodger.

As far as the Spanish Sahara went—the main topic of conversation in the nomad encampments—Omar was not optimistic. He had a deep-seated dislike of the Moroccan
government and he feared a take-over. The tribes in the south
of "Spain," he said, would resist them. There was talk of war,
and of a new force that would resist the Moroccans. (I now
know that he was referring to the left-wing Polisario Front, the
Front for the Liberation of Sekia el Hama and Rio de Oro.)
The Rguibat would probably fight against Morocco. But for
the Tradjakant it was more serious. There were Tradjakants
in Morocco who supported the Moroccan demand. Others in
Algeria and Mauritania opposed it. There was a danger of the
entire tribe splitting over the Spanish Sahara and fighting a
civil war. War was bad, he said, trade would suffer. Already
the caravans had stopped coming down from Morocco.

Then all of a sudden he clamped up.

"Why do you want to know, Nasrani?"

"What concern is it of yours?"

"Why is it that you always ask questions?"

He looked at me with scorn and then lapsed into a sulk. A
man with a wife and a house in Mali, a wife and a house in
Algeria, business connections in "Spain," and a hearty dislike
of Morocco, cannot be too careful when he talks politics to
strangers.

I wandered away, leaving him alone in his silence. I felt
alienated and distant and could have done with a cigarette. As

I lurked around the camp. feeling bored and useless, I came upon a deep green plant, a North African variety of the loco-weed. I bent down to examine it.

"Do not eat that, Nasrani," Omar shouted. "It will make you weak in the head."

Remembering the Sous-Préfet's advice, I didn't eat it. I tried smoking it, but it didn't work.

Lehia, 'Mood, and Kahil returned that afternoon. Lehia had found nothing, but 'Mood and Kahil, following fresh tracks, had come across a nomad encampment about half a day away. There were no camels for sale, 'Mood said, but the encampment did have something. Then he turned to me and produced from under his robes a thin, silver-stemmed nomad pipe and an old leather pouch full of tobacco.

"For you, Nasrani," Mood said. "You said yesterday that you missed tobacco."

I was suspicious at first. I feared that there was an ulterior motive behind the gift. How wrong I was; how ashamed I am now for thinking it.

The next morning Mohammed, who had come back during the night, spotted two outlines on the horizon, moving in our direction. I could hardly see them.

"It is two camels," he said with confidence. "From their size they are mother and child."

We waited a long time in silence, while they slowly meandered towards us. After an hour they were within sprinting distance, walking towards our own hobbled camels. In a split second the nomads were on their feet and rushing at the camels with their long graceful strides. The camels turned in terror. Too late, they were surrounded.

They galloped off in panic, trying to break out of the ever-decreasing circle, but wherever they ran they were headed off by humans. Suddenly they stopped in their tracks, frozen in fear. Ignoring the young one, the nomads went for the mother. Two of them grabbed her long spindly legs, two others took the neck. The Half-Child grabbed the tail. Omar, who had waddled up as fast as he could, just leaned. The she-camel crashed to the ground.

With her head pinioned down, she kicked in desperation. While a rope was being tightened around her forelegs, she fought back with a passion that seemed almost sexual. Sitting on her neck I felt her twist and lurch around in some masochistic orgasm. The hobbling operation completed, I looked around. Now I realized why she had twisted and lurched in such a fashion. Throughout the entire brawl between camel and humans, the Half-Child had been thrusting his little black fist in and out of her vagina. I looked down on the camel panting on the ground. She had had an orgasm.

No one was really interested in the abused camel. She was nothing but a hostage to keep the young one nearby the camp until dinner time. Allah will provide, Omar was fond of saying, and now Allah had provided. We studied the tender piece of living meat with gourmets' eyes.

We did not eat the camel that night. Dermas and el Kiad had not yet returned. It would have been inconceivable to have eaten such a meal without them. They trotted into camp the next day with a third nomad and a pathetic-looking camel, more like a donkey with a hump. The third nomad, setting eyes on the captured camel, looked very happy. For three days he had been searching for them, he said, after he had given thanks to Allah. For the first and last time on my journey, Tahar Omar looked as if he was about to lose faith in his God.

Omar was not only disappointed in God's will; he was disappointed in Dermas's and el Kiad's judgement of camels. What money Omar had made out of selling me *Mr. Wilson*, he now lost with this new purchase. More than just money was at stake; it was his pride too. He had lost face in front of a *nasrani.*

Then Dermas, by way of compensation, produced from behind his saddle the backside of a gazelle. It had been shot by the nomads from whom he had bought the camel, and they had given it to him to take back to Omar. Omar let out a burst of merriment and praise for God. In a moment his depression about the camel deal had been forgotten. Omar's knife quickly sliced off steaks, and long before they had properly grilled on the fire, eight pairs of yellowing and decayed nomadic teeth were tearing into them with gusto.

At an earlier time, according to Strabo, the whole of North Africa, from Carthage to the pillars of Hercules, abounded in wild beasts. "The reason why the name nomads or wanderers was bestowed on these people originated in their not being able to devote themselves to husbandry on account of the wild beasts."* Elephant, giraffe, ostrich, rhino, buffalo, lion, and antelope roamed the Sahara.

What has happened since then is depressingly predictable. Today, gazelle, jackal, and the occasional Addax antelope are the only large animals left. Even they are becoming an increasing rarity as soldiers, nomads, tourists, and "sportsmen" shoot them down from Land-Rovers with automatic rifles.

The Romans set the example, an example that was to be followed by the vast majority of "civilized" people after them. To feed the Roman public's insatiable lust for blood, Caesar threw four hundred lions into battle with four hundred gladiators. Later the Emperor Titus celebrated the opening of the Colosseum with nine thousand animals killed. Not to be outdone by his predecessors, the Emperor Trajan slaughtered

---

* Strabo, *Geography XVII.*

2,246 animals in one sitting. It is impossible to estimate how many hundreds of thousands of animals died in the ring, or how many millions must have been killed while being captured. But we should be wary of our condemnations. A society that gets its kicks from disaster films and horror movies is hardly in a position to judge too harshly the crowds who flocked to the Colosseum.

Yet right up until 1830, if the picture that Jean-Auguste Margueritte gives in his *Chasses de l'Algérie* is correct, North Africa still abounded in wild game. It was not until the invention of the breech-loading rifle that the killings turned into exterminations. In the last half-century alone, the ostrich, the leopard, and the hartebeest have disappeared. What animals are left are living on borrowed time. Already the Addax antelope is almost extinct, following one single hunt by French Meharists that turned into an indiscriminate slaughter.

The next day we loaded up to leave. We marched over a bitter, desiccated land. The caravan made no attempt to keep together, and soon I found myself with el Kiad, well ahead of the others. It was quiet and peaceful. In the distance we could hear the far-off shouts of the others calling to each other. We shifted south, then east, then south-south-east. I followed el Kiad through a series of dried-up river beds that had worn their way through the rocky terrain over hundreds of thousands of years, until we came onto a great plain covered with black slate. There el Kiad, like a compass needle wavering first one way then the other, until finally bearing onto course, swung south-east towards Bouir Ikrief.

The wind dropped and the sun was high above our heads. I could feel the heat around me. We were walking across layers of slate, scorching on their surface and razor-sharp on their edges. The lifeless surface was devoid of all colour save jet black. We walked in silence. Only able to communicate the simplest of words and phrases, life became a very simple affair. You ate, you slept, you walked, and you drank. Nothing else mattered.

The day wore on and our shadows grew longer. By late afternoon my feet were beginning to ache. But sunset cooled the air and gave me second wind. I walked through the early night enjoying the pleasure of an evening stroll.

After about an hour of night, the plain of black slates came to an end. In front of us was what appeared to be a garden growing out of the desert. I thought of the Koran's description of Paradise. "The Paradise promised to the righteous is as if rivers flow through it; its fruit is everlasting and also its shade."*

"Water," el Kiad said, pointing.

I began to walk towards it.

"Stay," he shouted. "We must wait for the others before we enter."

The next morning, after tea, Omar told me that we would be staying by the water-hole for another day because of the richness of the grazing. I was no longer surprised by any delays. I got up and explored the water-hole. The water was low, but a higher watermark showed that the hole had once seen better days. Around the hole were the tracks and droppings of gazelle, lizard, jackal, and desert hare. The grass and the bushes around were crowded with living things. After the silence and deadness of the black slate, it was like a bustling city. Birds chirped in the air and pecked fussily at the ground, while squadrons of black and golden butterflies hovered above the water. The most prominent of all the inhabitants of

* *The Koran.* 13:36, trans. Muhammad Zafrulla Khan, London, 1970.

this ecological city were the grasshoppers. They swarmed through the foliage in their thousands.

Although the grasshopper and the locust differ in their habits, their colours, and even the structure of their bodies, they belong to the same species. In a rainy season the hopper will multiply in numbers and spread out over fertile areas. After a drought the fertile area will have diminished, so the hoppers will concentrate, develop gregarious habits and breed, laying hundreds of eggs at a time. In three weeks the eggs will have hatched, and in another six weeks the newly born locusts will have reached maturity and be ready to breed in turn. Locust swarms, devouring all before them, can spread for hundreds of miles. *Exodus* tells how Egypt suffered a drought followed by a plague of locusts.

What I saw at that water-hole were the remains of a larger locust swarm that had been killed off by the continuous drought. They were desperately trying to eke out a living in the fertile areas that were left. As I looked at the swarms of locusts, Omar came up to me. "The will of God," he said, desolately, and waddled on.

That evening a herd of some fifty camel came down to the water-hole to drink. They marched in perfect order, heads following tails in one long line. There was no nomadic cameleer to urge them on from behind, only a king bull at the front to lead the way. Their movements were governed by a common consent that not even man, in the shape of Omar shouting at them because they were walking over his merchandise, could alter.

A series of minor and unmemorable delays kept us at the water-hole for another day. The cameleer who was responsible for the herd which we had seen that evening had discovered our presence. He negotiated the sale of another camel with Omar as he drank his tea, ate his food, and tried to cadge off his *nasrani*. He hung round the edge of our group like a bad smell that lingers and never goes away, taking but never giving, ingratiating but never helping. He had no tea, he told Omar. Omar gave him tea. He had no sugar, he whined. Omar gave him sugar. Finally Omar turned away from him in disgust.

"He has no dignity," he said, after he had gone. "He is not a man."

This was to be my last day with Lehia, el Kiad, 'Mood, and Kahil. From here we would all be going our separate ways. El Kiad and his son Mohammed were going west to do business with some Rguibat kinsmen. Lehia, 'Mood, and Kahil were returning to Chegga. Omar, Dermas, the Half-Child, and myself were going on to Taoudenni.

The next morning we were loading up to go when Kahil interrupted us with a shout. Two men on camels were galloping towards us. 'Mood and Mohammed raised their rifles with unconvincing melodrama. One of the camel-riders shouted out the beginnings of the salutation. Omar took it up. The rifles were not necessary, Omar motioned, so 'Mood and Mohammed lowered them with disappointment. The visitors were friends; they did not falter over the phrases.

As everyone went through the customary salutations, I saw two pairs of eyes observing me through indigo-blue veils. They were watching me with a mixture of irony and curiosity. Omar explained to them that I was a *nasrani* on my way to Taoudenni, and that I came from a country that was ruled by a woman. You would expect them to pity me in such a situation, but they didn't. They roared with laughter. As they laughed, I noticed that one of the newcomers had only half a right foot. I asked him why. He had lost the other half in a fight with a camel, he answered.

Omar sent off the Half-Child to find the cameleer and announced that there would be a feast. Departure was delayed for yet another day.

The Half-Child returned with the cameleer and a baby camel. A fire was built up and the cameleer, at the chance of free meat, made himself at home by the fire. This time Omar didn't mind. He was welcome. Everyone was welcome. I could no longer grudge Omar the money he had made out of the sale of *Mr. Wilson*. He was a rogue, but a generous rogue. The young camel that we were to eat had cost him a lot of money. I thought how gracious nomads are in their welcome, and how generous in their hospitality.

As we drank tea, Dermas led the condemned camel away to the place of execution, a cluster of rocks nearby. The camel was dragged along struggling. It was as if he already knew the fate that was awaiting him. The rest of the camp finished their tea and then walked over to join Dermas.

Mohammed produced a penknife for the killing but it was too small. Omar brought out his dagger but it was too blunt. Finally a use was found for my ridiculous sheath knife of heroic proportions. El Kiad took the knife from me, pointed the victim's head towards Mecca, and expertly inserted it into the throat, like a doctor injecting a patient.

The young camel gave a shudder and a fountain of blood spurted out of its neck. El Kiad took the knife out and the flow of blood rapidly increased. Gallons came out, completely flooding the rock holes around. Soon the blood overflowed the rock pools and trickled down the rocks in miniature waterfalls. The camel was still alive, but every line in its body seemed to have altered. It moaned, quivered, and shuddered in pain. As the life-force in it shrank, so the muscles in its body seemed to have tightened. The camel was taking a very long time to die. At last, summoning up all its remaining strength, it made one last unsuccessful lurch back to life, soaking everyone with its blood. It breathed deeply and then sank down to its death, its foreleg on the right side twitching hopelessly.

The killing was followed by the cutting. First the legs were stretched out and skinned. Then the hump was split open and the skin on either side of it was rolled back. Next the nomads tore the rib-cage out. Behind the rib-cage was a green balloon full of evil-smelling liquid. Dermas carefully took it out and deposited it several feet away from us. Omar held his nose.

"You may have to drink that if there is no water, Nasrani," he shouted gleefully and cruelly.

Everyone joined in the skinning. The dead flesh was cold and slippery and our hands were covered in blood. But it was innocent blood. And we were innocent too. We had killed for food, not for sport.

As everyone waited for the meat to cook, the gossip of the desert was exchanged and the politics of the tribes were discussed. The main topic of conversation was the Spanish Sahara and the sudden escalation in Morocco's demands for the territory. The two newcomers talked of rifles that had been taken across the border into "Spain." One of them told the nomads of the power of these magnificent guns.

"They fire and fire again and again without being reloaded. Bang—bang—bang—bang."

"*Automatique,*" said Omar knowledgeably.

"*Beserf.* Too much," the nomads exclaimed at this news.

Only Omar was against the threatening war. He said it would be bad for business. The others, especially 'Mood, were already fantasizing about how many Moroccans they would kill. 'Mood was waving his rifle around, miming future battles.

When the meat had cooked, the talk of war evaporated. The entire company attacked the meal. It began with the kidneys and went on well into the night. We ate, we slept, and then we ate again. Nothing was wasted. Our stomachs became bloated and our bodies immovable.

I woke again in the small hours of the morning. Clouds covered the sky and I could no longer see any stars. There was a roar of thunder. I felt a drop of rain strike me, and then another, and another. The rain was striking everything. I could hear the roar of thunder. I looked around me at the nomads sleeping it off. I imagined that the rain would wake them and they would dance around overjoyed. But none of them moved. I don't think they even felt the rain . . . or if they did feel it, then they didn't notice it . . . or if they noticed it, then they didn't care about it.

Postscript: Richard Trench came away from the desert with a newfound respect for these formidable people who are shaped by the unforgiving terrain in which they live.

NOTES ON THE CONTRIBUTORS

MICHAEL ASHER is one of the world's foremost desert explorers and the author of eighteen books, including *Last of the Bedu* and *Thesiger: A Biography*.

PETER CHILSON teaches creative writing at Washington State University, and his work has appeared in the country's finest literary magazines.

ROBYN DAVIDSON is an Australian writer and a desert traveler of some renown. She is the author of *Tracks*, which chronicled her 1,700-mile trek across the deserts of western Australia.

WILLIAM LANGEWIESCHE is a correspondent for the *Atlantic Monthly* and the author of *Cutting for Sign: One Man's Journey Along the U.S.-Mexican Border*.

GRAHAM MACKINTOSH has written *Journey with a Baja Burro* and *Nearer My Dog to Thee*. He lives in San Diego.

JUSTIN MAROZZI is a British writer who contributes to the *Spectator* and the *Financial Times*. He has penned *Tamerlane: Sword of Islam, Conqueror of the World*.

GEOFFREY MOORHOUSE is one of Britain's best-known travel writers and the author of eighteen books, including *The Nile*, *Apples in the Snow*, *The Diplomats*, and *Sun Dancing*.

JOHN WESLEY POWELL (1834–1901) became the second director of the U.S. Geological Survey and was instrumental in charting the course of the American West.

BAYLE ST. JOHN (1822–1859) in his short life wrote *Memoirs of Louis XIV and the Regency*, *Village Life in Egypt*, and *The Turks in Europe*.

JEFFREY TAYLER is a contributing editor to the *Atlantic Monthly* and the author of such works as *Facing the Congo*, *Siberian Dawn*, *Angry Wind*, and *River of No Reprieve*.

WILFRED THESIGER (1910–2003) was a British explorer and the author of such books as *Arabian Sands*, *The Marsh Arabs*, and *The Life of My Choice*.

RICHARD TRENCH is a British journalist of some note, and has written for the *Observer*, the *Guardian*, and the *Financial Times*.